Teach, Delight, Persuade

Scriptural Homilies for Years A, B, and C

James W. Kinn

HillenbrandBooks

Chicago / Mundelein, Illinois

TEACH, DELIGHT, PERSUADE: SCRIPTURAL HOMILIES FOR YEARS A, B, AND C © 2009 Archdiocese of Chicago: Liturgy Training Publications, 3949 South Racine Avenue, Chicago IL 60609; 1-800-933-1800, fax 1-800-933-7094, e-mail orders@ltp.org. All rights reserved. See our Web site at www.LTP.org.

Hillenbrand Books is an imprint of Liturgy Training Publications (LTP) and the Liturgical Institute at the University of Saint Mary of the Lake (USML). The imprint is focused on contemporary and classical theological thought concerning the liturgy of the Catholic Church. Available at bookstores everywhere, through LTP by calling 1-800-933-1800, or visiting www.LTP.org. Further information about the **Hillenbrand Books** publishing program is available from the University of Saint Mary of the Lake/ Mundelein Seminary, 1000 East Maple Avenue, Mundelein, IL 60060 (847-837-4542), on the Web at www.usml.edu/liturgicalinstitute, or e-mail litinst@usml.edu.

Cover photo © The Crosiers/Gene Plaisted, osc

Printed in the United States of America.

Library of Congress Control Number: 2009930767

ISBN 978-1-59525-026-1

HTDP

Contents

Preface

This book is intended for all kinds of people. It is based on the common lectionary that today is used extensively in Sunday worship by Catholics, Episcopalians, Lutherans, Presbyterians, and many other Christians. These scriptural homilies are primarily for those who preach at mass or Sunday worship. However, today many other people make use of these Sunday readings when they teach or preach the Word of God: directors of religious education, leaders of inquiry groups (such as RCIA), scripture study groups, prayer groups, religion teachers, and people who speak at a Sunday service.

Perhaps your experience is not so different from mine. We have heard our share of boring preachers: those who merely paraphrase scripture without any real insight, those who reduce the scriptures to a dead record of the past, and those who exhibit very little preparation of any kind. On the other hand, we have also heard homilists who are most engaging: those who are gifted storytellers, those whose personal experiences are powerful, those who have a delightful sense of humor, those who easily connect current events to scripture, as well as those who are adept at applying scripture to daily living. Such speaking gifts make their talks appealing and effective. All of these personal gifts are valuable for preaching God's word.

No matter what our personal charisms might be, if we strive to break open the Word of God based on the Sunday lectionary, we must constantly look for a deeper understanding of scripture. Vatican Council II encourages all of us to ground our preaching on scripture:

> . . . all the preaching of the church must be nourished and ruled by sacred scripture. For in the sacred books the Father . . . speaks with [his children]; the force and the power in the word of God is so great that it remains the support and energy of the church, the strength of faith for her sons and daughters . . . the perennial source of the spiritual life . . . . "For the word of God is living and [effective]" (Hebrews 4:12).[1]

---

1. Walter Abbott, sj, The Documents of Vatican II (NY: America Press, 1966), Dei Verbum, no. 21, p. 125.

The council calls the word of God "the energy of the church" and quotes scripture: ". . . the word of God is living and effective." Therefore, "all preaching of the church must be nourished . . . by sacred scripture." Our preaching based on scripture includes the "force and power of the word of God."

According to Saint Augustine, an eloquent preacher "should speak in such a way that he teaches, delights and moves"; then he quotes Cicero: "To teach is a necessity, to please is a sweetness, to persuade is a victory."[2] And he adds that teaching is primary, especially teaching the word of God. Such is the meaning of this book, *Teach, Delight, Persuade*.

There are some outstanding works that offer great insights into the three-year cycle of Sunday readings. Shortly after the publication of the *New Lectionary,* Reginald Fuller[3] Gerald Sloyan,[4] and Roland Faley[5] offered valuable scriptural commentaries on the complete Lectionary. Also, Mark Link[6] published complete homilies for the three-year cycle, which emphasized his forte of storytelling. But, as far as I know, no Catholic scholar has published a three-year series of complete Sunday homilies with the primary emphasis on scripture.

The main focus of this work is scripture exegesis. Scripture study was woefully lacking in the 1950's (when I was in the seminary). The explosion in the knowledge of scripture came in the last 50 years. Scholars have profoundly advanced our understanding of the entire Bible. They created a passion in me to follow their insights. Not everyone has been able to keep up with the mountain of solid scholarship. These homilies are one attempt to present these insights in homily form. Each homily is kept relatively short—only seven to ten minutes in length. That leaves room for personal stories, pastoral experiences, and applications to local needs or world events.

The theme for each homily is taken from the scripture readings for that particular Sunday in the common Lectionary. Often

---

2. Augustine, *De Doctrina Christiana* (On Christian Doctrine) (NY: Macmillan Publishing Co., 1958), Book IV, XII, 27. The quote from Cicero is from his Orations, 21, 69.

3. Reginald Fuller, *Preaching the New Lectionary* (Collegeville, MN: Liturgical Press, 1971).

4. Gerard S. Sloyan, *A Commentary on the New Lectionary* (NY: Paulist Press, 1975).

5. Roland Faley, TOR, *Footprints on the Mountain* (Mahwah, NJ: Paulist Press, 1994).

6. Mark Link, SJ, *Illustrated Sunday Homilies, 3 vols.* (Allen, TX: Tabor Publishing, 1990).

I include a careful exegesis of the Gospel or other reading. Where applicable, I explain the widely accepted modern forms of scriptural hermeneutics, such as form criticism and redaction criticism. The scriptural exegesis in these homilies flows from the valuable insights of scripture scholars of the last 50 years. Scripture scholars have profoundly advanced our understanding of scripture by opening up many new forms of criticism that are now widely accepted by the mainline Christian churches.

Each homily in this collection will try to do two things: 1. Understand just what the scripture writer intended to say in his situation or to discover just what the text meant to the author; 2. Discern what the text means now, in our situation today. Fortunately, recent scripture scholars put great emphasis on this point. Raymond Brown, my favorite scripture scholar, notes that modern literary criticism seems to be moving away from exclusive emphasis on what the author intended, toward including a broader emphasis on what his words actually convey to the individual reader. He adds, "the way the church in its life, liturgy and theology comes to understand the Bible is constitutive of the 'biblical meaning.'"[7] The Church today goes beyond what the Bible meant when it was originally written to what it means for us today. That is, from our perspective and in the light of our experience, we can find insights for a particular passage that are both true to its nature, yet would never have occurred to the scripture writer himself.

These homilies reflect the vision of Vatican II. They are the result of my 45 years of pastoral experience and preaching. They have all been tried out in parishes and often revised according to parishioner feedback. Many have been rewritten recently to reflect some of the social and religious concerns of this new century. The scriptural insights in them are the result of decades of modern scripture study. My preference has been the *Anchor Bible Series*,[8] which is an ecumenical series containing many of the definitive commentaries on the individual books of scripture. However, since these are homilies,

---

7. Raymond Brown, "The Meaning of the Bible," *Theology Digest*, 28, no. 4 (Winter, 1980), 312–313.

8. William F. Albright and David N. Freedman, gen. eds., *The Anchor Bible*

I have tried to use plain language and accessible style. To be consistent, all the scripture quotes will be from *The New American Bible*.[9]

For each Sunday there will be one complete homily that will often center on the Gospel. Occasionally, it will focus more on the Second Reading. For solemn feasts, I will offer more than one homily. The sequence will follow the seasons of the year: Advent, Christmas, Lent, Easter, Sundays of the year, and I will begin with the first Sunday of Advent—year A, year B and then year C. After all the Sundays of the year, I will add some of the great feasts of the year that do not usually fall on Sunday. Finally, there will be a biblical index, indicating all the readings actually used in these homilies. So if you are giving any kind of talk based on a particular passage of scripture, you can consult the index and find some homily suggestions.

Each homily is kept relatively short—only 7 to 10 minutes in length. That leaves room for your personal stories or adaptations, pastoral experiences, or applications to world events. I encourage you to make these homilies your own by incorporating the needs of your particular worshipping community into the scriptural insights offered here.

---

9. Donald Senior, gen. ed., *The New American Bible* (New York: Oxford University Press, 1990). Copyright © 1986 by the Confraternity of Christian Doctrine, Washington, D.C.

Part I

Advent

First Sunday of Advent

Year A

Isaiah 2:1–5; Romans 13:11–14; Matthew 24:37–44

Time and Eternity

I. Time has been a powerful influence in my life. From my youth
I have been very taken with how fleeting time is, how the years fly
along, how short a period is my life. Occasionally, I ask the question
of myself: How long do I have? Whether it's one year more or 20,
it's still a short time, because I am very aware that I have only this one
chance to do something worthwhile with my life. Such thoughts have
been a driving force throughout my life.

II. Today's readings encourage us to consider our view of
time, our sense of time and eternity in our lives. Many Christians of
the *past*—especially many preachers—so emphasized life after death
and eternity, that they lost all concerns for this life. Many preachers
seemed to say, "Don't be so concerned about material things, about
success and fortune; they will only distract you from the supernatural."
Or they told the poor, "You can't really change your circumstances;
but don't be discouraged; just wait for the chariot 'Comin' for to carry
you home.'"

Today many Americans go to the opposite extreme; they are
caught up in the American dream; they feel quite in control of their
life; they don't see the need for God in their daily lives; they manage
to ignore all thought of eternity. But most of us, I believe, are not
so crass. Rather we tend to hedge our bets; that is, we try to make
sure that we get all the satisfaction we can out of life now, just in case
the next life is an illusion. We are willing to do the minimum necessary to gain eternal life, but we are unwilling to follow Christ with
all out heart. We don't want to commit ourselves completely to the
Jesus way of life, just in case eternal life is not real, cheating us in the

end. We are unwilling to live entirely according to our hope in Christ, because his way and his values are too demanding.

III. Authentic Christianity asks us to take both this world and the next very seriously. Authentic Christianity never takes away the tension between life now and life after death. However, the *connection* between these two is not always clearly stated. The connection can be expressed this way: just because we believe in eternal life, our life now is more critical and filled with meaning, that is, all our work and daily achievement is an effort to make the quality of life around us a little more human and more Christian. All our efforts for material progress and psychological understanding are attempts to make all people more free and capable of becoming whole as human beings. And on the personal level, how we live as Christians now is what we will be for all eternity. Our *merit* before God consists not in so many pious prayers or good actions—like coins in a piggy bank—but in the kind of *person* we become. That is, whatever human development we gain now—whatever love, caring, acceptance, understanding we make a part of us now—that is the kind of person we will be for all eternity. And whatever deficiencies we have now—whatever selfishness, prejudice, enmity, lack of caring we have now—that will be a limit on us for all eternity. In other words, it is you and I, with exactly the character and qualities we have developed in this life, that will enter heaven. Our life will be transformed, but it will still be you and I.

IV. Saint Paul tells us today how we are to live out that tension of authentic Christian living, how we can take time and eternity seriously. "[P]ut on the Lord Jesus Christ," he urges us. Perhaps we can interpret his urging this way: Provide for yourselves and family; enjoy the world you live in; seek peace and satisfaction in your daily living. But also do all these things with the spirit and values of Christ: "[P]ut on the Lord Jesus Christ." Which means, have a sense of justice at work, try to show kindness to your neighbor during the day, have patience with your family, be charitable in speaking to others, have a Christian concern for others, accept the suffering that is a natural part of your life. This is how a Christian lives in time with a view of eternity. This is what we struggle to do in the short time we have in order to live as authentic Christians.

Year B

Isaiah 63:16b–17, 19b and 64:2–7; 1 Corinthians 1:3–9;
Mark 13:33–37

Waiting

I. Life is filled with *waiting*. Almost nothing worthwhile in life is sudden. All the important things are awaited, looked forward to, given time, hoped for. We begin life by waiting for our birth. Our parents wait expectantly for our first step, our first word. Soon we look forward to school and then to high school. In time we are anxious to graduate. We strive for the time when we can be on our own and independent. Then we wait for love and for one special love to come along; then we have to be patient for that love to grow and deepen. We look for a job that will satisfy us. We wait for our individual life to reveal its meaning and value. We watch our children grow up and move through all the stages of early life and wonderful changes. We expect the various transitions of our adult life that cannot be skipped: settling down, mid-life, later adulthood. Eventually we look forward to retirement. Finally, we reluctantly wait for death in hope. In all this waiting there may be furious activity: events may be set on timetables, projects may be rushed, schedules may be accelerated, activity may even be hectic. But life nevertheless develops slowly; human growth is gradual, love takes time, human caring takes patience. Waiting is the law of life, the measure of love.

II. Some of this waiting is neutral—wasted time. Such as our waiting for a bus or an elevator to get to us. Such is the waiting on the telephone or at the checkout line in the supermarket. This kind of waiting is like that of young people on the corner, just waiting for something to happen. Some of our waiting is filled with suspense and anxiety. As when we are in a doctor's office, waiting for an appointment. Such also is our concern when a child hasn't come home at night. Even more so, when we have a son or daughter in service or a child in trouble. Such is the anxiety when our life is enveloped in darkness or sickness, and we keep waiting for the light or relief. But some of our waiting is expectant or joyful. As that of a child waiting for Christmas to come. Or when we anticipate a vacation trip. Such also is the long expectancy of a mother awaiting the birth of her child. Or for a farmer waiting for his crops to grow through the summer sun and rain. Such is our joy when we anticipate the visit of a good friend or moving into a new home.

III. We Christians have a good start on waiting. This Advent season, which we begin today, gathers all these forms of hope and waiting together in one short time. And one beautiful symbol of that waiting is the *advent wreath* here in the sanctuary. This wreath, which we have just (blessed and) lighted, is a sign of our Christian waiting in its many forms. This wreath is first of all a symbol for Christ to come at Christmas. In the spirit of the Old Testament, we wait with God's people through a thousand years of prophecy and expectation for God's plan of salvation to be revealed in Christ. Today's reading from Isaiah expresses this expectancy: "Oh, that you would rend the heavens and come down." With them, we look for the rending of the heavens when God will send our Savior at Christmas. Each year we renew this sense of waiting, for it is a very human need to repeat this sense of anticipation for the unique event which changed all of human history.

Secondly, this wreath is a symbol of Christ's coming at the end of time or at the end of our life. This end of life is the only thing certain about our life. For us Christians, we also have the assurance of life after death flowing from Christ's death and resurrection. Without that assurance, our lives are suspended in time, disjointed, without a goal or final purpose. With that assurance, we are confident—along with Paul in the second reading—to follow Christ in faith ". . . as [we] wait for the revelation of our Lord Jesus Christ." And finally, the wreath is a symbol of our waiting for Christ to come into our lives more and more. For all of this waiting is not only the law of life and the measure of love; it is also the way of Christian growth. By all this waiting, we grow humanly through patience, courage, expectancy, and hope. This is part of the sense of the Gospel: the master ". . . places his servants in charge, each with his work." He means that as we fulfill those human tasks with patience and expectation, we grow into Christ.

IV. At the beginning of Advent, then, these readings offer help for us in all our human waiting. They remind us that without Christ, our hopes tend to die, our dreams fade away, our life has no ultimate direction. But with Christ, our joyful anticipations are not just fleeting moments. With Christ, our human growth has a model, a concrete human ideal. With Christ, all our human life transitions have a final goal and purpose. With Christ, all of our present living is a gifted moment.[1]

YEAR C

Jeremiah 33:14–16; 1 Thessalonians 3:12—4:2; Luke 21:25–28, 34–36

A SHORT TIME

I. One poem by Robert Frost is a favorite of mine. In it he describes his experience of riding out on horseback in a melancholy mood on one of the darkest nights of the year. He contemplates the cold, the snow and the darkness and thinks of his death:

> The woods are lovely dark and deep,
> But I have promises to keep,
> And miles to go before I sleep,
> And miles to go before I sleep.

II. Advent is often a melancholy time—a time for thoughts of death and shortness of life, and of what we might do with our life. In today's Second Reading, Paul is very conscious of death. This First Letter to the Thessalonians is his earliest writing, written at a time when he expected the end of the world to be coming soon. He wanted to answer a question for his converts: "How should we act if the end is near?" His answer is clear and direct: "[M]ay . . . you increase and abound in love for one another . . . so as to strengthen your hearts . . . at the coming of our Lord Jesus Christ." He seems to say to them: May you learn to love more and more in the time remaining for that is what you will be doing for all eternity. Now that's a nice thought for them and for us. But it doesn't seem to get through to us consistently, because we don't have a sense of urgency about all this. If we are young, we feel we are immortal. If we are middle-aged, we

---

1. Note: The four Advent candles can serve the same purpose as the Advent wreath.

are not regularly moved by the shortness of life. And none of us lives completely according to our hope in Christ. Many of us hedge our bets. That is, we follow Christ in half-hearted hope, but we also try to make sure that we get what we can now, just in case the next life is an illusion. We are unwilling to follow Christ with all our hearts, just in case that life is not real and we might be cheated.

III. In today's Gospel, Jesus assures us: "For that day will assault everyone who lives on the face of the earth. Be vigilant at all times." He wants us to live in that certainty and in the glorious hope that makes this short life even more valuable. He wants us to realize that he is certainly coming at the end of life. In my own life, I have been very conscious of the shortness of life. Now perhaps I have 10 to 20 years left. That is such a short time to accomplish something worthwhile in my life. It is such a short time to grow in love of God and neighbor. It is such a short time to really learn the way of Jesus and draw close to him. It is such a short time to become the kind of person I will be for all eternity. Such thinking is a driving, moving force for me.

IV. These are melancholy thoughts. They remind me of other passages in scripture, such as the classic lament of Job: "[M]y life is like the wind" (Job 7:7), in a moment it is gone and no trace is left of its passing; or the caution of James in his letter: "You are a puff of smoke that appears briefly and then disappears" (James 4:14). But these thoughts can add an urgency to our life: to do what we can with our time now, both to make our little part of the world a little better and to become the person we will be for all eternity. There is such a little time, "But I have promises to keep and miles to go before I sleep, and miles to go before I sleep."

Second Sunday of Advent

Year A

Isaiah 11:1–10; Romans 15:4–9; Matthew 3:1–12

Prepare the Way of the Lord

I. In modern times we have some difficulty understanding the message of John the Baptizer in these Advent readings. His message is: "Repent, for the kingdom of heaven is at hand!" In the old church, John's message was sufficiently clear; for then we put a lot of emphasis on *sin* and the commandments; so "repent" meant "get rid of your sins and turn away from evil." And for some people even today that is still the right medicine. But in the new church in general, we put more emphasis for Christian life on *commitment* to a person, on a way of life; therefore, "repent" seems rather an inadequate message to prepare for Christ. As a result, some of us may not understand John's message or not see it as appropriate for us. His preaching seems as vague as a prophet's preaching in the desert. So I would like to ask two questions today: 1. What was John's real message then? 2. How does that translate into a practical, modern Christian life?

II. First, what was John really saying to the people of his day? His theme was "repent" or as another translation has it, "Reform your lives! The reign of God is at hand." What he was asking for was a complete *reorientation of attitudes*, which John himself explained, "[D]o not presume to say to yourselves, 'We have Abraham as our father.'" That is, you cannot trust only in your Jewish heritage; you cannot place your confidence in the fact that you are Jews, God's chosen people. But he was also very practical, as we see in Luke's Gospel (3:11, 13–14): "Whoever has two cloaks should share with the person who has none." And to tax collectors he warned, "Stop collecting more than what is prescribed." To others he urged, "[D]o not falsely accuse anyone, and be satisfied with your wages." In a word, he teaches: prove your faith and change of attitude by your justice, kindness, and love. Only then will you be ready for God's kingdom that is now present in Christ.

All of this is quite similar to Christ's own preaching and message. His theme was the same as John's: "Repent, for the kingdom of heaven is at hand" (Matthew 4:17). Thus, for Jesus too the kingdom of God involves a call to repentance or reform, a *metanoia*; it demands a total transformation of life, a radical decision for God. Modern theologians describe that radical decision as accepting the mystery of Jesus as our plan of life and our interpretation of life's meaning. It means that all our deepest questions about human life— the source of life, the model for it, the purpose, direction, and goal of it—all of these are answered for us in the teaching and person of Jesus. In a word, we affirm that Jesus is the answer to all our human living.

III. The second question is this: How does all that translate into a practical, modern Christian life? The answer *today* is very different from the common spirituality of the last thousand years. For a thousand years, our lay spirituality has been a kind of imitation of religious spirituality, that of religious monks. Since the three vows of poverty, celibacy and obedience were considered "the way of perfection," lay spirituality was described as an approximation of that monastic life, that is, with a spirit of poverty, a chaste and faithful life in marriage, and an obedient following of the laws of the Church—along with some penance and devotional practices.

What we are finally learning in this twenty-first century is a *new form* of spirituality that is not just a watered-down version of monkish spirituality. Let me describe just two elements of this new spirituality. The first element of our spirituality concerns all the people we deal with all day long. The heart of our lives is people: incidental people we encounter in the stores or on the street, constant people in our work, essential people in our family and friendships. We are almost never without people; they are the constant factor of our daily existence. And Christ's secret for us in his way is to recognize that what we do to them, we do to him: "[W]hatever you did for one of these least brothers [or sisters] of mine, you did for me" (Matthew 25:40)—whether we realize it or not. We are to serve Jesus in others; we are to love all of them in the spirit of Jesus.

The second element is best expressed in the Letter to the Colossians, "[W]hatever you do, in word or deed, do everything in the name of the Lord Jesus" (Colossians 3:17). To act "in the name of the Lord Jesus" is to conform our life to his pattern, to act according to his teaching and example. This means that all we do is valuable in itself as following the way of Jesus and serving the needs of his people. True, almost all our actions are common and ordinary, but they are all part of the Jesus way, part of serving the needs of his people. As such, they are all sacred; they are the stuff of sanctity. This is what it means to "Repent, for the kingdom of heaven is at hand," for us who live in the world today. More and more, we see that the very life we live is the heart of our following of Christ.

Year B

Isaiah 40:1–5, 9–11; 2 Peter 3:8–14; Mark 1:1–8

Typology and John the Baptizer

I. Scripture often makes use of typology, in which one extraordinary person or one great event is seen as a type of another. Our readings today can help us understand better all biblical typology. The first reading, from Deutero-Isaiah, is one of the best-known passages of the Old Testament and a prime example of typology.

II. The first step in Isaiah's typology is the central event of the Old Testament, the exodus of God's people out of Egypt. That exodus was the original type or model. It was marked by the many miracles and signs of God for the sake of Moses and his people. It led to the promised land of Israel and a new way of freedom and living for the Israelites. The second step in Isaiah's typology is the return of the Israelites from the Babylonian exile back to Israel around 538 BC. Here the new Moses is Isaiah the prophet himself as the voice that cries out in the wilderness, "In the desert prepare the way of the LORD! . . . / Every valley shall be filled in, / every mountain and hill shall be made low." That is, their return will include miracles similar to those of the first exodus; God will again intervene in history, making their way smooth and bringing about the return from exile.

By this comparison, some consider Isaiah as the father of typology, as the first one to use the exodus as the type of God's major interventions in history. Our Gospel today offers the final step in this typology. Now the prophet is John the Baptizer; he is the voice in the wilderness "crying . . . : / 'Prepare the way of the Lord, / make straight his paths.'" Just as Moses prepared a way for the exodus and Isaiah prepared a way for the second return from exile, now John the prophet prepares a way for the advent of the Messiah.

III. This offers us a clear and theologically accurate way of understanding typology in scripture. It is not based on the conviction that history repeats itself; nor does it require that all the types were foreseen by the prophets involved. Rather it is based on the conviction that God's mighty acts in history follow a consistent pattern because God is true to himself and his purpose. In each case the eschatological event is defined as the revealing of God's glory. Isaiah prophesizes: "The glory of the LORD shall be revealed." This "glory" becomes a special word of salvation history; it refers to the saving presence of God who "comes with power." In the New Testament, John's Gospel constantly refers to this glory: for example, "[T]he Word became flesh / . . . / and we saw his glory, / the glory as of the Father's only Son" (John 1:14).

IV. Now, let us be practical. John the Baptizer exhorts us today: "Prepare the way of the Lord, / make straight his paths." This notion of the "way of God" is one of the richest expressions of the Bible. In the Acts of the Apostles, Christianity is called simply "the way." In John's Gospel, Jesus himself declares, "I am the way" (John 14:6). This way of Jesus is made concrete for us by his very life. The minimal element of following this way is to renounce sin—as indicated in today's readings. But the complete way of following this way is to respond to Jesus' invitation: "Whoever wishes to come after me must . . . take up his cross, and follow me" (Matthew 16:24) And the sense of that invitation is to be willing to offer our whole life for the cause of Christ. In the spirit of this invitation, let us try this Advent to offer our lives to follow Jesus our Savior in his way. Little by little we "Prepare the way of the Lord, / make straight his paths."[2]

---

2. *The New American Bible* prints poetry in a distinctive way. It sets it off with double spacing and with special indentation. We will follow that format for long poetic quotes. But for short quotes we will simply indicate the separate lines with a slash—as we did here.

Year C

Baruch 5:1–9; Philippians 1:4–6, 8–11; Luke 3:1–6

Luke's Way of Salvation

I. Christianity is a historical religion. Luke's Gospel proclaims a very human and historical religion: "In the fifteenth year of the reign of Tiberius Caesar . . . the word of God came to John." Luke wants us to know that the decisive phase of divine salvation began under a certain petty prince named Pontius Pilate and Jewish leaders named Annas and Caiaphas, in an undistinguished region of Galilee.
Not only that, but Jesus himself was an historical person, caught up like all of us in space and time and history. He himself willed to walk a totally human path: he was born under the emperor Augustus, precisely in Nazareth—a town from which no good can come (cf. John 1:46); finally he suffered under Pontius Pilate. He too was imprisoned in the here and now, with all the limitations of human existence. And the way of salvation he opened up for all peoples is also very historical and concrete. John, his precursor, preached, / "Prepare the way of the Lord . . ." by means of ". . . a baptism of repentance for the forgiveness of sins." And Jesus himself marked out certain definite ways of salvation for us: Repent . . . believe in the Gospel . . . be baptized with water . . . eat my body . . . keep the commandments. What all this means is that Christianity is a very historical and specific way of salvation.

For many people, it is too human; they would like their own religion to be entirely personal; they believe faith is an individual, internal commitment to God without careful regard for what we find in scripture or history and without a church community. They cannot believe that God could be so clear, human, and definite in his way of salvation.

II. Luke sees all this very differently. In our Gospel today, John urges: "Prepare the way of the Lord, / make straight his paths." John took these words from Isaiah the prophet as indicated in the first reading today. He wants everyone to prepare their hearts and lives in very definite ways to make a smooth way for God. This notion of the "way of God" is one of the richest expressions in the Bible. From the first book of the Bible, "the way" was a definite manner of life for God's people (e. g., Genesis 18:19). In the New Testament, we all hear Jesus proclaim that he is "the way" (John 14:6), meaning that he himself, his teaching, his example, his life is a very concrete model and way of salvation; in fact, "No one comes to the Father except through me" (14:6). And when Luke writes his second volume, the Acts of the Apostles, he frequently refers to Christianity simply as "the way." Throughout the Acts of the Apostles, when people ask about the way to salvation, they are told to believe and be baptized. They are told that Jesus' way includes certain sacramental actions as well as acts of justice, kindness, and love of neighbor. And it involves a community joined together in Christ with interdependence and definite authority.

III. And just as with John the Baptizer and Jesus, this Christian way is very human and rooted in history. Throughout Luke's Acts of the Apostles, this community fails badly, works through great divisions, is led by uneducated and sometimes inadequate people. Luke presents this community of Jesus as not completely formed and far from finished. Rather, it constantly unfolds in fits and starts; it very slowly grows in its understanding of the faith; it works through major uncertainties and divisions. It is very much a human and imperfect community but with organized norms and leaders.

IV. All of this is just as true for us Christians today. We follow an historical Jesus who is the norm for all our faith. He was himself utterly human, and he marked out for us certain definite ways of salvation, including definite sacraments, a faith that needs to constantly grow in its understanding of his word, with human leaders who taught with authority, and a community entrusted with maintaining that word and sacrament for all ages.

V. Let me conclude with Paul's words in the Second Reading today. Here Paul is pleading with his beloved church at Philippi to constantly grow in their human knowledge of Jesus and his way: ". . . this is my prayer: that your love may increase ever more and more in knowledge and every kind of perception, to discern what is of value, so that you may be . . . blameless for the day of Christ."

For Paul too, our faith is utterly human but entirely centered on Jesus the way.

Third Sunday of Advent

Year A

Isaiah 35:1–6a, 10; James 5:7–10; Matthew 11, 2–11

Wishes and Hopes

I. These next few weeks are a time of wishes and dreams, of stories and legends, of prophecies and hopes, of fantasies and imaginings. These days children have lots of wishes, TV produces legends and fantasies, Scripture is filled with prophecy, Scrooge has dreams, we fill our homes with trees, lights and decorations, children imagine Santa Claus coming and Frosty the snowman talking.

II. So it is timely to talk about wishes and hopes. There is a great difference between the two. *Wishes* are flights of fancy; they teach us what might be possible; they help us be playful with the unattainable. It is good to have wishes; without them life would be quite too grim and too rational. *Hopes* are based on reasonable foundations; hopes are expectations of what we might become, of what we expect to be. It is essential for us to have hopes; without them we would not even try to fulfill ourselves; without them we would be inclined to avoid reality; we would be overwhelmed by death.

III. There is no problem in having wishes; but there is in building a life on them. God is not someone who grants our wishes; he is someone who fulfills our hopes, who makes reality work. As an example of all this, take John the Baptizer. He could so easily have been a man of *wishes*, of dreams, of fantasies. For he was sent by God; he had every right to dream of great success. But most of the important people rejected him. When Jesus came, John might have at least expected to be certain that he was the Messiah. But he had his moments of doubt, as in the Gospel today: "Are you the one who is to come, or should we look for another?" He must have imagined that he would have some part in Jesus' later work, yet he was thrown into prison. Surely he wished to be exonerated and justified; but he was beheaded instead.

Rather, John was a man of *hope*, and only because of hope could he accept the reality of his life. He was nothing but "A voice of one crying out in the desert, / 'Prepare the way of the Lord'" (Matthew 3:3). He had many followers who later likely became disciples of Christ. For a short time he fulfilled his work and prepared a way for the Christ. But then his public life ended; he was put in prison and beheaded. So John did not base his life on wishes and what might have been, but on hope and confidence in God.

IV. We are often tempted to base our lives on *wishes*, on what might have been. At times we fantasize about being rich or successful; we dream about accomplishing something great in our lives. We wonder what our life would have been if we were married—or if we were married to someone else. We imagine a life free of all problems and difficulties. We would like to live without sickness or anxiety. We wish for our children to fulfill all our dreams for them; we expect that our friends will always be constant. But these things will probably not happen; they are only wishes and fantasies; they are not usually a part of human existence or the reality of life.

But we can be people of *hope*. Once the human heart is reconciled with itself and with reality, we can live out our hope. Once we make a truce with our own life, our own limitations, we can have courage in the face of reality. Hope shows us that only this occasionally gray life of ours is real. Hope tells us that by accepting this reality, we become our authentic selves. Hope lived out leads to certain fulfillment in Christ.

V. In these days of wishes and dreams and fantasies, we can be playful and imaginative. But these days are also days of hope, for the coming of the Lord is at hand. We have no assurance that God will fulfill our wishes. But he will fulfill our hopes. This is the promise and joy of Christmas.

Year B

Isaiah 61:1–2a, 10–11; 1 Thesslonians 5:16–24;
John 1:6–8, 19–28

Saint John and Fidelity

I. In the midst of Advent today, we celebrate *Gaudete*, Rejoice Sunday.
We hear Paul exhort us: "Rejoice always . . . in Christ Jesus." Also
Isaiah exclaims: "I rejoice heartily in the Lord." For many years we
wore rose-colored vestments on this Sunday, a joyful color, because
the Lord is near. Yet the dominant figure for today is John the
Baptizer. Perhaps by studying John the Baptizer, by understanding
what kind of person he was, we might experience a certain kind of
Christian joy.

II. Consider what happened to Saint John and what might
have happened. Many, perhaps very many people had come to John to
be baptized by him and to express their faith. So the leaders of the
people came out to ask him who he was. As an answer in today's
Gospel, he describes his divine call: "I am 'the voice of one crying out
in the desert, / Make straight the way of the Lord.'" And what success
did he have? He certainly had many followers and some of them later
became apostles of Jesus. But many did *not* prepare the way of the
Lord, especially the leaders of the people who refused to follow John,
believe in him, or to be baptized. He was even scorned by some of
the leaders; then he was put in prison. Finally, he was ignominiously
beheaded. Such was the earthly reward for the man of whom Christ
said, "[A]mong those born of women there has been none greater
than John the Baptist" (Matthew 11:11). His entire life had been for
one purpose, to which he was faithful. What had gone wrong?

What might have happened to John? He was sent by God;
he might have expected great success. He was the precursor of Jesus;
he might have dreamed that he would have some part in Jesus' later
work. He was faithful to his call; he could at least have hoped that he
would ultimately be exonerated and justified.

But John was faithful to his call. What might have been did
not distress him. Personal success did not occupy his attention. What

actually happened was what he cared about. Accepting the reality of his life was enough for him. Such was his faith.

III. Now compare John's experience to ours; look at what happens to us and what might have happened. All of us have plans and dreams and desires, especially when we are young. How seldom things develop just the way we hope! Along the way, most of us meet with some great difficulty—a chronic health problem, difficulty in our marriage, disappointments in our children. All of us have smaller but very real difficulties. We wonder, for example, why our lives are limited by such a job, or such relatives, or such a mediocre life. We see others having success, notable achievements, some notoriety, while we have little or none. We wonder sometimes, where did we go wrong?

And what might have happened to us? Without our children, we might have had more freedom. Without some chronic health problem, we would have had an easier life. With some success in our work, we might have had a strong sense of accomplishment. With better luck, we might have made a name for ourselves. If only things were a little different, we might have fulfilled our early dreams. Today, let us compare our life experience to that of John. What might have been must not disturb us. Personal success need not preoccupy us. Public acclaim is not essential for us. Accepting the reality of our life is all God asks of us.

IV. One powerful modern example for me is that of Mother Teresa of India, the Nobel Prize winner. When she was asked, "How can you continually work with the desperately poor and dying, especially when they continue dying? Don't you get utterly discouraged with such depressing work: How can you constantly live without any success?" Her answer was striking to me: "God has not called me to be successful; he has only called me to be faithful." She implied that success is not the hallmark of a Christian, fidelity is. The only success God asks of you and me is that we be faithful to the reality of our life as it comes to us humanly. Being faithful can be the source of lasting peace and joy.

Year C

Zephaniah 3:14–18a; Philippians 4:4–7; Luke 3:10–18

Prepare a Way for the Lord

I. We modern Christians are not used to the preaching of a prophet. All our life, we hear from Church leaders who are more comfortable being pastoral shepherds—consoling, correcting, encouraging us Christians to live good lives within the structure of the Church. We seldom hear the prophetic word of God in its Old Testament rough vitality. Only rarely do we hear the more insistent and demanding voice of our prophetic tradition. But in today's Gospel, we hear John the Baptizer; he is very much the great prophet, speaking to the people of his time. With a little imagination, we can hear John speak to us today in a similar fashion. Let us try to visualize John the prophet then and now.

II. First John had to *disquiet* those Jews who felt comfortable and secure. They felt secure because, "We have Abraham as our father" (Matthew 3:9). That is, we have this blood relationship and faith affinity with Abraham that are sufficient to establish our justification. John's answer rang out, "You brood of vipers! . . . Produce good fruit as evidence of your repentance" (Matthew 3:7–8); that is, it's not enough to be proud of your Jewish heritage, you must live like a true believer. If John were speaking to us today in his prophetic manner, he might say: "It's not enough to be proud of being a Catholic, to affirm all the truths of the Apostles' Creed; you must also commit your life to Christ and try to live as Jesus lived."

Secondly, John put some *teeth* into his prophetic preaching. He knew that some of his listeners were willing to be baptized and perhaps even to hear a call to do penance, but they wanted no interference in their way of making a living; they felt that no prophet had the right to restrict their work and livelihood. But John knew their lack of a sense of justice and warned them, "Do not practice extortion, do not falsely accuse anyone." If he were speaking to us today, his prophetic voice would be just as clear: "Don't tell me that 'Business is business,' or that religion has no place in your daily work. Living as a Christian involves every facet of your daily living."

Thirdly, John taught them about *true worship*. If some of the scribes and Pharisees would protest: We offer sacrifice regularly; we keep all the religious feasts, John would remind them of God's words to Amos the prophet: "I hate, I spurn your feasts, / I take no pleasure in your solemnities . . . / [rather,] let justice surge like water / and goodness like an unfailing stream" (Amos 5:21, 24). If John were speaking to us today, he might remind us of the words of Jesus himself: ". . . if you bring your gift to the altar, and there recall that your brother [or sister] has anything against you, leave your gift there at the altar, go first and be reconciled . . . and then come and offer your gift" (Matthew 5:23–24).

Finally, John taught them about *ethical values*. When someone wondered what they should do beyond keeping their responsibilities, he answered: Take on a new set of values; "[w]hoever has two cloaks should share with the person who has none." Today John the prophet would challenge us similarly: If you want to follow Christ, 'the man for others,' you need to accept his whole value system in which the love of neighbor is primary.

III. It's dangerous to ask a prophet, "What should we do?" But we can imagine what his response to us would be. When he answers, "Repent," he means have a total conversion of heart, a way of living that is different from the American Way. When he proclaims, "Prepare the way of the Lord" (Luke 3:4), he encourages us to live more and more according to the way of Jesus. This challenge of John the prophet rings out for all Christians throughout history— down to our day this Advent.

Fourth Sunday of Advent

Year A

Isaiah 7:10–14; Romans 1:1–7; Matthew 1:18–24

Bethlehem into Bedlam

I. In the year 1247, a hospital was founded in England, called St. Mary of Bethlehem. Two centuries later, it was converted into a hospital for the insane. In those days, the feeble-minded were chained and abused. Since there were no adequate treatments, medication, or counseling, the general environment was one of constant, irrational noise and confusion. In time the original name of Bethlehem was shortened to Bethlem and finally Bedlam—a word that has come into our modern English language as meaning any place of wild uproar and confusion. It is hard to believe that people could take such a glorious and peaceful name as Bethlehem and change it into the word "Bedlam," which means confusion and disorder.

II. Many people today are making Bethlehem into Bedlam. We would all like this season to be a time of peace and spiritual joy. But instead, we all experience some hectic times and turmoil. Shopping for gifts becomes a struggle of dealing with crowded stores and impatient mobs. Then trying to hide them from the young ones becomes a tense chore. Sending Christmas cards often seems an empty gesture or a trying job. Decorations are sometimes meaningless with nothing to do with the reality of Christmas. Last minute preparations can be tiring and anxious. What a Bedlam it seems at times! Such a picture is admittedly exaggerated but not totally unreal.

III. The real Christmas is found in Bethlehem. And today's readings can be very helpful. The Gospel tells us: ". . . this is how the birth of Jesus Christ came about . . . [His birth fulfilled the prophecy:] / 'The virgin shall be with child and bear a son, / and they shall name him Emmanuel,' which means 'God is with us.'" Here Matthew sees this quote from Isaiah as uniquely fulfilled in Jesus.

Such is Matthew's simple description of the Incarnation. What does it mean for us? Well it does *not* mean that God came to us under the appearance of man, that he was playing the part of a human being, that he looked like us so he could teach us in the surroundings of human life. *Rather*, it means that he became just as human as you and I are; he fully accepted all the limitations of human living; he took up our being born, our slow personal development, our gradual learning, our daily work, our tiredness and hunger, our fears and emotions, our suffering and dying. To go further, it means that Jesus transformed the meaning of this human existence and became the model of our human and Christian living.

IV. So this very human Jesus is our model for these hectic days of Advent. Thus, the joy of God-with-us can temper our hectic activity and foolish superficiality; our "peace on earth" can be found in the midst of our anxious preparations; our sense of God's loving presence is not driven out by noise and confusion. And—to speak more generally—only a thoroughly human Jesus can be a model throughout our life. His human example encourages us to have patience in the midst of frustration, kindness despite others' selfishness, constancy in the midst of monotony, peace in an anxious world, courage in the midst of pain, love in the face of indifference.

V. In a word, we are preparing for a real Savior and a human model, who does not save us *from* life but in the *midst* of our crazy modern life. With his help we can turn Bedlam back into Bethlehem yet.

Year B

2 Samel 7:1–5, 8b–12, 14a, 16; Romans 16:25–27; Luke 1:26–38

Incarnation Means Accepting Reality

I. Today's Gospel describes the incarnation of Jesus. With the "yes" of Mary, Jesus was conceived and became human in her womb. He was incarnated at that moment—*in carne,* "in the flesh." In preparing for Christmas today, let us meditate on what incarnation means for us.

II. First, the incarnation of Christ does *not* mean that God came to us merely appearing as a human being, playing the part of a human; nor does it mean that he wanted to teach us in a human context or milieu. Rather it means that he really became *human*; he was just as human as you and I are; he became a part of our world, he fully accepted our world, he became fully involved in it. That is, he submitted to all the accidents, human choices, injustices, and absurdities of human life. In the process, he took our being born, our slow human development, our work, our suffering and dying. And he made them his own, he transformed them, he made them Christian.

Secondly, because Jesus became incarnate, the entire nature of his revelation takes on a *this-world* significance. If our God is incarnate, then we cannot set as our goal and escape from this world; we cannot judge the entire world as evil. In fact, we see that God's revelation in Jesus is not only for the next world but intimately for this world; that is, the point of revelation is to make God's will and values known for our lives in *this world*. In a word, incarnation means that God has taken this world as his own, so that he can be found at the center of our world and of human life. This involves a new understanding of human life, a fresh beginning for our world, a whole new approach to God.

III. Two practical points seem to follow. First, because Jesus really became a part of our world and fully accepted human life, then we too are to be fully involved in this world. We are driven to accept the positive value of daily work, our human relationships, our worldly life in general. In a word, we Christians can find Christ in the midst of our world, and we try to see this real world in the light of Christ. Secondly, in Jesus our whole way to God is simplified. No longer must we be satisfied with partial truth about God as taught by the prophets, nor with rigid rules and precise religious practices as were required by the Pharisees, nor with private devotions or revelations as are followed by religious fanatics. In fact, our spirituality does not consist primarily in keeping rules, fulfilling spiritual exercises, practicing mortification, staying aloof from the world. Rather, there is only *one norm* for our holiness: it is Jesus and his way. For us he is the whole revelation about God; his only norm is a wholehearted acceptance of the real life that is ours; his way is one of love and compassion for all, which is very demanding but very concrete: "[L]ove one another as I love you" (John 15:12).

IV. What I have tried to say is that Christ's incarnation implies for us a total acceptance of our world, according to the concrete model that is Jesus himself. And today's Gospel gives us a picture of Mary who lived this acceptance so well: "May it be done to me according to your word."

Year C

Micah 5:1–4a; Hebrews 10:5–10; Luke 1:39–45

The Incarnated Christian

I. This fourth Sunday of Advent is dominated by the person of Mary. Each year on this Sunday, we read either the story of the annunciation of Christ's birth or, as this year, the visitation of Mary. In this Gospel, Mary is called "blessed" three times. This passage is the scriptural ground for our calling her the blessed Virgin. In this Gospel and in the entire Christmas story, we cannot look at Jesus without seeing his mother; and we can hardly look at Mary without meditating on the whole meaning of the incarnation. So what does it mean when we say that Jesus was conceived, was born, was incarnated in Mary?

II. First, it means that Jesus is really human in every way— just as human as you and I are. As a child of Mary, he took up our being born, our gradual learning, our failures, our tiredness and hunger, our emotions, our daily work, our suffering and dying. As a child of Mary, he became completely a part of our world, he accepted our human world, he was totally involved with it. And this incarnate child of Mary is the unique way God chose for our salvation. This human Jesus is God's preferred way to renew this world of ours. This life and death of Jesus is the substance of the New Covenant between God and us. Before the coming of Jesus, God's people sought the good graces of God mainly in prayer, atonement and sacrifices; they found holiness in keeping his Old Testament laws, in sacred places, in special feasts and rites prescribed by God. Only by fulfilling these divine prescriptions could they draw close to God and win his favor.

Once Jesus became incarnate, God began a new means of presence-with-us and a new way of salvation.

As today's letter to the Hebrews puts it: "Sacrifice and offering you did not desire, /but a body you prepared for me. . . . / Behold, I come to do your will, O God." That is, it was God's will that our redemption should be accomplished not through endless sacrifices and offerings but through the obedience of Jesus in his incarnation and his passion. As the theologian, Gregory Baum, put it: "In Christ is revealed that the way of God's presence is incarnation. God acts through the human. . . . Before Christ's coming, [people] sought the invisible God in temples and shrines; after his coming, they seek him in human life. What is revealed in Christ is that human life is the locus of the divine."[3]

III. Why is this so? Because all the moments of Christ's life were sacred. Not only his suffering and death, but all his human living was part of his saving work, a part of his holiness. Even his most human qualities and actions—such as anger and fear, hunger and thirst, learning and failure, suffering and trials—were sacred moments, means of grace. We have little difficulty affirming all these truths about Jesus. But what we need to realize is that, because of Jesus' incarnation, the same is true of our lives. That is, our entire human life can be a source of holiness and divine grace; all of human living can be sacred; all our human moments—everything except sin—can be sacred moments. This is the lesson that theologians are seeing more clearly and we are trying to understand in the beginning of the twenty-first century. One of the best scripture passages for this conviction is found in the Letter to the Colossians: "[W]hatever you do, in word or in deed, do everything in the name of our Lord Jesus" (Colossians 3:17). What it means to act "in the name of our Lord Jesus Christ" is to act according to the teaching and example of Jesus. Therefore, all our human actions, all our daily living is valuable in itself as a following in the way of Jesus and serving the needs of his people. Almost all our actions are common and ordinary, but they are all part of acting "in the name of the Lord Jesus Christ." So they are

---

3. Gregory Baum, *Man Becoming* (NY: Herder and Herder, 1970), p. 90.

all sacred; they are the stuff of sanctity, just as they were for Jesus, our incarnate Lord. That's some of what we mean when we affirm: "Human life is the locus of the divine."

Part II

Christmas

The Nativity of the Lord (Midnight)

Years A, B, and C

Isaiah 9:1–6; Titus 2:11–14; Luke 2:1–14

God's Christmas Gift

I. It happened some years ago in Pittsburgh. It was the middle of the Christmas rush, but a crippling teamsters strike prevented the department stores from delivering their goods. At such a time of the year, this could be disastrous for business. Large packages and gifts that were bought could not be delivered to the homes. But some stores came up with an ingenious idea. When a customer purchased a gift that was too large to carry home, the store provided a large photograph of the article with the message reading: "This is your Christmas gift. We regret the delay, but it will be delivered as soon as possible." Seeing the picture was not as good as possessing the actual gift, but it was a tolerable substitute.

II. Christmas is the most joyful time of the year! All of America gets caught up in this joyous season. But only we Christians can really appreciate the real cause of our joy: the coming of Jesus into our world. In the Gospel tonight the angel expresses this wonderful gift to the shepherds: "I proclaim to you good news of great joy that will be for all the people. For today . . . a savior has been born for you." This is the total gift of Christmas, the reason for our joy: a Savior is born to us; salvation is offered us; eternal life is promised us. But we cannot possess that gift of salvation now; we do not own that salvation now; we only possess an assured *hope* of eternal salvation. What we have right now is like a *picture* of the gift we will one day possess.

III. What we need to realize is that we possess *right now* part of that gift of salvation. For Jesus' coming not only opens up eternal

life; it also *transforms human life now.* This is also the profound meaning of Jesus' coming; this gift we possess right now. For Christmas
is God becoming human; it means that Jesus really experienced
all of human living in order to give new value to our life now. That is,
Christmas teaches us that the way of God's presence in the world is
incarnation. It means that God acts through the human, through
ordinary words, deeds, and human relationships. What is revealed at
Christmas is that human life is the locus of the divine. Because of
Christ's coming, there are no merely natural things for us anymore,
but all human actions have a Christian purpose and significance;
all human existence is a part of God's plan of redemption in Christ.
The locus of God's grace is human living—*now,* just as it comes to us
in all our human activity.

    IV. Perhaps another way of saying this would help. This
wondrous Christ child transforms our life—our values, our attitudes,
our motives. Because Jesus was born among us, everything we do is
sacred if we do it in the spirit of Christ. Our life now, just as it comes
to us humanly, is our following "the way" of Jesus. And Jesus himself
is the model for all our human living, for he is our incarnate, flesh,
and blood Savior.

    V. In a word, there are two parts to the amazing gift of
Christmas that is ours right now. The first part is a *picture* of what
God will grant us in Jesus our Savior. The second is the *actual gift*
now, the transformation of all human life into the following of Jesus.

The Nativity of the Lord (Dawn)

YEARS A, B, AND C

Isaiah 62:11–12; Titus 3:4–7; Luke 2:15–20 (or Luke 2:1–14)

CHRISTMAS IS FOR CHILDREN

I. A contemporary Christmas carol is entitled, "Christmas is for Kids." It's not a memorable song, but it expresses a very common conviction. For in America today, most of Christmas is centered on children. Movies are about Santa Claus or other Christmas fantasies. TV adds lighthearted stories to delight them. Streets are filled with Christmas cheer. Homes are decorated with trees and lights. Christmas carols are everywhere. Parents spend so much care in buying gifts especially for the children. By the time Christmas comes, they are filled with so much expectation and delight they can hardly stand it. People who celebrate this feast without children around, miss some of the excitement of Christmas.

II. In our church, too, Christmas is the most joyous, lighthearted feast of the whole year. We all get caught up in the joyous spirit of Jesus being born as an infant. Every church has a crib scene that attracts us to this little child. All of us, adults and children, are seduced into loving our infant Savior. This seems like a perfect time for all of us to learn one quality that Christ taught us: "[U]nless you turn and become like children, you will not enter the kingdom of heaven. Whoever humbles himself like this child, is the greatest in the kingdom of heaven" (Matthew 18:3–4). What is this quality of childlikeness that Jesus calls greatness? Scholars of the past emphasized the innocence or humility of children. But recent scholars rather emphasize the dependence of children. They recall that in ancient society children had no legal rights, no individual standing; they were entirely dependent on their parents for everything, so that, in adult

society, they saw everything as a gift to them. Even today, young
children are dependent on their parents for almost everything. What
Christ means, then, is that all of us need to gain this quality of
childlikeness; we need to realize that we do not have legal right or
standing before God; we do not have a claim on God's kingdom
through rank or status or strict merit; we can only receive everything
from God as a gift; we stand before God as his creature, without any
claim or strict merit of our own. This is the only proper attitude for us
before God; once we admit it, we have the necessary quality for
greatness: childlikeness.

III. Now Christmas is the best time for us to learn this
quality of childlikeness, for we can go to the crib and learn greatness.
Near the crib we see shepherds, who are poor and needy; they are
the opposite of self-satisfied and self-sufficient people. Then we see
Mary and Joseph, who surprise us with their simplicity and lowliness;
they are the opposite of external greatness or renown. Next we see
a manger that is cold, dark and rough, fit more for animals than an
infant—the very antithesis of worldly power and success. Then,
finally we come before our newborn Savior, who like any infant is so
tender and lovable; before him, it is useless to be sophisticated, rich,
or distinguished.

IV. All we can do before this crib is to admire and love this
newborn Savior. And we can learn from him what God considers
greatness: to admit that as his children, we are totally dependent on
his grace for our salvation. "[U]nless you turn and become like
children, you will not enter the kingdom of heaven" (Matthew 18:3).

The Nativity of the Lord (Day)

Years A, B, and C

Isaiah 52:7–10; Hebrews 1:1–6; John 1:1–18

The Word Became Flesh

I. "[T]he Word became flesh / and made his dwelling among us."
This is how John's Gospel, this morning, describes the birth of
Christ. John's way of thinking is so very different from the famous
Christmas narrative in Luke's Gospel. Let us try to follow John's way
of thinking. For John, Jesus is the Word of God, the whole truth
about God, the entire revelation of God to us humans. In the person
of Jesus, along with his life and teaching, God has taught us all we
need to know about human life, eternal salvation and God himself.
The reading from Hebrews, today, also describes Jesus as God's
final revelation:

> In times past, God spoke in partial and various ways to our ancestors
> through the prophets; in these last days, he spoke to us through a
> Son . . . who is the refulgence of his glory, / the very imprint of his
> being . . . .

When the great mystic, Saint John of the Cross, comments on this
passage from Hebrews, he asks us to imagine God speaking to us
about Jesus the incarnate Word; God would tell us:

> If I have already told you all things in my Word, my Son, and I have
> no other word . . . what revelation can I now make that would surpass
> this? Fasten your eyes on Him alone, because in Him I have spoken
> and revealed all, and in him you shall discover even more than you ask for
> and desire. . . . If you turn your eyes to him, you will find [my complete
> revelation]. Hear Him, because I have no more faith to reveal nor truths
> to manifest.[11]

---

1. *The Collected Works of St. John of the Cross*, trans. By Kieran Kavanaugh and Otilio
Rodriguez, (Washington, D.C.: ICS Publications, 1979), p. 180 (*Ascent of Mount Carmel*, Book
II, Chap. 22, #5).

That is, Jesus is the whole Word of God to us; by his very person, his teaching, and his actions, he expresses the whole truth about God and about our salvation. Theologians might add that all other religions can teach about God and lead to salvation, but only Jesus is the complete Word of God for us.

II. Near the end of John's Gospel, Jesus himself makes the famous claim: "I am the way and the truth and the life" (John 14:6). Theologians explain this quotation many different ways. My preference is that Jesus is the way *because* he is the truth and the life. That is, he is the way because he is the whole truth and revelation of God; when we see him, we see the Father; when we know him, we know the Father. And he is the way because he is the life, the source of all grace and life now and for eternity. Practically, this means that Jesus is the unique channel of salvation for all people: "No one comes to the Father except through me" (John 14:6).

III. But John's First Epistle takes us one step farther; it tells us that the word that Jesus speaks to us is *love*, for he is the absolute proof of God's love for us: "God is love. In this way the love of God was revealed to us: God sent his only Son into the world so that we might have life through him" [now and for all eternity] (1 John 4:8–9). Without Jesus, God himself would be impenetrable, unknowable; his love would be ethereal, abstract, and distant. But with Jesus who comes to us at Christmas time, we have the human and conclusive proof of God's love; because of Jesus, we can see the face of God. As Jesus said: "Whoever sees me sees the [Father]" (John 12:45).

IV. John's theology is very profound here! But there is a simple way for us to relate to his sublime teaching. On this Christmas morning, we all can understand how Jesus is the Word of God by looking at the crib here in church. When we see the infant Jesus, we know clearly that our God is thoroughly committed to our simple, suffering human life; we know that our God is most compassionate, approachable, and loving. Merry Christmas!

Alternate Christmas Mass

Years A, B, or C

Include Titus 3:4–7 (Mass at dawn) or Hebrews 1:1–6 (Mass during the day)

Christmas and God

I. The trouble with God for many Americans is that God seems so impersonal, so distant from us and not involved in our real life. By impersonal, they mean that God is the creator so far beyond this world that even our language fails us; they cannot be comfortable or draw near to such an intangible Lord of the universe. By distant, they mean God's place is in heaven and so far removed from our world; God's being is inaccessible to us, even unimaginable. And they fail to see that God is involved in our real world.

II. Christmas can change all that for them and for any of us who feel that way about God, if we let our faith grow along with our understanding of the real meaning of the incarnation. The reading from Titus today proclaims: "[W]hen the kindness and generous love / of God our savior appeared . . . / he saved us." This grace has appeared visibly for us all in Jesus our Savior, born on this day. This incarnation means that God became human, just as human as you and I are. He became fully involved with our world; he took up our being born, our daily human living, our slow personal development, our work and failure, our tiredness and hunger, our fears and worries, our suffering and dying. He experienced all of these and transformed them, so that he could be the model for human existence and show us how to live as children of his Father. So our God is not impersonal; in Jesus he is thoroughly human and personal. Only when we realize that Jesus is fully human can we relate to him and try to make him the model of our lives. Only such a Jesus can we be comfortable with and draw near to.

III. Before Christ's coming, God was distant from our world. As the reading during the day on Christmas describes it: "In times past, God spoke in partial and various ways to our ancestors through the prophets" (Hebrews 1:1). That is, before Christ's coming, people listened to the impenetrable God through the mysterious and very partial revelation of the prophets, or they sought to know God by visions or revelations. So they did not find God himself, for God was far away in heaven and quite incomprehensible to them. But with the incarnation of Christ at Christmas everything has changed. The reading from Hebrews continues: "[I]n these last days, he spoke to us through a son." John of the Cross offers an engaging commentary of this passage. He asks us to imagine God speaking to us; God would say to us:

> Jesus is my complete answer . . . he is all my vision and all my revelation; in giving him to you as brother, master and companion, I have spoken to you once and for all. I have no more faith to reveal, nothing more to declare. Set your eyes on him alone, for in him I have spoken and revealed to you all things, and in him you shall find more than what you ask and desire.[2]

Therefore, for us Christians God is no longer as far away as the heavens and as distant as the next life. *No,* our God is present to us in Jesus: he is as visible as our brother Jesus if only we make the effort to know him in faith. He himself reminds us: "whoever sees me sees the one who sent me" (John 12:45).

IV. Finally, it is understandable that many Catholics do not find God in their real lives, because they grew up with a spirituality that made place for God only occasionally on the margins of their daily living. That is, they were taught that, since they were not religious who took vows and followed religious rules, the best they could do was to "offer up" their work and daily living. Only occasionally could they make time for God on the margins of their daily living by observing sacred times, places and actions, praying, receiving the sacraments. These were the only supernatural actions that connected them with God. But our modern spirituality is very different.

---

2. *The Collected Works of St. John of the Cross,* trans. By Kieran Kavanaugh and Otilio Rodriguez (Washington, D.C.: ICS Publications, 1979), p. 180 (*Ascent of Mount Carmel,* Book II, chap. 22, #5).

It teaches us that all our human moments are sacred moments. It notes first that all the moments of Christ's life were sacred—not only his suffering and death—but all of his human living was part of his saving work, part of his holiness. Even his most human qualities—such as anger and fear, hunger and thirst, learning and failure, as well as his suffering and trials—were sacred moments, means of grace. So also all our human moments—including our weakest and inadequate moments—everything except sin—can be sacred moments, a source of holiness and grace. As Gregory Baum expresses it:

> In Christ is revealed that the way of God's presence is incarnation. God acts through the human. It is in ordinary words gestures, in interpersonal relations that God communicates himself to us. Before Christ's coming, people sought the invisible God in temples and shrines; after his coming they seek him in human life. What is revealed in Christ is that human life is the locus of the divine.[3]

That is, because of Christ's redemption and grace, all of human life is sacred, if we do it in the spirit of Christ. God and his grace are now a part of human life constantly, as long as we are in his grace.

V. Especially at Christmas time, we can learn that our God is not impersonal. Since Jesus is truly human, we can relate to him very personally. At Christmas our God is not distant from us, no longer impenetrable. In Jesus God has revealed all things to us; God spoke to us immediately and clearly in his Son. Before Jesus' coming, people only found God in sacred temples, in visions and prophecies, not in their daily lives. Now that Christ has come, we find God and his grace in our real daily lives, lived in the spirit of Jesus. For us, God's grace is present in all human relationships and all our efforts to serve God's people. Because of Christmas, our God is now personal and present to us in all our human living.

---

3. Gregory Baum, *Man Becoming* (New York: Herder and Herder, 1970), p. 90 (emphasis added).

The Holy Family of Jesus, Mary, and Joseph

YEAR A

Sirach 3:2–6, 12–14; Colossians 3:12–21;
Matthew 2:13–15, 19–23

A MODEL FOR CHRISTIAN FAMILIES

I. The church's intention in this feast of the holy family is to present Mary, Joseph and Jesus as a model for Christian families. Let us begin with a description of the holy family that we see literally or figuratively depicted in all the infancy narratives.

Consider Joseph first. Once he met Mary, his life changed drastically. He was filled with anxiety and fear over Mary's pregnancy. He "decided to divorce [Mary] quietly" (Matthew 1:19), until his fears were put to rest. At the time she was to give birth, he had to make a long, hard journey with her to Bethlehem. Once they were there, the only place for her to give birth was a miserable stable. After the birth of their child, Joseph was warned that "Herod is going to search for the child to destroy him," so he could not even return home but had to take his family to Egypt and hide out in exile. Only after the death of Herod could they finally return home to Nazareth.

Then consider Mary. She was thrown into confusion over an unnatural conception; then she was caught up in a scandalous situation worthy of divorce. She gave birth to her child in a poor, stinking stable. When she presented Jesus in the temple, Simeon warned her ominously that ". . . you yourself a sword will pierce" (Luke 2:35). Then, she was forced to flee the wrath of a tyrant and become an exile in Egypt. Later, she led a poor and unnoticed life in Nazareth. All of this adds up to a turbulent family life—more troubling than most of our family lives. Such a family is certainly not our idea of a happy family! But if we want to summarize in a simple way what the infancy narratives tell us about the holy family, this seems a fair description.

II. This year, we read Matthew's account of the holy family's flight into Egypt. Matthew knows that Egypt was a traditional place of refuge for those fleeing from danger in Palestine. Israel, God's chosen son, was called out of Egypt in the highpoint event of the Old Testament—the Exodus. Now Matthew presents Jesus as the new Israel who relives the Exodus experience; that is, Jesus, the son of God, is similarly called out of that land in a new Exodus. And he explains all this by means of the citation from Hosea (11:1): "Out of Egypt I called my son." Thus Matthew, at the beginning of his Gospel, already presents Jesus as the fulfillment of God's promises to his chosen people. Throughout his Gospel, he will gradually present Jesus as the one to save his people and lead them to the promised redemption.

III. Now all of this is very important from Matthew's point of view, but it does not tell us much about the holy family as a model for family life today. For that, consider the Second Reading. The Church chose this reading from Colossians as a summary of the virtues that form the basis of Christian family life. First mentioned are the widely recognized virtues of compassion, kindness and patience. By our baptism, we have been clothed with Christ (cf. Galatians 3:27), and so should put on these virtues that correspond to our new life in Jesus. And because we are all very human, we will need forbearance and forgiveness: "[B]earing with one another and forgiving one another . . . as the Lord has forgiven you, so must you also do." Aren't these obvious necessities, especially for spouses and parents? Such virtues cannot be taught to children by others; they must be caught in the home. And above all other virtues, we Christians and families should be clothed in love, which is the paramount virtue of Christianity as the bond of perfection. The reading from Colossians concludes with a summary of our whole modern spirituality: "[W]hatever you do, in word or in deed, do everything in the name of the Lord Jesus." That is, not only this or that activity can be a part of our life in Christ, but absolutely every action of our lives. As long as we try to follow Jesus, there is a saving character to all we do—even the most ordinary actions done without any conscious reference to Christ. Everything is meant to be the "stuff" of our life in Christ.

IV. The holy family did not live an untroubled life by any means, but they practiced the virtues mentioned in this reading. Similarly, our families have their constant challenges and faults, but by constantly learning to "put on" the virtues of Jesus, we can strive to make them holy, too.

YEAR B

Sirach 3:2–6, 12–14; Colossians 3:12–21; Luke 2:22–40[4]

THE PRESENTATION OF JESUS IN THE TEMPLE

I. Today's Gospel records the presentation of Jesus in the temple. It is a prime example of redaction criticism, and can help us understand this form of scriptural writing. Luke is the redactor, the one who structures this entire episode so as to blend tradition with his own theology. The result is his specific critique or the meaning of this story. Let us look at some of these elements of Luke, the redactor, to discover what he deliberately chooses to teach us here.

II. Luke bases his entire description of Jesus' presentation on another presentation in the Old Testament. In the First Book of Samuel (1:24–28), the parents of Samuel bring young Samuel to the priest, Eli, in order to dedicate him to God's service. The old man, Eli, accepts the dedication of their son at the sanctuary and blesses Samuel's parents. Building on this parallel, Luke adds other themes that are important to his own theology and Gospel development. The most obvious one is that of the fulfillment of the Mosaic law. Thus, Mary fulfills the law of the Book of Leviticus for her purification after childbirth; and Jesus is offered to the Lord in fulfillment of the Exodus law for the first-born male. Simeon and Anna represent the remnant of Israel who accept the Messiah. They await the fulfillment of the prophetic promise—"the consolation of Israel." Simeon recognizes Jesus as the one bringing salvation to God's people. All of this happens in the temple at Jerusalem, which for Luke is the symbol

---

4. Note: The first two readings are the same for all three years; only the Gospel changes each year.

of continuity between promise and fulfillment, between the new Israel and the offer of salvation to the entire world.

III. The centerpiece for Luke is the *Nunc Dimittis* of Simeon: "Now, Master, you may let your servant go / in peace." In this prayer, Luke unites the Mosaic law, the historical prophecies now being fulfilled, and the temple cult—all of them set the scene for the greatness of Jesus. Simeon continues with an ominous warning: "[T]his child is destined for the fall and rise of many in Israel." He prophesies that the entire mission of Jesus will be critical and divisive for his people; in making a decision for or against Jesus, people will be forced to declare themselves, and so will "fall or rise," be saved or not. Simon continues with a warning to Mary herself: ". . . and you yourself a sword will pierce." This sword will be a discriminating sword for Mary as well. By this symbolic language, Simon refers to the scandal of the cross and the anguish that Mary will feel at Jesus' death.

IV. Luke adds various other points to further his theology. Thus, he notes that Jesus will not only be the Messiah of Israel but also "a light . . . to the Gentiles." Luke is more concerned than the other evangelists about universal salvation, including Gentiles. Luke is also careful to include both men and women equally. In today's Gospel, Luke mentions both Simeon and Anna, along with Joseph and Mary, and previously Elizabeth and Zechariah. This is Luke's way of showing that man and woman stand together, side by side, equal before God.

V. Finally Luke concludes: "[The holy family] returned . . . to their own town of Nazareth. [Jesus] grew and became strong, filled with wisdom." He wants us to know that Jesus was really human; he had to learn and to grow in wisdom, to go through all the stages of human growth, with the gradualness of all human children. And Luke is careful to present Jesus as growing *in the context* of the human family; that is, the holy family is the context in which Christ is prepared for his saving mission and his whole future life. So Luke presents the holy family as the *paradigm* for all Christian family life, for the Christian family is the divinely provided context in which every child grows spiritually and morally as a human being. All of these facets are important to Luke's theology as he shows us by means of his redaction criticism.

YEAR C

Sirach 3:2–6; Colossians 3:12–21; Luke 2:41–52[5]

FAMILY VIRTUES

I. The Church's intention on this feast of the holy family is to present Mary, Joseph and Jesus as a model for Christian families. Scriptural scholars are not convinced that all the events of the infancy narratives are strictly historical. Without deciding that issue, let us describe the holy family that we see literally or figuratively depicted in these narratives.

II. First, consider the external characteristics of the life of the holy family. Once Joseph met Mary, his life changed drastically. He was filled with anxiety and fear over Mary's pregnancy; as a "righteous man" (Matthew 1:19), he considered actually divorcing her according to their laws. Just before she was to give birth, he had to make a long, hard journey with her to Bethlehem. Once they were there, all he could find as a place for Mary to give birth was a miserable stable. After the birth of their child, he was warned: "Herod is going to search for the child to destroy him" (Matthew 2:13). So he could not even return home but had to take his family to Egypt and hide out in exile. Only after the death of Herod, could they finally make the journey home to Nazareth.

Mary's life was just as turbulent. She was thrown into confusion over her unnatural conception; then she was caught up in a scandalous situation worthy of divorce. She gave birth to her child in a poor, stinking stable. When she presented Jesus in the temple, Simeon warned her ominously ("you yourself a sword will pierce") (Luke 2:35). Then she was forced to flee the wrath of Herod, the tyrant, and become an exile in Egypt. Later, she led a poor and unnoticed life in Nazareth. All of this adds up to a turbulent family life—more troubling than most of our family lives. This is hardly our notion of a happy family!

---

5. Note: The first two readings are the same for all three years; only the Gospel changes.

III. Now let us look at the internal characteristics of the life of the holy family. The second reading today—from the Letter to the Colossians—describes many virtues for family living. The Church chooses this reading so that we can imagine the holy family as a model for these virtues. The author begins by listing a number of domestic virtues, common in the Gentile world of his time and gives them a distinctly Christian significance. He encourages us to "put on" or clothe ourselves with these virtues, just as a baptismal candidate will put on a new, white garment as he comes out of the baptismal font. Such a moral exhortation is very common in the epistles; in most cases, the author also includes a list of vices that the newly baptized should "put off" or avoid. We find such lists often in the epistles as a kind of moral code for husbands and wives, parents and children, masters and slaves. Scripture scholars refer to such lists of virtues and vices as "household or domestic codes." They warn us that such codes were derived from Stoic, non-Christian teachings and passed into Greek-speaking Christianity. For example today, "Wives, be subordinate to your husbands, as is proper in the Lord." Many Stoic codes were founded on the Stoic notion of superiors and inferiors, *not on Christ's teaching* of the equality of all. Sadly, the Pauline writers, especially the non-authentic Pauline writers, basically accepted this Stoic approach without adding the corrective of Christ's teaching of the equality of all people who follow his way. This is what modern scripture scholars mean when they say that scripture is "culturally oriented"; that is, the writers followed the culture of their time without always correcting the deficiencies of the Stoic and other pagan influences. In our day, we are very aware of the limitations of scriptural writings that are "culturally oriented"—not only concerning the subordination of women but with other moral issues regarding war and slavery. We realize that we need to add the Christian sense of justice and equality of all people. Only that way can we arrive at the true and even revolutionary morality of Christ himself.

IV. Let us end on a positive note. We can all find plenty of inspiration today for Christian families in the first part of this reading to the Colossians. "Put on then, as God's chosen ones . . . heartfelt compassion, kindness . . . gentleness, and patience." These are critical virtues in any family; the motivation for doing so is that by baptism we have been clothed in Christ (cf. Galatians 3:27), and so should put on these virtues that correspond to our new life in Christ. And because we are all very human, we need forbearance and forgiveness: "[B]earing with one another and forgiving one another . . . as the Lord has forgiven you." I suspect husbands and wives know even more than I how necessary forgiveness is among spouses. Family life is such a close existence that it is bound to include offenses and human failures; it demands this Christian virtue again and again. "And over all these put on love, that is, the bond of perfection." And for our children, parents know that love is not taught by words; it is caught by them—in the home, more than anywhere else. God bless our families. They are the fount of our personality and of all our Christian living.

The Blessed Virgin Mary, the Mother of God

YEARS A, B, AND C

Numbers 6:22–27; Galatians 4:4–7; Luke 2:16–21

MARY, THE MOTHER OF GOD

I. Today's feast is entitled, Mary the Mother of God. The Second Reading is from Paul's Letter to the Galatians. Let us use this short reading to focus our thoughts today: "[W]hen the fullness of time had come, God sent his Son, born of a woman . . . so that we might receive adoption. As proof that you are children, God sent the spirit of his Son into our hearts, crying out, 'Abba, Father.'" That is, because Jesus was born of Mary, we are all redeemed and made children of God.

II. Paul's primary, amazing assertion, here, is that we are all sons and daughters of God. He means that by baptism we have the Spirit of God's Son dwelling permanently within us, so we can cry out with full confidence in this Spirit of his Son, "*Abba*, Father." This is Paul's unique way of describing our *intimacy with God*. Each of the great New Testament writers offers us a reason why we can relate to God intimately. Paul's teaching is very solid and most encouraging: our status as a child of God is initiated through faith and baptism; it is activated and realized through the indwelling of the Holy Spirit. This is a permanent status making us members of the family of God so that we come under the paternal care of God. For an *individual* to address God as Father was unheard of in the Old Testament; for Jesus to address God as "Father" was something new and unheard of, and unique to Jesus himself. Paul understood this and taught that all Christians could boldly use this same form of address to God. This original idea of Paul is based on the truth that we each have the Spirit of God's Son in us that encourages us to be so intimate with God that we can call him *Abba*, Father. What a great way to pray to God!

III. The Gospel today presents Mary as the mother of Jesus: The shepherds "found Mary and Joseph, and the infant lying in the manger." And then adds: "Mary kept all these things, reflecting on them in her heart." This passage is an incisive choice for this feast of the Mother of God, for it includes the two outstanding reasons why Mary is our mother and our model. First, Mary is the mother of Jesus, by whom we are all made God's children. As mother of Jesus, she is preeminent of all God's creatures. As "Mother of God" she is the mother of God's children. And secondly, Mary is the exemplar of faith. As she reflected on the all that happened, she slowly discovered the meaning of God's way of salvation; as she continued to fulfill God's will, she became "our tainted nature's solitary boast."

Alternative Homily for January 1

YEARS A, B, OR C

Numbers 6:22–27; Galatians 4:4–7; Luke 2:16–21

WORLD DAY OF PEACE

I. A tired businessman was just settling down to read the evening paper when his six-year-old son began to pester him. In order to give him something to do, he tore up a page of the paper. On one side was a crude map of the world and on the other a picture of a man. "Here's a puzzle for you," he told his son; "put this map of the world together again." His son happily went to solve the jigsaw puzzle. In 10 minutes he returned, his task completed. This surprised the father, because his son had no clear knowledge of geography. "How did you do it so quickly?" asked the father. "Well, all I did was to put the man right; when I did that, the world came out right!"

II. Today is the world day of peace (and the feast of Mary, the Mother of God). And this story exemplifies well a Christian approach to peace and solving social problems. We have to admit that Jesus did not produce any program for the renewal and transformation of social structures; he did not outline any political or cultural ethics; he has no practical answers for modern social ills; he has no detailed solutions for the grievances of one country against another or for territorial disputes. He does not even give an entirely clear statement on the morality of war or revolution. This is why Christians—even Catholic leaders—can have very diverse opinions about civil disturbances and revolutions within countries, about border disputes between countries, about practical solutions in Israel, Ireland, Afghanistan, and India and in many violently unjust situations in African or South American countries.

III. But there are ways that Christ, the Prince of Peace, *does* have an impact on peace in the world. One way is along the lines of the story we began with. For the whole thrust of Christ in the New

Testament is toward the reformation of the individual. This reformation is accomplished not by law and order but by the free decision of the individual person. That is, Jesus does not set up social laws to bridle cruelty and injustice, for that achievement would still leave us with a cruel world. Rather Christ positively teaches justice, forgiveness and love, so that people and institutions might really be changed. The implication is that radical social action alone is not sufficient to cure our social ills; we also need compassionate and just human beings. What a change there would be in so many social and political crises if the values of Christ were taken seriously: his identification with the weak, poor, underprivileged, and oppressed; his teaching on forgiveness of enemies; removal of prejudice and superiority in political situations. Such is Jesus' way of reforming the social order—not by specific social movements or political systems but by the reform of the individual members.

IV. In the Second Reading today, Paul offers us a strong motive for personal peace: "God sent his Son, born of woman . . . so that we might receive adoption. As proof that you are children, God sent the spirit of his Son into our hearts, crying out *'Abba*, Father.'" We are not just creatures who are nothing before God; we are also his sons / daughters, so that our fundamental attitude is that of a child of God. Such is the intimacy with God that we first received in baptism. No one can destroy that relationship except ourselves. Such is the permanent source of our personal peace before God our Father.

V. Finally, in the Gospel we hear, "Mary kept all these things, reflecting on them in her heart." Luke presents Mary as the exemplar of faith. Even she had to discover the meaning of God's way of salvation. We also need constantly to learn Christ's ways toward peace in our world.

The Epiphany of the Lord

YEARS A, B, AND C

Isaiah 60:1–6; Ephesians 3:2–3a, 5–6; Matthew 2:1–12

THE SYMBOLISM OF THE EPIPHANY

I. We have just read the main infancy narrative in Matthew's Gospel. It is the most engaging legend of three men from the East who follow the star to Jesus, whom they reverence as the newborn king of the Jews. On Christmas day, we read a very different infancy narrative in Luke's Gospel. It is the most wondrous story about the birth of a poor and humble Jesus, whom shepherds come to know as Savior and Messiah (cf. Luke 2:11). These are the only two fully developed infancy narratives in all the Gospels; Mark and John have no infancy narratives at all. There are two ways of approaching these narratives. In the past our approach was to reflect on these events and interpret them in a devout and spiritual way. The modern scriptural approach is very different. It understands them from the perspective of redaction criticism. That is, the redactor is the author of the Gospel, the evangelist who wrote it; the material he chooses to use and the particular way he develops it in his Gospel is redaction criticism. In other words, redaction criticism starts with the elements deliberately chosen by the Gospel writer and asks: What does Matthew want to tell us here? What is the meaning of the symbols chosen by him? What is the Christological significance of these narratives and symbols? Or more simply yet: Matthew constructed these symbolic narratives for a profound purpose; we need to discover his purpose and follow his emphasis.

   II. Let us try to do that now with Matthew's narrative of the Epiphany. Consider the important elements that Matthew presents to us. First, there is the *star*. In the Near East, people commonly thought that each individual had his or her own star; very important people were born under special stars. Even in our day, we speak of being "born under a good star," and so having a favorable horoscope and future. In the Book of Numbers, Balaam prophesies: "A star shall advance from Jacob" (Numbers 24:17). The popular notion was that when the Messiah appears, the star of Jacob would rise and be recognized by some. So Matthew wants us, his readers, to recognize the long-awaited Messiah. Second, there are *Magi*. The prophecy of Isaiah (in our First Reading) speaks of "Caravans of camels . . . / . . . bearing gold and frankincense / and proclaiming the praises of the LORD." The Magi from the East remind Matthew's readers that Christ is the Savior of the Gentiles. (Recall that at the time of his Gospel, after 80 AD, the church was growing fast in the Gentile world.) Third, there are *gifts*. As in the Psalm 72 (vv. 10–11): "The kings of Arabia . . . shall bring tribute. / All kings shall pay him homage, / all nations shall serve him." For he is the long-awaited royal king, even at birth; he is properly recognized by the great leaders of the earth. Finally, there is *Herod the Great*. He reminds believers of the hostility of Herod and his successors shown to Jesus both at his birth and his death. Along with him, the inhabitants of Jerusalem are also against Jesus. Together they represent the common hostility to Christ in the first century.

III. Now we see what Matthew deliberately chooses to teach the readers in his day with this legendary narrative: the emphasis is on the long-awaited Messiah who is the fulfillment of all the prophecies and is the incomparable King and Savior; and secondly, he stresses the simple sincerity of the Magi and their generous love of Jesus, despite heavy opposition.

Matthew's message for us today is similar. He proclaims that we are to follow this Savior of the entire world with sincere loyalty and generous love. In that spirit, let us respond today by bringing Jesus the gift of ourselves; let us try even more to make him the center of our life; let us simply follow him as our only King and Lord.

The Epiphany of the Lord (Alternate Homily)

WHAT THE MAGI MEAN FOR US

I. In 1940 at Chicago University, there was a meeting concerning atomic fission. Attending the meeting were brilliant scientists from around the world, including Albert Einstein. One man was assigned as personal secretary to Albert Einstein, to follow him every minute of the day and to take down everything that he said, not just scientific observations but absolutely everything; for example, "It's a nice day, today;" or "This coffee is terrible!" Later, a group of scientists took these notes of the secretary and studied, discussed everything he said. But for each sentence he spoke, they had to understand just what was the context, what was his purpose: whether he was joking, telling a story, or speaking as a scientist. Only then could they determine the significance of his speech. Scripture is a little like that. We have to understand what the scripture writer intended in each case: whether he was relating didactic fiction (as in the parables), or legend, or a moral story (as the Book of Jonah) or some kind of history (though not modern, documented history). And then we can discuss what his teaching means for us today.

II. So there are two things we do with any scripture text: first, we try to determine what the scripture really meant as intended by the author, and for this we have to know the type of literature he is using; secondly, we ask what that passage of scripture means for us today. For example, take the story of the Magi today. First, what kind of literature is this and what does Matthew intend? This passage is very likely a popular legend; it is only told by Matthew and is rather extraordinary. Matthew has transformed it into *midrash* or a moral story, by reflecting on various Old Testament prophecies. By this moral story Matthew shows how Christ is the fulfillment of these prophecies. Thus, in the Book of Numbers, Balaam prophesies: "A star shall advance from Jacob" (Numbers 24:17). Also, Isaiah prophesies: "Caravans of camels shall fill you . . . / All from Sheba shall come /

bearing gold and frankincense" (Isaiah 60:6). Again, Psalm 72 (vv. 10–11) foresees: "The kings of Arabia . . . shall bring tribute. / All kings shall pay him homage, / all nations shall serve him." Finally, Micah praises Bethlehem: "[Y]ou, Bethlehem . . . / . . . [F]rom you shall come forth for me /one who is to be ruler in Israel" (Micah 5:1). In sum, Matthew uses this popular legend to show the fulfillment of all these prophecies.

Also, this passage shows the mind of Matthew as proclaiming Christ the Savior of the Gentiles. Matthew's Gospel was completed after 80 AD. At that time the infant church was growing fast in the Gentile world—in Syria, Egypt, Ethiopia, Asia Minor, and Greece. In this context the Magi were representatives of these people, who had come to believe and worship Christ. The hostility of Herod the Great at Jesus' birth reminded Matthew's Gentile readers about the hostility of Herod Antipas at the time of Jesus' death and even the persecution of Gentile Christians by Herod Agrippa during the recent past (50–70 AD).

III. The second question we ask of any scripture passage is: What does this passage mean for us today? Modern scripture scholars are even more insistent on answering this question. The preeminent scripture scholar Raymond Brown notes that modern literary criticism seems to be moving to a broader emphasis on what the writer's words actually convey to the individual reader today. The original point of this story is the simple sincerity of the Magi and their generous love of Christ—despite the opposition of Herod and the Jewish leaders. The application for our time is not hard to find. Matthew's message for us today is similar. He proclaims for us that this child is the Messiah who is the unique fulfillment of all God's promises to his people throughout history. And secondly, that we are to follow this Savior of the world with sincere loyalty and generous love. No matter how the world and its leaders react to Christ or even how some church leaders fail Christ, we proclaim him as the unique Savior of all the world according to God's plan. We gladly pledge our lives to him and try to make him ever more the center of our lives.

The Baptism of the Lord

YEARS A AND B

Isaiah 42:1–4, 6–7; Acts 10:34–38; Matthew 3:13-17 (A);
Mark 1:7–11 (B)[6]

JESUS' BAPTISM AND OURS

I. The readings on this feast, the baptism of the Lord, can be very
instructive for us baptized Christians. All three readings today reflect
one theme. The first reading is one of the four "servant songs" of
Second Isaiah. The servant in general is Israel, God's chosen people.
But there are many individualized characteristics in these servant
songs that seem to indicate one individual who represents the collec-
tive Israel. Only in the New Testament do the scripture writers
identify Jesus as the individual fulfillment of these servant prophecies.
In Holy Week, we read all these servant songs and relate them to the
passion of Jesus. Notice how this first reading begins: "Here is . . . /
my chosen one with whom I am pleased, / Upon whom I have put my
spirit." The Hebrew word for spirit is *ruah* (that can also mean wind
or breath). The image is that of a force or power of God enabling his
servant to act in a manner beyond human capability. It is seen as the
power given to the long-awaited Messiah.

II. In the Second Reading, Jesus is the one fulfilling those
prophecies. "God anointed Jesus of Nazareth with the holy Spirit
and power," means that Jesus' ministry was Spirit-empowered at his
baptism. And his entire ministry is summarized simply: "He went
about doing good." That is, Jesus' baptism led to a life of good works.

Finally, the Gospel presents the Spirit as the one who
empowers Jesus and inaugurates his mission. The voice from God
affirms: "You are my beloved Son; with you I am well pleased"

---

6. Note: The first two readings are the same for all three years. The Gospel readings for year
A and year B are very similar.

(Mark 1; also, cf. Matthew 3). Thus God recognizes him as his unique Son who brings salvation to the world. From this moment of baptism on, Jesus is strengthened by the Spirit to fulfill God's saving will throughout his public life and even in his passion and death.

III. This feast, then, is the fitting conclusion to the entire Christmas season. These readings give us a glimpse of the promises of God in choosing Israel and preparing his people throughout their history for the coming of the Messiah, and they summarize all that Jesus did to fulfill our promised redemption.

They also teach us much about our own baptism. For each individual, baptism brings together the promises of God from the distant past and the redemption brought about by Christ and actualizes them in the life of the person accepting the faith. In addition, they remind us that baptism is the key and foundation sacrament; it is the most graced moment of our lives; it is the door to our future transition from death to life. Because of our baptism we are saved; yet like Jesus, we must live out that salvation now in this world. This same Holy Spirit was given to us at our baptism; that Spirit empowers us to follow in the way of Jesus with great confidence as real children of God; that same Spirit urges us to fulfill our mission by submitting to the will of God as it comes to us naturally in our ordinary Christian lives.

The Baptism of the Lord

Year C

Isaiah 42:1–4, 6–7; Acts 10, 34–38; Luke 3:15–16, 21–22

The Baptism of the Lord

I. The First Reading today is one of the "servant songs" from (Second) Isaiah:

Here is my servant whom I uphold,
my chosen one with whom I am pleased . . .
he shall bring forth justice to the nations, . . .
I . . . set you / as . . . / a light for the nations,
To open the eyes of the blind,
to bring out . . . those who live in darkness.

This all refers to Israel, but for us it is all embodied in Jesus. In the Gospel, the voice of God announces that Jesus personifies this long-awaited anointed one, the expected Messiah, who will carry out his mission gently and with humble self-sacrifice. Here in Luke, Jesus is baptized only "After all the people had been baptized;" that is, Luke presents him as the *last one* to be baptized by John, as the climax of John's baptismal ministry. Immediately after this, a *new era* begins with Jesus, the long-awaited Messiah, who is not just God's "servant" but his "beloved Son."

In a word, in these two readings we are to understand Jesus' baptism as a solemn investiture of the messianic role of establishing righteousness over all the earth. This baptism is the beginning of Jesus' public action and work as the Messiah. Finally, in the Acts of the Apostles today, Luke reminds us that "God anointed Jesus. . . . He went about doing good"; that is, his baptism led to a life of good works. His baptism was not just an isolated ritual; it was the start of all the work, action and living that accomplished our redemption. Remarkably, Luke alone has Jesus refer to the final action of his suffering and death as the completion of his baptismal commitment: "There is a baptism with which I must be baptized, and how great is my anguish until it is accomplished!" (Luke 12:50) To sum up: Jesus' baptism is the ritual inauguration of all his messianic work in fulfilling the Father's will; it is the start of his life's work. As such it is the model for our Christian following of him.

II. Saint Paul's constant teaching about our following of Christ stresses the same point. For Paul presents endless connections between the ritual of being born in Christ and the living out of that ritual, between beginnings and development in the way of Christ, between the ideal and the real life in Christ, between being and becoming a true Christian. He tells us again and again that the ritual of baptism must lead to a *life* after the model of Christ. For example, he tells us that we are saved, therefore we should work to be saved; we are already justified, therefore we should pursue justice; we are made holy, therefore we should seek holiness; we are children of the light, therefore we should walk as children of the light; we are new creatures in Christ, therefore we should be renewed day by day; we have put on Christ, therefore we should follow Christ more and more. What Paul means is this: Baptism is the beginning ritual; we need to live out that ritual by constantly trying to live in the footsteps of Jesus.

III. Jesus' baptism, without the carrying out of our redemption, would not make much sense to us. Our baptism, without the effort to live as Jesus lived, would be phony and ineffective. Let us continue to strive to become what we are, in Christ.

Part III

Lent

First Sunday of Lent

Year A

Genesis 2:7–9 and 3:1–7; Romans 5:12–19; Matthew 4:1–11

Faith Means Radical Dependence on God

I. My father was a steel worker most of his life. He was a strong, independent man. He worked in a Chicago sweatshop with a mud floor. During his sixty-fifth year, his arterial sclerosis got so bad he could hardly walk. One week after his sixty-fifth birthday, he had his right leg amputated. A few years later, he was confined to a wheelchair. At that time I was a young priest. On my day off, I would take him for a ride in the car. In order to get him in the car, I would lift him out of the wheelchair and carry him down the porch stairs to the car. But he didn't like being picked up; so he would grab the arm of the chair or the railing on the porch and hold on tightly. Until I convinced him to let go and trust me to carry him safely, we couldn't move. He was such an independent, strong-willed man, he didn't want to let go. It was always a problem for us.

II. Today's Second Reading and context is for theologians the most famous and most argued passage in all of scripture. On this passage alone is based the entire theology of original sin. That theology is derived from complex theological thinking, and it does not require an individual, historical Adam. The purpose of the passage is to show the superabundance of the saving act of Christ by means of a parallel between Adam and Christ. The primary theme is this: though the damage wrought by Adam was very great, the salvation wrought by Christ is greater. There are three steps to the parallel: 1. The fault of one man, Adam, had an influence on all; but the gift of Christ, unearned by us, abounds for all people. 2. One offense brought condemnation for all; but the gift of Christ brought acquittal for all, even after many offenses. 3. One offense brought about death's rule over all; Christ's gift is life everlasting for all. Paul's summation is: "[J]ust as through one transgression condemnation came upon all, so through one righteous act acquittal and life came to all." Adam represents the rejection of dependence on God and his law; Christ represents the radical trust in God's saving grace and his way.

III. The First Reading today is the original story of Adam's fall in the Book of Genesis. Adam here is the personification of Everyman. And his fall is one of disobedience and rejection of dependence on God. The Gospel account of the temptations of Christ is clearly messianic in character; that is, it gives a preview of the kind of messiah Christ is. But in the context of these readings today, the church intends to emphasize the obedience of Christ, his radical trust in God, his constant submission to the will of God—as all three of his responses to the devil indicate.

IV. What we touch here is the most fundamental relationship between us and God. What we face here is the most radical decision of human beings for all time. What we deal with is our essential choice of faith. That is: the *negative* choice rejects dependence on God and asserts: "I am an independent and self-sufficient human being; my decisions, attitudes, values and life are entirely mine to live; I don't need God in my life and don't want him." The other radical choice is that of *faith* which affirms a radical dependence on God: "I am a creature of God; I am saved only by the mercy of God, not my own works; I am really free to choose my way of life, values and attitudes, but all of my free, human living is part of God's way." This is what faith means. It means we live a truly free, human existence; we are not marionettes on a string, manipulated by God; we live according to our natural capabilities and our free choice in this real, human world. But we also live with a radical trust in God; that is, we are saved only by the love and mercy of God. We trust in God as the foundation of our existence; we let God be God, giving him glory for our human life and eternal salvation.

V. What faith means, finally, can be expressed by the example of my father. None of us is totally independent and self-sufficient. We all must let go of our self-sufficiency and trust in God, for he alone carries us by his grace and saves us by his love.

Year B

Genesis 9:8–15; 1 Peter 3:18–22; Mark 1:12–15

Reform Your Lives!

I. "The kingdom of God is at hand. Repent, and believe in the Gospel." That's how Jesus begins his first sermon. That's his Good News at the beginning of his public life. The words do *not* strike us very strongly; they sound strange to our modern ears. Yet somehow they must give us the real message of Jesus our Savior; they must give us some idea of what our Christian life is all about.

II. First, our Lord calls for a reform of life. He does not present a set of rules to follow; he does not demand a retreat from the world; he does not urge a monastic existence; he does not require a specific devotional life of prayer, sacrifices and penances. We cannot narrow down his call to any one of these forms or even to all of them. His call is more universal and demanding: a *metanoia*, a total change of heart, a radical decision for God, a complete transformation of one's life. Most of Christ's parables are a challenge compelling his hearers to respond to his message, to make a radical choice for God. Such a radical decision means that the mystery of Jesus becomes our interpretation of life's meaning. It means that all our deepest questions about human life—the source of life, the sense of it, the purpose, direction and goal of it—all of these are answered in the person of Christ. Secondly, he announces, "The kingdom of God is at hand." God's kingdom is never narrowed down to a legal system, a code of conduct, a ritual purity, and observance of sacred times, places, and rites. It can only be expressed adequately as doing the will of God or, in modern terms, as accepting the reality of our individual human life. This will of God is what we pray for mainly in the Our Father: "[Y]our kingdom come, / your will be done" (Matthew 6:10). This is the summary of Jesus' own life: "I come to do your will, O God" (Hebrews 10:7).

III. This notion of the kingdom of God does not resonate with our modern minds; it doesn't inspire us; it doesn't move us personally. The early church translated Jesus' preaching about the kingdom of God into the concrete *following of Jesus*, into living as

Jesus lived. In other words, the way of Jesus became their model for living, their plan of life. They understood what it meant to follow Jesus in terms of his invitation: "Whoever wishes to come after me must deny himself, take up his cross, and follow me" (Matthew 16:24). In their day, such sayings were common in the Greco-Roman world; they meant that anyone committed to a cause should be willing to offer their lives for that cause.[1] In Jesus' invitation, it meant that anyone who wants to be a disciple of Jesus must be so committed to Jesus as to be willing to live for him and his cause.

IV. What does all this mean to us at the beginning of Lent today? Let us hear Jesus' own sermon, "Repent, and believe in the Gospel." Let us try to do that by learning the way of Jesus here on Sunday and even at daily mass if possible. Let us more closely follow Jesus this Lent by loving our neighbor in patience, kindness, forgiveness, and caring. Let us try to follow Christ, the model for all our Christian living, as he put it: "[L]ove one another as I love you" (John 15:12).

YEAR C

Deuteronomy 26:4–10; Romans 10:8–13; Luke 4:1–13

OUR KIND OF MESSIAH

I. This Gospel of the three temptations of Christ is most familiar to us. But there is one point about today's Gospel that we may not readily realize: these three temptations of Jesus correspond fairly well to the type of savior that the Jews were expecting. That is, they were expecting a savior who would be a spectacular individual to liberate them form the rule of the Romans and so gain worldly power.

---

1. Edward Schillebeeckx, *God Among Us; The Gospel Proclaimed* (New York: Crossroad), pp. 202–203: "Long before the time of Jesus, for both Jews and Greeks (see already Plato, *Republic*, II, 361) the expression 'take up one's cross' meant to have the courage to die a violent death for a particular cause. . . . So what Matthew is saying in this story is that Christianity can result in a violent death. . . . What does this message mean for us . . . Christians who do not have to think of martyrdom and torture and only know the miseries of any human being . . . ? Briefly this. . . . Within our own surroundings, however small scale they may be, we must stand up for justice and love . . . even to our own disadvantage. This in itself will bring us suffering and persecution enough, which is what Matthew is ultimately concerned with."

For throughout the later Old Testament, they looked for God to give them back their promised land, so that they could again be an independent and free nation; they expected that if they kept their part of the covenant or testament, then God would send a messiah to restore their freedom and give them independence as a people and nation. So these temptations of Christ in today's Gospel correspond to their view of messiah. The temptation for Jesus was that he should show himself to be that kind of messiah. He should provide material abundance for his people again: "[C]ommand this stone to become bread." He should come in power to restore the kingdom of Israel: "I shall give to you all this power and their glory." He should do something spectacular: "Throw yourself down from [the temple]" and be miraculously saved by God. So if Jesus wanted to be recognized as the expected messiah, he must do such wondrous deeds, because these were the very signs the people expected. Despite all such popular expectations, Jesus rejected that kind of messiah. He would not be a political liberator, promising abundance; he had no desire to be a worldly ruler, defeating his enemies with great power; he was not a public miracle-worker, overwhelming any opposition by miraculous signs. Such expectations for the messiah were a continuous stumbling block for the Jews; they never did listen to him or understand his kind of messiahship. Even the apostles had a problem with such a messiah during Jesus' lifetime.

II. Here we are, 2000 years later, and we still have similar problems with such a messiah. Some of us look for a savior of material abundance. What value is Jesus to us, we think, if he can do nothing in the real world of achievement, success and status? "[C]ommand this stone to become bread"; bless us in our real life and help us attain some part of the American Dream. Then we would gladly accept your values and your way. Others want our savior to wield his power, to make his providence work for us. Isn't this part of his covenant with us: to take care of those who serve him well? If we are careful to follow his way and obey his law, we expect him to protect us from harm and take care of us. If only we could see the power of his providence in our lives, then we would give our whole lives to him. And many of us want our savior to do something spectacular. We may not express it, but in the back of our minds many of us look for him to make an obvious difference in our society. We dream of a God of

miraculous change to transform this world of ours; we wish for a
savior who will force this world to take notice of him; we pray for him
to appear in a public way that the world will be convinced and converted. But our Savior refuses to be that kind of messiah for us. He is
not a messiah who promises material abundance; he does not rule our
world with power; he is not a miracle-worker of spectacular deeds.
Therefore, we find it hard to give our whole heart to such a messiah.

III. This lent can be different for us. This lent we can
really hear Jesus explain what kind of messiah he is; this lent we can
fully understand just how he wants to save us in this real world of
ours; this lent we can accept this human and suffering Messiah as our
only Savior.

Second Sunday of Lent

Year A

Genesis 12:1–4a; 2 Timothy 1:8b–10; Matthew 17:1–9

Dreams and Visions

I. When you were a child, what did you dream of becoming one day?
Dreams or wishes are common for children. One thing I dreamed
about as a child was to drive around the country in a mobile
home—just touring all over our country, visiting all the national parks
and seeing many different people who make up this great country of
ours. But I know now that I'll never do that on a grand scale and that
doesn't distress me. But adult dreams are more compelling. As adults
we dream about our life; we dream about our children and their
future. It's good to have dreams, because "If you don't have a dream,
how you gonna' have a dream come true?" (From "Happy Talk")

II. Christ had a lot of dreams. The most important one he
told his friends before he died: [I have a dream: that all my followers
might learn to] "love one another as I love you" (John 15:12). Today's

readings deal with visions. The vision to Abraham deals with a promise: "All the land that you see I will give to you and your descendents forever. I will make your descendants like the dust of the earth; if anyone could count the dust of the earth, your descendants too might be counted" (Genesis 13:15–16). In today's Gospel, the vision given to the apostles deals with the glory of Christ and was intended to strengthen the faith of the apostles. All of us Christians share visions about human life and this world. Along with other believers, we share the vision that this world and the human beings in it are basically good and valuable, not thoroughly evil and corrupt; they can change and become better. The vision that Jesus had about his followers goes even further; he envisioned all Christians as bound together in unity: "[T]hat they may all be one, as you, Father, are in me and I in you" (John 17:21). We Christians have a similar vision for all the followers of Jesus.

III. But how are these Christian visions ever to become a reality? When is our God going to act in our history? How can these visions ever be carried out? Part of our answer comes from how God has already acted—as in the two readings today. First consider Abraham. God called him and asked for a response of faith. He tested Abraham profoundly by asking him to sacrifice his only son. And that son was to be the means of his countless descendants! Then God asked him to go to the foreign land of Canaan. This was not what Abraham wanted or envisioned, but he did follow God's call. Next consider Jesus. God's way of redemption in Christ was not to be accomplished by God's divine power, nor by a magical act, but by the suffering and death of Jesus. What a strange way of redemption! Peter and the apostles could not understand God's way; Jesus himself found it desperately hard to accept.

What do these two examples add up to? At least they mean that God does not carry out his vision by means of divine power, but rather by his call, by human faith in responding to his call, by human suffering and trial. So when we hear God's word today, "This is my beloved Son . . . listen to him," we have to see the vision in terms of Jesus. That is, our whole vision follows God's way of salvation as shown in Christ. Our personal Christian vision is carried out by our responding to God in faith, by accepting the fulfillment of that vision which consists of the reality of our actual human life. For us too, our vision is carried out humanly, by means of trial and suffering and the daily cross of human living.

IV. This is *not* the way we would like our dreams fulfilled; this is not the way we want to actualize our vision of human fulfillment, of love and unity in Christ. We want God to actualize our vision by his divine power and miraculous help. But he does not act that way. God will only accomplish his complete vision by his call and by our free response. He will only help us to fulfill our vision freely, humanly and with our determined effort to follow Jesus. There is only one way to fulfill our vision: "This is my beloved Son . . . listen to him," learn his way.

Year B

Genesis 22:1–2, 9a, 10–13, 15–18; Romans 8:31b–34; Mark 9:2–10

If God Is for Us, Who Can Be Against Us?

I. Delores was a young girl who was blind. Her father was a kind and tender man who took great care of her. After several years, she was able to have an operation on her eyes that permitted her to see for the first time. One of the greatest delights of her new sight was just looking at her father whom she could see as a strong man of noble appearance. She watched his every look and action. When he smiled at her or put his arms around her, she felt utterly happy. One day, as she was holding her father's hand, she told a friend, "Just think, I have had this father for several years and never really knew him."

II. In today's Gospel, the apostles have a momentary glimpse of the glory of God the Father and hear his one word to them; "This is my beloved Son. Listen to him." There are two important truths for the apostles and for us in this experience. First, God the Father hints that the one way we can constantly see him and know him is by seeing and knowing Jesus, his Son. Jesus alone is the concrete, human expression of the real person of God the Father. The more we know Jesus, the more we understand him, the more we grow close to him—to that degree we see and know the Father. Later, Jesus will tell Philip: "How can you say, 'Show us the Father?'" (John 14:9c). Whoever has seen me, has seen the Father" (John 14:9b). This is the genius of our Christian faith. We have a unique, human, clear expression of what our God is like in the person of Jesus.

III. The second lesson in the Transfiguration is found in Jesus' caution at the end: "[H]e charged them not to relate what they had seen to anyone, except when the Son of Man had risen from the dead." Mark makes this notion part of the main thrust of his Gospel. Throughout his Gospel, he slowly reveals his particular understanding of the person of Jesus: that he is not a wonder-worker, despite his miracles; he is not a savior of glory and power, despite his greatness. In fact, Mark presents this Transfiguration event immediately after Jesus' own instruction that "the Son of Man must suffer greatly . . . and be killed" (Mark 8:31). That not only tells us what kind of savior we have, but also what kind of God we have; that he is not a God of force or magic, but a God of compassion and love, who saves us by offering his only Son.

IV. The Second Reading tells us more about our God. This entire reading is an emotional assurance of our hope. Paul forcefully assures us that, even though we are sinners, even though we fail at times, we can have confidence without exception. For "Who will bring a charge against [us]? It is God who acquits us . . . [who did not spare his own Son]. Who will condemn [us]? It is Christ [Jesus] who died" for our salvation. In a word, no matter how often we fail, how long we have been separated from him, we need only ask our Father's forgiveness. His forgiveness is endless; his love is unconditional.

V. In a word, in Jesus we can see God, our Father, in clear, human terms. Through Jesus we know the God of endless forgiveness and love. With Jesus we hold the hand of our loving Father. "If God is for us, who can be against us?"

Year C

Genesis 15:5–12, 17–18; Philippians 3:17—4:1; Luke 9:28b–36

Transfiguration

I. The Transfiguration event, just described for us, causes all kinds of problems for scripture exegetes. Scholars are not sure what we are dealing with historically here, when it happened and which synoptic is the most objective. We will not try to answer these questions. We will only look carefully at Luke's account and draw some conclusions.

II. In all the synoptics—Matthew, Mark, and Luke—the Transfiguration comes shortly after Jesus' first announcement of his Passion and immediately after Jesus' saying on discipleship. It is clearly introduced by the evangelists as a corrective about Jesus' identification. The essential qualities of Jesus that we see in each Gospel context are these: 1. Jesus is one in whom God's power is present; he is God's Messiah; 2. He is the Son of Man who must suffer, be repudiated and put to death; he is the suffering Messiah; 3. He is to be followed as Messiah by our being willing to offer our life for his cause; 4. He is God's Son and chosen one to whom human beings must now listen to know God's kingdom. This much is true for all three synoptics. But Luke adds two special notes: 1. Luke alone mentions that Jesus' apostles had a glimpse of his "glory;" the clear inference for Luke is that he intended some connection between this episode and the risen state of Jesus; that there is a vague prediction here of Jesus' final victory as Savior of all; 2. In Luke alone, Moses and Elijah are withdrawn from the scene, leaving Jesus alone when the apostles receive the heavenly charge: "[L]isten to him."

III. Focus on this last note—that Luke removes Moses and Elijah from the scene before God commands, "This is my chosen Son; listen to him." There is just a hint here of the radical change God is making for all believers.

Elijah here represents all the prophets, all those who spoke of God in partial ways in the past, all who preached to believers with sacred words and divine wisdom, all who gave the partial vision of God's ways. As the Letter to the Hebrews puts it: "In times past, God spoke in partial and various ways to our ancestors through the prophets" (Hebrews 1:1). But that is no longer God's way of communicating to us. The great mystic, John of the Cross, comments on this passage from Hebrews:

> Any person questioning God or desiring some vision or revelation would be guilty of . . . foolish behavior . . . by not fixing his eyes entirely upon Christ. . . . God could respond as follows: If I have already told you all things in my Word, my Son, and if I have no other word, what answer or revelation can I now make that would surpass this? Fasten your eyes on Him alone, because in Him I have spoken and revealed all, and in him you shall discover even more than you ask for and desire.[2]

What he means is that God is no longer unknowable, incomprehensible; our God is as visible as our brother, Jesus, if only we make the effort to know him. "[W]hoever sees me sees the one who sent me" (John 12:45).

Similarly, Moses here represents the law and the commandments; he stands for all the 613 precepts of the Old Covenant with God, including all the sacred rites and sacrifices. Moses faithfully presented a way of righteousness for all believers; he indicated commandments that were to be kept, sacrifices that were to be offered, holy days that were to be observed. But all of these were concerned with occasional actions, with marginal activities—not sacred times, worship, and prayers. Now all that is being replaced and perfected by Jesus, the chosen one. For in Jesus we find that *all* the moments of his life were sacred—not only his suffering and death, but all his human living was a part of his saving work, a part of his holiness. Even his most human qualities—such as anger and fear, hunger and thirst, learning and failure, suffering and trials—all were sacred moments, means of grace. Everything he did was an accepting of his human condition and, in that sense, doing the will of God. So his whole life was grace-filled and sacred. In following him, we learn that all our human moments—including our weakest and most human actions—everything except sin—is our way of doing God's will and so are sacred moments, a source of grace. As the theologian, Bernard

---

2. *The Collected Works of St. John of the Cross*, trans. By Kieran Kavanaugh and Otilio Rodriguez (Washington, D.C.: ICS Publications, 1979), p. 80 (*Ascent of Mount Carmel*, Book 2, Chap. 22, #5).

Cooke, expresses this: "What is revealed in Christ is that human life [all of it] is the locus of the divine." By listening to Jesus and seeing him as "the way," we learn that holiness is not some special, marginal activity in our life—such as prayer or Sunday worship. *No*, it is all our living; it is what life in Christ is all about.

IV. What we learn especially from Luke's account of the Transfiguration is that Jesus is "the image of the invisible God" (Colossians 1:15), and the whole vision of God for us. And also that Jesus' way is affirming of all human life as our way of holiness and doing God's will.

Third Sunday of Lent

Year A

Exodus 17:3–7; Romans 5:1–2, 5–8; John 4:5–42

Stages of Faith

I. Many Catholics believe that faith is something you either have or don't have. And once you have faith, it's like owning a car; as long as you don't deliberately get rid of it or sell it off, it's yours. The truth is that there are as many different degrees of faith as there are people in this Church. Even more significantly, there are many stages of faith; there are numerous levels of growth in our understanding of who Christ is. Faith can constantly grow and mature all throughout life, just as it can slowly fade away. In today's Gospel, we see the development of faith exemplified in the dialogue between Jesus and the woman at the well; this dialogue can serve as a paradigm of our growing in faith and relationship to Christ all our life long.

II. Notice how John presents this encounter with Jesus. 1. It begins with a chance meeting, not as something she deliberately sought out: "A woman of Samaria came to draw water." 2. The dialogue starts with Jesus' request for water: "Give me a drink." 3. Quickly she begins to see a deeper significance in Jesus' response: I "would have given you living water." 4. Soon Jesus puts the dialogue on a very personal level: "You have had five husbands." 5. Then the woman realizes they are dealing with sacred matters, but still feels confident: "Our ancestors worshipped [God] on this mountain." 6. Eventually she realizes that this man is the Messiah: "I am [the Messiah], the one who is speaking with you." 7. Finally she brings her neighbors to Jesus, who also make a personal, mature choice for themselves: "[W]e have heard for ourselves, and we know that this is truly the savior of the world."

III. This encounter seems to be John's deliberate paradigm for human growth in faith.

1. Our beginning of faith is not something we sought out or desired. For almost all of us, chance brought us to Christ. Our parents happened to be Christian, so they brought us to the water of baptism. 2. Then, as a child, we came to realize that God is our heavenly Father who cares for us; we can pray to him for our material needs; we can expect his grace and protection. 3. In the early years of school and learning about our faith, we learned that God does make some difference in our lives; he makes demands that refer to our daily lives. Some of us practically stop our faith development here, for we prefer a God who leaves us alone; we like to believe in a good God up in heaven, but one who has little place in human living. 4. We don't want to think of faith in God as a deeper level of personal love that infiltrates all of human life. We just don't have room for him in our daily living. 5. Perhaps as an adult we came to realize that this God is the Lord of all life whom we need to recognize and worship. But we still believe that an occasional gesture towards worshipping him should be enough, for he is, after all, a forgiving God. This too is far from a mature faith. God wants us to worship him "in Spirit and truth." For our true worship in the Spirit, Jesus himself is our necessary food: "[U]nless you eat the flesh of the Son of Man . . . you do not have life within you" (John 6:53). The Eucharist *is* our constant contact for maintaining our life in Jesus. 6. A further aspect of mature faith is to realize the place of God in our lives. We come to realize that Jesus is the one who brings the final revelation about God; he is the entire Word of God's revelation to us; we are entirely dependent on his truth and grace; our destiny is in his hands. This is a critical

step for American Christians. For we Americans want to be self-reliant and self-sufficient; we want to possess our own life, control our destiny. We are not comfortable with feeling needy or dependent.

7. Finally, beyond all this, there are numerous other steps that we struggle to take all our life long. Such development only comes with time and effort, with saying "yes" to the individual reality that is our life. It depends on Jesus and ourselves as we try to make him the Lord of our own individual life: "[W]e have heard for ourselves, and we know that this is truly the savior of the world." Not only do we see Jesus as the Savior of the entire world, but we see him as our personal Savior, the center of our life, the model for our living. Let us continue to grow in this faith in Christ all our life long and especially during this Lent.

YEAR B

Exodus 20:1–17; 1 Corinthians 1:22–25; John 2:13–25

THE CROSS: GOD'S WISDOM AND POWER

I. A few years ago, there was an extraordinary personal article in the Chicago Sun-Times that was written by Benjamin Belden, a Chicago psychotherapist. Just two months before, his home had been completely burned-up by a 5-11 fire. The picture of his burned-out home in the paper, with all the ice formations resulting from water poured on the fire, was entitled, "Ice monument." He got out of the fire with everything destroyed; he only saved the clothes on his back and his dog. That fire changed his life. In the article he describes how, before the fire, he was caught up in "life's two great illusions," as he called them. He suggested that these two illusions were common to a lot of us. Grand illusion number one is: "I am special, and because of this, it can't happen to me; tragedies happen to other people." And grand illusion number two is: "Someone wonderful will come and make my life work—anybody but me." Along with these two illusions were the additional feelings: "It shouldn't have happened to me; fate should be kinder; it was so unfair." He felt cheated, angry, bitter. But with the help of many people, he found another road, what he calls "the

tougher path to freedom and acceptance." He learned to accept life
as it is, right now, without qualification, without feeling cheated
or wronged. He found new life deep inside himself, making him a
richer person and a better counselor.

II. These two grand illusions Dr. Belden talks about are very
common human traps. They are similar to the two illusions that Saint
Paul mentions today: "Jews demand signs and the Greeks look for
wisdom." That is, the Jews expected and demanded signs and spectacular miracles that would show divine intervention; they looked for
a messiah who would inaugurate their nation's sovereignty over the
Gentiles by another display of God's miraculous *power*. While the
Greeks searched for *wisdom* or a philosophy that would give a satisfac-
tory explanation of human life and the whole cosmos. This wisdom,
they thought, would release them from the snares and obstacles of
human existence; this philosophy would make them unaffected by
common human trials.

III. There are modern forms of these two grand illusions that
affect us all. The first illusion is best expressed by the question: "Why
did this happen to me?" Sometimes it seeks to bargain with God:
"If only you would cure me now or grant this one success, then I will
serve you well." Sometimes it seeks a more permanent solution:
"Give me a life without illness, disappointment or anxiety, and then
I will commit my life to you." Often it is just a confused cry: "What
did I do to deserve this?" Or: "Why doesn't God do something?"
Such is the modern search for God's *power* to makes things right.

The second illusion for modern Americans is: "Everything
ought to make sense in this world of ours." It concentrates on the
obvious problem of evil; that is, the apparent contradiction between
suffering, injustice, and misery on the one hand, and the providence
of a loving God on the other hand. It recognizes the unfairness and
injustice of so much human living and wants to shout: "Things ought
to go well for those who are innocent; God should smooth things
out for those who try to serve him; there ought to be obvious justice;
things ought to make sense." Such is the modern search for *wisdom*.

IV. God's answer to these two illusions is the *cross of Christ*.
This human cross of Jesus is all of God's power and wisdom; it is
God's unique plan of salvation. His *power* does not destroy us; it does
not change the world by magic, by making everything fair and just,

because then we would not be free and human. Nor does he change the world by force, by forcing us to be morally just and follow his laws; because then we would be robots, not humans. Rather, he saves the world by the cross of Christ as the greatest possible human proof of his love. He saves us by compassion, forgiveness and love, for that alone can save *free* human beings.

And his *wisdom* is equally gracious. As Jesus expressed it: "[T]ake up [your] cross daily and follow me" (Luke 9:23). He means that human life is necessarily prone to illness, suffering, loneliness, and anxiety. Christ's way does not do away with all of them, for such an existence is not human. Rather his way is to accept them and suffer through them. His wisdom is that we follow Jesus; his wisdom is found in the purpose and direction that Christ offers; his wisdom includes the courage that comes from hope in him.

V. All the wisdom of Christianity is summarized simply by Saint Paul here: "Christ the power of God and the wisdom of God." This cross will always be a deep mystery for us. But it is God's real answer in Jesus, and the only way for real human living and salvation.

Year C

Exodus 3:1–8a, 13–15; 1 Corinthians 10:1–6, 10–12; Luke 13:1–9

God in Human Life

I. In a restaurant, eight young adults were discussing religion. I heard them quite distinctly, because they were arguing loudly and uninhibitedly. The tenor of the discussion was negative and critical; they found religion rather restrictive. One man was being very candid after a few drinks, and he eventually dominated the conversation. He contended, "I would be happy to believe in God, if I could only find a God who would let me alone, let me live my life, just love me without all kinds of demands and restrictions. All the religions I know, present a God who ties us down and makes all kinds of demands on us." Most Americans with faith problems about God have difficulty not with his existence but with his providence, his influence on their lives, his rules and commandments, his apparent control of human life.

II. Today's readings offer some reflections on God's providence, on his influence in our lives. In the First Reading, God describes himself as "I am who am"; he is the God of existence. Some modern Americans limit their notion of God to this: he exists in his heaven but has no place in human living, similar to the kind of God sought by the young man in the restaurant. That is, we can live our life here on earth by taking care of things ourselves. We don't need magical solutions or interventions of God, nor do we need his laws, rules or restrictions. This notion of God doesn't leave much room for God in human living; it has been described as the notion of God of the *American practical mind*. In terms of our life now, it implies a worthless God, a meaningless God. It can only be maintained by those who reject the whole Bible, for both the Old and New Testaments present a God who is thoroughly involved in human existence.

Other Americans go to the opposite extreme and put no limits on God's activity. They assert that all things depend on God; all natural events, good or bad, are his doing; all human actions are willed by God. Good things are a reward from God; evil things are his punishment. We don't always understand God's ways, but he knows what he is doing and some day we will realize the wisdom of his providence. This notion of God is that of the *pietistic religious* or the *fundamentalists*. Such a notion of God's activity can find some foundation in the early books of the Old Testament. But the New Testament clearly corrects this notion. And one of the clearest denials of this notion is in today's Gospel. Here Christ asks the rhetorical question: "Do you think that because these Galileans suffered in this way they were greater sinners than all other Galileans? *By no means!*" (emphasis added). Twice in this reading (see also vv. 4–5) Jesus rejects absolutely any connection between death and God's punishment, between God's action and human guilt. We have to conclude that at least some human events have nothing to do with God's direct intervention.

III. All we have done so far is eliminate the two extremes: God does nothing; God does everything. That much seems clear. But Scripture and the Church have not given an entirely explicit answer.

I think we can find a more complete answer if we concentrate on human freedom. If we humans are really free, then we are not marionettes on a string, manipulated by God. If we are really free, then we can choose to disobey his will and do even senseless, harmful, inhuman things. If we are really free, then things cannot go well always, life will not consistently be just and equitable, and human beings can mete out reward and punishment entirely contrary to God's judgment.

IV. What all this implies is that God's providence doesn't arrange things in our *external* world. He does not make a farce of human freedom, does not interfere with the freedom he gave us. Rather, his providence and care of us in *internal*; his influence is within our hearts and minds. That is, if we are committed Christians, then God does have a profound influence within us, without interfering with our freedom. Thus, from him we take our whole outlook on life. In his calling us as Christians, we freely choose a way of living. In his word we find our values for life. In Christ we choose to have a model for all our living. In Jesus we have an adequate motive for loving all people. In him we establish our dreams and found our hopes. The deeper our individual commitment as Christians, the more all these are a part of us. *This* is the way God provides for us; this is the way God influences us freely and humanly. We remain entirely free, yet he provides everything for us internally. "In him we live and move and have our being" (Acts 17:28). He is a God who draws us by love and by the model of Jesus. This is God's wonderful plan for us as free human beings.

Fourth Sunday of Lent

Year A

1 Samuel 16:1b, 6–7, 10–13a; Ephesians 5:8–14; John 9:1–41

Christ the Light

I. Scripture uses light frequently as a symbol. The primary symbolism of light refers to God himself. God was the creator of light in Genesis; his presence and protection were represented by a column of fire in the great Exodus. At the Transfiguration of Jesus, God appeared as a cloud of light; he dwells in inaccessible light. But the secondary symbolism of light refers to REVELATION. Isaiah speaks of the light of revelation to God's people—"a light for the nations" (Isaiah 42:6). Paul speaks often about the light of the Gospel. The most concentrated use of light as a symbol is found in the Johannine Gospel and Epistles. John tells us that "God is light" (1 John 1:5) and his light is seen in Jesus who is "the light of the world" (John 8:12). But even more does he emphasize that Jesus is the revelation of God. His entire Gospel can almost be summarized by saying that Jesus is the Word of God, the total revelation of God to us. For John, whatever light God wanted to communicate to us about himself, he did by means of the light of Christ.

II. Today's readings deal with fire and light. Let us focus on the Gospel and John's symbolism of Jesus as the "light of the world." Here, as with any passage of Scripture, there are two steps for understanding it. The first step is the exact literal meaning of the text as written. This event occurred during the feast of Tabernacles. During this festival week, the Jewish people went up to Jerusalem and camped near the temple in huts. They prayed for early winter rains while processing from the pool of Siloam to the temple; the court of the temple was strikingly lighted by immense torches. During this feast Jesus opens the eyes of a blind man and proclaims: "I am the light of the world." The implication is that he is the Messiah, as Isaiah predicted, who would be a "light for the nations" (Isaiah 42:6) and would open the eyes of the blind. This is the main point of the whole passage: Christ is the Messiah and the light of the world. Some additional points are worth noting. The washing in the pool of Siloam and the curing of blindness are symbols of baptism; in the early catacomb art, this healing of the blind man is a common symbol for baptism. Also, this Gospel begins and ends with the connection between sin and blindness. Jesus first insists that physical blindness is *not* caused by sin, and he ends by telling the Pharisees that their spiritual blindness—their refusal to believe—*is* caused by sin, by not wanting to see, by choosing *not* to believe.

III. The second step in understanding scripture is the practical meaning of the text for us today. In this case, the interpretation for us is found by answering the question: "How is Christ the 'light of the world' for us?" The complete answer involves Jesus as the meaning of life, the model for living, the source of our hope, the entire truth about God. But today let us concentrate on just one aspect of Jesus as the "light of the world:" his value system for life. Until the last couple centuries, people acquired their value system, their norms for living, their religious interpretation of life, the same way they acquired their language and culture. They were born and raised into such a system and culture, and there were few options for the rest of their lives. But today in America, there are many options existing in our society. 1. There is the value system so prevalent in the 1960's: the counter-culture, centered on freedom, integrity, and individual expression. 2. There is the value system of the "me generation:" "Eat, drink and be merry, for tomorrow you die." 3. There are the pervasive values of the "American Dream," which include economic success, social status, and material possessions. 4. Or there is the value system of Christ, which involves submission to God, openness to the person of Jesus, equality of all, honesty, justice, respect for all and response to others' needs.

IV. If we choose this value system of Christ and try to make him the model for our life, then he is eminently the "light of the world" for us. The challenge for you and me this Lent is: How much do I accept this light of Christ? To what extent am I growing into Christ and his values? Our life-long struggle is to make Jesus the primary light of our life.

Year B

2 Chronicles 36:14–16, 19–23; Ephesians 2:4–10;
John 3:14–21

Two Worlds—Two Spiritualities

I. Catholics have two different ways of looking at the world. Both
of them are based on scripture and both of them are somewhat
valid. But whichever view of the world we choose determines our
form of Christian living and spirituality. Let me delineate these two
ways clearly.

II. The first Catholic view of the world is that the world is
suspect. It is based on these words in John's First Letter: "Do not love
the world. . . . For all that is in the world [is] sensual lust, enticement
for the eyes, and a pretentious life" (1 John 2:15–16). [Old translation:
"the lust of the flesh, the lust of the eyes, the pride of life."] So the
best thing for a Christian to do is to *flee* the world as much as possible.
Such was the leading theme and title of countless books of the twelfth
and thirteenth centuries: *De Contemptu Mundi* (on the contempt of
the world). In these books, not only *excessive* love of the world but all
love of pleasure, riches, and self was suspect. This approach to the
world was the basis of monkish spirituality; religious men and women
fled the world by entering a monastery. For a thousand years this was
the normative spirituality for all monks and religious. The three vows
of poverty, celibacy, and obedience were constantly seen as "the way
of perfection," the superior way of following Jesus. Everyone else—
who were not religious or monks—could only follow a watered-down
version of this way of perfection as best they could in their secular
lives. If they could not follow the ideal of poverty, they could at least
lead a simple life; if they were married, they could still be chaste; if
they were not bound by religious obedience to a superior, they could at
least control their self-will. Such a spirituality stressed human sinfulness and the *evils of the world*. It was an *eschatological spirituality*,
looking toward the other world. The problem with such a spirituality
was that it was only possible for one percent of Christians—for monks
and nuns. For everyone else it was an impossible ideal that could only

be practiced in a *marginal* or inferior way. Yet, to a large extent, this was the spirituality we grew up with in the old Church.

III. Since Vatican II, there is a very different view of the world that is developing in our modern Church. This view is based on the words of Jesus in John's Gospel today: "God so loved the world that he gave his only Son . . . not . . . to condemn the world, but that the world might be saved through him." That is, God's purpose in creating and redeeming the world in Christ was to love the world and sinful humanity, not to condemn it. So the best thing a Christian could do is to *love* the world. In the words of Pope Paul VI, shortly after the Vatican Council: "We will love our time, our community, our technical skills, our art, our sport, our world." What is pleasing to God, then, is for us to grow and become mature human beings after the model of Jesus. We are to feel responsible for our world, seek to direct it, give meaning to it and work to develop it. Consequently then, for example, parents should strive for a good home for their families along with decent living conditions and a good education. They should have some recreation and pleasure in their families. They can seek positions of authority and responsibility. What all of this means is that our family, home, job, free time, spiritual activities, sexual life, relationships to others are all essential to holiness. Such spirituality stresses the need *to love* sinful humanity and to try to form this imperfect world in the spirit of Christ. It is an *incarnational* spirituality, concerned with forming this world; it is life affirming, aware of God's grace and presence in our world. It is a spirituality at the *center* of our life, involving every moment of it.

IV. In a word, what it means to follow Jesus in this way is to commit our whole lives to his cause. We do that not by abandoning the world but by living our worldly life in the spirit of Jesus. We do that by accepting the reality of our life, just as it comes to us. We do that by having the same attitude toward the world that God himself has: "God so loved the world that he gave his only Son . . . not . . . to condemn the world, but that the world might be saved through him."

Year C

Joshua 5:9a, 10–12; 2 Corinthians 5:17–21; Luke 15:1–3, 11–32

Guilt and Reconciliation

I. Some years ago, a discussion group I had was talking about guilt. One of the young men in the group claimed that he never felt guilt or any reason for guilt. As we talked about it, it seemed he didn't want to ever face God or himself with such an admission, so he covered over his guilt and refused to admit it. He preferred to ignore his common, human condition which is such that we all hurt others at times, we do act selfishly occasionally, we do treat others sometimes with impatience, anger or injustice. According to Dr. Carl Menninger, this approach to guilt is very common today; that is, guilt is handled by refusing to admit it, by suppressing it, by forcing it into the subconscious. But there it does not stay suppressed; it festers and becomes toxic.

But the opposite extreme also does violence to us. That is, obsessive guilt stunts our growth also. Some people see faults and guilt everywhere. They expend all their energy and nerves in avoiding offense against endless laws, rules, and imagined requirements. They demand perfection of themselves and cannot tolerate the flaws of our human condition. Anxiety hangs like a fine mist over their lives. Their capacity to enjoy life is impaired; even their finest human relationships and achievements get infected with guilt.

II. A Christian sense of guilt understands that to be human is to be imperfect. We Christians have a benign view of human beings; we know that human nature is basically good but imperfect. We do not expect human beings to be perfect; we expect them to fail, to be weak at times, to be selfish, to hurt others. We are not really surprised by our faults; we are compassionate toward others' faults. In fact our Catholic sacraments are built on an acknowledgment of the flaws of our human condition. The genius of the sacrament of Reconciliation is that it permits us to face ourselves with compassion, to acknowledge our guilt and then to be healed with God's forgiveness. This sacrament of reconciliation is a normal means of forgiveness determined by Jesus for our individual assurance of God's forgiveness. For us there is no lingering guilt, no fear, only the comforting assurance of God's forgiveness and total healing.

III. Today's Gospel is the parable of the prodigal son. This parable of Jesus serves as a perfect paradigm or model of our sinfulness and God's forgiveness. Notice the progressive steps experienced by the prodigal son. The first step back is his "Coming to his senses . . . ." He realizes that "he squandered his inheritance on a life of dissipation;" he offended his father and harmed himself. For us too, the first step is to admit our sin and guilt, to realize that we hurt someone. Then the prodigal son ". . . got up and went back to his father." He decided to make a new start, a new beginning; he wanted to be reconciled with his father. We too, at times, need to seek reconciliation. The very word, reconciliation, means "walking together again;" so even the name of this sacrament reminds us that this sacrament is where forgiveness *is*, according to Jesus. Thirdly, the prodigal son say, "Father, I have sinned against heaven and against you." And his father "ran to his son, embraced him and kissed him." That is, the son admitted his guilt to his father, who welcomed him with open arms. What a comforting view Jesus gives us of our forgiving God, who welcomes us with open arms. We know our God is a God of compassion and endless forgiveness, so we can face our own guilt with compassion. Finally, the father says, "[L]et us celebrate with a feast, because this son of mine was dead, and has come to life again." The emphasis in this parable is on the father's joy at his son's return; no one is sad or half-hearted; there is only joy and relief. This is our common experience in the sacrament of reconciliation—a sense of joy and relief.

IV. All of this is why we Christians can admit our guilt and deal with it realistically. This is why we can face ourselves compassionately as imperfect and sinful. For we have only get up and go to our father, to make a new beginning, to be embraced and forgiven; to be welcomed with joy.

Fifth Sunday of Lent

Year A

Ezra 37:12–14; Romans 8:8–11; John 11:1–45

I am the Resurrection and the Life

I. These last three weeks, the Gospel readings have been taken from John's Gospel. The central half of John's Gospel has a common pattern. It consists entirely of six miracles, each one joined together with a discourse of Jesus, along with either a debate with his adversaries or an explanation for the disciples. Each of these discourses of Jesus takes up the theme that the miracle symbolizes; they show that Jesus' miracles in John are always signs. As signs, they show what kind of Messiah and Savior Jesus is. For example, in healing the paralytic, Jesus shows that he is the Savior—because the word Greek word for "savior" really means healer. The multiplication of the loaves is deliberately connected by Jesus with the Eucharist, which is our food for eternal life. The cure of the blind man, last Sunday, leads Jesus, the light of the world, to warn the Pharisees of their spiritual blindness in not believing in him. And here today, the restoration of Lazarus to life is clearly a sign of Jesus as the Lord of eternal life.

II. At the outset of this sign, Jesus asserts that this miracle will lead to his glory, meaning his death, resurrection and glorification. In fact, in John's Gospel, the Lazarus miracle and its fame become the prime and immediate cause of the condemnation of Jesus. And throughout this narrative, we hear numerous phrases repeated by Jesus that recall his promise earlier in chapter five of John: "[T]he hour is coming in which all who are in tombs will hear [the voice of the Son of Man] . . . and . . . those who have done good deeds [will come] to the resurrection of life" (John 5:28–29). And the entire impact of this passage is found in Jesus' assertion: "I am the resurrection and the life; whoever believes in me, even if he dies, will live."

That is, in Jesus our Savior we are saved from death itself by our sure hope of life after death forever.

III. Throughout this narrative, John makes use of symbolism. Lazarus himself represents all faithful Christians. Later John will use the same kind of symbolism for the beloved disciple at the foot of the cross and again for Peter when he is forgiven by Jesus. In these three instances, the one whom Jesus loves—"See how he loved him"—takes on the symbolic significance of all true believers. The raising of Lazarus is also symbolic. In fact, it has a twofold dimension: first it refers to the raising of every Christian when he initially accepts Jesus in faith; secondly, it refers to the future, final Resurrection. John is telling us that whoever comes to Jesus in faith will never experience spiritual or total death, for the believer has already passed from death to life. Notice how John weaves these two aspects of rising with Christ into his narrative: first he tells Martha, "whoever believes in me, even if he dies, will live," for he has already passed from death to spiritual life in Jesus; and then he promises final Resurrection: "[E]veryone who lives and believes in me will never die." John constantly affirms that each believer has already risen with Jesus by means of his faith in him and will one day rise with him to everlasting life. To conclude, the raising of Lazarus is a sign of our twofold Resurrection in Christ: both realized now and completed in the future.

IV. What does this narrative say to our hearts? It tells us that we are already risen with Jesus to a spiritual life that will never end. And it promises us that we can expect to rise with him in glory after this earthly life. This hope is the heart of our faith and our central reason for living as Christians. We can see this amazing hope as the horizon for all our living, meaning that all life is meant to be lived with that assurance of everlasting life as the constant horizon we see clearly before us. To say this even more simply: such is the love that Christ has for us now and for all eternity.

Year B

Jeremiah 31:31–34; Hebrews 5:7–9; John 12:20–33

Unless the Grain of Wheat Dies

I. Fr. Mike Adrian, a Claritian priest I knew on Chicago's south side, spent 12 years as a missionary in New Guinea. He worked with people in a small village there. They were very primitive people whose ancestors had actually been headhunters. Their entire means of sustenance came from gathering food. They fished and they cut down sego trees; their basic food, their main source of starch and carbohydrates was the pulp of the sego trees. The missionaries tried to teach them to grow crops and raise animals but without success. They convinced a few people to plant seeds in the ground, but when nothing happened the next day or so, they became impatient with the process and gave up. They had to experience the natural process of seeds dying, germinating and eventually growing before they could accept such a valuable addition to food gathering.

II. In today's Gospel, Jesus tries to explain the mystery of his atoning death with two paradoxes that are a part of human experience. First he describes the familiar paradox of nature: that a grain of wheat, left to itself, produces nothing; only when it is buried and appears to have died, does it bring forth fruit—in far greater abundance than its original form as seed.

The second paradox Jesus uses in the Gospel is the human paradox: "Whoever loves his life loses it, and whoever hates his life in this world will preserve it for eternal life." He means that anyone who selfishly seeks the good life, following his own desires, will lose fullness of life now and in eternity. On the other hand, anyone who sets aside his own selfish interests for the cause of Christ will find fullness of life now and in eternity. This is similar to Jesus' other invitation: "If anyone wishes to come after me, he must deny himself and take up his cross daily and follow me" (Luke 9:23). He means that everyone who wants to be his disciple must be willing to offer his entire life for the cause of Christ. Luke's Gospel makes it clear that this invitation of Jesus is not about literally dying for Christ, for by adding the word, "daily," he makes it clear that he is speaking figuratively and referring to a way of life that embraces all types of Christian endurance as a way to follow Jesus. Practically, it means accepting all of human life in the spirit of Christ just as it comes to us naturally. Notice that these sayings are directed to all of Jesus' followers without exception.

III. To put these words of Christ into practice is the essence of Christian morality and spirituality; this is the heart of our life in Christ. What does this invitation of Jesus mean in modern times? "Saving our life" and "loving our life" refer to selfishness and self-centeredness, which is the all-pervasive and primary human fault. Modern equivalents would be: to look out for number one, to ignore the needs of others, to be self-reliant without God, to control our life and destiny. On the other hand, "losing our life" and "denying ourselves" refer to concern and love for others. Modern equivalents would be: spending ourselves, helping others, accepting human life just as it comes to us, admitting our dependence on God. All of this means that our entire Christian spirituality is a Christological spirituality; it is a constant "dying with Christ." It means that Christ's whole way of living and his cross are the unique symbol and model for all of Christian living. Karl Rahner explains further: "The Christian, every Christian at all times follows Jesus by dying with him;" he calls it "dying by installments." He adds that for each of us, this dying is entirely individual and unique. Quite simply it consists of accepting the will of God as found in our daily life, just as it comes to us humanly. We adults need to learn this way of Christian growth all our life long. We need patience with this process of growth, for this seed of selfishness and self-centeredness only dies slowly. But if we are patient, we will slowly bring forth the fruit of Christ.

Year C

Isaiah 43:16–21; Philippians 3:8–14; John 8:1–11

Christian Self-Renewal

I. Paul today gives us a picture of what it means to be a real Christian: "I even consider everything as a loss because of the supreme good of knowing Jesus Christ my Lord. For his sake I have accepted the loss of all things and I consider them so much rubbish, that I may gain Christ and be found in him." Even more simply Paul affirms: "For to me life is Christ, and death is gain" (Philippians 1:21). In other words, no matter what he does or experiences in his life, the model of his life, the center of his existence, the primary value for him is Jesus the Lord. If we accept that definition of a real Christian, then there are not many real Christian around. Yet I think that our parish claims some in the recent past and even today.

But there is something else mentioned in all three readings today that is not beyond you and me, and is much more attainable by all of us. The First Reading asserts, "Remember not the events of the past"; in the Second Reading, Paul speaks of "forgetting what lies behind but straining forward to what lies ahead"; and the Gospel includes Jesus' warning, "Go, [and] from now on do not sin any more." The common note in all of these is to forget the past, to draw a line on the past, to start anew, to renew ourselves; and in fact this is what God wishes us to do.

II. The thrust of these remarks in the three readings today is that we should not have a negative concentration on the past but seek a positive improvement for the future; our emphasis should not be on simply giving up things but a denial of self; we should seek not simply discipline but a building up or renewal of self. In other words, let us forget the past—no matter how foolish or sinful it was—and strive to renew ourselves positively in some way, in order to prepare for the new life in Christ at Easter. Let me give some examples of forgetting the past, or positive self-renewal.

For a person who is grossly overweight, self-renewal might mean a decision to get back in shape again. For an anxious person, self-renewal might mean finding the deep cause of one's anxiety and dealing with it. For a shy and retiring person, self-renewal means beginning to gain self-confidence. For a self-assertive, dominant person, renewal would involve listening to others, being sensitive to others. For an oversensitive person, self-renewal means learning to put things in perspective and to ignore slights. For married partners who have drifted apart, renewal might mean making a marriage encounter or simply beginning to dialogue about their own relationship. For parents who do not understand their teenagers, self-renewal means making a new beginning of honesty and openness with them. For someone who detests his work, renewal means learning to appreciate his work *or* changing it. For someone who is in a constant state of sin, self-renewal means finding some way out of it and starting again.

III. Most of us are not Saint Pauls. We are not entirely happy with the things of God *or* with the things of this world; we are a little confused and slightly screwed-up. We are afraid of the risk of being open and committed to Christ. We are not willing to say the all-inclusive "yes" to God, afraid to pay the price. Maybe we are not ready to go all the way with Christ; yet I suggest we are not as far away from human wholeness or sanctity as we might think. We can take one giant step forward now; we can begin one important self-renewal now: "[F]orgetting what lies behind but straining forward to what lies ahead." We make no claim to be ideal Christians. We only struggle continually to be disciples of Christ, to learn his way, to strain toward our model of human living, Jesus the Lord.

Palm Sunday of the Lord's Passion

YEAR A

Isaiah 50:4–7; Philippians 2:6–11; Matthew 26:14—27–66 (or 27:11–54)[3]

MATTHEW'S GOSPEL (YEAR A)

I. We have just read the Passion according to Matthew. Why does Matthew so often remind us that the words of the prophets are being fulfilled? Why do we get the impression that everything was foretold? The reason is that Matthew wants to teach his Jewish readers the significance of Jesus' passion, death and resurrection in terms of their own religious tradition. For in their tradition, whenever God's people were in trouble, the prophets reminded them that God would send someone to save them, just as he had done in the past, for God always keeps his promises. Further, in the last few centuries before Christ, after the age of the prophets ended, the scribes still studied the prophets to find God's hidden purposes in history and to discern God's will in the events of their lives. According to their custom then, they would find in the words of the prophets meanings that went beyond the intent or knowledge of the prophets. So Matthew wants his Jewish readers to understand how God's hidden purposes are imbedded all along in the words of the prophets, and how Jesus is actually the culmination of God's promises.

Only by appealing to their prophetic tradition again and again, could he overcome the scandal of the cross and the tragic failure of Jesus' rejection by the leaders. Once he shows them that even this terrible failure and scandal is part of God's hidden purpose, then they can begin to understand that all their hopes and all God's promises have been fulfilled beyond their wildest dreams.

---

3. Note: After the Passion, a short homily may be given.

II. Matthew's method works not only for his Jewish contemporaries, but also for us who find God's hidden purpose hidden in the ancient teachings of the prophets. We too can be impressed with the amazing way that God keeps his promises and brings salvation to all who believe. We can even be confident that Jesus will be with us always and be our support in all our struggles to follow him. One thing holy week teaches us then, is that our God is ever faithful to all his promises.

YEAR B

Isaiah 50:4–7; Philippians 2:6–11; Mark 14:1—15:47 (or 15:1–39)

MARK'S GOSPEL (YEAR B)

I. We have just read the Passion and death of Jesus our Savior in Mark's Gospel. Throughout history, our primary focus on the Passion has been that Jesus died for our sins and won for us eternal life. Modern theologians, of course, also proclaim that this is the unique achievement of Christ for all people. But increasingly, they add another focus: that Jesus in his life, Passion, and death is the model for our human living now. They more and more emphasize that Jesus is the exemplar of what it means to be human; he is the model of what human life is for, and how it is to be lived.

II. Let me use scripture to explain this. In the synoptic Gospels (Matthew, Mark, and Luke), Jesus himself never says exactly "imitate me," but he does ask us often to "follow" him. He means that we are to offer up our Christian lives for the sake of his cause. John's Gospel is more direct. After washing the feet of the apostles, Jesus explains, "I have given you a model to follow, so that as I have done for you, you should also do" (John 13:15). That is, he wants us to follow his example as one who serves. Later in the same chapter, Jesus urges us to follow his example of love: "I give you a new commandment; love one another. As I have loved you, so you also should love one another" (John 13:34). This is a new commandment because it has an entirely new model, Jesus himself. The epistles continue this emphasis. In today's second reading, Paul urges: "Have among your-selves the same attitude that is . . . in Christ Jesus" (Philippians 2:5), meaning to imitate his humility and obedience. And more generally, Paul adds: "[P]ut on the Lord Jesus Christ, and make no provision for the desires of the flesh" (Romans 13:14), but follow the example of Christ. In a similar way, Peter encourages us all in his epistle: "[T]o this you have been called, because Christ also suffered for you, leaving you an example that you should follow in his footsteps" (1 Peter 2:21).

II. All of this adds up to a new focus for theology. Jesus our Savior not only won for us the forgiveness of sin and eternal life. As Savior, he is also the exemplar of what it means to be human; he is our model for all our Christian living now. Throughout this holy week, let this be our invitation and encouragement.

Year C

Isaiah 50:4–7; Philippians 2:6–11; Luke 22:14—23:56 (or 23:1–49)

Luke's Gospel (Year C)

I. We have just read the passion of our Lord Jesus Christ in Luke's Gospel. This passion dominates holy week and is central to our whole Christian faith. Let me make two observations that might help us focus our reflections this holy week.

II. First, notice what this Passion, death and Resurrection of Jesus tells us about our *God*. For the essential paradox of Christianity is not precisely that Jesus died and rose again; rather the eternal paradox is that *only after* the disgraceful kind of death Jesus suffered, did God raise him to victory. That is, Jesus' human fiasco—of rejec-tion, passion, failure, and humiliation—is forever a part of God's revelation of his kingdom and our way of salvation. His cross is the clearest sign of Christianity and of God's love. Without the cross, the Resurrection of Christ might give us an understanding of God as triumphal, victorious and heavenly. But because of the cross of Christ—along with his resurrection—we have God's understanding of himself as a God totally involved with our suffering and sinful world, a God who is forever known as compassionate, forgiving and loving in the whole struggle of human living. He does not do away with suffering, but shows us a way through it.

Second, notice what Jesus' passion tells us about our *human life*. What we learn only slowly is that this passion of Jesus is the paradigm for our whole Christian life. It is not only the means of the world's redemption; it is the model for our Christian life. Jesus our Savior makes this clear several times in the Gospels. He invites us to *follow* him and somehow die with him. And Luke's Gospel says it best for me: "If anyone wishes to come after me, he must deny himself and take up his cross *daily* and follow me" (Luke 9:23, emphasis added). This means that our whole spirituality as Christians is a Christological spirituality, a constant, natural dying with Christ. The great theologian, Karl Rahner, comments on this very passage, "The Christian, every Christian, at all times, follows Jesus by dying with him." This dying is entirely individual and unique for each one of us. Concretely, it consists of accepting the will of God, as seen in the sometimes difficult, daily life that comes to us humanly. This holy week, as we meditate on Jesus' Passion and Resurrection, let us learn what it tells us about our God, and what it means for our daily following of Jesus our model.

Part IV

Easter

Vigil of the Solemnity of Easter Sunday: The Resurrection of the Lord

Year A

Genesis 1:1—2:2 (or 1:1, 26–31a); Genesis 22:1–18 (or 22:1–2, 9a, 10–13, 15–18); Exodus 14:15—15:1; Isaiah 54:5–14; Isaiah 55:1–11; Baruch 3:9–15, 32—4:4; Ezra 36:16–17a, 18–28; Romans 6:3–11; Matthew 28:1–10[1]

Our Kind of Redeemer

I. In the musical Pickwick, there is a song entitled, "If I Ruled the World." Some of the lyrics are these:

> If I ruled the world, every day would be the first day of Spring,
> Every heart would have a new song to sing,
> And we'd sing of the joy every morning would bring.
> If I ruled the world, everyone would say the world was his friend;
> There'd be happiness that no one could end,
> No, my friend, not if I ruled the world.
> Every head would be held up high,
> There'd be sunshine in everyone's sky,
> If the day ever dawned when I ruled the world!

These lyrics from "If I Ruled the World" describe a beautiful world. What a Utopia the author expresses! If he ruled the world, what a great world we would all have. Apparently, he would do away with all evil, all suffering, all sin. He would rule out injustice and dishonesty; he would magically put an end to poverty and starvation; he would rid

---

1. Note: The seven vigil readings are the same for every year. The epistle each year is always Romans 6:3–11. The Gospel changes each year. The homilies below reflect all the readings of this preeminent feast.

the world of prejudice and hatred; he would change us into selfless, kind and loving people.

II. But our God *does rule* this world of ours. And we wonder why he does not give us such a world. Christ is the glorious Savior whom we honor this Easter day. We wonder why he is not that kind of Savior. We wonder why he does not redeem us by turning all the evil in the world to good. We wonder why he doesn't *magically change* all of our human suffering into joy.

Yet Christ tells us clearly he is not that kind of redeemer; in his Passion this holy week, he tells Pilate, "My kingdom does not belong to this world" (John 18:36). That is, he did not come to rule this world, to dominate his subjects. He did not come to magically change human wills, to guarantee honesty, justice, and kindness. He did not come to change us into robots—even good robots. Rather, he came to save *free* human beings, who must ever be imperfect and free or they are no longer human.

III. But there is another possibility. For Christ, our risen Savior, is king over all peoples. He could at least exercise his *power* over humanity. He could redeem us by condemning the evil in this world. He could confront evil with force, destruction, and vindictiveness. He could suppress human wickedness and *force* human beings to obey him. This is the kind of savior the apostles themselves expected. They expected Jesus to be a redeemer of force and condemnation, at least on the small scale; for they hoped that he would crush the evil of Roman rule, destroy the injustice to his people, suppress the pagan lack of faith, and restore the kingdom of Israel. So Jesus had to tell them again and again that he was not that kind of redeemer. He explained to them: "God did not send his Son into the world *to condemn* the world, but that the world might be saved through him" (John 3:17, emphasis added). That is, he insisted that he did not come to condemn our sinful world, or to crush wickedness and injustice, or to suppress human evil by force. He knew that human beings are selfish, alienated from one another and hostile to God; but he did not respond with hostility and condemnation. For he came to *save* human beings, not force or condemn them.

IV. If we want to know our God and his way of redemption, we need only look at his way of acting throughout history. The vigil readings we just heard tonight teach us that throughout the Old

Testament, God revealed himself by his *actions*. When his people wonder what kind of God he is, the answer comes back to what he *does*; he makes himself known by acting in history: he chose his people, he delivered them from Egypt, he made a covenant with them, he sent his prophets to correct and console them and he forgave them endlessly. All of this shows that God is a God of love and compassion. But the definitive revelation of God came only in the New Testament. With an entirely gratuitous love, he sent his Son to redeem us by his suffering and death: "[T]he love of God was revealed to us [finally and conclusively]: God sent his only Son into the world so that we might have life through him" (1 John 4:9). This concept of God's love, embodied in Jesus' self-giving, is the greatest proof of God's love, the perfect expression of his kind of redemption. This conviction about God's love and redemption is the unique possession of Christianity. Our God *does* rule the world in the only way that is faithful to himself and to us *free human beings*: he leaves us free to follow his Son in suffering and love; he reveals himself as our God of unconditional *love* and compassion and ultimate hope.

Year B

Genesis 1:1—2:2 (or 1:1, 26–31a); Genesis 22:1–18 (or 22:1–2, 9a, 10–13, 15–18); Exodus 14:15—15:1; Isaiah 54:5–14; Isaiah 55:1–11; Baruch 3:9–15, 32—4:4; Ezra 36:16–17a, 18–28; Romans 6:3–11; Mark 16:1–7[2]

God throughout History

I. The readings tonight place before us the entire panorama of God's work throughout history. Let us study all this scripture and see what it tells us about our God and his way of being present to us. Throughout this history, we are able to know God by his actions, by what he has done for his creatures. In the first reading—from Genesis— God is the source of everything that exists. God wanted to share his

---

2. Note: The seven vigil readings are the same for every year. The epistle each year is always Romans 6:3–11. The Gospel changes each year. The homilies below reflect all the readings of this pre-eminent feast.

goodness with the whole of creation, especially with intelligent human beings who mirrored his intelligence. "God looked at everything he had made, and he found it very good" (Genesis 1:31). So, God showed himself to be the creator and source of all life.

II. But God knew this would not be enough for humans to know him. He had to become embroiled in human history—with all its successes and failures. So God identified himself with one people, Israel. He chose this people, he made a covenant with them, he forgave them again and again, he delivered them from Egypt and gave them the promised land. He drew them to himself: "I will be your God, and you will be my people" (Leviticus 26:12). That is, he made them a people peculiarly his own; he revealed himself as a compassionate God, the God of the eternal covenant.

III. Yet he knew this would not be enough for them. So through his prophets, he prepared his people for his complete revelation. With an entirely gratuitous love, he sent his Son to redeem us by his suffering and death: "In this way the love of God was revealed to us [finally and conclusively]: God sent his only Son into the world so that we may have life through him" (1 John 4:9). In Jesus, we have God's total revelation: "Whoever has seen me has seen the Father" (John 14:9). In Jesus we have the whole plan of God for our eternal salvation, the ultimate cause of all grace: "No one comes to the Father except through me" (John 14:6). Now we know that God has bound himself to us forever in love. And he has proven this love for us in the great work of redemption that we celebrate tonight.

IV. But God had still not finished his involvement with us and his presence among us. God's ultimate act of presence in our world could only come once Jesus had finished his work of redemption. As Jesus promised: "I will ask the Father, and he will give you another Advocate to be with you always . . . [and] teach you everything" (John 14:16 and 26). That means, our God actually enters into our individual lives in the person of the Holy Spirit. This Holy Spirit is the presence of God within each of us to help us understand the entire mystery of God's work in our world. This "Spirit itself bears witness with our spirit that we are children of God . . . through which we cry, 'Abba, Father' "(Romans 8:16 and 15). This Holy Spirit is the final presence of God in us, remaining in us always. Because of his presence, we can be constantly intimate with God as our Father, for we are really his children and heirs of eternal life.

V. What an amazing history God has with our world! He has embroiled himself with us in a constantly growing involvement and intimacy. God is not only our creator, who gave us his covenant and his promises, but he fulfilled those promises wonderfully in Jesus, our Redeemer, who is the revelation and proof of his love. Finally, he sent the Spirit of Jesus to dwell with us so that we can most intimately call him *Father*.

YEAR C

Genesis 1:1—2:2 (or 1:1, 26–31a); Genesis 22:1–18 (or 22:1–2, 9a, 10–13, 15–18); Exodus 14:15—15:1; Isaiah 54:5–14; Isaiah 55:1–11; Baruch 3:9–15, 32—4:4; Ezra 36:16–17a, 18–28; Romans 6:3–11; Luke 24:1–12[3]

CHRIST'S VICTORY, CHRIST'S WAY

I. Easter does not grab us the way Christmas does. Easter does not have the appealing story of Christ's birth or the light-hearted joy to attract us. The readings of Easter deal with unsettling scenes and uncertain people: an empty tomb, wrappings lying on the ground, frightened women, groping apostles, angelic instructions, reports of anxious women, and unsettling appearances. We have to listen to the entire group of readings tonight and throughout the Easter season to put together the evidence, to appreciate the significance of this feast, to understand the enormity of this event. Let us concentrate during this Easter vigil on two points: 1. The incredible, unique achievement accomplished by Christ; 2. The significance of this model offered for our lives.

II. Peter describes the incredible achievement of Jesus this way: "Blessed be . . . God . . . who in his great mercy gave us a new birth . . . to an inheritance that is imperishable . . . kept in heaven

---

3. Note: The seven vigil readings are the same for every year. The epistle each year is always Romans 6:3–11. The Gospel changes each year. The homilies below reflect all the readings of this pre-eminent feast.

for you" (1 Peter 1:3–4). In the book of Revelation, Jesus himself describes this achievement as unique for all people: "I am the first and the last, the one who lives. . . . I hold the keys to death . . ." (Revelation 1:17–18). To say it clearly, this victory of Christ over death today is what makes our faith unique among all religions and all peoples. For all other religions, no matter how valid their starting point and how valuable as a means of opening the human heart to God, must impart hope to pass through the zero point of death. In fact, if faith does not lead to a hope beyond death, it is not worth spending our whole life on it. It is Jesus Christ alone, who was crucified and rose from the dead, who was not just a religious phenomenon but also accomplished a *successful transition to life with God.* No other religious figure has given evidence of such a hope. So for us Christians, Jesus Christ is the door of life, who by his death and Resurrection has guaranteed our transition from this life to eternal life with God.

Jesus himself tells all his followers: "*No one* comes to the Father except through me" (John 14:6, emphasis added). That is, all Christians who rise to life with God from this world, rise because of Jesus and his Resurrection at Easter.

III. The other significance of Easter is that this dying and rising of Christ is also a *model* for us. His dying on the cross and then rising to new life is a paradigm of all Christian living and of different levels of our spiritual life. The first level is that of dying to sin. As Paul tells us tonight: "[W]e who were baptized into Christ Jesus were baptized into his death. . . . Consequently, you too must think of yourselves as [being] dead to sin and living for God in Christ Jesus" (Romans 6:3 and 11). This dying to sin is the essential dying with Christ in order to live with him forever. The second level of imitating Christ's death and Resurrection is described in many ways by Paul and by Christ himself: "If anyone wishes to come after me, he must deny himself and take up his cross daily and follow me" (Luke 9:23). What Paul and Jesus mean is that we must offer our lives for the cause of Christ by accepting the sufferings and struggles of daily life just as they come to us naturally. And the third level of imitating Jesus' death and Resurrection is all-inclusive. Jesus himself gives the central norm for Christian living: "As I have loved you, so you also should love one another" (John 13:34). Jesus offers himself as the model, the example of Christian living; as he loved others completely and selflessly, so we are to follow his example. He wants us to see all our sufferings and efforts to love others as our way of following his pattern and example.

IV. Paul simplifies all this for us: "We were . . . buried with [Christ] through baptism into death, so that, just as Christ was raised from the dead . . . we too might live in newness of life" (Romans 6:4).

Easter Sunday: The Resurrection of the Lord

Years A, B, and C

Acts 10:34a, 37–43; Colossians 3:1–4 or 1 Corinthians 5:6b–8; John 20:1–9

What Kind of Victory Is Easter? (Colossians 3)

I. Easter is the victory of Christ over death. His victory over death today is what makes our Christian faith unique among all religions of the world. For Christ alone has accomplished this transition from earthly life to eternal life with God and has given evidence that he is the door of life. His victory at Easter is the basis for his claim: "No one comes to the Father except through me" (John 14:6). That is, all Christians who rise to life with God from this world, rise because of Jesus and his Resurrection at Easter.

II. This victory of Christ today reveals for us the *essence of God* as nothing else can reveal him. For the essential paradox of Christianity is not precisely that Christ died and rose again; rather the exact paradox is that only after the disgraceful death of Jesus, did God raise him to glory. That is, Jesus' human fiasco of failure, suffering, and death is forever part of God's revelation of his kingdom and God's plan of salvation. His cross is the clearest sign of Christianity and of God's love. Without the cross, the resurrection of Jesus might give us an understanding of God as triumphal, victorious and heavenly. But, because of the cross of Jesus—along with his Resurrection— we experience God's understanding of himself as a God who is totally involved with our suffering and sinful world, a God who is forever known by us as compassionate, forgiving, and loving in the midst of all our human suffering and living. This is the principal revelation of God's own nature; because of Easter we know that our God is completely understanding, forgiving and loving.

III. This victory of Christ, his dying and rising, is also a *model for us*, a paradigm of all of Christian living and of the different levels of our spiritual life. Let me explain. The first level of our dying and rising with Christ is clearly expressed by Saint Paul in the epistle last night: "[W]e who were baptized into Christ Jesus were baptized into his death. . . . Consequently, you too must think of yourselves as [being] dead to sin and living for God in Christ Jesus" (Romans 6:3 and 11). Here Paul expresses the essential level of our dying and rising with Christ: we are to die to sin in order to live with Christ now and in eternity. But Saint John gives us a second and more positive way of imitating Jesus' dying and rising; John in his Gospel quotes Jesus himself: "This is my commandment: love one another as I love you. No one has greater love than this, to lay down one's life for one's friends" (John 15:12–13). This is Jesus' only commandment in John's Gospel, the one that includes all the others. This is the ideal and summit of Christian living. And Jesus then refers directly to his example in dying for us; "No one has greater love than this . . . ." He means that this is the extreme model of love; he means that his one commandment is inseparably joined to the cross, to his suffering and dying. He means that we must be ready to offer our lives for him if necessary. But he also means that his great love is a general model for all our living, an example of how we are to love in all our Christian living. That is, Jesus himself is our way of love, our ideal norm for human living. For example, Jesus' love is our model in his sensitivity to others, in his kindness, in his acceptance of all people, in his forgiveness of others, in his constant selflessness. Let me boldly assert that we are all far from living this ideal. At our Baptism we began a life of commitment to die and rise with Christ; we ritually died to sin. We also know that we have a whole lifetime to approach this model. This Easter we can personally accept Jesus' model of loving as our way of dying and rising with him. This Easter we can at least agree that all our spirituality is Christological. This Easter Sunday we can be encouraged by the Second Reading: "[Y]ou have died, and your life is hidden with Christ in God. When Christ your life appears, then you too will appear with him in glory."

IV. Such is the encouragement we hear this Easter: our God is absolutely compassionate in the midst of all our human living and failure; and Jesus our Savior is our model for life: "[L]ove one another as I love you" (John 15:12).

Years A, B, and C

Acts 10:34a, 37–43; Colossians 3:1–4 or 1 Corinthians 5:6b–8; John 20:1–9

What Easter Reveals about God and Human Life (Acts 10:34, 37–43)

I. Experience seems to be the primary criterion for credibility these days. We can have no better connection with someone than the personal experience: "I know how you feel," or "I've been through that myself." Modern theologians claim that human experience is the best point of departure for theology and that our knowledge of God must start with what we know and experience. They call this approach "theology from below," because it begins with human experience and history. The opposite of this is "theology from above," which starts with revelation or dogma. So when we talk about our Christian hope, we look for an historical sign that authorizes our hope and gives validity to it. Tonight we happily experience that sign which gives validity to our human life and clarity to our knowledge of God. The sign we seek is called Jesus of Nazareth, crucified and risen. The manifestation of that sign is called Easter. This amazing sign is unique to Christianity; it is the fundamental affirmation of the New Testament. Let us focus tonight on this sign and what it tells us about God and our human hope.

II. The final word of the New Testament about Jesus' life, death, and Resurrection is that this is how God's love is expressed: "In this way the love of God was revealed to us: God sent his only Son into the world so that we might have life through him" (1 John 4:9). It implies that God chose this way of showing himself and his love because there was no clearer way, no more realistic and human way. Not sparing his own Son is God's way of saying there is no restraint on God's love for us. Easter shows us a God who is totally involved with our suffering and sinful world, who assures us of his absolute compassion in all our human living, who forever binds himself to us by a bond of love that can never be broken in this life.

III. Easter not only reveals God to us; it also reveals much about our human existence. Throughout history, Christians learned that Jesus died and rose to save us from sin and grant us *eternal life*. This is the point that Peter makes at the end of his sermon in the first reading this morning: "[Jesus] is the one appointed by God as judge of the living and the dead. . . . [E]veryone who believes in him will receive forgiveness of sins through his name." This remains the heart of our faith. But modern theologians increasingly focus on another aspect of what Jesus accomplished. They emphasize what Jesus did for our *human living* now. They teach that Jesus is the exemplar of what it means to be human; he is the model of what human life is for, and where it is leading. In the Gospels, Jesus' life is presented in narrative form; his concrete life focuses our attention on his teaching, his actions, his virtues and his final sacrifice; thus his life is an example of what it means to be fully human. So the following of Christ, the imitation of Christ becomes our norm for human living, so that all our thinking and our conduct can be shaped by the model provided by Jesus. This is what Saint Peter emphasizes in his letter: "[T]o this you have been called, because Christ also suffered for you, leaving you an example that you should follow in his footsteps" (1 Peter 2:21). And Paul told us in the epistle last night: "[Y]ou too must think of yourselves as [being] dead to sin and living for God in Christ Jesus" (Romans 6:11). He means not only that we should be free from sin but also positively committed to Christ, psychologically aware of that union, with his approach to life and his attitude towards others. In a word, Easter focuses our attention on Jesus as the *model* for all our Christian living now.

IV. This Easter let us concentrate on these two meanings of Easter. 1. There can be no more forceful way for God to prove his love for us than in offering his Son for our salvation. 2. Jesus' life and death offer us a concrete model of how we should live our human life. This feast of Easter is the unique sign and proof for our faith and our life in Christ.

Second Sunday of Easter (Divine Mercy Sunday)

YEAR A

Acts 2:42–47; 1 Peter 1:3–9; John 20:19–31[4]

FAITH AND DOUBT

I. One verse of the First Reading today gives a succinct summary of the faith-practice and life of the apostolic church: "They devoted themselves to the teaching of the apostles and to the communal life, to the breaking of the bread and to the prayers." We can learn from them how to strengthen our faith today.

II. The early Christians knew that conversion to Christ was not enough. If their faith was to grow and be intelligent and strong, they first had to learn more about the teaching of Jesus and about his life. They shared these accounts of Jesus' life and teaching regularly in their Sunday worship. In fact, these oral accounts and instructions evolved over several years and were finally written down for themselves and for us today. This was the very process that led to the four Gospels. Consider one example of these oral accounts—the one we find incorporated in John's Gospel today. John is wrestling with the very real problem in the post-apostolic church. That is, how could

---

4. Note: These readings may also be used in years B and C for the sake of the RCIA candidates.

one believe in the risen Lord without having personally verified that he is risen? His answer is: faith comes through hearing the word of God, through hearing the risen Christ speak through his disciples. They needed to hear Jesus and to know him through those who experienced him personally; only then would their faith be not naive and uninformed. Nor can our faith be naive and uninformed today. We need to hear the same evidence, the same narratives about Jesus constantly. Only then will our faith be strong in the face of our increasingly uncommitted world.

III. Secondly, the apostolic church expressed their faith by "the breaking of the bread." This action was not the Eucharist but it did have a distinctly sacred character. We know from the Acts of the Apostles that such celebrations and prayer were distinctive marks of the early Christian community. And so is it with us. Our Sunday worship and prayer are our means of renewing and strengthening our relationship with Jesus. Modern psychology and our own experience affirm the absolute necessity of such regular actions; for all human friendships must be constantly expressed and fed or they fade away, become dormant or dead. Since our relationship with Jesus is also a human friendship, it follows the same norm. So unless we express that friendship externally at mass and communion with some regularity, it will fade away.

IV. Thirdly, the early church expressed their faith by a "common life" or fellowship. In some instances that common life was quite extreme in the form of a freely chosen sharing of possessions in common. Clearly our Christian life today is very different; still it must have some form of sharing, some sense of community. For in our faith too, "No man is an island," but needs the support of others. This parish as a whole, our school, and the various groups within the parish are the support that we absolutely need to follow Jesus faithfully. Admittedly, we are far from the ideal Christian community here in our parish, but the early Church was also far from the ideal, as we see abundantly in Paul's epistles.

V. This is how the early church strengthened their faith in the midst of an unbelieving and contradictory culture. We too are increasingly challenged in our faith by the experiences of our life and the questioning of modern American society. We need all these helps to maintain and increase our faith in Jesus; that is what we do each

Sunday here, as we experience Jesus in word and sacrament. That is how we can strongly affirm with Thomas today: "My Lord and my God!"

Year B

Acts 4:32–35; 1 John 5:1–6; John 20:19–31

Faith for Modern Americans

I. How did the early Church strengthen and develop their faith? What were their very real problems regarding faith in Christ? Today's readings offer clear answers to these questions and say much to us about faith in our modern American society. First, in the Gospel, John is wrestling with a very real problem in the post-apostolic church; that is: How could one believe fully in the risen Lord without having seen him? The first part of his answer is arresting: even to see Jesus is no guarantee of faith; even the disciples had to make a leap of faith when they saw him; Thomas only made that leap of faith with difficulty and with Jesus' unique assurance and evidence. Others in Jesus' day did not take that step. Thomas finally made that leap of faith: "My Lord and my God!"

II. But the second part of John's answer is more positive and helpful to us. In verse 23 Jesus gives the Holy Spirit to the disciples and, along with the Spirit, the power to forgive sins, as the Council of Trent officially interpreted this verse. Throughout John's Gospel and Epistles, this Holy Spirit is the "new Advocate" who is to take the place of Jesus for all his disciples; that is, whatever Jesus was to the disciples who accompanied Jesus during his public life, the Holy Spirit was meant to be for those who came after Jesus' departure. Thus, Jesus was their physically present teacher, their friend, the source of apostolic authority, the one who revealed to them personally the whole truth about God and salvation. Remember how, in John's Gospel, Jesus taught, "[It] is better for you that I go [to the Father]. For if I do not go, the Advocate will not come to you . . . to be with you always, the Spirit of truth" (John 16:7 and 14:16–17). *Now* here, in today's Gospel, we have the inauguration of the invisible presence of Jesus in his Spirit. This *Holy Spirit* of Jesus is to be the ever-present teacher and friend, "the Spirit of truth" who would reveal to later disciples the entire revelation about God and salvation, just as Jesus did in his day for a small number of disciples. And only because of this new presence of the Holy Spirit of Jesus in his future disciples can a new type of faith emerge: faith for those who have *never seen* Jesus personally. Here John gives the early Church the crucial answer to their deepest faith problem: What about faith in Jesus once he is gone? And his answer is stronger and clearer than any other Gospel writer: those who come later will have the invisible presence of Jesus in the Holy Spirit. They can have the same kind of divine help in their faith and will be even more blessed because of their faith. His conclusion is the so-called ninth beatitude: "Blessed are those who have not seen and have believed."

III. Finally, in the Second Reading, John answers another problem for the early church. That is: How can we live our faith in Jesus in this secular world that is so opposed to God in so many ways? By "this world" John consistently means unbelieving human society, organized in opposition to God and subject to sin and death; he means all those who reject God and Christ and live only for this world. John's answer is most forceful: "[W]hoever is begotten by God conquers the world. And the victory that conquers the world is our faith." That is, our faith is strong enough to overcome this secular world, but only a faith that is not just a set of dogmas but also a personal commitment to Jesus Christ. For John sees Jesus as the revelation of God's saving love to whom we are to commit our lives; John calls him "the way and the truth and the life" (John 14:6). He sees Jesus as the heart and center of our lives, the only channel of salvation. This is true even for modern America. We are surrounded by a desacralized America in which science and technology ignore the sacred. Our world is one in which the exclusive concern is with the self, the present, the practical, the material. Our world is one in which the great human actions of being born and dying, of belonging and relating are deprived of the sacred. Yet, even this world is overcome by our faith— by answering the ultimate questions of human existence which the world cannot answer; by helping us experience the invisible presence of Jesus in us by his Holy Spirit; by helping us understand God's plan of salvation in Jesus, even in such a world; by teaching us the way to human fulfillment in the midst of a world which will ever be in opposition to God. In a word, John encourages us today in just such a modern world: "Blessed are those who have not seen and have believed."

Year C

Acts 5:12–16; Revelation 1:9–11a, 12–13, 17–19; John 20:19–31

Jesus Is the Alpha and the Omega

I. Every year we have this same reading on this second Sunday of Easter. Most years we hear a homily on this Gospel—on Thomas's faith in the risen Lord and our faith in Christ. This year, let us do something different; let us consider the Second Reading, taken from Chapter 1 of the Book of Revelation. Revelation (or Apocalypse, which is the Greek word for revelation) is a mysterious and complex book. The last 20 years have seen an explosion of our knowledge on the Book of Revelation. We now know that there are probably three separate authors who contributed to this book, and that only the first three chapters are clearly Christological. The rest of Revelation (Chapters 4 to 21) seems to come from John the Baptizer or his disciples and has a decided Old Testament apocalyptic flavor. The common misunderstanding of Revelation is that this book is a symbolic code predicting the exact persons and events that will lead up to the end of the world. This is clearly false. Yet throughout our lives we will hear from many self-styled prophets who will predict the end of the world, based on their interpretation of the book of Revelation. Some of these predictions will be bizarre; some of them will be quite ingenious. But they will all be false, for Revelation does not have that purpose.

II. Now consider our reading today. There are two different aspects of faith presented. First, the author relates his own overwhelming vision of Christ the Lord, an ecstatic experience of the risen Christ. Now that's the kind of faith experience we would love to have in our life! If only we could experience Christ this way once, we imagine it would be easy to believe in Christ whole-heartedly, to commit our entire lives to him, to accept any troubles or sufferings.

Most likely very few Christians have had such an ecstatic vision of God. But, according to one sociological survey, an appreciable minority of Catholics has had some kind of profound experience of God in their lives or in their prayer life. Yet even such an experience of God, as I can attest, does not alleviate all life's sufferings or even take away all uncertainty. We still need the constant help of God's grace.

III. The second aspect of faith comes from the words of Christ in this vision: "I am the first and the last, the one who lives. Once I was dead, but now I am alive forever. . . . I hold the keys to death." That is, Jesus describes himself as the glorious Lord of life, the first and the last revelation about God and our life. He even hints at a primary truth of Christianity: that the human Jesus is the final, clear, and complete revelation about God and life; he is all that God chooses to speak to us about himself and about human life and salvation. In Jesus we know enough about our transcendent God to commit ourselves to him with our whole hearts. Saint John of the Cross wonderfully describes this unique place of Christ. He asks us to imagine that God is speaking to us about Jesus and revelation:

> If I have already told you all things in my Word, my Son, and I have no other word, what revelation can I now make that would surpass this? Fasten your eyes on him alone, because in him I have spoken and revealed all, and in him you will discover even more than you ask for and desire. You are making an appeal for [private] revelations that are incomplete, but if you turn your eyes to him you will find them complete. For he is my entire . . . vision and revelation. [5]

God wants us to be assured the *all* his revelation is found uniquely in Jesus. So we need no other private revelation, no public apparition, no mysterious apocalypse, no charismatic preacher, no end-time prophet. God would also add that we can grow in our knowledge and friendship with Christ all our life long: "This is my beloved Son . . . ; listen to him" (Matthew 17:5); all my truth and love are found in him.

---

5. 1. *The Collected Works of St. John of the Cross*, trans. By Kieran Kavanaugh and Otilio Rodriguez (Washington, D.C.: ICS Publications, 1979), p. 80 (*Ascent to Mount Carmel*, Book II, chap. 22, #5).

Third Sunday of Easter

Year A

Acts 2:14, 22–33; 1 Peter 1:17–21; Luke 24:13–35

The Journey to Emmaus

I. This Gospel of the journey to Emmaus is one of the most tender stories in all of scripture. It is also most significant for our Christian understanding of suffering in our lives. The story really begins for these two disciples with the suffering and death of Jesus. For them the tragic end of Jesus' life was a grave disappointment. The end of Jesus' life was a complete fiasco for them; he was overcome by his enemies, rejected by the religious leaders, deserted by the apostles, judged a failure by the people. The two disciples see this as the failure of all their hopes: "[W]e were hoping that he would be the one to redeem Israel." They did not see this tragedy as the hand of God at all. They only found themselves "in the soup." They were distressed, so they ran away from Jerusalem to Emmaus to take themselves out of the painful situation. They found no redeeming value in all they had experienced, so they got out of the mess.

II. Then Jesus appears to them as a fellow traveler. He gets them talking and listens to their pain. When their painful story is finished, he slowly and kindly explains the real sense of all that happened. The central point of the entire event is found in the words of Jesus: "Was it not necessary that the Messiah should suffer these things and enter into his glory?" Here in Luke the meaning is clear: his suffering and death were the fulfillment of many prophecies and writings of scripture; so it was *necessary* for Jesus to suffer in order to fulfill the prophecies of God's suffering servant. All the apostolic writers struggle to explain this great scandal of a suffering Messiah. Each evangelist tries to throw light on this central mystery of our faith. The Letter to the Hebrews explains that such a suffering Messiah was *fitting*: "[I]t was fitting that [God] . . . in bringing many children to glory, should make the leader to their salvation perfect through suffering" (Hebrews 2:10). Peter emphasizes that all this was an *example* for all of us: "Christ . . . suffered for you [in just this way] leaving you an example that you should follow in his footsteps" (1 Peter 2:21). John stresses that his suffering and death for us is the best *proof* of God's love: "In this way the love of God was revealed to us: God sent his only Son into the world . . . as expiation for our sins" (1 John 4:9–10).

III. Here in Luke this event can be seen as a paradigm about suffering in our lives. Sometimes we go through a great suffering— a chronic physical illness, the failure of a primary relationship in our life, the feeling of God's absence in our prayer and life or a personal tragedy. It is very hard to see the will of God in this experience. We wonder why this evil came to us; we even see it as an unmitigated evil. Our inclination is to try to run from it, somehow to avoid the painful situation. We need to focus on Jesus, on his own suffering, on the explanation of scripture: "Christ . . . suffered for you, leaving you an example that you should follow in his footsteps" (1 Peter 2:21). Like the apostles, we too learn only gradually and with great reluctance that the only truly human way of redemption is one of embracing the entire human mystery of pain and suffering as the way of purification and human maturing. Like the disciples at Emmaus, we can learn from Jesus that the very suffering and confusion help us find new life. Like them, we too can apply Jesus' words to ourselves now and throughout our lives: "Was it not necessary that the Messiah should suffer these things and enter into his glory?"

Year B

Acts 3:13–15, 17–19; 1 John 2:1–5a; Luke 24:35–48

Faith Equals Life

I. Many Americans see faith as a purely individual commitment. That is, they believe in the identity of their deepest self with God, and that this connection is totally independent of any church or other institution. This is the claim of Harold Bloom in his book, The American

Religion. He asserts that a profound negativity toward all institutions afflicts our society; thus, there is a deep distrust of government, church, and any social organizations. Even helping the poor becomes entirely an individual choice and activity; personal acts of compassion become their way of showing non-conformity, of doing their own thing. Many believe in their own theology, their independent faith, their separate religion.

II. Today's readings offer a commentary on such an American Religion. The First Reading contains a short sermon of Saint Peter the apostle. There are many such sermons in the Acts of the Apostles, which describes the early life of the church. Such sermons contain no argumentation in them but merely the kernel or core of our faith, called *kerygma* in Greek. In this sermon, the *kerygma* or core of our faith that Peter points out has three parts: 1. The prophets foretold the coming of Christ, the Messiah. 2. He died and rose from the dead and will come again. 3. Therefore, we must reform our lives and turn to God. This, for the early disciples, is the substance of the Gospel and the core of our faith.

But how can we know that we really turn to God, really believe this *kerygma*, this good news? How can we truthfully say, "I am a believer; I am a Catholic?" The Second Reading and the few verses following it (which we did not read today) tell us loudly and clearly, "Whoever says, 'I know him,' but does not keep his commandments is a liar. . . . This is the way we may know that we are in union with him: whoever claims to abide in him ought to live [just] as he lived. . . . Whoever says he is in the light, yet hates his brother [or sister], is still in the darkness" (1 John 2:4–6, 9). Three times this reading shouts it out: faith is not merely affirming truths; faith is also obeying Jesus' commands, trying to live as he lived, loving our brothers and sisters.

III. And this entire Easter season is full of readings that describe the early church and what was required of those believing in Jesus. As one example: "[The Christians] devoted themselves to the teaching of the apostles and to the communal life, to the breaking of the bread and to the prayers" (Acts 2:42–44). "The breaking of the bread and the prayers" (though not Eucharistic) clearly indicates that such common worship and prayer are distinctive marks of the early

Christian community. Also the "communal life" and fellowship were invariably the constant norm of faith in the early church.

In summary then, especially at Easter time we have a ringing response to the American Religion. In these readings of the Acts of the Apostles, faith is not just something known but something lived. Words and faith affirmations *are* indispensable, but so are sacraments—more than in any other religion. Sacramental actions make the reality of Jesus present for his followers according to Jesus' will. Our entire tradition of faith is living for us in the history of our Catholic community. Our faith is constituted by these traditions and living community, and it cannot exist without them.

YEAR C

Acts 5:27–32, 40b–41; Revelation 5:11–14; John 21:1–19

LOVE AND AUTHORITY

I. In John's Gospel we can learn a great deal about love for Christ and about authority in his church. For the hero of the Johannine community is the "beloved disciple." He is never named—even though we used to think of him as John himself. Throughout John's Gospel, there is a consistent and deliberate contrast between the "beloved disciple" and Peter the apostle. Thus, at the last supper, the beloved disciple rests on Jesus' chest, while Peter has to signal to Jesus; during Jesus' trial, the beloved disciple accompanies Jesus into the high-priest's palace, while Peter only enters with his help; most important, at the foot of the cross, we find the beloved disciple standing there, but Peter and the other apostles have abandoned Jesus; then in the early Easter event, the beloved disciple outruns Peter to the tomb and only he is said to believe the evidence he sees there; finally, when the risen Jesus appears to them on the shore, as in today's Gospel, the beloved disciple is the first to recognize him and tells Peter that it is the Lord. In general, we see a constant one-upmanship of the beloved disciple over Peter; both in Jesus' life and death, the beloved disciple is quicker to believe in Jesus and closer to him in love.

II. Now consider our Gospel today. This Gospel and all of Chapter 21 in John's Gospel is an addition to the Gospel. It is, of course, canonical and authentic, but it is a later addition to the original Gospel of John. Surprisingly in the original Gospel of John (Chapters 1–20), there is no special authority given to Peter or anyone else. None of the passages from the synoptic Gospels that indicate authority—especially that given to Peter—is found in John's original Gospel. For in John's Gospel there seemed to be no need for an institutional structure or authority. Apparently, that's because all Christians have the new Advocate, the Holy Spirit, as the Spirit of Truth. This Advocate will guide the members of the Johannine community into all truth and will remind them of all that Jesus taught them. According to Raymond Brown, the premier scholar of John's Gospel, this lack of human authority, even for interpreting the Gospel, led to many difficulties regarding faith and scripture interpretation and practical Christian living. But this addition about Peter in today's Gospel is a moderating force in the Johannine community, persuading the Johannine Christians that the pastoral authority practiced in the apostolic church was instituted by Jesus himself. Yet even here, where the authority of Peter is introduced, his position as leader does not exempt him from the Johannine criterion of loving Jesus. The threefold question and affirmation of love assures the Johannine community (and us) that Peter is an authentic disciple and one who is properly given pastoral authority. Yet the authority only comes after his expression of love for Jesus.

III. There are two points that follow from all this, according to the Gospel of John. First, authority in *necessary* in the church of Christ—necessary for leadership, for understanding the teaching of Jesus and necessary because Jesus himself chose it for his followers. In fact, according to Raymond Brown, that branch of the Johannine community that rejected any form of authority in the church soon died out as a recognizable group. The reliance on the Holy Spirit present in each member was not enough to maintain the unity or even the survival of that group. The second point is even more significant. It is that our personal love of Jesus is more important than our having a position of authority in the church. For all of us—whether in a position of authority in the church or not—what matters most is our individual, personal love for Jesus. Especially is this point significant for women in general and for all who are presently left out of certain forms of leadership in the church. In a word, John's Gospel tells all of us: what is primary is not a position of authority but of personal love of Christ. Love of Jesus is essential both for feeding Christ's sheep and for being a beloved disciple of Jesus. That's something the whole church—and each of us too—needs to learn.

Fourth Sunday of Easter

Year A

Acts 2:14a and 36–41; 1 Peter 2:20b–25; John 10:1–10

Jesus Is Lord and Christ

I. During the twentieth century, there were many articles and books written about "the search for the historical Christ." Even popular journals, such as Time and Newsweek, pointed out that we do not have the exact words of Christ and we have no eyewitness account of the resurrection itself. Such articles need not trouble us, if we keep in mind the literary form of the Gospels and epistles. For the Gospels are proclamation history, which proclaim Christ as the Lord and Savior of all the world. They were not written as proof documents, but professions of faith in the historical Jesus and his teaching. With such popular articles as a background, we need to recall two points. First, post-Vatican II theology is definitely new and different, principally because of the explosion of our knowledge of scripture and a solid respect for that new insight into scripture. Secondly, the essentials of our faith do not change. The core doctrines of our faith are just a handful of truths; they can be understood by us in a new way with new emphases; but they remain the same core doctrines that Saint Peter taught in the First Reading today.

II. Let us take a closer look at this First Reading today, along with the First Reading last Sunday. These two short passages make up the first sermon that we have from the early church. In this sermon, Peter gives us the core *kerygma* or the essential truths of our faith, both then and now. Very simply, these truths relate to God, Christ, his life, death and resurrection, baptism, faith and, by implication, the community of believers or church. As Peter put it:

> Jesus . . . was a man commended to you by God with mighty deeds, wonders and signs, which God worked through him in your midst . . . . [He was] delivered up by the set plan and foreknowledge of God . . . . [He was crucified and rose again.] . . . God has made him both Lord and Messiah. . . . Repent and be baptized . . . in the name of Jesus Christ . . . and you will receive the gift of the holy Spirit. (Acts 2:22–23, 36, 38)

This is the unchanging rock of our faith; it will always be so.

III. Now a few words of explanation about Peter's sermon. First, notice the response of his listeners; it is the same question all sincere people have to the preaching about Jesus: "What are we to do?" That is, if all of this is true, what does that mean for our lives; how are we to follow him? Peter answers: "Repent [or reform] and be baptized." He means they must reassess Jesus and his significance; they cannot think of him as an impostor who failed and was crucified but rather the emissary of God and the bringer of human salvation. And such reform probably had some of the meaning it had for Jesus himself—a radical transformation of life with a whole new value system, new attitudes, a new way of living. "Be baptized" means more than forgiveness of sins; it means God's whole gift of salvation and his joining them to a community of believers. It includes a new relationship to God and a wondrous hope.

IV. The other point that needs explaining is Peter's proclamation: "[L]et the whole house of Israel know for certain that God has made [Jesus] both Lord and Messiah." In Hebrew thought, "Lord" and "Messiah" are functional terms, meaning that from the Resurrection onward, the risen and exalted Christ exercises the functions of Messiah and Lord. So he rules over his people, he forgives them, he nourishes them with word and sacrament, he commands their obedience. In a word, all that God does toward his people is now done through Christ. In today's Gospel Jesus describes himself both as the good shepherd and the gate of the sheepfold, indicating that he is the one who nourishes his people by word and sacrament and so gives them life. This is a comforting and all-inclusive view of Jesus our Lord.

V. In our readings today, then, we have the unchanging core of faith expressed by Peter and by Jesus himself. We see Jesus as the total revelation of God and the source of salvation for all who believe.

Year B

Acts 4:8–12; 1 John 3:1–2; John 10:11–18

Jesus Is the Good Shepherd

I. "I am the good shepherd," proclaims Jesus in today's Gospel. This image of Jesus as the good shepherd was by far the most popular picture of Jesus in the catacombs and in the early church in general. In their own personal experience, Christians were very familiar with all the implications of such an image. They knew that a good or model shepherd is concerned for his sheep, he leads them with care, defends them, serves their needs, even suffers for them. We modern [sub]urbanites are not so familiar with this image, and some of us might prefer to translate this entire image of shepherd into something more familiar—such as savior or leader. And in fact, today's readings suggest that to us. So let us study today's readings and see Christ our Savior with an open eye and heart.

II. A. In the First Reading, we see a Savior who heals us. Peter asserts that the crippled man is healed in the name of Jesus and then expands this to assert that we are ALL healed and saved by Jesus. Peter uses the same word for both healing and saving: *sosthenai*. He wants us to see Jesus as Savior, as a healer who makes us whole, as one who saves. Yet Peter learned well from Jesus that he is not a magical and universal healer; he does not take away all our pain; he does not heal us by transforming our human life into something else. Rather, he heals our sickness with comfort, our suffering with courage, our loneliness with friendship, our anxiety with hope.

B. Peter's second point is that Jesus is Savior as the source of salvation: "There is no salvation through anyone else, nor is there any other name under heaven given to the human race by which we are to be saved." This is an extravagant claim—that Jesus is the *only one* who fully deserves the name "Savior." He means that whoever is ultimately saved—no matter what his sincere faith or religion—is saved only by the grace and redemption of this unique Savior. Modern theologians would be quick to affirm that all religions can help people of faith to be saved; but if they come to salvation with God, they do so only by means of the unique saving grace of Jesus. Jesus alone has merited the grace of salvation for all.

C. Thirdly, our Savior seeks out those who "do not belong to this fold." Which means that his salvation is not only for the Jews but also for us Gentiles and for those who do not yet believe. In fact he accepts anyone in the world who believes in him—without exclusiveness, without preference, without limits of any kind. Most other religions are based on some kind of elite group; they have a preference for one ethnic group or for males or for those who follow a rigid code of spiritual practices. None of this is true of our Savior; he permits no superiority, no preference and no exclusion.

D. Fourth, our Savior can honestly say, "I know mine and mine know me." The Hebrew word for "know" does not mean simply to perceive or be familiar with; rather it includes personal involvement. Jesus does that constantly with his word and sacrament—as we experience here each Sunday. And he does that personally through his Holy Spirit given to us individually at baptism. He knows and cares for each of us, he is concerned for us, he intercedes for us so that "whatever you ask the Father in my name he will give you" (Jo. 16, 23). No other religious leader can make such claims.

E. Finally, he points to the highpoint of his care and personal involvement: "I will lay down my life for [them]." By his dying and rising, he gives us the final proof of his love for us and the assurance of his promise of eternal life: "No one has greater love than this . . ." (John 15:13).

III. This is the image of Jesus our Savior. He is our Savior who heals us even now. He is the *only* Savior worthy of the name in the whole plan of God. He excludes no one, gives preference to no one. He cares for each of us individually, even to the extreme of laying down his life for us. Only he can claim, "I am the good shepherd," the unique Savior of all.

Year C

Acts 13:14, 43–52; Revelation 7:9, 14b–17; John 10:27–30

Faith Involves a Choice

I. This entire Easter season is a time when the church leads us to reflect on what our faith is all about, on what Easter means to us. We try to deepen our understanding of Christ's death, resurrection and glorification; we try to appreciate what it means for us to affirm that Jesus is our Redeemer, Savior and Lord. This is the perfect time to reflect on our faith as a choice we make, not just once, but constantly.

II. Here in our parish and throughout our country, people are making choices about their Catholic faith. In the last 10 years, so many people in our parish have made a choice for Christ. Because of our RCIA (Rite of Christian Initiation of Adults) several non-practicing Catholics have returned to the practice of their faith. Generally, they were young people who had very little Catholic education as children and had not practiced their faith for years. In addition, many people from various backgrounds have learned about Jesus through the RCIA and have chosen to follow Jesus. This is great news!

III. But not all the news is good, both here and throughout America. The number of Catholics in America who chose *not* to grow in their faith is increasing steadily in the past 25 years. Such people think of themselves as Catholic and protest that they believe in God. But they have very little external contact with Jesus in terms of mass and Eucharist. One way that sociologists describe this is that every year another one percent of Catholics joins the group of non-practicing Catholics. So that in the past 25 years, there are twenty-five percent less Catholics who are regularly going to mass on Sunday. A crushing statistic is that on any one Sunday now, only one-quarter of Catholics attend mass or receive communion. This is a most distressing problem for me as a priest. Agreed, church attendance alone is *not* a clear indication of internal faith. But I am forced to conclude that for many of them, their faith is fading away. They are doing serious harm to their faith—and that of their children—and they hardly realize it.

IV. Today's readings offer some commentary and suggestions for this situation. The common theme of today's readings is acceptance or rejection of Jesus Christ. In the First Reading, many "Gentiles were delighted when they heard this and glorified the word of the Lord . . . [and they] came to believe"; while some Jews "reject" the word of God. Notice that people are free to reject Christ personally or really respond to him. In the Second Reading, the author of the book of Revelation sees those who are saved before the throne of God because they "have survived the time of great distress"; that is, it takes a real commitment to follow Christ, especially in difficult times. And in the Gospel, Jesus proclaims, "My sheep hear my voice . . . and they follow me." That is, to hear and respond to Jesus' word is the decisive factor which will determine our eternal life. All of these readings teach us that Jesus expects faith in him and living according to that faith.

V. This Easter season is meant for us to strengthen our commitment to Jesus the Good Shepherd. The liturgies of this season encourage us to renew our choice to follow him, for he is our whole interpretation of life's meaning; he is the model for our living; he wants to be the center of our lives, the constant friend with whom we share our life. In the readings for daily mass this week, Jesus himself suggests one powerful external source of our friendship with him: "[U]nless you eat the flesh of the Son of Man . . . you do not have life within you. . . . [T]he one who feeds on me will have life because of me" (John 6:53 and 57). Jesus himself insists that only if we experience him in the Eucharist regularly and try to make him our friend, can we be real Christians and grow in love of him.

Fifth Sunday of Easter

Year A

Acts 6:1–7; 1 Peter 2:4–9; John 14:1–12

I Am the Way and the Truth and the Life

I. "I am the way and the truth and the life," is one of the most familiar of all Jesus' claims. For John, it is a summary of his entire Gospel. What does John mean here? What is Jesus telling us about our relationship to him? How is he "the way and the truth and the life" for us?

II. The critical problem with this quotation is the relation of these three nouns to one another. Throughout history, the Fathers of the Church and scripture scholars have related these three nouns in every possible way; emphasizing one or other of them. Fr. Raymond Brown, the preeminent Johannine scholar, considers all these alternatives in his lengthy commentary on John's Gospel and then chooses this explanation:

> [T]he way is the primary predicate, and the truth and the life are just explanations of the way. Jesus is the way because he is the truth and the life. . . . He is the way because he is the truth or revelation of the Father . . . [And] he is the way because he is the life . . . the channel through which the Father's life comes to [all people]."[6]

He gives two reasons for seeing "*the way*" as dominant. First, in verse 4, Jesus asserts, "you know the way;" and verse 5 continues with Thomas's question, "how can we know the way?" So "the way" is the *focus* of the entire exchange between Jesus and Thomas. Second, the last part of verse 6 only mentions Jesus as the way: "No one comes to the Father except through me." So Fr. Brown concludes:

---

6. Raymond Brown, *The Gospel According to John (Anchor Bible, vol. 29A)* (New York: Doubleday, 1970), p. 621.

These verses simply explain how Jesus is the way to the Father. He is the way because he is the truth or revelation of the Father, so that when the disciples know him, they know the Father (v. 7). And he is the way because he is the life; that is, since he lives in the Father and the Father lives in him (vv. 10–11), he is the channel through which the Father's life comes to us.[7]

In a word, Jesus presents himself as the only avenue of salvation, meaning there is no other way for human beings to attain salvation, except through Jesus, for he is the unique way to the Father, the only source of grace and eternal life. As a theologian I must quickly add that people of all religions can come to eternal life through their faith in God and by living according to their faith; but the door of salvation has been opened for all by means of the redemption won by Christ.

III. There is also a secondary meaning to this passage, which is also true and most significant for us: Jesus is the way as the norm or model of life. Fr. Raymond Brown points out the long tradition in the Old Testament of a way of life in conformity with the law of Moses, and in the Acts of the Apostles which describes the whole Christian life as simply "the way." Many of the saints understood Jesus' words this way, when they insisted that Jesus is the way because he is the model for us to follow, the image we are to imitate. For example, the mystic Saint John of the Cross teaches:

Christ is the way. For he is our model and light. . . . A man makes progress only through imitation of Christ, who is the Way, the Truth and the life. . . . Accordingly, I should not consider any spirituality worthwhile that would . . . run from imitation of Christ. [8]

Notice what this implies for our faith. It means that Jesus wants us not only to believe in certain truths, but also to follow a way of life patterned on him. We do that by struggling all life long to make his values and attitudes our own, to live as he lived. That means we Christians are unique among all religious groups of the world. For all other religions follow sacred writings, ultimate truths, moral laws. We go beyond all that; we alone follow a *person*, Jesus Christ. He is

---

7. *Ibid.*, p. 628.

8. *The Collected Works of St. John of the Cross*, trans. By Kieran Kavanaugh and Otilio Rodriguez (Washington, D.C.: ICS Publications, 1979), p. 124.

not just someone we believe in; he is our model for living; we try to make him the center of our lives.

IV. Let me conclude by bringing us back to the beginning, to the primary meaning of these amazing words of Jesus. When Jesus tells Thomas, "I am the way. . . . No one comes to the Father except through me," he means he is the unique source of grace for all people, no matter what their religion. He is the only door of salvation, the unique way to everlasting life. We are proud to acclaim him as "the way and the truth and the life."

Year B

Acts 9:26–31; 1 John 3:18–24; John 15:1–8

I Am the Vine; You Are the Branches

I. "Children, let us love not in word or speech but in deed and truth." This counsel comes from the Johannine author, exhorting us about Christian living. This whole reading from John's First Epistle seems to consist of various notes from John about Christian living. Notice the points he makes: 1. Faith is not merely professing certain truths but living according to them. 2. God expects two things of us: faith in Jesus Christ and love for others. 3. If we are committed to God, we can be at peace with him and confident in prayer. 4. The external test of our union with God is whether we keep the commandments. 5. The internal test is the gift of the Spirit. To summarize all this, we see that John holds together things that are often separated from one another in our thinking: faith and works, belief and obedience, prayer to God and love of our neighbor. It is not a matter of either-or but of both-and. And the result of all this is an intimate union with God: "[Then we] remain in him, and he in [us]."

II. In the Gospel, the Johannine author gives an expansion on a parable of Jesus: "I am the vine, you are the branches." Last week John gave us the comforting image of Jesus as good shepherd; today he adds the comparison of the vine and the branches. This image is even more intimate and personal, for it describes our relationship with Jesus in the language of indwelling, of "remaining together" in friendship: "Remain in me, as I remain in you. . . . Whoever remains in me and I in him will bear much fruit, because without me you can do nothing." This reminds us of the theology we learned as children: that we must be in the state of sanctifying grace—without serious sin—in order to merit and bear fruit in Christ. Modern theology would only add that this abiding in the grace of Christ is a personal relationship, an intimate indwelling and remaining together in friendship. It involves being open to transformation into Jesus throughout our life—slowly becoming like the one in whom we believe.

III. Let me explain this a different way. When young people come to the rectory to prepare for marriage, I always find a few minutes to talk to them about their whole future life as married Christians. I try to explain to them that authentic Christian living requires that we live according to the truths we profess, and that we continually nourish that faith with Christ's word and sacrament. Some of them don't really get the idea; they feel that a minimal acceptance of truths and keeping the commandments is all there is to Christian faith. Today's readings from John teach us that our life in Christ is much more than that. It involves faith and works; it includes prayer and keeping the commandments; it grows by frequent union with Christ in word and sacrament; its goal is true friendship with Jesus. Jesus himself encourages us to develop a personal friendship with him; he invites us to remain in him; he wants to be the center of our lives, the model for our living. "Remain in me, as I remain in you . . . [and you] will bear much fruit."

Year C

Acts 14:21–27; Revelation 21:1–5a; John 13:31–33a, 34–35

My Commandment: Love One Another as I Have Loved You

I. When King Henry VIII of England wanted to divorce his wife for phony reasons, in order to marry Anne Bolyn, Thomas More refused.

So Henry VIII threw Thomas in prison to force him to agree. According to the play "A Man for All Seasons," while Thomas was in prison, his daughter, Meg, visited him and lovingly argued with him:

> Father, you always taught me that only good men were worthy of positions of authority and leadership. But you are the most just, the most kind man in England. You deserve to be free and rewarded with authority, not rot here in prison.

Thomas More responded very gently to his daughter, the love of his life:

> Meg, what kind of world would this be if virtue were always rewarded and vice were always punished? How many would try to appear virtuous just for the reward? We would be virtuous for all the wrong reasons and our virtue would be pharisaical. No, God wants us to be virtuous for love of him, and he is wise in not always rewarding virtue in this world.

II. Today's Gospel implies a lot about virtue, morality and motivation for us Christians. There are three points that Jesus makes here. First, Jesus gives us a *new commandment*. This is the *only* commandment Jesus gives us as his own. How is it *new*? Fr. Raymond Brown, the premier scholar on John's Gospel, teaches that it is new because it is connected with the Last Supper, the Eucharist, and the entire new covenant. All of this is the fulfillment of the prophecy of Jeremiah: "The days are coming . . . when I will make a new covenant with the house of Israel" (Jeremiah 31:31). Now at the Last Supper, Jesus gives us the "cup [of] the new covenant" (Luke 22:20), and the commandment of the new covenant. This commandment is the summary of the Ten Commandments of Moses, so central to the Old Testament, and it supersedes them.

III. Secondly, Jesus clarifies what this one commandment of the new covenant consists in: "As I have loved you, so you also should love one another." Very clearly, Jesus says his love is a *model* for our love. When Jesus repeats this command in Chapter 15, he immediately adds: "No one has greater love than this, to lay down one's life for one's friends" (John 15:13). So there he means that his love is a model for us in the *intensity* of that love—by being ready to sacrifice everything for love of him. But in our Gospel today, Jesus is speaking more generally, for ordinary people like you and me, who will not have to die for our faith. Here he intends his love as a general model for all our loving, an example of how we are to love, a concrete expression of what our love should be in all of our living out of this covenant. That is, Jesus himself is our way of love, our concrete norm for human living. Such a love is not a selfish love, motivated by reward or success; that's the point Thomas More made earlier. It is not a phony love, for it includes all the negative aspects of love, as it did for him: anger, fear, sadness, disappointment, and rejection. It is not a namby-pamby love, for it includes the hard aspects of love: forgiveness, sacrifice, suffering, and risk. It is a mature human love; it includes sensitivity, sexuality, kindness, acceptance, communication, sharing of self. Whatever psychologists describe as part of mature love is found concretely in Jesus and is a model for our loving. The whole summary of Christian life is found in Jesus' command today: "As I have loved you, so you also should love one another."

IV. Finally, Jesus points to our living this command and adds: "This is how all will know that you are my disciples." Very soon after these words were written in John's Gospel, many Christians suffered and died as martyrs after the example of Jesus their crucified Lord. And Christian apologists would point to the impact made by Christian love and martyrdom as a standard argument for the superior love of Christianity. Happily, we are not called to such an extreme following of Jesus. But we are "commanded" to make Jesus' love the model for us in all our following him. Though you and I fail often, we can never lose sight of this wondrous, real, concrete model for all our living. In that way, as long as Christian love is in the world, the world is still encountering Jesus. "This is how all will know" me and my love.

Sixth Sunday of Easter

Year A

Acts 8:5–8, 14–17; 1 Peter 3:15–18; John 14:15–21

Our Relationship to God: Father, Son, and Holy Spirit

I. The Church year has a plan to it. The various seasons of the Church year have very different purposes; there is an ebb and flow to the liturgical year. Advent and Christmas is a time of expectation and fulfillment; Lent is a time of renewal and growth; the ordinary time from Pentecost to Advent is a time of action, of living the faith; this Easter season is a time of meditation. Throughout this Easter season, we meditate on the central mysteries of our faith that tell of God's love, of Christ's redemption and of the Spirit's presence in us. At Easter we meditate on the Resurrection and the appearances of Jesus. In this present week, we try to appreciate the Ascension of Christ and his becoming our Lord and glorious Savior. At Pentecost we concentrate on the continued presence of Jesus with us through his Spirit. And we do all this especially in the context of John's Gospel and Jesus' own meditative discourse with the disciples at the last supper. Much of this discourse of Jesus at the last supper is a reflection on our relationship with God: Father, Son and Holy Spirit.

II. Start with last Sunday's Gospel reading, in which Jesus told Philip: "Whoever has seen me has seen the Father" (John 14:9). That is, in Jesus we know God the Father in a human, visible way for Jesus is the best revelation of God to us; he is God inasmuch as God reveals himself to us. Recent scripture scholars lead us to a conclusion: the *revelation of God* is a person, Jesus Christ. They mean that in Jesus we see concretely and know with assurance all that God intended to reveal about himself; in Jesus we know that our God is most kind, he is accepting of all people, he is so understanding of our human condition, he is endlessly forgiving. We know all this about

God because we see all this in Jesus, who is the revelation of God the Father.

Then, in today's Gospel reading, Jesus promises "another Advocate to be with you always, the Spirit of truth . . . ." And the very next words of Jesus are: "I will not leave you orphans; I will come to you." What Jesus means is that his Spirit, whom he sends us, will be his continued presence with us. John's Epistle explains, ". . . the way we know that [God] remains in us is from the Spirit that he gave us" (1 John 3:24). All this means that the Holy Spirit is the truth and love of God in us; he is God inasmuch as we individually possess God. The conclusion we are led to here is that *the possession of God* is a person, the Holy Spirit.

III. This season of Easter is the liturgical time for us to meditate on our wondrous relationship to God; the time to be convinced that God our Father is as gentle and loving with us as was Jesus himself; and the time to be assured that the Spirit of Jesus is the constant presence of Christ and God in us and the loving teacher of his way. If you are like me, one thing tends to hold us back from a complete conviction of all these intimate relationships to God. When we compare ourselves to other Christians, doubts begin to arise. We do not see ourselves as holy as some others we know; we are not as popular with other people; we do not see ourselves as outstanding personalities; we may not think of ourselves as charming or attractive. But with Jesus, public status means nothing; charm, popularity and notoriety are not necessary qualities. What is most significant is that we believe in these relationships to God that Jesus emphasizes, and that we strive to live ever more faithfully as children of such a Father. Jesus wants us to realize that only one personal quality is important to him: "[T]hose who hear the word of God and act on it" (Luke 8:21; cf. also 11:28).

Year B

Acts 10:25–26, 34–35, 44–48; 1 John 4:7–10; John 15:9–17

God Is Love

I. Today's readings are among the best commentaries on the love of God for us in all of scripture. In John's Epistle, he offers the simple affirmation: "God is love;" surprisingly, this is the only place in scripture for this wonderful description of God. Yet it is easy to miss the whole force of John's assertion, because we tend to see this as a general, self-evident truth, a philosophical abstraction about God, telling us that the essence of God is love. But John had something quite different in mind; he made this assertion about God in a typically Jewish fashion; he meant it as a summary of God's way of acting. He was drawing a conclusion from the very way God treats his people: he creates them, chooses them as his own, makes a covenant with them, forgives them, leads them to freedom, and promises them a redeemer. Throughout the entire Bible, the scripture writers come to know God and describe him by his actions. Then, in our Second Reading, John describes God's love by his pre-eminent, greatest action: "In this way the love of God was revealed to us: God sent his only Son into the world . . . as [an] expiation for our sins . . . so that we might have life through him." That is, God reveals who he is above all by Christ's life, death and redemption. By Christ's life and death we know that God is love; by this supreme act of human love, we know that God's love is selfless and unconditional.

II. And John is also quite practical in this passage. He is aware that many Greek philosophers claim to know God with their esoteric philosophy. For them, philosophical knowledge was the supreme human achievement and perfection. John implicitly rejects such knowledge here; he implies that such knowledge is not enough for us. Rather, the acid test for anyone claiming to know God is—strangely—love of the brethren. Only the one who experiences human love and returns it, really knows God, for real love is the essence of God. Anyone who has never experienced real human love cannot understand what God is like.

III. But we modern Americans have another problem understanding all this. Today, human love is the most talked-about and the most confusing of human affections—as evidenced by countless talk shows, TV dramas, movies, and fiction books; some would argue that love is a quagmire for Americans today. Perhaps today's Gospel would help us cut through the phony ideas about love. Jesus offers himself as a concrete human *model* of love; he urges us simply: "[L]ove one another as I love you;" he means that he himself is our way of love, our supreme norm for human loving.

Let us look at Jesus and see what kind of love he offers as our model. First, his love is not a phony love, for it includes all the negative aspects as well, just as it did for him: anger, fear, crying, sadness, and disappointment. Second, it is not a namby-pamby love, for includes all the hard aspects of love: rejection by others, forgiveness, sacrifice, great risk and suffering. And it is a mature human love, for it includes sensitivity, understanding, patience, compassion, acceptance, self-giving. Whatever modern psychologists describe as part of mature love is found in Jesus. Listen to what a woman psychologist affirms about Jesus:

> From a developmental frame of reference, it is certain that Jesus of Nazareth was a whole, self-realized and completed personality . . . His active, continual demonstration of love exemplifies what human love could be . . . . [Acceptance of all, sensitivity,] dependability, understanding, a generous spirit, the ability to experience another as oneself, keeping one's word, the ability to affirm life fully in the face of death—these are all traits which flow from a supremely well-defined and developed consciousness.

In sum, she affirms that Jesus our Lord is the model of human wholeness.

IV. So for us Christians, scripture equivalently tells us that the whole summary of Christian life is found in Jesus' assertion: "Love one another as I love you." And modern psychologists add that the complete example of mature human love is found concretely in Jesus our Lord.

Year C

Acts 15:1–2, 22–29; Revelation 21:10–14, 22–23;
John 14:23–29

Division in the Church

I. Ever since Vatican II in the 1960's, this First Reading from the Acts of the Apostles is one of my favorite readings. It is a critical reading for our Catholic Church today. Let me show you why.

II. The situation in the early church was critical. The explicit question was this: Do Gentile converts have to be circumcised, to eat only certain meats, to observe the 613 laws of the Mosaic Law? This was important enough. But implied in this practical problem was a more crucial question: Is this new Christian way just a new form of Judaism or is it a whole new church? The apostles had to establish some norm, some uniformity, some peace. The so-called Council of Jerusalem was called to do just that—as indicated in our reading today from the Acts of the Apostles. After prolonged discussion by the apostolic leaders, the solution was offered by Peter and finally by James, the Bishop of Jerusalem, who was a most conscientious observer of the Mosaic Law. In James' words, ". . . we ought to stop troubling the Gentiles" (Acts 15:19). They explained in their decision that the Holy Spirit had been given to them as well as to us. We are all one in Christ as proven by the external evidence of the charisms of the Spirit and by our baptism. We are all saved by the grace of Jesus Christ and by faith, not by observance of the law. So, "It is the decision of the holy Spirit and of us not to place on you any burden beyond these necessities, namely, to abstain from meat sacrificed to idols . . . and from unlawful marriage." That is, Gentiles are not required to follow all the Jewish laws, but need only do what even the Book of Leviticus asked of them. In general, the council did not decide how exactly the Christian Church was related to the Old Testament law; they did not solve the critical theological issue, as important as that was. Rather, they only gave a practical Jewish solution. It amounted to this: Jewish Christians should "stop troubling the Gentiles"; they should not force them to follow their ways, not condemn them. They did not decide what was absolutely true or false, or uniformly right or wrong, or what everyone had to do. They wanted both groups to exist side by side in mutual acceptance and peace.

III. Our situation in the Church today is also critical. There is a multitude of questions facing the universal church, especially after the great changes of Vatican II and our accelerated knowledge of scripture in the last 50 years. On one side, many people are concerned or troubled over different theological approaches such as liberation theology, or moral questions regarding medical or sexual ethics, or concerns springing from the explosive developments in scripture studies, or sacramental practices regarding mass, Eucharist, reconciliation, and marriage.

On the other side, many people are distressed over recent disciplining of several theologians, or strict regulations from Rome regarding Catholic universities, or rejection of inclusive language texts, or exclusion of women from many facets of the Church, or even Roman restrictions put on national conferences of bishops.

IV. In the face of all this, some say it is imperative that the Church establish some norms in these cases, some clear direction, some peace; she should insist on uniformity. But the solution today could well follow the same lines as in the early Church. Both sides in this deep division need to remember that the essence of our faith is not at issue; almost all these problems deal with secondary matters, not essential truths or morals. And most of all, we need to realize that we all have the same faith, we all belong to the one body of Christ through baptism. Conservative Catholics should not so quickly condemn liberal Catholics; they should not argue bitterly with them or try to force them to follow their way. Nor should liberal Catholics ridicule or totally dismiss conservative Catholics. In the great majority of cases, it is simply not necessary to decide what is absolutely true or false, what is uniformly right or wrong. Both sides can exist side by side in peace and acceptance. After all, we follow Jesus our Savior who earnestly prayed for *unity but not uniformity* among his followers. Both sides need the spirit of Jesus and of the early church: "It is the decision of the holy Spirit and of us not to place on you any burden beyond these necessities."

Ascension of the Lord

YEAR A

Acts 1:1–11; Ephesians 1:17–23; Matthew 28:16–20

I AM WITH YOU ALWAYS

I. "I am with you always, until the end of the age" is the great assurance of Jesus today. In Matthew's Gospel, these are the triumphant last words of Jesus to his apostles and to us. But in Twenty-first century America, it is so easy to wonder about these words. We have very little experience of the presence of Christ when we drive through our town, when we read our newspapers, when we see the condition of our society. Is Jesus really alive and well and living among us?

II. Let me try to show how Jesus is present to our world and in our individual lives. First, he is irrevocably a critical part of our *world*. This feast of the Ascension is the day that Christ is publicly established as the Lord of our world. As the second reading today puts it: "[God raised Christ from the dead] "seating him at his right hand in the heavens. . . . [H]e put all things beneath his feet and gave him as head . . . to the church, which is his body, the fullness of the one who fills all things . . . ." That is, on this day of the Ascension, we celebrate the conclusion of Christ's redemption; after dying and rising, he ascends to glory and is crowned victorious. This is his final victory, the completion of his work; this is his exaltation and glorification; this is the day on which he is publicly acclaimed Lord and King, on which he is glorified as Messiah and universal Savior for all time. As a result of this redemption, completed on this day, our whole world is graced forever, our existence is *a redeemed existence*, our God has communicated himself clearly and conclusively and our hope is secure. Our faith in Christ assures us that from this moment, human existence is never purely a natural existence but one that has eternal significance in every facet of its being, and our whole world is so graced by Christ that everything in our world has a new value and worth.

II. Secondly, Christ can be intimately present in our *individual lives*. Let me preface this with the experience of Victor Frankl, the psychiatrist, as described in his book, *Man's Search for Meaning*. Victor Frankl had spent years in a Nazi prison camp in the Second World War. In those years he developed the basis for his psychology. During the horror of those years, he noticed that most who survived that experience, who did not fall apart, had something to sustain them. In his words, "The salvation of man is through love and in love. A man who has nothing left in this world still may know bliss in the contemplation of his beloved."[9] That is, he saw that his fellow prisoners needed some cause, some person, some love to keep them from falling apart. That person was very much present to them and sustained them. Clearly, he was not speaking about physical presence, for they were generally separated from their love. But the psychological or spiritual presence was very real, strong, and life sustaining. And this is how Christ is present to us in varying degrees. As Paul expressed it: "I live by faith in the Son of God who has loved me and given himself up for me" (Galatians 2:20). That faith includes all that is most human in our lives: the substance of our dreams and hopes, the basis for our motivation and courage, the model for our behavior, our whole value system, our ultimate purpose and direction of life. In a word, Jesus can be present to us in all that is most real for us, in all that is internal and enduring, in all that builds up the human spirit.

III. These are two important ways that Christ's words are true: "I am with you always." That is, our world is essentially redeemed because Jesus is the final, universal Savior for all people. And our individual existence is alive with his Spirit in all that makes us fully human.

---

9. Victor Frankl, *Man's Search for Meaning* (New York: Washington Square Press, 1963), p. 59.

YEAR B (THEME FROM EPHESIANS 1:17–23)

Acts 1:1–11; Ephesians 1:17–23; Mark 16:15–20

CHRIST, OUR UNIQUE AND UNIVERSAL LORD

I. "[God] put all things beneath [Christ's] feet and gave him as head over all things to the church, which is his body, the fullness of the one who fills all things . . . ." This is how today's reading from the Letter to the Ephesians summarizes the meaning of the feast of the Ascension. Theologians explain this scripture in various but similar ways: the Ascension means the final victory of Christ, the completion of his work; it marks his becoming Lord and King over all people; it represents his final exaltation and glorification. The point of such theology is that even after the Resurrection from the dead, Jesus is not publicly acclaimed as Lord and King, he is not formally the victorious Savior of all, he is not yet glorified as the Messiah. Only after his Ascension is he glorified and completely victorious as Savior of all people. As Peter proclaimed on the day of Pentecost: "God has made him both Lord and Messiah, this Jesus whom you crucified" (Acts 2:36). To express this another way: We Christians are all Jesus people; on this day he becomes formally our Lord. So on this day, we rejoice in his victory, the victory of our only Savior and Lord.

II. Let me try to say this in a way that is more personal for us. This victory of Christ we celebrate today is what makes our faith unique among all religions. All other religions, no matter how valid their starting point and their value as a true means of opening hearts toward God, must impart hope for believers to pass through the zero point of death. In fact, if faith does not lead to a hope beyond death, it is not worth spending our whole life on it. It is Jesus Christ alone, who rose from death and ascended to God, who accomplished this successful transition to life with God. No other religious figure has given evidence of such a hope; no one else can rival this unique accomplishment of Jesus our Lord.

III. Jesus makes this very claim in John's Gospel for all his followers: "I am the way and the truth and the life. No one comes to the Father except through me" (John 14:6). He asserts that he is the unique way to the Father, he is the door of eternal life for all his followers. Theologians explain that absolutely no one has a natural right to the eternal life that God offers us. But if we come to salvation with God, we do so only because of the justification won for us by the grace of Christ, our unique Savior.

So on this feast of the Ascension, we exult in the words of scripture: God showed his strength by "raising [Christ] from the dead and seating him at his right hand in the heavens, far above every principality . . . and dominion, and every name that is named not only in this age but also in the one to come." In a word, today we acclaim Christ as our unique redeemer and the door of life with God.

YEAR C

Acts 1:1–11; Ephesians 1:17–23; Luke 24:46–53

CHRIST, OUR UNIQUE LORD, IS WITH US ALWAYS

I. "[God] put all things beneath [Christ's] feet and gave him as head over all things to the church, which is his body, the fullness of the one who fills all things . . . ." This is how today's Second Reading summarizes the meaning of this feast of the Ascension.

Theologians explain this scripture in various but similar ways: The Ascension means the final victory of Christ, the completion of his work, his becoming Lord and king over all people, his final exaltation and glorification. Their point is that even after the resurrection from the dead, Christ is not formally the victorious Savior of all, he is not yet glorified as their Messiah. Peter, the apostle, expresses all this quite simply: "God has made him both Lord and Messiah, this Jesus whom you crucified" (Acts 2:36). To express this another way: We Christians are all Jesus people; on this day he becomes formally our Lord; on this day we rejoice in his victory, the victory of our only Savior and Lord.

II. Let me try to say this in a way that is more personal for us. This victory of Christ that we celebrate today is what makes our Christian faith *unique* among all religions. All other religions, no matter how valid their starting point and their value as a true means of opening hearts to God, must enable believers to ultimately pass through the zero point of death. That is, if any faith does not lead to a hope beyond death, it is not worth spending one's whole life on. But it is Jesus alone, who accomplished such a successful transition to life with God and so gave evidence of our hope. So our Christian faith is unique among all faiths because of Christ's victory over death that we celebrate today.

III. In today's Gospel, Luke gives us Jesus' final words to his disciples: ". . . I am sending the promise of my Father upon you; but stay in the city until you are clothed with power from on high." What did Jesus mean by "the promise of my Father"? In Luke's second book, the Acts of the Apostles, he explains in Jesus' words, ". . . wait for 'the promise of the Father about which you have heard me speak . . . you will be baptized with the holy Spirit.'" Then Luke recounts the coming of the Holy Spirit at Pentecost. What Luke wants us to learn from all this is that the era of Jesus ends with the Ascension; the historical presence of Jesus on earth and his redeeming death establishes our faith as real and historical. But now as Jesus departs, God knows that Christians of all time need more than a memory, more than some ancient history. So God begins the new era by sending the Holy Spirit on all believers. This new era, which had been historically founded on the real history of Jesus our Savior, now has the Spirit of Jesus alive in each one of us individually until the end of time. Next Sunday we will celebrate the feast of Pentecost, the coming of the Spirit of Jesus. This Holy Spirit continues the work of Jesus in us by helping us understand the meaning of all that Jesus taught us and by being with us always to make us true disciples of Jesus.

Seventh Sunday of Easter

Year A

Acts 1:12–14; 1 Peter 4:13–16; John 17:1–11a[10]

Apostolic Tradition

I. A few years ago, the Chicago Sun-Times surveyed Catholics in
the Chicago area. They asked specific questions about why Catholics
remain bound to the community of the church. The number one
reason mentioned by Catholics was: "a faith to pass on to their children." The second important benefit Catholics found was: "aid in
holding their marriage and family together." And the third reason for
appreciating their faith was the reception of the sacraments. This is
a very positive and encouraging finding; it means that those benefits
of the Church relate to the intimate dimensions of a person's life, such
as marriage, children, family, and life-cycle, are the prime reasons
for turning to religion. A further observation of this study was that
Catholics, more than any other religious people, stress ritual and
sacrament. On the other hand, about a third of those who do not
emphasize sacraments said they might leave the church. And other
surveys in recent years have shown that many Catholics have become
marginal in the practice of their faith during the last twenty-five
years. Many of them try to live their Christian life outside the church
structure and worship, without any public expression of their faith.
They seem to believe they can have faith without religion, or a belief
in God that is entirely internal.

II. Today's readings make some important points regarding
such issues. In the First Reading, from the Acts of the Apostles, Saint
Luke implies that the handing on of tradition is a matter of apostolic

---

10. Note: In many Christian churches, the Ascension is celebrated on the Seventh Sunday of
Easter. In those cases the Second Reading and the Gospel for the seventh Sunday may be read
on the Sixth Sunday. For the sake of completeness, here is a homily for each Seventh Sunday of
the three-year cycle.

tradition. For him, the twelve Apostles had been appointed by Jesus himself as a *sign* of the Christian community and as the *foundation* of that community. Their function was to give witness to the original saving events of Christ's ministry and Resurrection. They are the bridge and foundation of faith and Church. In the Gospel, Christ commits his words to them: "[T]he words you gave to me I have given to them . . . and they have believed that you sent me." And he established the unity of the church in the common sharing of word and life in Christ: "[K]eep them in your name . . . so that they may be one just as we are" (John 17:11b).

III. What does all this say for our Church today? First, what does it say to those on the periphery of the church, without much contact or communal expression of faith? These readings and scripture in general demand frequent enrichment by *word and sacrament*. Jesus tells us it requires an effort to remain united with him. He wants his followers to be "one just as we are [one, Father]." Scripture and Jesus himself are insistent about the handing down of tradition by means of the apostles, and about enrichment by word and sacrament. And experience teaches that those who give up regular contact with the Church, in time will more and more give up contact with Christ; for habitual contact with Christ demands a common sharing of word and sacrament, which is received only in his Church.

IV. These readings are also significant for us. For we are a community founded on the Apostles and on the word and sacrament they handed down to us. We can only continue to grow close to Christ by constantly experiencing his word and sacrament in the midst of this community, along with the support of others who share our faith. The Catholics who answered the Sun-Times survey understood these essentials of life in Christ. Together with them, we see how such a faith binds together the intimate dimensions of human life along with the word and sacraments of Christ and the constant handing down of tradition by a living community.

Year B

Acts 1:15–17, 20a, 20c–26; 1 John 4:11–16; John 17:11b–19

That They May Be One Even As We Are One

I. Several years ago, Time magazine's cover story was entitled: "U.S. Catholicism: a Church Divided." The article described the Catholic Church in America rather accurately as a less tumultuous Church than that of the first years after the Second Vatican Council. But it also presented the church as still "troubled by colliding purposes and visions." Here are some of the statistics mentioned: 1) eighty percent of Catholics have generally accepted the changes in the church; 2) about half are constantly practicing their faith; 3) a leading problem for many is with authority in the Church, especially regarding sexual ethics; 4) some twenty percent of Catholics have ceased their constant practice of the faith and have become peripheral Catholics, partially because of the problems with authority and sexual ethics. These Catholics still believe their Christian faith but are trying to live their Catholic life outside the church structure, without external expression of that faith and worship. Though they would not describe their situation in these terms, they seek to have faith without religion, belief in God without external expression of that faith in a believing community.

II. The readings today deal with the handing down of tradition. For Luke, in the Acts of the Apostles, faith depends essentially on apostolic tradition. For him the 12 Apostles were appointed by Jesus himself as a *sign* of the Christian community and as the *foundation* of that community. Their function, throughout the Acts of the Apostles, was to give witness to the original saving work of Christ's ministry and Resurrection. Without that historical experience and testimony, the church would not exist. Luke presents the Apostles as the bridge and foundation of faith and Church.

In John's Gospel today, we heard Jesus pray to the Father for the disciples: "Consecrate them in the truth. . . . As you sent me into the world, so I sent them into the world . . . so that they also may be consecrated in truth." He means that the disciples are to be consecrated by means of the Holy Spirit so they can impart the truth of Jesus, which is God's word and commandments. Here Jesus connects consecration and mission inseparably. Just as Jesus' mission was to reveal the whole "truth" about God, so the disciples continue to impart this same truth with the help of the Spirit of Truth. In this chapter, Jesus prays that "they may be one" and they may proclaim the truth. Throughout Jesus' entire farewell speech to his disciples, his primary concern is for dedication to truth and unity for his followers.

III. In a word, these final words of Christ to his disciples remind us that his primary concern for his followers was for truth and unity. In John's Gospel, Christ is the Word of God, the whole truth about God and his salvation. Above all then, his disciples are to be ministers of his word, proclaiming that truth which is Jesus. And Jesus' farewell prayer is for unity among his followers; his prayer is made ineffective by division and disunity.

IV. What Jesus wants for his Church today are the same two qualities: truth and unity. Truth must mean that we cannot depend merely on our own opinions and interpretations; that method of believing leads to endless diversity and countless divisions in the church of Christ. For all the essential truths of our faith we need the help of scripture and the authority of the church. Secondly, the followers of Jesus must show the one quality Jesus prayed for: unity. Notice, Jesus does not demand *uniformity*. There was great diversity in the early church; each scripture writer was unique in his description of Jesus, and each community was strikingly different. But with constant effort, their unity was maintained. Today, after Vatican Council II, there is greater room than ever in this one church of Christ for differing views, opinions, approaches, and attitudes. But we cannot call ourselves true followers of Jesus if we separate ourselves from his community of believers. "I pray . . . also for those who will believe in me through their word, so that they may all be one, as you, Father, are in me" (John 17:20–21).

Year C

Acts 7:55–60; Revelation 22:12–14, 16–17, 20; John 17:20–26

The Glory of Christ and Our Unity with Him

I. "[Stephen], filled with the holy Spirit . . . saw the glory of God and Jesus standing at the right hand of God." This vision of Stephen and the readings today in general, continue the theme of the feast of the Ascension: the final victory of Christ our Lord and his enthronement at the right hand of the Father. The Gospel reading from John is dominated by two concepts—glory and unity. If we understand what John means by these two words, we can understand much of today's readings and of this Ascension time.

II. First, the word, *glory*. In John, the glory of Christ refers to the entire redemptive action of Jesus: his Passion, death, Resurrection and Ascension. All of this final action of Jesus is what constitutes his glorious victory, our redemption, God's glory. This Ascension time is when we celebrate the completion of that redemptive work, the public glorification of Jesus as Lord and King, the unique accomplishment of Jesus our Messiah. This victory of Christ is what makes our Christian faith unique among all other religions. For all other religions, no matter how valuable as a true means of opening our hearts to God, must help people pass through the zero point of death to life with God. If faith does not lead to a hope beyond death, it is not worth spending our whole life on it. And it is Jesus alone, who by his rising from the dead, accomplished the successful transition to life with God. No other religious figure has given evidence of such a hope. So for us Christians, our hope of everlasting life with God has been guaranteed by the death and resurrection of Jesus. Today's Second Reading proclaims: "Blessed are they who . . . have the right to the tree of life and enter the city through its gates." Jesus our Savior is that unique door of life for us Christians. In his words: "No one comes to the Father except through me" (John 14:6).

III. Second, the word, *unity*. Unity is the one petition of Jesus for all his followers: "I pray . . . also for those who will believe in me through their word, so that they may all be one, as you, Father, are in me and I in you."

The model and principal of this unity is the shared life and love of the Father and the Son. Jesus' whole life was dominated by his sense of unity with God. Especially in John's Gospel, all that Jesus taught was only a revealing of who God is; all that he did was only a carrying out of God's will; all that Jesus accomplished as Messiah was by means of his suffering and death, as his Father willed. So the unity Jesus prays for in all of us, his followers, is after this model. All that we are to believe is what Jesus revealed to us about God and salvation; how we are to love is modeled on the constant love and dedication of Jesus: "As I have loved you, so you also should love one another" (John 13:34). Practically then, what we are to do is to accept all the human events of our life, just as they come to us, in the spirit of Jesus—for that is God's will for us. This unity is the ideal and goal of our Christian life. It is also to be the characteristic of Jesus' community of followers, his church: "[S]o that they may all be one . . . that the world may believe that you sent me" Such unity in his church would be enough to teach the world about Christ.

IV. Notice finally, that Jesus did *not* pray for uniformity; his church was never intended to be uniform, with absolutely everything the same. There is ample room in this Church of Christ for differing views, opinions, approaches and national diversity in non-essentials. We must only accept different opinions and tolerate ambiguity in our worldwide diversity. We cannot break away from our human church because its leaders or members are far from perfect. We can still rejoice in our unity: "[O]ne Lord, one faith, one baptism; one God and Father of all" (Ephesians 4:5–6).

Pentecost

YEARS A, B, AND C

Acts 2:1–11; 1 Corinthians 12:3b–7, 12–13; John 20:19–23

RECEIVE THE HOLY SPIRIT

I. This Gospel for Pentecost is short but very significant for our Christian life. Let us try to understand just what Jesus teaches here and draw some conclusions from the context. Notice this reading is from John's Gospel; the words he uses are tightly bound up with his theology.

II. Earlier in John's Gospel, Jesus made a solemn promise to his disciples: "Peace I leave with you; my peace I give to you" (14:27). This promise follows immediately after Jesus assures them: "The Advocate, the holy Spirit that the Father will send in my name— he will teach you everything and remind you of all that [I] told you" (14:26). In all of this Jesus is speaking about a *permanent* source of peace that he would give them when "I will come back to you" (John 14:28). *Now,* in today's Gospel, Jesus greets the disciples twice with "peace;" then immediately he "breathed on them and said to them, 'Receive the holy Spirit.'" Fr. Raymond Brown, the pre-eminent Johannine scholar, explains that *here* we have the fulfillment of Jesus' promise at the Last Supper, in which he indicated that his gift of peace would not be ephemeral; he would come back to his disciples and grant them a permanent source of peace. Now here he grants them his *spirit* as their permanent source of peace and the enduring presence of Jesus *in* his Spirit. For John, the Holy Spirit *is* the permanent presence of Jesus with us, the source of our confidence and hope.

III. Then Jesus "breathed on them and said, 'Receive the holy Spirit. Whose sins you forgive are forgiven them, and whose sins you retain are retained.'" This is part of his essential gift of the Holy Spirit—the power to forgive or retain sins; this includes the authorized judgment given to the disciples. This text is one of the very few texts of Scripture that the church has formally defined. The Council of Trent saw in this text the basis for the church's authority to forgive post-baptismal sins. In a word, Jesus tells us that by this Holy Spirit we have a permanent source of forgiveness of sins that can constantly reestablish our peace with God.

IV. Finally, let us consider the surrounding chapters in John's Gospel. In them, Jesus explains much more about our new Advocate, the Spirit, who is with us always: "[I]f I go, I will send him to you . . . the Spirit of truth, he will guide you to all truth. . . . He will teach you everything and remind you of all that [I] told you" (John 16:7, 13 and 14:26). That is, Jesus, who once spoke in the flesh, now speaks to us through his Spirit. His Spirit is now our personal teacher to lead us into all truth about Jesus; he is our constant guide in living the way of Jesus; he is our help in learning what it means to follow Jesus; he is our intercessor in prayer. To sum up: Jesus wants us to realize that his Spirit is with us always as our advocate, our companion, our teacher, our source of grace and forgiveness. In a word, whatever Jesus was for his apostles, his Holy Spirit is for us now. On this Pentecost our prayer is very simple: Spirit of Jesus, guide us into the whole truth about Jesus that we may better understand and follow the way of Jesus.

Years B and C (Alternate Homily on the Holy Spirit)

Acts 2:1–11; 1 Corinthians 12:3b–7, 12–13; John 20:19–23; also using the five Paraclete sayings in John's Gospel: 14:16–17; 14:26; 15:26; 16:7–11; 16:13

The Work of the Spirit

I. "[N]o one can say, 'Jesus is Lord' except by the holy Spirit." Thus Saint Paul teaches today, that even the simplest assertion of faith can only be made with the help of the Holy Spirit. He implies that everything of grace and faith is attributable to the Holy Spirit. All that we are as Christians, all that we have of Christ's grace and life, is attributed to the Holy Spirit. But the rest of today's readings do not get very specific about what the Spirit does. Have you ever heard a sermon on what is the work of the Holy Spirit and what is not? Today, I'm going to try to do just that. It will not be all explicit Scripture or defined doctrine, which we simply don't have, but only one theologian's considered opinion.

II. First, consider what the Spirit *does not do*. The Spirit does not *arrange* the human events of our life. He does not make things go well for us when we obey God's commands; he does not reward us now for being good. Nor does he make things go poorly for us when we sin; he does not punish us here and now for following our own way instead of the way of Christ. He simply lets us live our human lives in real freedom with all the accidents, illnesses, troubles, uncanny events, and occasional tragedies of all human lives.

Also the Spirit does not take care of our *bodies*, so that we will not be sick or become tense and nervous. Even if we were saints, the Spirit would not directly take care of our bodies and our psyches for us. If we never exercise and often eat unhealthy foods, we will eventually have an unsound body. If we do not get sufficient rest and occasional time off, we will eventually become unhealthy.

Finally, the Spirit does not give us constantly satisfying *prayer*. He does not always fill us with consolation and delight. He does not make us feel the presence of God when we pray. At times the Spirit does this wonderfully in our prayer; but after we have made some progress in prayer, we necessarily go through difficult or dark prayer.

III. Now consider what the Holy Spirit *does do* for us. First, in Chapters 14 to 16 of John's Gospel, Jesus makes clear just what the Spirit does for us in terms of *learning his truth*. Jesus repeatedly calls the Paraclete "the Spirit of truth." He tells the disciples that the Spirit "will teach you everything and remind you of all that [I] told you" (14:26). For the disciples that promise of Christ meant that the Spirit would help them understand so many things about Jesus and his redemption, about his teaching and way of life. For us it means much the same. But to be more specific: 1. We need the Spirit for every act of *faith:* "No one can say, 'Jesus is Lord' except by the Holy Spirit." We need the Holy Spirit to lead us through the stages of prayer, to help us when we do not know how to pray: "[T]he Spirit . . . comes to the aid of our weakness; for . . . the Spirit itself intercedes with inexpressible groanings" (Romans 8:26). The Spirit helps us understand the meaning of Scripture: "he will guide you to all truth" (16:13). Jesus, the Word of God is our entire interpretation of life and the Spirit of Jesus will instruct us to know and follow this Word.

Secondly, the Holy Spirit can give us strength in all the human events of our life. He gives us *grace* to live the way of Jesus. He helps us to accept whatever happens to us as Jesus did—with his kind of patience and absolute trust in God. With the grace of the Spirit (all grace is from the Spirit) and the example of Jesus, we come to realize that these very human events, accidents, troubles, and crosses are the very stuff of human holiness. The Spirit of Truth helps us see that the mystery of human suffering, freely accepted just as it comes to us, is the way of Jesus and the plan of God for our purification.

Finally, the Spirit leads us to *love*. He instills us with the assurance of God's love for us: ". . . the love of God has been poured out into our hearts through the holy Spirit that has been given to us" (Romans 5:5), especially through Baptism and Confirmation. The Spirit convinces us of God's love for us individually; we possess his Spirit as the proof of his love. And he helps us to love others in Christ: "[S]erve one another through love . . . [and] live by the Spirit" (Galatians 5:13, 16). He moves us to follow the concrete example of love that we have in Christ: "[L]ove one another as I love you" (John 15:12).

IV. So on Pentecost, let us turn to the Holy Spirit with all our hearts. Not to arrange our lives for us, not to care for our bodies, not to fill us with constant consolation, but rather as "the Spirit of truth" to help us in faith, in prayer, in understanding Scripture, in learning the way of Jesus. Let us ask the Spirit for grace to follow in the way of Jesus, to accept our individual lives just as they are, in the spirit of Jesus. Let us go to the Spirit of Love who pours out the love of God in our hearts and leads us to serve one another in Christ. Our prayer on this Pentecost is simple but urgent: "Come, Holy Spirit, come."

The Most Holy Trinity

Year A

Exodus 34:4b–6, 8–9; 2 Corinthians 13:11–13; John 3:16–18

Defining God

I. Our Catholic theology must sound very complicated to many of you. And modern theology might seem even more confusing. In recent years, I have reached a better understanding of the central dogmas of our faith, the central core of both former and modern theology. I would like to simplify things for you today; on this Holy Trinity Sunday, let me try to express this core of our faith. The concepts are deep, but they are few in number, and they tie together our understanding of God, of salvation, and of Christian life. The outline of all this is one sentence in Paul today: "The grace of our Lord Jesus Christ and the love of God and the fellowship of the holy Spirit be with all of you." Here is the outline of our faith, expressed in terms of our Christian experience: grace, love and community; and the order is important: Son, Father, Spirit. For it is in Jesus Christ and his life, death, and Resurrection that we encounter the love of God for us, and this encounter leads to our incorporation into the church in which we participate in the common life of God's Spirit.

II. To express this more fully, let us begin with an assertion that the heart of our faith is found in this claim: in Jesus of Nazareth, God has revealed and communicated himself once for all—unmistakably and completely; for Jesus is the image, revelation and manifestation of God for us. In his historical person, his teaching and his public life and death, he is the complete *revelation of God* for us; he is the definition of God's eternal nature; he is all that we know about God and all God intends to reveal to us. As Jesus told Philip: "Whoever has seen me has seen the Father" (John 14:9). More specifically, the cross of Christ and his Resurrection is not only the source of our redemption, it is also the complete definition of God for us. John's Epistle expresses it simply: "God is love. In this way the love of God was revealed to us: God sent his only Son into the world so that we might have life through him" (1 John 4:8–9). That is, he defines God simply as self-communicating love, and the evidence for that, our human understanding of that is Christ's life, death, and Resurrection. It further suggests, that the whole of salvation history is also God revealing to us who he is; thus, God is the one who saves us, the one who communicates his love for us in Jesus. His cross and resurrection is the recapitulation of the Old Testament—even though it was only vaguely indicated there—and is the core of the New Testament. So if this is the way God reveals himself to us in all of Scripture, then this must be the inner essence of God himself; he is simply self-communicating love.

III. Now consider the Holy Spirit who is the source of all grace for us Christians; Paul asserts "No one can say, 'Jesus is Lord,' except by the holy Spirit" (1 Corinthians 12:3); that is, even the simplest statement of faith needs the grace of the Spirit. And John insists that the Spirit is the permanent presence of God in each of us individually: ". . . [the Father] will give you another Advocate to be with you always, the Spirit of truth" (John 14:16). The work of the Spirit is to " teach you everything . . . [and] guide you to all truth" (John 14:26 and 16:13). That means the Spirit is the source of our individual understanding about God and of our ability to follow in the way of truth. He is the permanent presence of Jesus in each of us. To say this clearly, the Holy Spirit is our *possession of God*, here and now, individually.

IV. We can sum up what we know about God this way: Jesus is the whole revelation of God for us, who proves that "God is love." And the Holy Spirit is the possession of God in each of us individually. All of this is implied in the simple formula of Paul today—the same words that we use in our greeting at the beginning of mass each Sunday: "The grace of our Lord Jesus Christ and the love of God and the fellowship of the holy Spirit be with all of you."

Year B

Deuteronomy 4:32–34, 39–40; Romans 8:14–17; Matthew 28:16–20

The Holy Trinity in Our Lives

I. My father was not particularly good at writing letters—nor was he very pious. But in one of his rare letters to me while I was in the seminary, he offered this advice: "There is one gift which no one can give to a man but himself; that is, to feel at ease, to be alone in his own company, in the presence of the Lord, satisfyingly alone." It has been 60 years since he wrote that letter, but I will always remember that letter from my father. For my father taught me then that to be a man means to be at ease, to be comfortable with oneself and to live in the presence of God. Such advice, I believe, would not be welcome to many Americans today—especially for those who distract themselves with noise and activity all day long, are not comfortable with being quietly alone, are not inclined to even ask themselves the ultimate questions about their lives. But today's feast of the Holy Trinity invites us to reflect on the core of our faith and ask such questions.

II. Today's readings have much to say to men and women today—especially about what it means to be a Christian. First, they indicate that by baptism we have a new relationship with God the Father that is very real and that others do not possess. In the Hebrew Scriptures (the Old Testament), God is given many titles such as creator, lord and guardian. But he is rarely referred to as father and never in the sense that we call him Father. Similarly with other religions: the Moslems have 99 names for God in the Koran, but not one of them is father. The Hindus know God, but they do not call him father. But for us it is different. By baptism we possess the life of God, a new relationship of love; because we are really his daughters and sons. As Paul says in today's second reading, "[Y]ou received a Spirit of adoption, through which we cry, *'Abba*, Father!'" That means we are not merely his creatures nor his puppets, we are God's sons and daughters. Because of that real, family relationship, his love for us is unconditional and permanent.

III. By baptism we have a new relationship to God the Son. In today's Gospel, Christ calls us to "make disciples of all nations." We are not just intellectual believers, we are disciples; that means we have Jesus as our own way of holiness. "I am the way" (John 14:6) means that we have a concrete model for becoming selfless, accepting, understanding and kind. "Love one another as I love you" (John 15:12) means we have a motive for love that is strong enough even in the midst of our impersonal and disjointed society. "[T]ake courage, I have conquered the world" (John 16:33) means that we have an undying source of encouragement and hope. Jesus is really one of us human beings, and he is the unique and universal plan of God for our salvation.

IV. Finally, in baptism we have a new relationship to God, the Holy Spirit. In John's Gospel, the Holy Spirit is the permanent presence of Jesus with us, his disciples; that is, what Jesus was to his disciples, the Holy Spirit is to be for us today. Just as Jesus was the friend, teacher, advocate and constant source of grace for his disciples, so the Holy Spirit is our permanent source of grace, our friend, teacher and advocate. Jesus explains all this: ". . . I will ask the Father, and he will give you another Advocate to be with you always, the Spirit of truth. . . . He will teach you everything and remind you of all that [I] told you" (John 14:16, 17, 26). Jesus affirms that the Spirit is his constant presence within us to be our constant guide, to teach us everything, to help us learn what it means to follow Jesus.

V. This is what the mystery of the Holy Trinity means to us. It means God is our Father who loves us as his children. It means Jesus is our model and our motive for how we live. It means the Spirit is the continued presence of Jesus within us to lead us in his way.

YEAR C

Proverbs 8:22–31; Romans 5:1–5; John 16:12–15

THE TRINITY AND THE MEANING OF LIFE

I. Passages is a book by Gail Sheehy. It describes the psychological passages adults make as we pass through the ages of the twenties, thirties, and forties. In it she describes a man called Aaron, a top French designer and businessman. Then she lets him describe his mid-life crisis:

> I have always used my work as a substitute for solving problems in my life. I packed my life with activity in order to avoid major personal decisions. What I do is give up autonomy by creating a high-demand situation, so that I must always jump from project to project, never really allowing time to think about what I'm doing it all for. Since I turned 40, it's become clearer to me that the reason I do this is I really haven't wanted to scrutinize what my life is all about.[11]

Aaron is a typical study of many Americans who avoid the basic questions of life by leading a distracted, pragmatic life. We will return to Aaron in a few minutes.

II. In the readings today, we have an implicit treatment of the Christian experience of the triune God. In the Second Reading, Paul affirms that God is the source of our redemption. But it is through Jesus Christ that this redemptive act is performed: "[W]e have been justified by faith . . . with God through our Lord Jesus Christ." And it is through the Holy Spirit that ". . . the love of God is poured out into our hearts," so that we can experience that redemptive action. In the Gospel Jesus confirms that the revelation he brings us is from the Father, and the Holy Spirit makes that revelation meaningful to each succeeding generation: "the Spirit of truth . . . will guide you to all truth." All of this helps us to understand the three persons of the Trinity insofar as they relate to us. That is, Christ is God in his self-revelation; he is the total, final, and *complete revelation of God*; he is God inasmuch as he reveals himself; he is the best way of knowing what God is like. This means that the revelation of God to us is a person, Jesus Christ. "[I]n [Christ] dwells the whole fullness of the deity bodily" (Colossians 2:9).

The Holy Spirit is the experience of God that we have as individuals; the Spirit is the source of our personal relationship to God; just because we have the Spirit of his Son, we are children of God. And he is the one who makes God's revelation meaningful to us as individuals; he is the present cause of all faith, love, and understanding that we have of God. Thus the Spirit is God

---

11. Gail Sheehy, *Passages* (New York: E. P. Dutton, 1976), p. 333.

inasmuch as we possess him; he is God in us and for us. This means the *possession of God* is a person, the Holy Spirit. "This is how we know that we remain in [God] and he in us, that he has given us of his Spirit" (1 John 4:13).

III. Now let us return to Aaron who was "slow to scrutinize what [his] life was all about." He, like many Americans today, prefers to avoid scrutinizing the enigma of human existence. Yet it is only with difficulty and constant activity, that he can submerge the questions and threats to his human existence. For his rational nature urges him to make some sense out of his existence. He must face the threat of limited time and of death; he must face the threat of nothingness. He must ask some questions about all of reality: why is there anything at all? what is its source? He must face the reality of suffering and evil; and he must face the threat of emptiness and meaninglessness.

In the face of all these threats to human existence, he does have a choice: he can decide that reality is completely void, empty, meaningless, accidental, irrational, and hopeless; or he can decide that reality is ordered, reasonable, with primal meaning and value, with an ultimate source and goal. These two alternatives are each of a whole; he cannot pick and choose parts of each. If he chooses the first, then all human life is meaningless and irrational. If he chooses the second, then all of reality has meaning and sense. But that second alternative implies that God exists as the ground of that life, meaning, value, hope, and goal. That second alternative, then, includes the ultimate truth, sense and value of reality. And that fundamental faith does not come from reason alone but from grace; it comes from the Spirit as does all grace. Christ tells us that this is the work of the Spirit—to lead us to this fundamental truth and to all truth: "[T]he Spirit of truth . . . will guide you to all truth." Without our triune God, our human life is ultimately empty, meaningless and hopeless. With faith in God, everything makes sense and has great value.

The Most Holy Body and Blood of Christ

Year A

Deuteronomy 8:2–3, 14b–16a; 1 Corinthians 10:16–17; John 6:51–58

Why Regular Communion?

I. For seven years, I was a chaplain at the University of Chicago Hospitals. Occasionally, visiting the Catholics there, I met a man or woman who had lost interest in religion. As they put it: "I'm not much of a Catholic, Father," or "It's been a long time since I practiced my faith." One reason they would be so open with me is that being in the hospital is conducive to serious thoughts about faith. Those experiences taught me that there is a direct connection between possessing a strong Catholic faith and feeding that faith regularly by mass, worship and especially Communion. The connection I would like to describe is not one of obligation or sin but of human friendship.

II. First consider that all human friendship and love demand *presence and signs of affection*. This is most obvious with a child. He comes to his mother to be embraced, kissed, protected, consoled, and loved by her. How often he needs her actual presence, her personal care, her individual attention to him. He needs more than words; he needs the actual experience of her love. And married partners need regular signs of affection and presence. If a husband is hardly present to his family because of his work, he puts a great strain on the marriage. If a wife is never kissed anymore, she wonders: Does he still love me? And friends need regular contact and presence. If friends no longer have regular presence—by being together, sharing themselves, doing things together—they can only keep that friendship alive by writing, phoning, or e-mailing. If they do none of these things, their friendship dies or at best is dormant for a time. In your own experience, you have had so many friendships in your lifetime that eventually faded out and were no longer a part of your day-to-day living. This is the universal law of human friendship: all human friendship demands some presence, some signs of affection. Now our relationship to Christ is a human friendship, especially on our part. Therefore, it demands presence, some signs of affection. We can experience that presence and affection in many ways: private prayer, reading Scripture, prayer or study groups or other sacraments. But, in my experience, those who do not have regular contact with Christ in Sunday mass and Communion, don't have adequate contact with him in any of these other ways either. And so, time and distance destroy that love and friendship—as they do all human friendship. This is just what Jesus emphasizes in the Gospel: "[U]nless you eat the flesh of the Son of Man and drink his blood, you do not have life within you." He means that without the Eucharist, we cannot maintain our life in Christ, our friendship with Christ.

III. Secondly, friendship must be an individual and *personal relationship*. For example, it's never enough for the father of 12 kids to say he loves them all. He must show his care for each individual child, otherwise the children are starved for affection. Similarly, it's not enough for us human beings to know that God loves all his creatures and that Christ redeemed us all. We need a personal, visible, individual assurance of God's love. And this is the *genius* of our sacraments: that it makes God's love for us visible; it makes Christ's redemption individual for us. Notice that we receive all the sacraments individually, one at a time; that is one way God assures us that his love is for each one of us. And in the Eucharist, Jesus comes to us personally to constantly prove his enduring friendship: "Whoever eats my flesh and drinks my blood remains in me and I in him [her]."

IV. Finally, friendship is based on *sharing something together*. There is always a common source of friendship; friends might be related to each other, might work together, might spend leisure time together; but they must also share something of themselves or they are just acquaintances. The basis of true friendship is sharing their feelings, their hopes and dreams, their lives—and sometimes one critical part of their lives, such as a birth, illness, personal trouble or great joy. Now with Christ we can share all that is most deeply human in us. But the most crucial relationship we share is that he redeemed us by his suffering and death. And it is particularly in mass and Communion that we recall this critical part of his life; as Paul reminds us today: "The cup of blessing that we bless, is it not a participation in the blood of Christ? The bread that we break, is it not a participation of the body of Christ?" That constant sharing in Christ's great act of love is our means of maintaining our love and friendship with him.

V. I have tried to answer the question: Why go to mass and Communion regularly? The answer is: our friendship with Jesus cannot survive strong without such regular contact. It follows the same norms as any human friendship.

Year B

Exodus 24:3–8; Hebrews 9:11–15; Mark 14:12–16, 22–26

Eucharist as Covenant

I. "Absence is to love as wind is to fire: it extinguishes the small and enflames the great." A friend once gave me a banner with these words on it; it impressed me deeply. "Absence is to love as wind is to fire: it extinguishes the small and enflames the great." Absence does make the heart grow fonder sometimes. Yet for friendship to endure over time, friends frequently need actual presence as well as some signs of affection. For example, small children need to be hugged and kissed frequently for them to know that they are loved. And married partners need regular signs of affection. If a wife is never kissed anymore, she wonders: Does he still love me? All human love demands some presence and signs of affection.

II. Today is the feast of *Corpus Christi*, Latin for "the Body of Christ," referring to the Eucharist. The readings this year consider the Eucharist under the aspect of *covenant* or commitment. The First Reading describes how Moses ratified the Old Testament covenant with blood. He sprinkled blood on the altar and on the people. Why was it necessary in the Bible for the covenant to be ratified in blood? The idea seems to be that the death of the animal victim has a finality about it which makes it—and therefore the covenant it ratifies—irrevocable. In this way, sacrifice is expressive of the offerer's total commitment to carry out the terms of the commitment. Notice that before the covenant is complete, the people have to become participants. In the Sinai covenant, this is achieved when Moses sprinkles the people with blood after first sprinkling the altar, which represents God himself. Then in the Gospel reading, Jesus tells us, "This is my blood of the covenant." Again the death of the victim is necessary to show that the covenant is irrevocable. And we the people of the new covenant become participants in Jesus' sacrifice by receiving the blood of Jesus in the Eucharist. That is why the mass is a necessary part of Jesus' once-for-all sacrifice on Calvary; so that we can complete the sacrifice on our part by receiving the blood of the sacrifice under the form of wine. This is one reason for the recent addition of receiving the Blood of Christ; by it we complete the sacrifice of Christ on our part.

III. One other aspect of this parallel between the old covenant of Moses and the new covenant of Christ is critical. It deals with the carrying out of the covenant. For the people of the old covenant, it meant carrying out all the 613 commands of the Mosaic Law. For us in the new covenant, it means carrying out especially the one law of Christ that he left us at the same time as the institution of the Eucharist: "I give you a *new* commandment: love one another. As I have loved you, so you also should love one another" (John 13:34, emphasis added). That is, we carry out this covenant especially by living out this one commandment of Jesus: to love one another for his sake, after his own *model* of love. Notice that Jesus calls this his *new* commandment, meaning his one command of the new covenant.

IV. We began this talk with the universal principle for human love: all human love demands some presence, some signs of affection. So also does our *friendship with Jesus.* And one of the principal ways he does this for us is in the *Eucharist.* For in the Eucharist, Jesus is present to us individually. He is present to you, one to one. Here he is not only the Savior of all; he is your individual Savior and friend. Also, as Jesus carefully notes in Mark's Gospel today, here you receive the "blood of the covenant, which will be shed for many." So it is the sacrificing Jesus that you receive, the Jesus who makes his covenant with you, his sign of affection for you. If we are to carry out our part of this covenant with Jesus, we need that frequent presence and sign of affection. We cannot just experience it on rare occasions; we need it again and again.

V. "Absence is to love as wind is to fire: it extinguishes the small and enflames the great." Unless we are confident that our love for Jesus is a great love, we need his presence and sign of affection often; we need to receive the Eucharist often, lest that love be extinguished.

YEAR C

Genesis 14:18–20; 1 Corinthians 11:23–26; Luke 9:11b–17

THE FAITH OF THE AMERICAN PRACTICAL MIND

I. On any one Sunday in America, only twenty-five percent of Catholics actually attend church. Some of these twenty-five percent go every Sunday, some on most Sundays, some occasionally and some seldom. So the 25 percent does not represent the very same people each week. In the absence of exact figures, let me suggest that thirty-five to forty percent of our people attend church with some regularity. That still leaves sixty percent of our people who have very little external contact with Jesus in terms of mass and Eucharist. On this feast of the Body and Blood of Christ, let us consider the theological issues involved in Catholics falling away from the active practice of their faith.

II. In America today, there seems to be a growing segment of people who are comfortable with the faith of the American practical mind. Such a faith involves a belief in God who leaves us alone, lets us live our own life, lets us free to live our human life without all kinds of demands and restrictions. It believes that God is in his heaven but has little influence in human living. Providential solutions and direct interventions by God are not expected or realistic. The general outline of the commandments is enough for one's ethical life. A basic faith, along with baptism, is sufficient for salvation. They have almost no contact with the church structure; their faith is individualistic and internal. They believe they can have *faith without religion*. As a result, they do not see the need to connect with God in daily living. As long as their life is not threatened in any major way, they can be quite self-sufficient; if their job is secure, their marriage is stable, their children are adequately provided for, their family does not have any chronic health problems, then they feel in control of their life. Such an American practical mind sees no need for regular contact with God through worship or supporting the parish community. In a word, they have *no felt need for God* in their daily life. I believe this is the underlying reason for their indifference to the traditional practicing of their faith, including regular mass and Eucharist.

III. How can we respond to such an attitude of the American practical mind? Why are regular mass and sacraments so essential for a personal relationship to Jesus? For me the best reasons are found in Scripture. Scripture testifies that our faith is centered on God's word and sacrament. Without word and sacrament there is no Catholic faith. All that we believe comes from God's revealed word found only in the living tradition of the church. And sacraments are essential to our following of Christ. We Catholics are a sacramental people, more than any other religion. Jesus himself insists: "[U]nless you eat the flesh of the Son of Man and drink his blood, you do not have life within you" (John 6:53). And also in our Second Reading today, when Jesus instituted the Eucharist, he twice added: "Do this in remembrance of me;" that is, Jesus wants us to do this again and again. Along with baptism and penance, these sacraments are essential to our Christian faith. Our Christian faith is an historical religion; its essential elements were determined by Jesus himself. We cannot be Christians and refuse to accept the historical foundation of our faith, which is Christ and his way. That means Christ himself rejects faith without religion. Let me commend all of you—for doing what Christ wants each Sunday: hearing his word, receiving his sacrament and connecting with his faithful people. Only with the word and sacrament of Christ's community can we effectively follow Jesus as "the way and the truth and the life."

Part V

The Second through Tenth Sunday in Ordinary Time

Second Sunday
in Ordinary Time

Year A

Isaiah 49:3, 5–6; 1 Corinthians 1:1–3; John 1:29–34

Universal Salvation

I. What is proclaimed in all three readings today is universal human salvation in Christ. In the First Reading, (Second) Isaiah prophesies, "I will make you a light to the nations, / that my salvation may reach to the ends of the earth." We extend that to Christ who will not be just a light to Israel but to all the earth. In the Second Reading, Paul reminds the people of Corinth—as he does often in this letter— that they are only a part of the universal church so they must not isolate themselves from the whole body of Christ. For they are called together with all who in every place profess the Lord Jesus. And in the Gospel, John the Baptizer affirms that Jesus is "the Lamb of God, who takes away the sin of the [whole] world." So at the beginning of Christ's public life, the church today reminds us that Jesus our Savior is the source of universal human salvation.

II. But modern people have problems with such an assertion—on two counts: that his salvation is not human and that it is not universal.

First, some claim that Christ's salvation is not really *human*. They draw a caricature of traditional apologetics something like this: God is a divine being facing humanity from beyond history; he has decided, for the sake of human salvation, to reveal some of his marvelous truths to us; if we believe these truths on his authority, then we will be rewarded with eternal life. Faith, then, is the obedient acceptance of a heavenly message, independent of its meaning for us and its effect on human life now. So existence within the Church, and especially regular worship in church, appear to them as an exotic territory with no relation to the landscape of their daily experience. Religion is like a tropical garden artificially maintained in a modern city—belonging to a strangely different realm. In a word, they see religion as irrelevant, extrinsic, and inhuman. What is most real to them is their subjective human experience, their inner human needs. So they look for help when they are afraid because of the frailty of life; when they feel alone in an automated world, an impersonal society; when they are confused by the injustice and evil in our hard, never-improving world; when they are distressed by hatred and antagonism; when they are troubled by the selfishness and unconcern around them; when they despair because of the death of a loved one. They argue simply: what can religion do to alleviate all these basic human needs; what value is God for the here and now?

We can answer them by noting that our God is most real for us in those very mysteries of human existence. For when we are afraid, Jesus tells us with authority, ". . . do not worry about your life . . . your Father knows [what] you need" (Luke 12:22 and 30). When we feel alone, he teaches us to pray, "Our Father." When we are confused by the injustice on the world, he assures us, "[T]ake courage, I have conquered the world" (John 16:33). When we are distressed, by hatred, we see Jesus' example of love of enemies. When we see self-ishness everywhere, we also see a real cure: "[L]ove one another as I love you" (John 15:12). And finally, when we face death, we do it with great assurance: "I am the resurrection and the life" (John 11:25). All of these faith responses are most humanly relevant and are intrinsic to our life now.

III. The second problem with Jesus as the source of universal human salvation is that his salvation is not really *universal.* That is, Jesus' salvation is not for all people, not really operative in the lives of all people. They argue that all humans experience the same inner and outer drama of their lives—the same fears, struggles, confusion and distress. And while such experiences lead many people to turn to God in faith, they do not lead them to faith in Christ. In other words, God and faith may be universal, but Christ is not.

By way of response, I agree that every person is summoned by life itself to reflect on one's own actions, to see answers to the mysteries of human living—to turn to many different religions; and in them they find partial answers; in them their understanding of human life is somewhat hidden, partial and provisional. But in Christ those answers are complete and definitive. For in Jesus we find God's specific answers to the mystery of life; in him we see God's gracious plan for us; in Jesus we find the model facing the troubles of human living; in him we have the final word of God to us, by which we can be saved. As the Letter to the Hebrews puts it: "In times past, God spoke in partial and various ways . . . ; in these last days, he spoke to us through a son . . . / who is . . . / the very imprint of his being" (Hebrews 1:1–3). Notice how this Christian response affirms both the universality of divine grace and at the same time the uniqueness of Christ and his way.

IV. The scriptures today assert that Jesus' salvation is truly human and universal. It is truly human, for it arises directly from our human experience. It is truly universal, for it is the complete word of God for all people.

Year B

1 Samuel 3:3b–10, 19; 1 Corinthians 6:13c–15a, 17–20; John 1:35–42

Our Call in Christ

I. The readings today are about being called. In the first reading we hear Samuel's call as a young man to be a prophet. The church intends Samuel's call as a type of Jesus' baptism. For at Jesus' baptism, he responded to his Father's call to take up his mission. And in the Gospel, John hints at Jesus' own baptism: "I saw the Spirit come down . . . and remain upon him" (John 1:32). Then he also relates the call of the first disciples to follow Jesus permanently. All these calls are types of our call to follow Jesus. You and I have been called directly and individually in baptism to be a son or daughter of God and a permanent follower of Jesus our Lord. Over half the world has not heard about God's plan of salvation in Christ; over half the world has not been called individually as you and I have.

II. The crucial question for all of us who are baptized in Jesus and have responded to his call is HOW do we fulfill his call, how do we live and be faithful to this call to follow Jesus? There have been countless historical answers to this question. The early church saw the ideal response to Jesus' call as that of *martyrdom*. "If anyone comes to me without hating . . . his own life, he cannot be my disciple" (Luke 14:26). Starting in the fourth century however, the call to leave all and follow Christ was understood ideally by many as a call to the eremitical life; that is, leave the world behind, separate yourself from the evil world and become a hermit. From about the eleventh century on, the ideal of following Christ was found especially in *religious life*. The "way of perfection"—as it was called for centuries—consisted of the three vows of poverty, celibacy and obedience. Religious life, dedicated to keeping these three vows, was the "better way" to respond to the call of Jesus. Everyone else who was not a monk or nun could only imitate the religious way of perfection as best they could. So lay spirituality for a thousand years was mainly an approximation of that kind of life: by a chaste and faithful life in marriage, a spirit of poverty, an obedient following of the laws of the church, along with some penance and devotional practices. This usually meant that all daily secular living could only be "offered up" along with some pious practices and devotions. There was not much change in this basically monkish spirituality throughout the last thousand years, until modern times. Now after the Second Vatican Council, we are finally seeing a *new spirituality* at the heart of our living in the world. *Now* our spirituality, our living out of our call to follow Christ, is no longer just an approximation of monkish spirituality, no longer involving devotional practices at the margin of our daily existence. Our new spirituality involves *the whole of our living*. Today let us focus entirely on the central element of our new lay spirituality: how we relate to people all day long.

III. The heart of our lives is *people*: incidental people in stores and on the street, constant people in our work, essential people in our family and circle of friends. We are almost never without people; they are the heart of our daily existence. And Jesus wants us to understand that what we do to them, we do to him. He so identifies himself with his followers that the way we are to love him is to love and serve others: Whatever you do to them, you do to me (cf. Matthew 25:40). Even though we almost never consciously make this connection between Jesus and others, *he* makes it constantly, and will make it also at the last judgment. He wants us to know that everyone does have a relationship to him. He wants us to serve and love him in others; he wants us to try to live as he lived with others. So we try more and more to show kindness at home and respect of our neighbors; we try to accept all people whatever their race, color or social standing; we will show some of the compassion of Jesus to those who are suffering or disabled; we will be more generous to the poor and needy; we will have great regard for justice in our work; we will strive to be reconciled with others when they ask our forgiveness.

IV. The foundation for our new spirituality is still our baptism in Christ. This is how Jesus wants us to fulfill our call to follow him. Our motivation is the powerful one that Jesus himself gives us: "Whatever you did for [them] . . . you did for me" (Matthew 25:40).

YEAR C

Isaiah 62:1–5; 1 Corinthians 12:4–11; John 2:1–11

CANA AND DECISIONS

I. Cana is a very familiar story to us. But the symbolism of Cana is not so familiar. Like most of the miracles narrated in Saint John's Gospel, this sign too is loaded with symbolic meaning. Thus, "My hour has not yet come" is a reference to the "hour" of the passion; the water "for . . . ceremonial washings" hints at the messianic purification accomplished on the cross—"the blood of . . . Jesus cleanses us from all sin" (1 John 1:7); and the result—"Jesus . . . revealed his glory"—adumbrates the cross and resurrection as the supreme glorification of Jesus. In a word, the transformation of water into wine at Cana is a sign that points toward Jesus' transforming the old order into the new Christian covenant.

II. In a similar way, all the miracles and sermons in John's Gospel are signs directed to "the Jews" in an effort to convince them that Jesus has done away with the Old Testament laws, rites and feasts. Only John's Gospel argues this way with the Jews in general; it sets before the Jews a crisis, a decision, between Old Testament ways of laws, rites, and feasts and the new way of faith in Jesus and his way of living, free of old laws and rites. In this bold approach, John's Gospel is more liberal than James and Peter certainly, but even more than Paul, for John saw no abiding significance in Jewish cults and feasts. He simply encouraged a break with their entire religious culture and tradition. This was most revolutionary; it took them some time to realize how really separate they were from the old traditions. Only with time could they learn they were a new group, they were simply "Christians."

III. Our situation today is different; ours is no longer a crisis regarding old religious culture and new ways of living. But in the spirit of John's Gospel we are asked to make our personal decision about Jesus, a decision between the Christ way and the way of the world. We need to affirm our own identity in our American society today, not to sell out to a whole new set of values. For our society is an efficiency-oriented society and it affects us all. It has its own set of values; the prime virtue is ability; the supreme law is achievement; the organizational norm is profit; the goal is success; the meaning of life is improvement of material living and prosperity. Now none of these values is bad in itself, but they can cause us to lose sight of higher Christian values and our comprehensive meaning to life. Jesus' words *do apply* here: to find your life is to lose it (cf. Luke 9:24); to find our life in self-sufficiency is to lose our life in God. That is, if economic values are primary, then we have made the wrong decision. If we buy the whole package of our secularist society, then we cannot center our life in Christ.

IV. The essential decision is not so different from the one in John's Gospel; it is also revolutionary regarding our own culture. It is to decide for Jesus, that he becomes our plan of life and our interpretation of life's meaning, that we want him to be ever more the center of our lives. Today's Gospel ends, "his disciples began to believe in him." If we make a similar decision to really believe in him, he becomes our plan of life and our interpretation of life's meaning. This is not a decision we make once at baptism; it is a decision we make again and again in our life, always trying to improve on this lifelong commitment to Jesus and his values.

Third Sunday in Ordinary Time

Year A

Isaiah 8:23—9:3; 1 Corinthians 1:10–13, 17;
Matthew 4:12–23

The Way of Christ

I. All of us see Jesus through different glasses. As Joachim Jeremias, the scripture scholar, puts it:

> Rationalists depict Jesus as a preacher of morality; for idealists he is the epitome of humanity; esthetes prize him as the genius of artful speech; socialists perceive in him the friend of the poor and a social reformer; and by countless pseudo-scholars he is made out to be a character in a novel.

For us Christians, it is critical that we know what kind of savior he was, what was his cause, what is his message to us. Only a good sense of scripture can give a whole picture of Christ. *Today in this Gospel,* we see Jesus at the beginning of his public life giving us an indication of his whole ministry, cause, purpose, and way.

II. Much of that Jesus summarizes in one sentence; it is the theme of his entire public life: "Repent, for the kingdom of heaven is at hand."

He calls us to "repent" or to reform our lives. He does not merely present a set of rules to follow; he does not demand a retreat from the world; he does not demand a monkish existence; he does not require a specific devotional life of prayer, sacrifices, and special practices. We cannot narrow down his call to any one of these forms. His call is more universal and demanding: a *metanoia*, a total change of heart, a complete transformation of one's life, a radical decision for God. Most of Jesus' parables are a challenge compelling his hearers to respond to his message. Such a radical decision means that the mystery of Jesus becomes our plan of life, our interpretation of life's meaning. It means that all our deepest questions about human life—the source of it, the sense of it, the model for it, its purpose, direction, goal, and hope—all of these are answered in the person of Christ.

Then he continues, "The kingdom of heaven is at hand." This kingdom of God is never narrowed down to a legal system, a code of conduct, a ritual purity, and observance of sacred times, places, and rites. It can only be adequately expressed as doing the will of God. This will of God is what we pray for at the heart of the prayer of Jesus: "[Y]our will be done / on earth as in heaven" (Matthew 6:10). This will of God is the common denominator of the Sermon on the Mount. This will of God is the summary of Jesus' own life: "Behold, I come to do your will, O God" (Hebrews 10:7). For Jesus, this doing the will of God means accepting whatever came to him with submission and love. That is especially how Jesus is our model as we try to accept our human lives in the spirit of Jesus. For many modern theologians, following Jesus means accepting the reality of our lives just as it comes to us. God's will is that we accept everything that comes to us naturally just as Jesus did.

III. In the longer form of this Gospel for today, Matthew summarizes Jesus' public life and work this way: he proclaimed "the Gospel of the kingdom, and [cured] every disease and illness among the people." He implies that the message of God's kingdom that Jesus brought is aimed at all people in all their dimensions; not only at their soul, but at the whole person, body and soul, their whole concrete, suffering existence. For Jesus our Lord is not only a preacher and adviser; he is also a healer and helper. And he is for all people, not only for the strong, healthy, capable, and righteous, but also for the weak, sick, incapable, sinning, and outcast. He does not take away all human failure, illness, and tragedy; but he begins to transform the curse of human existence into blessing even now.

IV. This is how Jesus himself describes his whole mission and message at the beginning of his public life. He shows himself to be the unique Savior of the whole person and of all kinds of people. Pope Benedict XVI puts a new light on Jesus' essential proclamation today: "The kingdom of heaven is at hand." In his book, *Jesus of Nazareth*, our Holy Father explains:

Christ uses these words to refer to himself: He, who is in our midst, is the Kingdom Of God. . . . The new proximity of the kingdom . . . is to be found in Jesus himself. Through Jesus' presence and action, God has here and now entered into history in a wholly new way. The reason why *now* is in a unique sense . . . the time of joy, is that in Jesus it is God who draws near to us. . . . Christ uses these words to refer to himself: He, who is in our midst, is the "Kingdom of God" . . . .[1]

Year B

Jonah 3:1–5, 10; 1 Corinthians 7:29–31; Mark 1:14–20

Repent and Believe in the Gospel

I. "Repent, and believe in the Gospel." This is the first sermon of Jesus at the beginning of his public life. Here Jesus gives us the theme of his whole ministry, cause, purpose and way. Much of that is summarized in this one sentence. He introduces his sermon by the claim, "This is the time of fulfillment"; that is, the event that the Old Testament looked forward to, is about to happen; God is beginning to act eschatologically; his fulfillment of all his promises is now beginning. Let us today try to understand Jesus' sermon, so that we can learn what our Lord is all about, what is his plan of salvation.

II. "Repent" or reform your lives is the opening challenge. He does not merely present a set of rules for us to follow; he does not demand retreat from the world; he does not require a monastic existence separate from the world; he does not propose a specific devotional life of prayer, sacrifices, and special practices. We cannot narrow down his call to any one of these forms. His call is more universal and demanding: a *metanoia*, a total change of heart, a complete transformation of one's life, a radical decision for God. Most of the parables of Jesus that he will relate throughout his public life are a challenge compelling his hearers to respond to his message. Such a radical decision means that the mystery of Jesus becomes our plan of life, our interpretation of life's meaning. It means that all our deepest questions

---

1. Pope Benedict XVI, *Jesus of Nazareth* (N. Y.: Doubleday, 2007), p. 60.

about human life—the source of life, the sense of it, the model for it, its purpose, direction, goal and hope—all of these are answered in the person of Jesus himself.

Then he continues, "The kingdom of God is at hand." This kingdom of God is never narrowed down to a legal system, a code of conduct, a ritual purity, an observance of sacred times, places, and rites. The only way to adequately express this kingdom of God is doing the will of God. This will of God is the common denominator of the Sermon on the Mount. It is the summary of Jesus' own life: "Behold, I come to do your will, O God" (Hebrews 10:7). What does Jesus mean by doing the will of God? For many modern theologians, it does not mean that God determines all of our life for us or directly arranges all that happens to us. Rather it means accepting the reality of our life just as it comes to us. It is based on the model of Jesus' own life; just as Jesus accepted whatever came to him with submission and love, so we try to accept all the common, weird and accidental events of our life in the spirit of Jesus.

III. The last part of this Gospel today gives us a practical example of Jesus' message for us today. For Jesus' calling his apostles is a good illustration of what it means to "repent, and believe in the Gospel." "Come after me," he tells them. That is, he does not ask them to accept certain timeless truths; rather he invites them to be personally attached to him. One difficulty we constantly have with Jesus' preaching in the Gospels is that he constantly refers to believing in the kingdom. The whole notion of kingdom is foreign to us in America, who don't naturally relate to kings and kingdom. But already in the early church, Paul, Peter, and John translate his message for us in a clearer form. They translate "believe in the kingdom" into "believe in Christ," commit yourself to Christ. In our own time, theologians talk about the kingdom in similar terms. As Pope Benedict XVI affirms:

> [T]here is a growing tendency to hold that Christ uses these words to refer to himself: He, who is in our midst, is the "kingdom of God". . . . The new proximity of the Kingdom of which Jesus speaks—the distinguishing feature of his message—is to be found in Jesus himself. Through Jesus'

presence and action, God has here and now entered actively into history in a wholly new way.[2]

For us today, then, to "believe in the kingdom" is, quite simply, to believe in Christ.

Year C

Nehemiah 8:2–4a, 5–6, 8–10; 1 Corinthians 12:12–30; Luke 1:1–4; 4:14–21

Christ the Liberator

I. In today's Gospel, Jesus is in the synagogue in his hometown of Nazareth. After reading a passage from the sixty-first chapter of Isaiah, he asserts that the passage is now being fulfilled in him and his kingdom. He claims that he is the servant of God that Isaiah spoke of, who would liberate God's people by preaching, delivering the oppressed and healing the sick. In the Gospel of Luke this is the first sermon of Jesus. When he gave it, it was a startling sermon, so much so that it was not well received. Jesus had to act out this sermon throughout his public life. He had to show them practically that he was the expected Messiah by healing the sick, by giving sight to the blind, by releasing from sin, by comforting them, by raising some from death and by preaching the kingdom of God.

II. But his hearers were not at all satisfied with his sermon. They had critical problems with such a liberator or messiah. Most of all they could not accept this passage as relating to Jesus himself. For he was one of their neighbors; he grew up with them; he lived for many years in Nazareth with them. In the Gospel next Sunday, we will hear their reaction to this sermon: "Isn't this the son of Joseph? [So] . . . they were all filled with fury. They rose up, [and] drove him out of the town" (Luke 4:22 and 28–29). In a word, they found him to be the *wrong person* to claim to be such a messiah. He was too familiar to them; he was a prophet without honor in his hometown.

---

2. Pope Benedict XVI, *Jesus of Nazareth* (N. Y.: Doubleday, 2007), p. 60.

The other problem they had with Jesus' sermon was a common problem for most of the Jews of Jesus' time. That is, he was the *wrong kind of messiah*. They were not looking for a preaching, healing, helping messiah. They wanted a political liberator; they wanted to be a free people again, free of Roman rule. They wanted a king to make them a nation again with their own laws, authority, and government. This was the kind of messiah they were given to expect by God's word itself in the Old Testament. But Jesus did not take away injustice; he did not destroy the Roman rule; he did not give them back freedom; he did not make them a strong nation, chosen by God. He was simply the wrong kind of messiah.

III. The Second Reading today is a very appropriate choice. Paul asserts here that "all the parts of the body, though many, are one body, so also Christ. For in one Spirit we were all baptized into one body." That is, the church, the assembly of the baptized, is the extension of Christ's body in this world. Now the members are diverse and their gifts are diverse, but the gifts are meant to be for the benefit of the whole body, the church. The implication is that the Church is supposed to carry out the work of Christ, the Messiah. That is, all of us who are baptized into Christ are called to carry out these words of Isaiah in our day; we are meant to follow in the steps of Jesus the liberator and messiah. Each of us has our own unique gifts and abilities; each of us is meant to use our gifts, whatever they are, for building up the body of Christ.

Now there are obvious difficulties with Paul's proposal here. A common attitude in the church years ago was that the laity are the *wrong people* for the job, because the church was constituted by the pope, bishops, priests, and religious. It was their job to preach, to teach, to administer, to carry out the work of the Church. Now they are changing the game; they now claim that all the baptized make up the body of Christ and should contribute to building up his body—even with proper lay ministries. Such a view of the church is still a new development and not fully accepted by all. In a word, the laity are the *wrong people* for the job of forming the church.

The other problem with all this is that, for many people today, Jesus is the *wrong kind of messiah*. They don't want to commit themselves to follow a messiah who will not overcome the constant suffering and injustice around the world or who cannot liberate humanity from hunger, hate, violence, and war. They won't follow a messiah who does not change our suffering, unjust, and evil world into a world of justice, peace, and love. If Jesus can not make our world a world free of suffering and injusice, then they will never be satisfied with him and certainly will never commit their lives to him.

IV. But we are still called to follow Christ who is *this kind of messiah*. We acclaim him as Savior in the midst of suffering, injustice, and human evil. We do not expect him to magically change our own nature and that of all humans into something other than human. We will always be free, so our world will never be perfect. But it is also our individual call to follow in the way of Jesus our model and build up this body of Christ in our own limited way. That means, for example, that doctors can free some from disease; teachers can free from ignorance; priests can teach God's word; parents can give food and shelter and formation to their children; businessmen can free some from poverty; social workers can free some from pain; those who visit the elderly can free them from loneliness; all workers serve the needs of people in some way; and lay ministers in the church can help people in their faith. Paul reminds us today of our motive for following this kind of Messiah: "[Y]ou are Christ's body, and individually parts of it."

Fourth Sunday in Ordinary Time

Year A

Zepheniah 2:3; 3:12–13; 1 Corinthians 1:26–31;
Matthew 5:1–12a

The Beatitudes in Matthew

I. The beatitudes are filled with mystery and idealism. They are addressed "to [all] his disciples" who have clearly chosen to follow Jesus. Together they make up the spiritual charter of Christ's kingdom, a program of life that is in fact modeled on the life of Jesus himself. Let us try to understand the wisdom of Jesus' beatitudes. Each beatitude in Latin begins with the word *beati*, which means blessed or happy or, more accurately, fortunate. There are always two parts to a beatitude, indicating if you do this, then that will follow. The first part of each beatitude—fortunate are those who are poor, who mourn, who hunger, who weep, who are persecuted—is absurd to those without faith. On the natural level, such assertions are preposterous and contradictory. And even for us Christians, they only begin to make sense at all because of the second part: "theirs is the kingdom of heaven . . . / they will be comforted . . . / they will inherit the land . . . / they will be shown mercy." All of these are variations on the last promise of Jesus: "for theirs is the kingdom of heaven." That is, Jesus relates all these beatitudes to the next life and the reward that God offers to those who follow Jesus. So Jesus calls such people fortunate in view of the reward that awaits them. The logic here is expressed clearly by Saint Paul in his letter to the Romans: "I consider that the sufferings of this present time are as nothing compared with the glory to be revealed for us" (Romans 8:18). That is, we Christians live our whole life against the horizon of hope; for us, everything has an added value because of what it will mean for us for all eternity.

And when we encounter suffering in our life and accept it willingly, we are fulfilling the will of God in a notable way, perhaps even a heroic way. Such actions are especially rewarded by God, for they are our way of living out the following of Jesus in difficult circumstances.

II. But we can still ask a further question of Jesus concerning these beatitudes: Why are all these negative experiences singled out for beatitude? We can approach this question by looking at the parallel beatitudes in Luke's Gospel, for in Luke, Jesus also adds opposite conditions as maledictions: "[W]oe to you who are rich . . . / who are filled now . . . / who laugh now . . . / [whom] all speak well of" (Luke 6:24–26). For an answer, look at the common *result* of the conditions Christ is condemning. Those who are rich are not needy; all their material wants are fulfilled. Those who are full and satisfied, do not easily question the meaning to life; they are comfortable and satisfied with their independent life. Those who laugh do not feel injustice or powerlessness; they feel quite self-sufficient. Those who are well spoken about are the successful, the capable; they esteem highly material progress and human advancement. On the other hand, those who are poor are in need of help and of something to hope in. Those who hunger, look for some comfort and satisfaction; they seek some meaning beyond their meager existence. Those who weep, feel injustice and wrong; they are inclined to recognize their dependence on God. And those who are not well spoken about and looked down upon are left out of the material and technological progress; they are more inclined to be open to God and to ultimate questions of life.

Of course none of these beatitudes is an absolute. The hungry and suffering do not always turn to God and the rich and powerful sometimes realize their need for God. But history and experience seem to concur with Christ's beatitudes and woes.

III. In a word, what Jesus our Lord teaches us in these beatitudes is a set of values and attitudes that is diametrically opposed to the easy answers of society. His values and attitudes lead us to see everything in the light of eternity: "[T]he sufferings of this present time are as nothing compared with the glory to be revealed for us" (Romans 8:18). Finally, I might add one note of my own: whatever our circumstances in life—rich or poor, successful or not, well off or suffering—we are truly blessed if we live out our relationship to God above everything else.

Year B

Deuteronomy 18:15–20; 1 Corinthians 7:32–35; Mark 1:21–28

The Authority of Christ, the Word

I. In his memoirs Napoleon Bonaparte, one of the greatest military leaders of all time, wrote this about the authority and power of Christ:

> I know men, and I tell you that Jesus Christ is not a man. Superficial minds may see a resemblance between Christ and the founders of empires. . . . That resemblance does not exist. Between Christ and anyone else in the world, there is no possible term of comparison. With what authority does he teach men to pray! You speak of Caesar, of Alexander, of their conquests and the enthusiasm they enkindled in the hearts of their soldiers. But can you conceive of a dead man making conquests with an army faithful and entirely devoted to his memory? How different is the power of the God of the Christians and the perpetual miracle of the progress of the faith and the government of his church!

For Napoleon, the authority and power of Christ over human beings is much greater than that of any one who ever lived.

II. Today's Gospel speaks of the authority and power of Jesus. Here Mark describes the beginning of the public life of Jesus. He simply relates one miracle of Jesus, an exorcism, and then tells us that Jesus "taught . . . as one having authority." In fact, his authority is foremost in this episode: "What is this? A new teaching with authority? He commands even the unclean spirits and they obey him." Throughout his Gospel, Mark relates numerous miracles as a sign of Jesus' power, but his primary emphasis is on the teaching authority of Jesus. The miracles are illustrations of the power of Jesus' teaching with authority. In Mark Jesus is not primarily the great miracle-worker, but rather the great teacher, the living word. He came to teach us the way to salvation through faith and Christian living, not to miraculously change our life here into something other than human.

III. And this is the kind of power and authority Jesus exerted throughout history. As in Napoleon's words, the authority of Jesus is over people's minds and hearts. It was not the authority of conquest, nor the power of political rule, nor the miraculous change of human life into something magical.

Such is the authority and power of Jesus in our day also. It is not the power of pietistic Christianity; it is not the power that fits our own illusions, such as when we think that everything ought to make sense and justice should prevail in our world, or when we believe that things ought to go well for us, or when we think that God is at our disposal as long as we serve him. *No,* Jesus' power does not work like this; he leaves our lives thoroughly human and therefore somewhat frail, common and difficult. But his power *does* work in our minds and hearts. His power secures for us all that we really need as human beings to live our lives with hope, courage, meaning, and purpose—all those things without which we cannot be whole, cannot become what we are, cannot live noble lives (even though very human).

IV. What I'm trying to say is expressed well in a simple poem I received from the Missionaries of Africa:

> God has not promised skies always blue,
> Flower-strewn pathways all our lives through;
> God has not promised sun without rain,
> Joy without sorrow, peace without pain.
> But God has promised strength for the day,
> Rest for the labor, light for the way,
> Grace for the trials, help from above,
> Unfailing sympathy, undying love.

Year C

Jeremiah 1:4–5, 17–19; 1 Corinthians 12:31—13:13;
Luke 4:21–30

In Praise of Love

I. One of the most sublime passages in the whole Bible is this second reading today. Paul's thoughts are so lofty, his expression so enthusiastic, and his poetry so engaging that we are rightly impressed with his exuberant praise of love. Let us try to get our minds around this wonderful passage.

II. First, in general. Just as *wisdom* was praised in the book of Wisdom, so *love* is praised here as the greatest of all human gifts. No distinction is made between love of God and love of neighbor, so we can reasonably conclude that Paul means *both*. What Paul said just before this is significant; Paul had just completed a list of gifts that were most evident in the church of Corinth; he indicated that there is a hierarchy of charisms, according to how they contribute to the good of the body of Christ. Speaking in tongues is at the bottom of the list, because it does not contribute much to the welfare of Christ's body. Miracles and healing come next, for they profit individuals. Teachers and prophets are more important practical gifts for so many. Quite important are the apostles with their ability to spread the word and clearly build up the body of Christ. But for Paul, there is one gift that surpasses all of these evident gifts in the early church: "Strive eagerly for the greatest spiritual gifts. But I shall show you a still more excellent way." His "more excellent way" is that of love.

III. In extolling love, he first deals with the *necessity* of love. He insists that love is so necessary that without some love of God and neighbor, even the greatest gifts are worth nothing. Theologians add that this is literally true; without sanctifying grace—or, in modern terms, our basic relationship to God—nothing is of any value. In v. 1, he asserts that no matter what gifts or abilities we *have*—such as extraordinary gifts of preaching, speaking in tongues or other superior talents—all are worth nothing if they are held in selfishness or pride. In vv. 2–3 he comments on *doing* or accomplishing. He asserts that even performing miracles, or giving away endless riches, or helping others by healing or teaching—all of these are of no value before God if they are only acts of philanthropy or humanitarianism, without love. In a word, Paul insists that everything turns to ashes without some love of God and neighbor; even the greatest gift or action becomes rotten if it proceeds from a rotten motive.

IV. Then Paul deals with the *qualities* of love, or the measure and proof of our love. His development here is straightforward and practical. He chooses 15 qualities that were neglected by the people of Corinth; many of these same qualities are important for us American Catholics. "Love is patient;" in our anxious, nervous, touchy world, patience is *the* modern virtue. "[L]ove is kind;" our world is often cold and impersonal with little caring, kindness, consideration. "[Love] is not jealous;" it is willing to have attention paid to others, is happy when they are praised. "[Love] is not pompous;" it does not try to impress others with personal importance or achievements. "[Love] is not rude;" it is respectful of others and avoids needless clashes of opinion. "[I]t does not seek its own interests;" it is not wound up in its own little world of needs and troubles; "Me first" is contrary to love. "[Love] is not quick-tempered" or prone to anger, as many men are; when things go wrong or others cross us, we may not lash out with vulgar words or verbal violence. "[I]t does not rejoice over wrong-doing," as many women do; we cannot delight in spreading gossip. "[Love] bears all things . . . endures all things;" it realizes that occasional offenses occur in any friendships, so friendships can only survive if we are willing to excuse and forgive. All these are realistic qualities that take love out of the imaginary or purely romantic world. If we want to improve our love, Paul teaches, this is what we need to work on.

V. We Christians believe that at the end of our life we will be judged not on external accomplishments but on the quality of our love: "So faith, hope, love remain, these three; but the greatest of these is love." For Paul, love is not just a crucial human virtue, it is the whole summary of what we strive for as Christians.

Fifth Sunday in Ordinary Time

YEAR A

Isaiah 58:7–10; 1 Corinthians 2:1–5; Matthew 5:13–16

YOU ARE SALT AND LIGHT

I. "The radical cause of most human inertia, failure and unhappiness is an ugly self-image." This is the opinion of Dr. Maltz in his book, Psycho-Cybernetics. Other leading psychologists in the U. S. agree to this strong assertion; as one author put it, "I am sure that almost all human neuroses and moral evils stem from this one common cause: the absence of true love of oneself." On the other hand, they assert, "A deep understanding of, and a serious effort to achieve true love of self is the beginning of all human growth and happiness."[3] Also: "Most contemporary psychotherapy . . . is designed to help a person toward one thing: to help one adopt a kindly, positive and accepting attitude towards oneself."[4] In summary: "There is a growing consensus of opinion that there is one . . . fundamental and essential need: a true and deep love of self, a genuine and joyful self-acceptance, an authentic self-esteem, which result in an interior sense of celebration: 'It's good to be me; I am very happy to be me.'"[5]

II. What would Christ say about all this? Very simply, he tells us that self-love is not only good, it is also the starting point for following him: "[Y]ou shall love your neighbor as yourself" (Matthew 19:19). Our love of self, the value and care of ourselves is the *Christian norm* for love of others! We have to value and love ourselves first, if we are going to love others well. Today's Gospel strongly affirms this attitude. Jesus himself cries out to all his disciples: "You are the salt of the earth . . . . You are the light of the world." The point we easily

---

3. John Powell, S.J., *The Secret of Staying in Love* (Niles, IL: Argus Communications, 1974), p. 18.

4. *Ibid.*, p. 19.

5. *Ibid.*, p. 13.

miss is that Jesus does not tell us to become the salt of the earth or to make ourselves the light of the world. Rather he affirms that we *are* salt and light already, because Jesus has called us, and we have responded to his call. Most of the world has not heard this call of Jesus or has not responded to it. Jesus wants us to know that by our faith in him, by his grace and new life, we *are* salt and light. So Jesus wants us to manifest what we are: "[Y]our light must shine before others."

IV. Saint Paul recognizes the great value of what we are now in Christ; He begins with the assurance that our essential salvation and intrinsic goodness is from God. Through baptism and our faith, we are already given that wondrous relationship of love and acceptance by God as his sons and daughters. That relationship is constant and almost indestructible; it establishes our fundamental value and goodness by itself; it does not depend on our social position or our natural abilities. Then, in a dozen different ways, Paul urges us to deepen, to grow, to progress in that reality, to live according to our status as children of God. For example, Paul tells us that we are children of light; therefore, we should walk as children of light. We are saved in Jesus our Savior, so we should work to be ultimately saved. We are new creatures in Christ; therefore we should be renewed day by day. We have put on Christ; therefore we should grow into our model, Jesus. In a word, God has made us his sons and daughters, so we are of great value and worth already; let us become more and more what we are. We add to our essential value before God by the love that we show others, by living in the way of Christ. This struggle to put on Christ more and more makes us more effective salt and light.

V. Jesus concludes his teaching in the Gospel by adding a caution: "[I]f salt loses its taste . . . [i]t is no longer good for anything but to be thrown out and trampled under foot." What he means is that those who lose their faith, who no longer even try to respond to his call are no longer the salt of the earth. Similarly, our light can be extinguished; our faith can weaken and die out.

VI. So what these two encouraging parables say to us is this: by baptism and faith in Christ our Savior, God has already made us salt and light; he has given us our essential justification, goodness, and worth. None of this can be taken away from us. So we are salt for others by affirming our faith and deepening it by how we live it. We are salt for others by our kindly, accepting attitude toward them. We are salt by constantly affirming, "It's good to be me; I'm happy to be me."

Year B

Job 7:1–4, 6–7; 2 Corinthians 9:16–19, 22–23; Mark 1:29–39

Ministers All

I. Today's readings give us a photograph of three very different lives. The first reading describes Job's miserable life experience:

> I have been assigned months of misery . . . .
> If in bed I say, "When shall I arise?" . . . .
> I am filled with restlessness until the dawn . . . .
> My days / . . . / come to an end without hope . . . .
> I shall not see happiness again.

Job feels restless, depressed and hopeless.

The Second Reading describes part of Paul's life:

> [A]n obligation has been imposed on me, and woe to me if I do not preach [the Gospel]. . . . I have made myself a slave to all so as to win over as many as possible. . . . All this I do for the sake of the Gospel, so that I too may have a share in it.

He freely serves the Gospel and God's people; he runs so as to win the race.

The Gospel focuses on one day in the life of Jesus. His day begins by his curing Peter's mother-in-law. Later, "The whole town was gathered at the door." He cured many of them; he cast out devils. Then before dawn, he got up and went off to pray. His apostles would not let him alone; they found him and explained: "Everyone is looking for you." So he went off to other towns to preach to them.

II. Now these are short vignettes of three very different people of faith. It doesn't take much reflection for us here today to identify with one of these three photographs. Job is easy to identify with. We have all had days when we felt depressed, tired, dragging; when human problems and tragedies crowded into our lives.

Paul reminds us of different times in our lives when we feel compelled to serve our job or our family; we do it willingly but feel as if we are running a race in search of a finishing line. And in keeping faith with our responsibilities, we are pulled every which way; we feel as though we are asked to be "all things to all [people]" (1 Corinthians 9:22).

The day in the life of Jesus that Mark describes for us in the Gospel, also resonates with some parts of our lives. Single parents or parents who both work can feel the constant press of obligations that never let up. They try to find some quiet time, but people always find them and make demands on them.

What is common to all three vignettes is this: these three Christian heroes feel compelled to do things they have not chosen; their lives at times are driven by other people or circumstances. They are not in control of their lives; they can only say "yes" to life as it comes to them. And this is exactly their fulfillment of God's will, their ministry to God's people, and their very human way to holiness.

III. This leads to the one point I want to make today: Our common and ordinary lives are very often driven by demands of our work or family; but that is precisely our form of ministry to others; that is our simple, human form of ministry. What I mean is: To the extent that we minister to human needs, to that extent we are ministers of Christ. For example, the job we do each day, ministers to some human need; this is true not just for medical personnel or social workers or teachers, but for all of us; even those who are far removed from the people they help, such as office workers, business people and garbage collectors. Also the care we take of our family; I dare say, most of us easily recognize this as our way of service to them. Or the kindness and acceptance toward acquaintances all day long. Or just listening to others' troubles. Or putting-up with boring, inconsiderate people. Or occasionally ministering to pain or sorrow by visiting the sick or going to a wake. All of these are everyday forms of serving one another. Most of them we feel compelled to do, we are not in control of them; they just come to us day after day. All we need do is say "yes" to them. And that "yes" is our fulfillment of God's will; that is how we minister to others; that is our very common way of holiness; that is our way of walking in the footsteps of Job, of Paul, and of Jesus.

Year C

Isaiah 6:1–2a, 3–8; 1 Corinthians 15:1–11; Luke 5:1–11

Here I Am Lord; Send Me

I. Today's Gospel tells of a fishing boat on the Lake of Gennesareth. The apostles had been fishing all night and caught nothing. Yet at Jesus' command, they caught a great multitude of fish. Luke had a symbolic purpose in mind for this miracle narrative; that is, for Luke, the lake is the world, which Jesus wants to make over into a "new world." The boat is the barque of Peter, the Church, including all of us Christians. The fish are the people to be Christianized, as Jesus himself indicated. And they are to be won over to this Christian way of life by Jesus' special grace, helping the apostles to make a human catch.

II. All three readings today make some reference to a vocation or call—the call of Isaiah, of Paul, and of Peter. In each case there is a sense of inadequacy, sinfulness, and unworthiness. Isaiah laments, "I am doomed! . . . I am a man of unclean lips." Paul describes himself as "one born abnormally . . . the least of the apostles." And Peter begs Jesus, "Depart from me, Lord, for I am a sinful man." Such a sense of weakness and inadequacy is a constant biblical pattern; that is, those whom God calls, express diffidence, fear and incredulity in the face of a call, and only with the help of God, do they slowly come to accept God's call. For the more they experience their weakness and absolute need for God's grace, the more God is willing to grant them his powerful help. Paul expresses this common Christian pattern very well: "I will rather boast most gladly of my weaknesses, in order that the power of Christ may dwell with me. . . . For when I am weak, then I am strong" (2 Corinthians 12:9–10). That is, once Paul realizes his own weakness, he freely acknowledges that all grace is from God. Only then can God's power be actualized in his ministry.

III. Much the same can be true of us. We may have a hard time believing that we have a notable vocation to Christian service. Some of us think of our baptismal call as a simple and common call. We may not realize that Jesus' invitation is for *all* his followers:

"If anyone wishes to come after me, he must deny himself and take up his cross daily and follow me" (Luke 9:23). What Jesus means is that every one of us should offer our life for the sake of his cause. He was referring to a common saying of religious and political leaders of his day: If you want to be my disciple, then commit your life to follow me in your entire life, in all your living, even to death.[6] This means that our baptism and confirmation are a call to follow Jesus in the very life that is ours. So we need a sense of vocation as parents, for we are trying in our simple way to form our children in the way of Jesus. We need to think of our daily work as a vocation to serve the human needs of God's people. If we are sick or struggling through some trial we need to see that trial as a way of following Jesus, our suffering Savior. If we are elderly or widowed, we need to know that God is with us even now. In a word, we need to be deeply convinced that whatever our circumstances of life, that is *our way* of living out our Christian calling; that is the *actual reality* of our following of Christ; that is our real *call* to discipleship.

IV. In the spirit of today's readings, each of us needs to respond to God's call by declaring, "Here I am, [Lord] . . . send me." In saying that, we are simply affirming that we will try to live this real life that is ours with the values of Jesus, with his attitude toward people and events, with a sense of commitment to his will, with some realization that what we do to others is done to Jesus himself. Today, let us each renew our commitment to follow Jesus and to deepen our sense of vocation in the real life that is ours. Today and often, we need to hear God's call in our real lives and respond: "Here I am, [Lord] . . . send me."

---

6. Edward Schillebeeckx, *God Among Us: The Gospel Proclaimed* (New York: Crossroad, 1987), pp. 202–203; see footnote on page 59.

Sixth Sunday in Ordinary Time

Year A

Sirach 15:15–20; 1 Corinthians 2:6–10; Matthew 5:17–37

Christ and Morality

I. What is the relationship between law, virtue, and love? How can we
reconcile commandments, legalism, and Christian freedom? What
does Jesus teach about law and morality? Today's Gospel is one of the
best passages for understanding his teaching on the relation of law
and morality. But it is not easy to interpret. Let us try to do it now.

II. The Pharisees in Jesus' time, considered the Mosaic law to
be the summary of all wisdom, human and divine, a complete and
sure guide of conduct, an assurance of good relations with God. This
value of the law Jesus did *not* accept—as is evident from his own
non-observance of the Sabbath rules and the laws of Levitical clean-
liness. Yet in the beginning of our Gospel today, Jesus asserts that
his mission is not to *annul* or destroy the Mosaic law but rather
to fulfill it or bring the law to final perfection. He meant that his
disciples were to follow exactly *his* complete and perfect understanding of the law. He explains what he means by six examples (four in
this Gospel and two next Sunday). In each of these six examples,
Jesus presents an antithesis between the *old* understanding of the law
and *his* pronouncement of the perfect law. There is no easy, consistent
pattern however.

In the first example, Jesus not only prohibits murder but even
anger, which can lead to murder. Then he insists that fraternal relations are more important than cultic duties; that is, we must first
be reconciled with our neighbor before we bring our offering to God's
altar. In the second example, Jesus not only prohibits adultery, but also
lustful desires that can lead to adultery. Again, he insists on internal
disposition not just external acts. In the third example, he takes up
the question of divorce. Regarding divorce, there were two governing

views at the time: the conservative opinion (Shammai) which only permitted divorce in the case of adultery, or the liberal opinion (Hillel) which permitted divorce for lesser causes. Jesus rejects both views and does not permit divorce for any reason at all. Here and in three other Gospel citations, Jesus' teaching on divorce is very strict. In the fourth example, Jesus not only prohibits false oaths, but also implies that truthfulness should be secured by the inner integrity of the person, without the deceits and lack of trust surrounding some oaths and vows of the time. In the fifth example—which will be read next week—our Lord rejects "an eye for an eye" retaliation of revenge and proposes non-resistance. In the last example, Jesus teaches not only love of neighbor but also love of enemies, after the example of God.

III. Now let me try to summarize Jesus' moral teaching here in two statements. First, the whole structure of human morality that Jesus inculcates is based on internal responsibility to God and the highest universal principles. As Rollo May observes, "the essential point in Jesus' ethics was his shifting the emphasis from the *external* rules of the 10 commandments, to *inward* motives." Morality for Jesus does not consist simply in the avoidance of evil acts but in the positive internal desire for good, because God's claim for obedience is an absolute, total demand, claiming our whole person in all our relations. Secondly, in these six examples, Jesus presents a morality that is even *more demanding* than that of the Old Testament: "I have come not to abolish [the moral law] but to fulfill" (Matthew 5:17). But he bases his whole *motivational structure* on the universal principle of love. Recall here, the summary command of Jesus in John's Gospel: "This is *my* commandment: love one another as I love you" (John 15:12, emphasis added; cf., John 13:34). So the pivot of Jesus' moral revolution is love; it is not just the center of his morality; it is the entire structure.

IV. To sum up. Our Lord's righteousness goes beyond that of the Scribes and Pharisees, because he is not concerned with negative legalisms but with positively doing the will of God. He is not concerned with carefully following complicated legalisms but with loving attitudes after Jesus' own model. His first concern in not with the complexities of law but with the demanding ideal of love. In a word, his morality is internal, all encompassing and loving.

Year B

Leviticus 13:1–2, 44–46; 1 Corinthians 10:31—11:1; Mark 1:40–45

What Kind of Messiah Is Jesus?

I. What kind of Messiah is Jesus? How does he save us? What challenges does his kind of salvation imply? All of these questions are important to Saint Mark and we see hints of them in today's Gospel.

II. This short miracle story follows the basic pattern common to all such stories: 1) the diagnosis—in this case that the man was a leper, along with his request for healing; 2) the cure by word and touch; 3) The demonstration—here the command, "go, show yourself to the priest," in accord with the law as mentioned in the First Reading today. But this miracle story adds something that is often characteristic in Mark's Gospel; it hints at Mark's central motif of the messianic secret. Notice what Jesus tells the one who is cured: "See that you tell no one anything." That is, Mark wanted to correct a false notion that Jesus was mainly a miracle-worker, whose principal ministry and purpose was to perform wondrous acts. For Mark, miracles are only a subordinate feature of Jesus' ministry. Jesus' main purpose is to preach the Good News of salvation. Later in his Gospel, especially in Chapter 8, Mark will add the full exposition of his "messianic secret": that Jesus is not a messiah of power and glory but a messiah of suffering and death, showing that God's salvation is one of compassion, forgiveness, and love. So even when Mark relates miracles as a sign of Jesus' power, his primary emphasis is on the teaching authority of Jesus. Mark wants us to see Jesus not as the great miracle-worker, but rather as the great teacher, the living word. For Jesus came to teach us the way to salvation through faith and Christian living, not to miraculously change our life here into something other than human.

III. This leads to a valuable lesson for us today. Years ago, we still looked for a God who would do away with the suffering and evil in our world. If we prayed hard enough and were very devout, we hoped that God would change our little world, so that justice might prevail and things might go well for us. If we lived according to his commands and tried to follow his way, then he would take care of us; he would make our life more easy and free of trouble. Didn't we sometimes think like that years ago? But Mark implies that Jesus is not that kind of redeemer; he did not come to rule the world, to protect his followers from harm, to transform our world into an earthly paradise. No, Jesus came to save human beings, who must ever be imperfect and free or they are no longer human. Rather, he confronts the evil in our world with compassion, forgiveness, and love. Jesus wants us to accept the suffering involved in all our human living just as he did. Like him, we try to face all our challenges with acceptance. Like him, we confront the evil in our world with a mature and constant following of Jesus, our suffering Messiah.

IV. One final note. Even though Jesus told the leper not to make public what he did for him, this common man proclaimed to all what Jesus did. In the old church, for the most part, only priests, religious, and the hierarchy proclaimed Jesus. Increasingly today, the laity are involved in numerous way of proclaiming Jesus and ministering to others in the church—as communion ministers, as lectors, as home and hospital visitors, as catechists or teachers. This is a challenge for all of us to accept; we need to see this as a welcome development in our church. All of us need to learn that we are each ministers to one another. Paul goes even further today in counseling the people of Corinth and all of us; he gives us a one-line summary of Christian living: "[W]hether you eat or drink, or whatever you do, do everything for the glory of God."

Year C

Jeremiah 17:5–8; 1 Corinthians 15:12, 16–20; Luke 6:17, 20–26

Why Are the Beatitudes True?

I. The beatitudes we just read are filled with mystery and idealism. They are poetic ideals that express Christ's value system. They are very difficult for us to get a grip on them, to understand why they are true. We cannot understand them at all with human reason alone. Without faith, Jesus' beatitudes are ridiculous or absurd. They are particularly difficult for us to understand living in our modern American culture.

II. There are two forms of the beatitudes in the Gospels. We are more familiar with the eight beatitudes found in Matthew's Gospel. Here in Luke, there are only four beatitudes, along with four contrasting woes. Scholars suggest that Luke's form is more likely the original form that Jesus gave us. Also, Luke's four beatitudes and four woes give us a hint toward understanding Jesus' rationale; he inclines us to look at the common *result* of the conditions Jesus describes. First consider the *woes*. Those who are rich are not needy; most of their material wants are fulfilled. Because they do not feel needy, they are less inclined to depend on God for anything. Those who are full and satisfied do not easily raise questions of meaning; for the most part they are comfortable and satisfied with their life. Those who laugh do not feel injustice or lack of power; they feel quite independent and in control. Those who are well spoken about are the popular or successful, and in our society they are usually the skilled and technologically capable; they are content in their public position.

On the other hand, consider the *beatitudes* and their likely results. Those who are poor are in need of financial help and for something to hope in. Those who are hungry look for some comfort and satisfaction; they need something to give their life meaning. Those who weep feel injustice and lack of power; they easily look to God for some consolation and ultimate justice. Those who are not well spoken about and looked down upon, are left out of our technological and economic progress; they are more inclined to seek acknowledgment from God.

Of course none of these woes or beatitudes is *absolute*. The poor and hungry do not always turn to God, and the rich and powerful sometimes do see their need and dependence on God. But history and experience show some general truth and rationality to Jesus' beatitudes and woes.

III. The First Reading from Jeremiah today, suggests another way of interpreting these beatitudes and woes. "Blessed is [one] who trusts in the LORD," asserts Jeremiah. That is, trust in the Lord is understandably the attitude of those who are poor, hungry, hurting.

Such people cannot put their trust in human beings and the American dream; they can only turn to God with hope in his promises; they can only find meaning to life in the ultimate answers Jesus offers. Just because they find no immediate fulfillment in their life now, they look for real human fulfillment in the promises of God.

On the other hand, Jeremiah asserts: "Cursed is the [one] who trusts in human beings, / who seeks his strength in flesh, / whose heart turns away from the LORD." Often enough trust in human ability and power is the attitude of the rich, the satisfied, the successful. As long as their life now is satisfying and superficially meaningful, they are not inclined to look elsewhere. As long as they have found partial answers to human living in the American dream of success, status and possessions, they are not inclined to look farther for ultimate answers.

IV. In a word, what Jesus our Lord teaches in these beatitudes and woes is a set of values and attitudes that are diametrically opposed to the easy answers of secular society. His values and attitudes lead us to see everything in the light of eternity. The mystery and idealism of his teaching is totally bound up with the ultimate questions of human life and with our amazing hope. He insists that religion and life are ultimately questions of our relationship to God. He would add, I believe, that whatever our circumstances in life—rich or poor, successful or hurting—we are truly blessed, if we prize our relationship with God above everything else.

Seventh Sunday in Ordinary Time

YEAR A

Leviticus 19:1–2, 17–18; 2 Corinthians 3:16–23; Matthew 5:38–48

LOVE YOUR ENEMIES

I. Today's Gospel continues our reflection on the Sermon on the Mount. It addresses two issues: 1) retaliation or responding in kind; 2) attitudes towards enemies. These are two of the most difficult teachings of Christ—so demanding that we seldom preach about them. Such principles of Christ we might not really believe or at least would like to forget about. Let us listen to Jesus.

First Jesus refers to the Hebrew law of *talion* or retribution: ". . . an eye for an eye and a tooth for a tooth." In the Old Testament (Exodus 21:24 and Leviticus 24:19–20), this norm was meant as a limit for retribution; it was an improvement on the harsh retribution of the time; it counseled that retribution should not go beyond what is proportionate.

Even this moderate law is now repealed by Jesus. He counsels a response to personal injury that is non-violent, that does not seek retribution at all. This principle of Jesus is one of those that distinguish Christianity from pagan or merely rational morality—in fact from most other religions. Reason tells us that if others are decent to us, we will be decent to them. Most religions would agree: Do unto others as they do to you. But Jesus went beyond all that—as much as we would like to forget that. Jesus here tells us that we cannot reciprocate in kind. We cannot let our rightness depend on another's conduct. We cannot simply meet evil with evil, hatred with hatred. We must be willing to break the vicious cycle of injustice in our cruel world. If we Christians are not willing to do this, who will?

II. Second, Jesus remarks: "You have heard that it was said, 'You shall love your neighbor and hate your enemy.'" There is no explicit Old Testament command to "hate your enemy," but there are some approximations to this norm (See Psalm 137:8–9 and 139:19–22). Such hatred and retaliation is a clear example of protology, that is, a teaching of an Old Testament that is corrected in the New Testament. Jesus deliberately rejects such Hebrew morality and insists on his ideal of love of enemies. He also points out that his norm is far removed from pagan ethics or merely human wisdom: "[I]f you love those who love you, what recompense will you have? . . . Do not the pagans do the same?" Jesus leaves no doubt about his ideal: ". . . love your enemies and pray for those who persecute you."

III. What *motivation* does Jesus offer for us to love our enemies? His motive is deceptively simple: "[L]ove your enemies . . . that you may be children of your heavenly Father, for he makes his sun rise on the bad and the good, and causes rain to fall on the just and the unjust." That is, our dealings with others should reflect the way God himself deals with all people, both the good and the bad. For God sends his natural gifts of rain and sunshine to all people equally. Perhaps we might add that, as long as we are here on this earth, God not only gives natural life to all, he also offers his grace and forgiveness to all, he provides eternal salvation equally for all who believe. God is most generous to "the good, the bad and the ugly." Jesus tells us to "be perfect, just as your heavenly Father is perfect"; love your enemies as well as your friends.

IV. Such teachings of Jesus in the Sermon on the Mount were extreme in his day and seem just as extreme for us today. One modern writer summarizes much of the Jesus' teachings here as a *social revolution*, one that turns social relations between people in a society upside down:

> Jesus' sayings, especially those that were collected into the Sermon on the Mount, were subversive of almost everything his contemporaries took for granted. He spoke of turning the other cheek instead of taking revenge, of loving one's enemies instead of hating them, of doing good to those who hate you, and of forgiving them all seventy times. . . . That alone would

have revolutionized social relationships . . . as well as the relationships between different groups and classes, and between religions and nations.[7]

In all honesty, you and I must admit that we often fail to follow these teachings of Jesus. But we must admit that this is the ideal that Jesus himself taught and lived. And no matter how often we fail in this, let us at least never give up following his example.

Year B

Isaiah 43:18–19, 21–22, 24b–25; 2 Corinthians 1:18–22; Mark 2:1–12

Encounters with Christ

I. What does Jesus really do in today's Gospel? The first obvious answer is that he does something amazing; he performs a miracle; he accomplishes a cure of body and soul. But secondly, Jesus also proves something; he proves that he can forgive sins; and he offers the cure of the paralytic as an external proof of his ability to forgive sins: "[T]hat you may know that [I have] authority to forgive sins . . . ," he then performs the cure as proof of God's forgiveness through him. And it seems reasonable to infer that he can also give that power of forgiving sins to others. Such an inference is probably one of the reasons why Mark included this event in his Gospel: to show that his followers can forgive sins. But he also does a third thing: he affects a person. He talks to this man personally and treats him as a person. In all Jesus' encounters, Jesus relates to people in a personal manner and people respond to him accordingly. For example, in some instances the one who is cured reacts by jumping around and praising God, or by following Jesus with great joy or by telling others about Jesus' goodness to him.

III. Jesus does the same three things for us by means of the sacraments. These three points form the basis for a new and profound theology of the sacraments. What does Jesus do for us by means of his

---

7. 1. Albert Nolan, *Jesus Today; A Spirituality of Radical Freedom* (Maryknoll, N. Y.: Orbis Books, 2007), pp. 50–51.

sacraments? First, he *does* something: he forgives sin, he gives grace, he cures us. This effect of the sacraments is what we all learned about them from our childhood: "sacraments are outward signs, instituted by Christ, to give grace." Actually, Scripture presents Jesus as the explicit author of only three sacraments: baptism, Eucharist, and reconciliation. The others came from the early Church, with the inspiration of the Holy Spirit. What I want to stress here is that Jesus himself made our church a sacramental church. Jesus intended that we not only believe in him; we must also make use of his sacraments to be authentic Christians.

III. Secondly, his sacraments are a *proof* of something, a proof of his concern for us as individuals, an individual proof of his love. They make Christ's death and resurrection apply to us individually; we receive them one person at a time. Jesus knows it is not enough for us to be convinced that God loves all of us in general; each of us needs to know that he loves *me* individually. We each need our Father's personal embrace; we need to experience his love in a sensible way. He does this by making each one of us his child in baptism, by forgiving each of us in reconciliation, by loving each one personally in the Eucharist. This is the *genius* of his sacraments: God proves his love for us as individuals in a sensible way.

IV. But above all, each sacrament is an *encounter with Christ*. It is not just a gift, not just a proof, but also an encounter with Christ himself. The primary effect of the sacraments is a personal love for Christ. What I mean is that in reconciliation, for example, we not only receive forgiveness of sins; we have an encounter with Jesus himself, with his forgiveness, his kindness, his love. And he wants our personal response to be our sincere effort to follow him. Even more obviously in the Eucharist, we not only receive grace and spiritual nourishment, we are united with Jesus himself as the one who loves us and gave up his life for us. Saint Ambrose expressed this well 1600 years ago: "You have shown yourself to me, Christ, face to face; it is in your sacraments that I meet you." This encounter with Jesus in his sacraments is a strong source of our friendship with Jesus. Just as all human friendship demands regular, external contact, so our friendship with Jesus requires regular, external contact. And we have that especially in the sacraments. That is why we come here Sunday after Sunday: that we maintain and develop our friendship with Jesus, as he himself implied: "Whoever eats my flesh and drinks my blood remains in me and I in him" (Jo. 6, 56).

V. This is what Jesus intends by his sacraments: he *does* something in giving us his grace; he also *proves* his love for us individually; and finally, he *encounters* us personally as our friend. Such is the genius of the sacraments that Jesus gave us.

YEAR C

1 Samuel 26:2, 7–9, 12–13, 22–23; 1 Corinthians 15:45–49; Luke 6:27–38

LOVE YOUR ENEMIES

I. During the Civil War, President Lincoln made a speech in which he referred to the Southern Confederates as "erring human beings," rather than as enemies of the United States. An elderly lady complained to him, "Mr. President, how can you refer to such slave-holding rebels as 'erring human beings'; they are actually sworn enemies of the Union and of freedom." Lincoln replied calmly, "Why, madam, *do I not destroy my enemies when I make them friends?*" President Lincoln's attitude toward the enemies of the Union made it possible for the United States to survive the great Civil War and then to reconstruct our nation. His was a profound example of the command of Jesus in our Gospel today: "Love your enemies."

II. "[L]ove your enemies," seems to be an *authentic and original* command of Jesus himself.[8] It is a norm that goes further than all previous ancient wisdom. Thus, in the Old Testament, there are several instances of hatred of enemies; one shocking example is found in Psalm 137 (v. 9): "Happy the [one] who shall seize and smash / your little [children] against the rock!" Other religions held similar norms; thus, Confucius specifically rejected love of enemies. And the Dead Sea Scrolls of the Qumran community expressly commanded hatred toward outsiders. Only Jesus gives us such a radical command; only Jesus counsels a practical universalism that

---

8. Joseph Fitzmyer, *The Gospel According to Luke, I–IX* (Vol. 28 of the *Anchor Bible Series*) (New York: Doubleday, 1970), p. 638.

knows no bounds of nation, class, race, gender faith, or moral condition. This is one principle that distinguishes Christianity from pagan ethics, non-Christian religions and mere rational morality. Reason tells us that if others are decent, we should be decent to them; do unto others as they do to you. That is quite rational, but "do good to those who hate you" makes no sense rationally.

III. What exactly does Jesus *mean*? What is he asking us, his followers to do here? Clearly, he is telling us that we cannot reciprocate in kind. We cannot let our rightness depend on another's conduct. We must not just meet evil with evil, hatred with hatred; we must be willing to break the vicious cycle of injustice in this cruel world of ours. Just because others are small-minded, we must not be picayune; even when they show ill-will, we cannot get aroused; just because they are antagonistic, we must not be offensive; when they are vicious, we must not respond in kind.

IV. Why does Jesus talk like this? Doesn't he realize this is entirely too much for ordinary human beings? What *motive* does Jesus offer for such a radical position? Does he refer to the pervasive suffering in our world as a reason for such extreme compassion? Or is he trying to establish a perfect moral order? *No*, the motive he offers us is simply divine: "Be merciful, just as [also] your Father is merciful." That is, be good children, imitate your Father, who makes no distinction between friend and foe; who lets his sun and rain fall equally on all; who "loved us [when we were sinners] and sent his Son as expiation for our sins" (1 John 4:10).

God simply loves all people without condition, as long as they are alive; he offers salvation and forgiveness to all; he loves even sinners and evil people. We can show that we are sons and daughters of such a God by our love of enemies.

V. Let me be honest here. I don't follow this command of Jesus very well; I find it extremely difficult to love my enemies. On occasion, with time and God's grace, I can manage some degree of love of enemies. Perhaps some of you are willing to admit a similar failure in trying to follow Jesus. I would offer two words of encouragement to sincere Christians who fail in this very radical way of Jesus. First, we need to admit that this teaching of Jesus is really our ideal; we are really called to this extreme; we cannot reject this outright but must struggle to approach this goal in our life. And second, knowing that we fail badly regarding this ideal, we should not be so quick to condemn other Catholics because they fail badly or church leaders for their abuse of authority. In a word, all of us are humbled when we hear Jesus' command: "[L]ove your enemies, do good to those who hate you."

Eighth Sunday in Ordinary Time

Year A

Isaiah 49:14–15; 1 Corinthians 4:1–5; Matthew 6:24–34

What's First in Our Lives?

I. Jesus has a challenge for all his followers today in this Gospel: "No one can serve two masters. . . . You cannot serve God and mammon." We need to understand exactly what Jesus means if we are to accept that challenge. "Mammon" refers to money and possessions. To serve mammon means to make money and material possessions the most important things in one's life, the primary goal of life. Jesus' teaching amounted to a clear condemnation of the pagans of his time, because for them, who didn't believe in God, there was nothing else they could put first in their life but riches, pleasure and power. They could easily identify with the formula, "Let us eat and drink [and be merry], / for tomorrow we die" (1 Corinthians 15:32; cf. Isaiah 22:13). Let me boldly assert that none of us here is so crass; we do not find ourselves in that category.

II. But Jesus' challenge was also for those who believe in God but choose to live their lives independently, according to their own standards. In our day, many Americans try to find that kind of compromise. They believe in a household God; that is, they admit a place for God in our society and life, but the God they acknowledge is an innocuous God, a convenient God with no disturbing features, no inconvenient demands. Such a God is a household God—nice to have around the house but not interfering with our lives. He pardons all our human faults and lets us continue in our selfish ways. He harms no one, interferes with no one, is useful to no one. Such a God makes possible a religion that disturbs nothing and imposes no obligations. With such a God, it is very easy to serve God and mammon *together*, at the same time. That is, such Christians can cater to their own desires for money, power, pleasure, and possessions, while at the same time acknowledging their household God. Since he makes no demands on their way of life, does not interfere with their own program, they can acknowledge him and still feel unhindered in their lifestyle. They admit that God is a value, but only when he is convenient. They try to have the best of both worlds; that is, they admit an innocuous God and a harmless religion but also get all they can out of this world.

III. What Jesus proposes in this Gospel is that we make God *primary* in our lives, that we serve God above all. To serve God means to carry out his will, to obey his commandments, to seek his kingdom, to make a radical decision for God in our life. For Christians, it means to make a radical commitment to live as Jesus lived, to make him the model for our lives. It does *not* exclude material needs, human satisfactions or positions of authority. But it subordinates everything to this principle: "[S]eek first the kingdom [of God]" (Matthew 6:33). The model for this norm is Jesus himself; the whole summary of his life and preaching is that God and his will come first; the heart of the prayer he taught is: "Your kingdom come, / your will be done" (Matthew 6:10). He did not require that his followers give up all money, possessions, and status; he only insisted that all such things be subordinate to God and his kingdom. Jesus' God is a God of freedom; he does not require us to reject everything else in our world; he only wants us to prefer God to any other human desire, to make our personal relationship to God our Father dominate all of our living.

IV. If we do not recognize this as a real challenge, then we probably have made our own compromise, we have chosen to believe in a household God. If we want to respond to the challenge of Jesus, today, we need to hear how all-encompassing it is: "[S]eek first the kingdom [of God] and his righteousness, and all these things will be given you besides."

Year B

Hosea 2:16b, 17b, 21–22; 2 Corinthians 3:1b–6; Mark 2:18–22

Change in the Church

I. Today's readings deal with written laws and long-standing traditions, with new adaptations and institutional change. The Gospel is a pronouncement story in Mark; that is, it is one of several in Mark's Gospel that illustrate the growing conflict between Jesus and the Jewish authorities. Here the focus is on fasting; the accusation is that Jesus and his disciples do not keep the traditional fasts. Jesus' specific answer is that they do not need to fast as long as he, the bridegroom, is with them. But his two parables about wineskins and clothing make a more universal point, namely that the laws and practices of the past are not appropriate in the new covenant with its own character and norms. He implies that Christianity has a radically new nature with a vital change of outlook. In fact, Jesus' entire public life was spent in dealing with opponents to change. Just because he was a revolutionary, their opposition led to his death. His new covenant was not a new set of laws but a vital new spirit. As Paul reminds us today: he is the minister "of a new covenant, not of letter but of spirit." That is why our Christian faith is unique among all religions. All other religions follow definite moral laws, sacred writings, traditional practices. We Christians go beyond all that; we alone follow a person, Jesus Christ. So whenever Christians get caught up in laws and institutional practices, they lose some of the focus of their faith in Christ. In Paul's words, ". . . the letter brings death, but the Spirit gives life."

II. These Scripture readings today can be a profound help to us Catholics today, especially because of changes in our institutional Church. Some conservatives get very caught up in the laws, practices, and traditions of our Church. Whenever any of these traditions is changed or abrogated—even by some Church leader— they feel betrayed by the institutional church. And when a major transformation is instituted, as after Vatican II, they become positively distressed: "What have they done to our Church?" Other people would like to see more inclusion of women in the Church or more democratic procedures in the Church, as was positively recommended by the Vatican Council. When they see little change in such areas over many years, they get impatient and ask: "When will the Church ever learn?" Or they even choose to leave the Church, believing the institution will never change.

Today's readings speak to both of these positions. Paul reminds us all that our Church is primarily "not of letter but of spirit." That is, the ultimate norm for us Christians is not law but the Spirit of Jesus himself. We do not center our faith on law but on the person of Jesus Christ. And Scripture also represents the early Church as one that struggled for a whole century with the problems of Jewish laws that were not in sync with the new spirit of Jesus. The Church slowly transformed itself, at an agonizing pace, into a new community open to both Jews and Gentiles alike.

III. What we all need to learn is that our Catholic Church is like all large institutions; it must constantly adapt to society in order to remain a leaven in the world; but also as a large traditional institution, it can only transform itself very slowly. In addition, one overriding attitude should dominate all concerns about change in this church of Christ: we are *not* primarily people of law, authority or human tradition, for these will always be imperfect and flawed; *no*, we are followers of Christ; he is the complete revelation of God; he alone is the model for our living; his Spirit is the primary guide and strength. No matter what happens in our institutional church, the Spirit remains with us individually and that "Spirit gives life."

Year C

Sirach 27:4–7; 1 Corinthians 15:54–58; Luke 6:39–45

A Good Tree Produces Good Fruit

I. In a restaurant one evening, I overheard eight young adults discussing religion, God and freedom. I heard them quite distinctly, because they were arguing loudly and uninhibitedly. The thrust of the discussion was negative and critical; they found religion rather restrictive. One man was feeling no pain after a few drinks and dominated the conversation after a while. He contended: "I would be happy to believe in God, if I could only find a God who would leave me alone, let me live my own life, just love me without all kinds of demands and restrictions. All the religions I know present a God who ties us down and makes all kinds of demands on us."

II. He was expressing rather well a common American notion of religion and God. Let us call it the religion of the American practical mind. Let me try to describe religion as understood by the American practical mind. Such a religion is happy to believe in a god who leaves us alone, lets us live our own life, lets us free without all kinds of demands and restrictions. It believes that god is in his heaven but has very little place in human living. The general outline of the commandments is enough for us humans to handle our lives without magical solutions or interventions from god. We do not have to make much room for god in our daily lives. We only need a basic faith in him along with baptism and a life that is not evil. Our God is compassionate and loving; he will save us because of our faith.

III. Today's Gospel and what follows it in Luke offer a response to such a religion of the American practical mind. At the end of the Gospel we just read, Jesus uses two fruit tree images to make the point about the source of a person's actions. It is the fruit that tells whether the tree is healthy; also the fruit tells whether it is a fig tree or a thorny tree. By this simple metaphor, Jesus means that the kind of faith we have is proven only by our actions, by our fruits. Immediately after this reading in Luke, Jesus asks: "Why do you call me 'Lord, Lord,' but not do what I command? [Anyone] who comes to me, listens to my words, and acts on them" (Luke 6:46–47). That is, Jesus insists that those who call upon him as Lord must demonstrate the reality of their relationship to him by their actions. In Chapter 8, Jesus makes the same point twice more; he reminds us that our whole relationship to him demands that we hear the word of God and act on it (cf. above). Without acting upon God's word, our faith is phony. Jesus' argument here is quite straightforward. Goodness or evil comes from the heart; a good Christian is one who takes Jesus' words to heart and deliberately tries to live them. Faith in God is not just intellectual assent, not just calling out, "Lord, Lord"; rather faith is only real when it becomes the motivation for our acting and living. Faith is a commitment to God as the Lord of our lives; it is a relationship to Jesus as the love of our life. Jesus' call to faith involves an all-encompassing commitment: "If anyone wishes to come after me [and be my disciple], he must deny himself and take up his cross daily and follow me" (Luke 9:23). Theologians paraphrase this by referring to a common saying in Jesus' time, used by political and religious leaders: If you want to be my disciple, then you must have the courage to die for a particular cause.[9] Jesus' challenge, then, to each of his followers is to be willing to die for his cause or more commonly to offer his whole life for Jesus and his way. The call of Jesus is no minimal invitation but a total dedication to his cause.

IV. Jesus' parables about good and bad trees today, offer a strong response to the American practical mind. That is, our Christian faith is not a faith in a distant god that has nothing to do with human living. It is not merely an intellectual faith that lets us be free to live independent lives. Rather, Jesus wants us to prove our faith by the fruit of our lives; he tells us we can only be Christians if we hear the word of God and act on it. The faith Jesus wants us to strive for is that which grows constantly in his values, attitudes, and commitments, to make him the most important person in our lives, the center of our lives. Lest we think this is impossible, let us remember that our God is most compassionate and loving. He forgives all our sins and failures; he is patient with our stumbling and muddling through. He does not expect us to be perfect, but only that we never give up on this goal. His call is profound but most forgiving.

---

9. Edward Schillebeeckx, *God Among Us; The Gospel Proclaimed* (New York: Crossroad, 1987), pp. 202–203; see footnote on p. 59.

Ninth Sunday in Ordinary Time

Year A

Deuteronomy 11:18, 26–28; Romans 3:21–25, 28;
Matthew 7:21–27

Understanding Scripture

I. Martin Luther was inspired by our passage from Romans today:
". . . a person is justified by faith apart from works of the law . . . ."
He concluded from this passage that we are saved by faith alone
and not by good works. This became one of the foundation stones of
the Lutheran Church. I would like to use this passage in Paul today
to help us understand both the teaching about justification by faith
and how to interpret all of Scripture. My intention is not to criticize
Luther's approach, but to help all of us interpret Scripture. The
primary point I wish to make is this: the number one fault of those
who misunderstand or misuse Scripture is having a selective view of
Scripture. From the time of the early Church until today, most of the
heresies, splinter sects, and bizarre teachings outside our Catholic
Church or within it have come from concentrating on one or two
passages of Scripture and ignoring others that qualify or restrict that
meaning. We can make Scripture say almost anything, if we concentrate on one passage and ignore related passages.

II. Take, for example, Paul's profound statement today: ". . . a
person is justified by faith apart from works of the law." In the context
Paul asserts that the works of the Mosaic Law are not the source of sal-
vation but only faith in Jesus Christ. His constant point is that Jewish
Christians are no longer bound by the 613 Mosaic laws of the Old
Testament. He insists that though "all have sinned. . . . They are jus-
tified freely by [God's] grace through the redemption in Christ Jesus."
He means that our beginning of salvation, our original justification

[in baptism] comes from God alone; we do not achieve our own justification, but receive it as an unmerited gift of God. Our good works do not strictly merit the grace of salvation. Our faith is the root of all justification, for by our faith we appropriate God's saving grace.

But scripture also contains the Letter of James, who asserts: "[A] person is justified by works and not by faith alone" (James 2:24). In the context, James is arguing that mere intellectual faith is of no value to anyone, it is dead if it is not active in our living. His comparison helps: "[J]ust as a body without a spirit is dead, so also faith without works is dead" (James 2:26). My point is: there is no contradiction between Paul and James, rather they complement one another. Paul insists we are justified by the grace of God and we receive that grace by faith not by our own achievement. Paul never denies the value of good works for ultimate salvation; he only insists that keeping the Mosaic Law does not strictly merit justification. James, on the other hand, insisted that mere intellectual faith is of no value to salvation, but only real faith that is evidenced by good works. Also, Paul was focusing on our *first acceptance* of Christ and his justification, while James was speaking about *living out our faith* as a lifetime commitment to Christ. Both emphases are true and critical. To emphasize one and ignore the other is not to understand Scripture.

Happily, today both Catholics and Lutherans affirm all that we just described in Paul and in James. In October, 1999, at Augsburg, Germany, representatives of both the Lutheran and Catholic Churches signed a joint declaration on the doctrine of justification; it read in part: "Together we confess: by grace alone in faith in Christ's saving work and not because of any merit on our part [we are justified]." This agreement means a new day has dawned in Lutheran-Catholic relationships, for the central Lutheran teaching of justification by faith alone is now accepted by the Catholic Church. Both churches reached this milestone of agreement because they no longer focused only on one passage of Scripture, but were willing to accept the real meaning of both Paul and James and see how they complemented each other.

III. Now add Jesus' words in today's Gospel: "Not everyone who says to me, 'Lord, Lord,' will enter the kingdom of heaven, but only the one who does the will of my Father in heaven." He means that superficial faith in Jesus is not enough for salvation, but doing "the will of my Father in heaven" is also required. Jesus adds two comparisons about houses built on rock or sand. Again his point is that faith is more than hearing Jesus' word; it requires acting according to one's faith.

IV. This teaching about justification by faith in Paul is so complex; only after 400 years did the Catholic Church and the Lutheran Church come to agree that both faith and living out that faith are necessary for salvation. But they could only come to this stunning agreement by comparing the passages in Paul and in James. As difficult as this example is, it teaches us not to concentrate on only one passage of Scripture and ignore other similar passages. Such a narrow view so often leads to a false teaching, as the history of Christianity teaches endlessly. Our faith is completely founded in Scripture, but we have to look at God's word with both eyes, not just one!

Year B

Deuteronomy 5:12–15; 2 Corinthians 4:6–11; Mark 2:23—3:6

Sunday, the Lord's Day

I. Joey was only six years old; he was visiting his grandma. Since it was Sunday, his grandma took him to church. After the service, she showed him around the church. Joey was very taken with a large plaque hanging on the wall that had many names set in polished brass. "Who are these people?" asked Joey. "They are all the people who served their country," answered grandma; "They died in service. So we honor them." Joey was very silent and thoughtful. Then he asked, "Did they die during the nine o'clock service or the ten-thirty service?"

II. The First and Third Readings today are about keeping holy the Sabbath day. The first reading is part of the actual giving of the Ten Commandments in the Old Testament. It gives the reason for the third commandment, the Sabbath observance. Here, the motive for keeping the Sabbath is humanitarian; that is, the Israelites were to remember their years of slavery in Egypt in the past, and to be concerned with the well being of slaves and their own households by providing one day of rest each week.

The Gospel reading from Mark consists of two conflict stories regarding the Sabbath observance. Jesus responds here to the Pharisees' legalism that overloads the Sabbath observance with rigid norms. In the first instance, Jesus' disciples are stripping grain on the Sabbath to satisfy their hunger. Jesus' defense is taken from a biblical precedent: the high priest rightly gave the sacred bread to David's hungry soldiers. Similarly, Jesus' disciples are exempted from the law on the basis of human need and hunger. In the second instance, Jesus heals a man on the Sabbath. His defense is similar; that is, an act of mercy takes precedence over the law. In both instances, Jesus implicitly rejects the notion that religion is centered on law, for then the real meaning of faith would be lost.

III. What do these readings say to us about keeping the Lord's day holy in terms of work and worship on Sunday? Today, our problem is not so much extreme legalism but rather laxity in observing Sunday. For us, it's not a question of observing Sunday too exactly but of not observing it at all. Nevertheless, let me try to apply the same norm of Jesus to our day. First, regarding Sunday rest from work. Notice that our law still includes the notion of not doing servile work, the work traditionally done by slaves or servants. Many of our questions regarding work on Sunday can be answered by considering real human needs or acts of mercy. As long as we are acting from necessity or real human need, we are acting morally.

Second, regarding worshipping God on Sunday. The new Canon Law (promulgated in 1983) still says we are "bound to participate in the mass" on Sunday. Here again, we can use Jesus' norm of human need—in this case, our very real need to constantly feed and strengthen our faith. For us there is simply no greater need than to maintain our faith in Christ and increase our love for him. And regular mass and Eucharist is the essential means of doing that, as Jesus himself assures us: "Whoever eats my flesh and drinks my blood remains in me and I in him [her]" (John 6:56). Jesus wants to be the center of our lives, the model for our living. He can only be that if we relate to him regularly in the mass and Eucharist. That is how we personally make "the Son of Man . . . lord . . . of the Sabbath."

Year C

1 Kings 8:41–43; Galatians 1:1–2, 6–10; Luke 7:1–10

Acceptance of All People, Not All Beliefs

I. All three readings today are remarkable in that they teach acceptance of all people. This is more remarkable, the more we realize the source of these three references; for all of them are spoken by religious Jews, God's chosen people, about Gentiles, who often epitomize the alien, the foreigner, the unbeliever. Thus, we have Solomon praying: "To the foreigner [who prays to you, Lord,] . . . listen from your heavenly dwelling . . . that all the peoples of the earth may know your name . . . ." In the Gospel, the Jewish elders ask Jesus to help the centurion, a non-Jew, "for he loves our nation and he built the synagogue for us." And Jesus responded most positively to the centurion, even though his essential mission during his lifetime was only to the Jews.

The Second Reading also implies acceptance of the Gentiles, though Paul explicitly makes a different point. Paul is shocked: "I am amazed that you are so quickly forsaking [God] . . . for a different Gospel." Then Paul asserts twice—and such repetition is unique in all of Paul's writings: ". . . if anyone preaches to you a Gospel other than the one that you received, let that one be accursed," condemned by God. The false teaching he is concerned with here is that Gentiles must follow the whole Jewish law in order to be saved. He insists that we are all saved by the grace of Christ and the mercy of God, not by the works of the law. He concludes: accept Gentile believers, but be absolutely intolerant of any teaching that asserts our salvation results from keeping the law.

II. Together, these readings offer some guidelines regarding other groups within Christ's church and outside his church. The guidelines come from Jesus, our only Savior and Lord, and from Paul, the passionate Jew who became the Apostle to the Gentiles. Jesus understood his ministry as essentially directed to the Jews—only after his Resurrection, does he show a determined effort to reach all peoples. Yet even in his public life—especially in Luke's

Gospel—Jesus occasionally reaches out to people of all beliefs. And Paul, though famous for his dramatic move to preach the Gospel to the non-Jewish world, in today's reading he is most insistent on believing all the essential teachings of Christ. Still, in his Letters to the Corinthians (especially 1 Corinthians 7–11) he clearly admits that other views than his are acceptable and agrees that some of his views are less than absolute in matters that do not clearly come from Christ.

III. What does all of this imply for us in the Catholic Church today? Let me suggest three guidelines. First, we Christians are asked, as much as possible, to have a positive attitude toward all different groups of Catholics. Today there are a multitude of different cultures and outlooks in our one Catholic Church. Even recent popes have admitted that we are bound to have pluralism in our theology. There is more room than ever for great diversity. Second, the group of defined doctrines must be accepted by all Catholics, no matter which way they lean. But that number of defined doctrines is limited in number. Third, whatever the beliefs of others—inside or outside our church—we must love them all in the spirit of Christ. We cannot accept all beliefs, but as Christians, we must accept all people.

Tenth Sunday in Ordinary Time

Year A

Hosea 6:3–6; Romans 4:18–25; Matthew 9:9–13

It Is Love That I Desire, Not Sacrifice

I. "[I]t is love that I desire, not sacrifice." In today's Gospel, Jesus quotes these words of Hosea. The real life story of Hosea is stunning! Let me describe his life situation. Many of the Israelites of his time were idolatrous, worshipping false gods. And the rituals they used for worship were based on the fertility rites, involving sexual intercourse. So Hosea uses his own marriage to Gomer as a parallel example in his preaching. Hosea believed he was following God's will by marrying Gomer who had been a prostitute. After a few years of marriage to Hosea, Gomer tired of him and reverted to her promiscuous ways. Hosea was hurt and angry, so he threatened her. Gomer then left Hosea and their children and separated from them. After some time, Gomer came to her senses and realized that she foolishly rejected a good and faithful man. Hosea still loved her, but he was only willing to take her back if she promised to be faithful to him alone.

Now in preaching to his people Hosea drew an obvious parallel to his own marriage. The Israelites had been like a prostitute in worshipping other gods with their fertility rites. He tells them that if they wish to avoid their fall and decline as a people, they must come back to their God; God will accept them back if they will promise to be faithful to God alone. Hosea prophesies in the name of God, "[I]t is love that I desire, not sacrifice, / and knowledge of God rather than holocausts." He meant that their hypocritical sacrifices to other gods must be replaced by real worship and love of God alone. And that required real knowledge of God and faithfulness to him alone in all their living.

II. In the Gospel, Jesus refers to these very words of Hosea, the prophet. Jesus is forced to defend himself against the Pharisees for eating with Gentiles and sinners. He asserts: ". . . learn the meaning of the words, 'I desire mercy, not sacrifice.'" That is, what is primary with God is love and repentance of sinners, not empty formalities regarding food customs and cult. Then he concludes: "I did not come to call the righteous but sinners." That is, Jesus did not come to call the self-righteous people, like the Pharisees, but rather sinners who are willing to repent; he comes to save those who know their dependence on God's mercy.

III. There are two modern problems that are appropriate applications of these Scripture quotations. The first problem might be expressed this way: "Why should I bother to worship regularly, to go to Sunday mass regularly? What God really wants is 'mercy not sacrifice.' The only important thing is that I live my life decently." Let me try first to give a very human answer. No human commitment or friendship can continue strong over a long period of time without some regular external expression of that friendship. If two friends no longer do anything together, never see each other, never write or call, then that friendship fades away. It becomes dormant and, if never renewed again, dies out. Isn't that true of the friendships you had in your own life? So many friendships you had long ago have disappeared in your life, because you gave up all contact. So also with our faith and friendship with Jesus. If we never express that faith externally and publicly, our faith slowly fades away, our whole relationship with Jesus lies dormant. And the one regular external contact we have with Jesus is Sunday mass and Eucharist. The most important thing Jesus requires is love and friendship with him, not empty words or phony ritual acts. "[I]t is *love* that I desire, not sacrifice" (emphasis added). Mass and Eucharist is our way of maintaining our love and friendship with Jesus.

IV. The other modern problem is the other extreme. It might be expressed this way: "Religion is mainly worship. As long as I have faith and continue to go to mass regularly, I am a good Catholic. But I have to live my own life. Religion has no place in business, in politics, in the bedroom." The words of Hosea the prophet are a strong response: "[I]t is love I desire, not sacrifice, / and *knowledge* of God rather than holocausts" (emphasis added). The knowledge of God that is found in Scripture requires love of God and faithfulness to him in all our living. Our knowledge of God, our religious commitment to God cannot be phony or hypocritical; it must be real; it must involve a life in Christ. Jesus is our whole knowledge about God and his love is our model for our Christian love. Such a knowledge and love is worlds apart from merely going to mass.

V. "I desire mercy, not sacrifice," are the words of Hosea and of Jesus. They teach us that our sacrifice is only real is we sincerely try to live according to our model, Jesus.

YEAR B

Genesis 3:9–15; 2 Corinthians 4:13—5:1; Mark 3:20–35

WE ARE BROTHERS AND SISTERS OF CHRIST

I. The final scene in today's Gospel is stunning! Jesus asks: "Who are my mother and [my] brothers?" Then instead of pointing to Mary and his family, he indicated those surrounding him and believing in him: "Here are my mother and my brothers." Even for us, this saying, at first hearing, contains a harsh note about Jesus' own family, a kind of rejection of them. But to his actual listeners, his comment was even more shocking, for in their culture, they placed a higher value on family or blood relationship than we do. The real surprise here is that Jesus does not hold blood relationship as primary. Rather, the most important relationship to Jesus consists of doing "the will God." That is, Jesus wants his followers to have the same single-minded dedication to his Father's will as he had.

This same incident is also found in Matthew and Luke; it is supremely important in all three Synoptic Gospels. In each Gospel Jesus tells us that genuine relation to him consists not so much in descent from common ancestry as a voluntary attachment to him involving the acceptance of God's word as the norm of one's life: "[T]hose who hear the word of God and act on it" (Luke 8:21).

It is difficult for us to realize how radical this teaching of Jesus is. He means that for all of us Christians, the primary relationship he recognizes is not through blood or other earthly connections but through hearing and acting upon the word of God. He wants us to know that this relationship is powerful and spiritual so that we are even more intimately united with Jesus than we would be by a purely physical relationship. In the Synoptic Gospels, this is the primary foundation for our intimacy with Jesus throughout our Christian lives: we who keep God's word are brothers and sisters of Christ.

II. Let me tell you, then, what this teaching of Jesus means to me today. The more I study Scripture, the more I am convinced that Jesus' preference is not for the rich, the famous, the successful, the people of status. No, Jesus esteems highly the common, dedicated people—those who are usually unnoticed, who know their dependence on God, who struggle to follow the way of Christ, despite their faults. Also, as I grow older, I recognize such people as true Christians. They are not usually outstanding in the world, they are not much publicly acclaimed, not especially renowned, not super-achievers. But they are "blessed" in the critical way that Jesus esteems people: "[They] hear the word of God and act on it" (Luke 8:21). They excel in this central quality of Jesus himself and so are real disciples of Jesus, following his example.

III. All of this relates to so many of you here today. You make no claim to be perfect Christians; you are not, generally, people of status. But you are true Christians, for year after year you continue to struggle to "hear the word of God and act on it." That means that Jesus claims you as his brothers or sisters; he wants to relate to you with tender care and love. What he says is easy to understand, but you and I have to take him at his word. As long as we struggle to do the will of God in our lives, he loves us intimately, more than a brother or sister!

Year C

1 Kings 17:17–24; Galatians 1:11–19; Luke 7:11–17

Women in the Church

I. Two nuns were driving down a country road in a sparsely populated area. As luck would have it, they ran out of gas. There wasn't much traffic, so they decided to walk in search of a gas station. About a mile down the road they found a gas station and an old pump but no attendant. They were desperate, so they looked around for something to carry some gas in. Out in the back was the only container they could find—a bedpan. So they filled the bedpan with gas and carried it back to their car. As they were carefully pouring the gas from the bedpan into the gas tank, another car drove by. The driver stopped and watched the two nuns pouring something from the bedpan into their gas tank. "Wow!" he said out loud; "that's what I call real faith!"

II. In the First Reading today, Elijah brings back to life the son of a widow and then "gave him to his mother." In the Gospel, Jesus raises to life the son of the widow of Naim and then "gave him to his mother," as Luke reports. Luke uses the identical Greek word as in the Elijah event. Luke is hinting here that Jesus is the new Elijah. Each reading concludes with wonder and faith in the prophet Elijah or in Jesus. These are two of the greatest miracles of the bible—raising someone to life. They are performed for women, for widows, for single parents, for women of faith. I would like to use these readings as an occasion to speak about women of faith, women in the Catholic Church today.

III. Let us begin with a summary of Jesus' attitude. In the Gospels, Jesus shows great solidarity with sinners, the oppressed, the poor, and the outcasts. In fact, he comes to all people, male and female, slave and free, rich and poor. He wanted to build an inclusive community; all those who are left out of society in any way are to be included in his community. In Jesus public life, this is the primary sense in which Jesus is catholic or universal: he is for all people; he accepts no barrier of race, sex, or class. Each person is valuable in his kingdom with no superiority among them.

IV. What does this say today, to us and to the church of Christ. First, is says that our *language* should reflect this attitude of Jesus. Therefore, our language should be inclusive, especially in our liturgies. At a gathering in Rome some time ago, an American priest remarked:

> In the United States we are [becoming] conscious of the importance of avoiding in our liturgical texts all semblance of sexism, racial slurs or anti-Semitic words or phrases . . . . Revising our liturgical texts to free them of exclusive language must not be perceived as giving in to radical groups, but rather as part of the normal development and proper inculturation of our . . . rites.

A few years ago, we received the new translations from Rome, which corrected many of the constant masculine pronouns but needs more work to make it really inclusive.

Second, in recent years, the status of women in the church has improved greatly. Women are now lectors, communion ministers and ministers of care. And girls are now altar servers. Women are slowly more prominent as pastoral ministers, pastoral coordinators, and teachers of theology and scripture. But they are far from equal in many other forms of authority and ministry in the church. Finally, all of us can help the situation by using inclusive language in our own speech, by respecting all women as equals and by being open to positive steps toward equality in our church. All of this is necessary if the church of Christ is to be really inclusive and Catholic. Only then will the church of Christ reflect the attitude of Jesus himself.

Part VI

The Eleventh through Twenty-first Sunday in Ordinary Time

Eleventh Sunday in Ordinary Time

Year A

Exodus 19:2–6a; Romans 5:6–11; Matthew 9:36—10:8

God's Unconditional Love for Us

I. One of my all-time favorite musicals is "Fiddler on the Roof."
At one point in "Fiddler," there is a tender moment between Tevya
and his wife, Golda. Tevya asks his wife of 25 years, "Do you
love me?" Golda responds, "For 25 years I have washed your clothes,
cooked for you, listened to you, consoled you, borne your children.
Do I love you?"

But he kept asking her, "Do you love me?" and she answered
the same way. For Golda, all the events and constant giving in their
life together was proof enough. But Tevya wanted more; he wanted
to know he was loved with affection, for his own person, unconditionally. *Both of them are right!* Real human love must be proven by deeds
and events *and* it must be selfless and unconditional. All human loves
are less than perfect; they fail in one or other aspect. For example,
some loves are merely temporal or changeable; some are marred by
self-interest; most are conditioned on the goodness and response
of the friend. Think about your own life. How many people in your
life love you selflessly and unconditionally—and have proven it?
For most of us, we would mention some of our parents, spouse, other
family members, or very dear friends. Isn't that the limit for most
human beings?

II. In today's reading from Romans, Paul takes up this question of love in terms of God's love for us. At this stage of Scripture,
the answer was still not entirely clear. In the Old Testament, God's
relationship to his people was ambiguous. Thus, God made several
covenants with his people, Israel. The main covenant was with Moses

on Mount Sinai. There, he bound his people to follow his 10 commandments with the understanding that, should they fail to remain
faithful, he would punish them. After that time in the Old Testament,
the Hebrews knew that their God was a gracious God, but there
was always the worry that if they totally disregarded their God, they
could be rejected. Accordingly, they seldom called God, "Father," and
when they did, it was only in the sense of being his elected people,
never as his individual children.

III. In the New Testament, the Scripture writers are still
working through their relationship to God. They saw Jesus referring
to God as Father and teaching them to pray, "Our Father." Slowly
they came to know it in a wonderful, biological sense: that God is
really their Father and cares for them individually as a loving parent.
In today's reading, Paul is struggling with the quality of God's love.
First, he shows that God's love is not just a theological speculation,
a vague conviction that God will keep us from harm. No, for Paul,
God's love has been *proven*; the proof came very concretely in the
event of the cross. For Paul sees Jesus as the whole revelation of who
God is, the best expression of God for us. And Jesus' entire life and
revelation is summed up in his self-giving death. This means that
God's entire being is summed up for us in his self-communicating
love. God proved his love in this wondrous Jesus event, which is the
central event of the history of the world.

Secondly, Paul shows that God's love is unconditional,
gratuitous, for our sakes: ". . . only with difficulty does one die for a
just person. . . . But God proves his love for us in that while we were
still sinners Christ died for us." That is, his love does not demand
goodness on our part; he simply loves us because *God is good*; even our
sinfulness cannot destroy God's love for us, as long as we are alive.
Only after Paul struggled with these ideas could he help us understand God's unconditional love. John followed the same kind of
reasoning in his first letter; he came to the same insight and reached
the grand conclusion of all of scripture and God's revelation: "God
is love. In this way the love of God was revealed to us: God sent his
only Son into the world so that we might have life through him"
(1 John 4:8–9). Scripture gives us no clearer understanding of God's
relationship to us than these insights of Paul and John: we know
certainly that God is love, because he proved his love and because he

loves us gratuitously and unconditionally. In fact, this self-giving death of Jesus is the ultimate purpose of all salvation history and of God's eternal plan to redeem us; it is the proof that God is self-communicating love, that his love is real. So the conclusion of Scripture is that God is love because he loved us unconditionally and proved that love in Jesus, our Savior.

Year B

Ezra 17:22–24; 2 Corinthians 5:6–10; Mark 4:26–34

The Future of the Church

I. Several sociological studies in the last 20 years have taken a hard look at the future of the Church. The common conclusion is that there is a personnel crisis looming on the horizon for the Catholic Church.

They predict a constant decrease in the number of priests and an even worse decline for nuns. But when they surveyed the laity in the parishes, they found some surprising results. That is, Catholics still believed strongly in priest leadership and would support it even if it were changed from the exclusively male and celibate form. But they believed even stronger in the importance of local Christian communities, so that they could envision parish life continuing even without a resident priest. They seemed to welcome the challenge for greater lay involvement and for training lay ministers. The single greatest consensus found in one study was the self-confidence parish communities have in themselves and their community. This strong faith of the people of God bodes well for the Church of the future, even though there will be numerous changes and transformations of religious life and parish life.

II. Today's Gospel has two simple parables of Jesus. The first is the parable of the seed growing secretly or, more accurately, the parable of the patient farmer. The farmer plants the seed and then he just goes about his daily activity without anxious thoughts or active steps for the growth of the crops. Yet the harvest comes quite naturally, without his special efforts. So it is with the kingdom of God, says Jesus. The seed, that is the word of God, is planted by Jesus. The seed germinates; it grows irresistibly from an insignificant beginning to a full harvest, quite freely and naturally. At the time Jesus spoke this parable, he may have been intimating that the kingdom of God does not come the way the Zealots would like it to come, by the violent overthrow of the Roman power and the liberation of Israel. He also intended that God's kingdom would not come by means of a political Messiah, a social reformer. It only comes by sowing the seed and waiting for it to grow humanly and freely.

III. Jesus' second parable about the kingdom of God is that of the mustard seed. The mustard see, "the smallest of all the seeds," is planted in the ground. Soon it grows into a shrub large enough to shelter birds. We note that "a tree which shelters the birds" was a common metaphor for a mighty kingdom that protects its people. The meaning is obvious here too: out of most insignificant beginnings, almost invisible to the human eye, God creates his mighty kingdom that embraces all the people of the world. This parable was probably an answer to some who doubted the mission of Jesus. Could this wretched band of apostles and followers be the beginning of God's kingdom? Jesus' answer here is clear: Yes, it is; you can be certain of it.

IV. Theologians insist that our Catholic Church is not identical to the kingdom of God but only a prominent part of God's kingdom. Nevertheless, let us limit our focus to our church alone. It seems obvious today that this Catholic form of the kingdom of God grows by fits and starts; it seems to meander back and forth within the continents of the globe. Consider, for example, the many changes of Vatican II, the falling away of some Catholic populations in Europe, along with the increase in Africa, the lack of priests in North and South America. Why can't the leadership of the Church hold things together more securely, so that the failures and depletions might not happen? Jesus' parables remind us that the seed of God's word germinates irresistibly but quite naturally and freely. God is the patient husbandman—not controlling or forcing the growth. His kingdom is offered to all people of the world; some will follow him freely, others will not. But we can be assured of the final greatness of his kingdom, for it is, finally, God's kingdom; it will come.

Year C

2 Samuel 12:7–10, 13; Galatians 2:16, 19–21; Luke 7:36—8:3

Human Understanding

I. "Nobody understands me," is the common cry for help. The most desperate cry for help and understanding that I experienced in all the years of my priesthood was from a young woman who came to see me years ago. She was not a Catholic but came to the rectory anyway and poured out her story to me for hours at a time. We'll call her Kathy. She had been adopted as a child, and her adoptive parents felt that her real mother was "no good." They held that against Kathy and never really accepted her, no matter how hard she tried to win their love. A few years before, she had married a man who was actually a bigamist and had no respect for her. Her little girl was autistic, wrapped up in her own world and unable to respond in any positive way to her mother. Her friends were either mixed-up emotionally or were on drugs. They confused her and at times just used her. One of them raped her. Over a period of two years, she tried to commit suicide three times. She would call me up—usually late at night; she would be crying, swearing, screaming for hours on the phone. Her frequent complaint was, "Nobody understands me." There was almost nobody she could turn to who could understand her horrendous problems. Sometimes I pointed out that nobody fully understands another person; we don't even fully understand ourselves. Over a period of three to four years, I listened and talked to her for over 400 hours! Toward the end of my appointment, she began by fits and starts to gradually pull herself together. Now, years later, she has come a long way; she lives in California, married to an understanding man.

II. All of us need people to understand us, to listen to us, to accept us. That's why we continually relate so many stories about ourselves to others, and why they are happy to have us listen to them. That's why we seek good listeners or understanding people as friends.

III. Among all the Gospels, the passage that arguably shows best the understanding of Jesus is today's Gospel. Here Jesus shows a great sensitivity and understanding to his host, the Pharisee, and at the same time to the woman who was a sinner. Jesus was a guest in the Pharisee's house, and yet some customs or laws were broken on his account or at least in his presence. The woman should not have been there at all, for she was a notorious sinner; she unbound her hair in the presence of men, which was a disgrace; she made a disturbing scene of weeping and administering to Jesus. Christ recognized all these irregularities for the Pharisee, but he also was sensitive to the woman. He knew her reputation and understood her great sorrow and repentance; he also saw some kind of faith in her and her personal attraction to himself. With great sensitivity to them both, he told a parable about a man who had two debtors, one who owed him a large sum and one who owed him a small amount; he forgave them both the debt. Then he asked the Pharisee, "Which of them will love him more?" Finally he concluded that this woman truly loves much because so much has been forgiven her.[1] What an understanding of human nature and of these two people! Jesus understood the Pharisee's rightful concern and still tried to bring him to acceptance of this woman and the whole situation. And he was certainly sensitive to the woman's whole-hearted repentance and filled her with joy and determination for the future.

IV. Let me draw two conclusions from Jesus' understanding here. First, we can each be confident in going to Jesus with any human problem, knowing that he will understand us and accept us, for he knows and accepts our screwed-up human situation, and only looks for faith—and sorrow, if necessary. Secondly, we can remind ourselves today how much everyone needs understanding and how they sometimes look to us to listen to them and understand. It's nice to know that we follow Jesus, a man of profound sensitivity and understanding.

---

1. The Hebrew language does not distinguish between a purpose clause and a result clause. Simple logic suggests that the woman's love is a response to Jesus' forgiving "her many sins." Also Jesus' next sentence, ". . . the one to whom little is forgiven, loves little" implies that love is the result of the forgiveness.

Twelfth Sunday in Ordinary Time

Year A

Jeremiah 20:10–13; Romans 5:12–15; Matthew 10:26–33

Faith Means Radical Dependence on God

I. My father was a steel worker most of his life. He was a strong, independent man. He worked in a Chicago sweatshop that had a mud floor. During his sixty-fifth year, his arterial sclerosis got so bad he could hardly walk. One week after his sixty-fifth birthday, he had his right leg amputated. A few years later, he was confined to a wheelchair. At that time, I was a post-grad at the seminary, working on my doctorate. On my day off, I would take my dad for a ride in the car. In order to get him in the car, I would lift him out of the wheelchair and carry him down the porch stairs to the car. But he felt insecure being picked-up; so he would grab the arm of the chair or the railing on the porch and hold on tightly. Until I convinced him to let go and to trust me, we couldn't move. He was such an independent, strong-willed person, that he never learned to let go easily. It was always a problem.

II. Today's Second Reading and context is for theologians the most famous and most argued passage in all of Scripture. On this one passage alone is based the entire theology of original sin. That theology is derived by complex theological thinking that does not require an individual, historical Adam. The purpose of the passage is to show the superabundance of the saving act of Christ by means of a parallel between Adam and Christ. The primary theme is this: though the damage wrought by Adam was very great, the salvation wrought by Christ is greater. There are three steps to the parallel: 1) the fault of the one man, Adam, had an influence on all; but the gift of Christ, unearned by us, abounds for all; 2) one offense brought condemnation for all; but the gift of Christ brought acquittal for all, even after many offenses; 3) one offense brought about death's rule over all; Christ's gift is life everlasting for all. Paul summarizes the entire argument this way: "[J]ust as through the disobedience of one person the many were made sinners, so through the obedience of one the many will be made righteous" (Romans 5:19). Adam represents the rejection of dependence on God and his law; Christ represents the radical trust in God's saving grace and his way. Let me add one idea here from the end of today's Gospel: Jesus assures all that faith in him and witness to him will lead to salvation, and refusal to believe in him will lead to destruction (v. 20).

III. What Paul touches here is the fundamental relationship between God and us. What he deals with is the most radical decision for all human beings. What he treats is our essential choice of faith. That is: the *negative* choice rejects dependence on God and asserts: "I am an independent and self-sufficient human being; my decisions, attitudes, values and life are entirely mine to live; I don't need God in my life and don't want him." The other radical choice is that of *faith* which affirms a radical dependence on God; it freely affirms, "I am a creature of God; I am justified only by the grace of God; I hope to be saved by the mercy of God, not by my own works; I am really free to choose my way of life, values, attitudes, but all of my free, human living is part of God's way." This is what faith means. It means we live a truly free, human existence; we are not marionettes on a string, manipulated by God; we live according to our capabilities and our free choices in this real, human world. But we also live with a radical trust in God; that is, we are saved only by the love and mercy of God. We trust in God as the foundation of our existence; we let God be God, giving him glory for life and salvation.

IV. What faith means, finally, can be expressed by the example of my father. None of us is totally independent and self-reliant. We all must let go of our false self-sufficiency and simply trust in God, for he alone carries us by his grace and saves us by his love.

Year B

Job 38:1, 8–11; 2 Corinthians 5:14–17; Mark 4:35–41

The Wind and Sea Obey Him

I. Today's Gospel is a wonderful real-life parable. Just to read it or hear it proclaimed can move each of us in any trouble that confronts us. But the more we study it, the more it can teach us.

II. Start with the event described here. Fishermen, who are used to the sea, are caught up in a storm—a storm so violent that even they are terrified. But Jesus, their leader, is *asleep*! They think that he does not care for them: "[D]o you not care that we are perishing?" He answers them with a reproach: "Why are you terrified? Do you not yet have faith?" After Jesus calms the storm, the disciples are filled with awe at him. Mark wants his readers and us to go beyond such awe to a here-and-now faith in the struggles of life. He is suggesting to us that when the storms of life, the difficulties or worries enter our life, we need to recall that Jesus is with us to calm the storm or to ride it out. He tells us to trust that Jesus will take care of us, no matter what troubles come into our lives.

III. This is certainly a valid understanding of Mark's historical parable. But there is more to Mark's faith and wisdom here. He ends with the question, "Who then is this whom even wind and sea obey?" Mark himself answers this question in his Gospel by gradually revealing his "messianic secret." Thus Mark proclaims that Jesus *is* the Messiah, but he is the Messiah of suffering and death. So we should not imagine that Mark is telling us that in all the storms of life, Jesus will take away the struggle, the danger, the suffering; all of that was actually a part of Jesus' own way of redemption, and they are integral parts of our salvation in Christ. So what Mark assures us in this Gospel, is that Jesus is in the boat with us; we can weather any storm with his help.

IV. Paul teaches something similar in the Second Reading: "[T]he love of Christ impels us, once we have come to the conviction that one died for all . . . so that those who live might . . . live . . . for him who for their sake died." And he goes on to explain that we do not look upon Jesus as a wonder-worker, but rather as the crucified one. He is our Savior by offering himself in love; this great love of Jesus is what impels us to live by his values. For Paul, as for Mark, our salvation is not a glorious salvation, not a cheap salvation; it is salvation that is fully human, carried out amidst the storms of life.

V. Perhaps Pope Pius XI can help us understand this better. One day a bishop was making his regular report to Pius XI and confided all the great troubles he had within his diocese. The pope listened carefully to his troubles; then he pointed to a small picture on his desk. It was a cheap print representing Jesus calming the waves, as in today's Gospel. He went on to explain:

> See this picture. The first day I set foot in this room after being elected pope, I felt weighed down under the heavy responsibilities of this burden placed on me. When I entered this room, there wasn't much in it. I walked over to this desk and found this little picture, left here by chance. This simple picture restored my confidence, for I felt that no matter what the storms or demands on this bark of Peter, I could always be sure that Jesus was with me in the boat. And now every time anxiety or grief disturbs me in my ministry, the sight of this picture makes me again place my trust in God.

For us too, no matter what storms of life surround us, we try to remember that Jesus is in the boat with us, not to calm every storm, but to help us ride it out with him.

YEAR C

Zechariah 12:10–11; 13:1; Galatians 3:26–29; Luke 9:18–24

JESUS IS EQUALLY FOR ALL

I. Today's second reading is one of my favorite passages in all of Scripture. In order to understand Paul here, we need to follow his argument. In the first three chapters of his letter to the Galatians, Paul builds to a crescendo; his whole effort is to show that no one is justified by keeping the law and the prescriptions of the covenant; he even asserts that "We, who are Jews by nature . . . know that a person is not justified by works of the law but through faith in Jesus Christ" (Galatians 2:15–16). His entire argument is that all Christians are one by their baptism in Christ; all are equal by their faith in Christ. So far his argument seems theological and abstract. Then in our reading today, he makes a practical application that is easier to understand; he concludes that faith and baptism in Christ transcend all barriers of nationality, race, social standing, and gender. The Galatians understood his point but must have found it absurd. For the Jews were God's chosen people, whereas the Greeks were considered unbelieving, uncircumcised pagans. Even Greeks who believed in Christ had not been a part of God's chosen race for 1500 years as were the Jews. And social differences were just as overwhelming; most of the Roman Empire consisted of slaves with no rights, no status, and no place in free society. And finally, the Roman Empire was strictly a male-dominated world; women were mere possessions, just a little above slaves. Now, in the face of such realities in their society, Paul dared to say: "There is neither Jew nor Greek, there is neither slave nor free person, there is not male and female; for you are all one in Christ Jesus." Paul knew very well the real differences of nature, history, and culture; he was not indifferent to those real distinctions. But he insisted on the ultimate, all-important fact of their unity in Christ. Nothing could outweigh this essential unity and equality: "[Y]ou . . . have clothed yourself with Christ." He meant that no distinction could be as important as that unity. He doesn't mean that unity destroys distinctions, but that it ties them together and rules them. "Concentrate on this," he urges, "you are all one in Christ; your essential unity is the only important element." This very challenge, in terms of Jews and Gentiles, was the primary struggle of the early church—which almost tore that church apart.

II. And Paul's challenge is a constant task for us 2000 years later—for we constantly distinguish according to race, social status, color, and gender. I cannot honestly say that such distinctions do not lead to prejudice at times for me. I suspect we all need to face this ageless challenge of Paul today in three ways. First, some of us are still basically prejudiced. To have members of another race living in our building, working alongside us, belonging to our club or organization, or worshipping together with us, is still repugnant to us. Second, many of us still are disturbed by certain differences we perceive in other people: "Why do they dress in such a bizarre fashion?" "Why are they always late for things?" "Why can't they be a part of our culture?" "Why don't they raise themselves up by their own bootstraps?" Such attitudes are common in our American society; we find it so difficult to overlook or accept such differences. And finally, almost all of us fail to really know or appreciate other cultures. There are so many distinct cultures even here in our parish: Filipino, Hispanic, African-American, Chinese, Scandinavian, Slavic, Italian, German, Polish, Irish, and many others. They are all strong cultures, rich in tradition. We all have a long way to go to fully appreciate and understand such a variety of peoples.

III. The question comes naturally: "Why should we bother; why should we even try?" The answer is because Jesus came to form an inclusive community. Because all those who are left out of the prevailing culture were included by him in his ministry. Because Jesus is catholic, or universal, he calls all human beings to solidarity with one another across all the barriers of race, gender, and class. Because in Jesus' Church, there can be no superiority, no preference of any kind. As Paul puts it so forcefully today, "you are all children of God in Christ Jesus . . . [so] there is neither Jew nor Greek, there is neither slave nor free person, there is not male and female; for you are all one in Christ Jesus."

Thirteenth Sunday in Ordinary Time

Year A

2 Kings 4:8–11, 14–16a; Romans 6:3–4, 8–11;
Matthew 10:37–42

Become What You Are

I. Several years ago, a best-selling book, Seasons of a Man's Life, was published. It was a groundbreaking and engaging book on human adult development. It was the first to formally document that our adult life develops through a sequence of eras or seasons, unfolding in an orderly progression. That is, as young adults we first take on adult responsibilities with a new life-style; around 30 years of age, we deal with the structure and ambitions of our life; in the late 30's, we settle down and find our niche; in the early 40's, we face mid-life transition and the rest of our life; at 50, we settle into later life and a definite life-style; in the 60's, we deal with older life and loneliness. These same authors admit that these eras of human development are certainly variable in individual lives but seem to be more or less universal and grounded in human nature—in our very biological and psychological make-up. This work is a further development on what so many modern psychologists describe, namely, that becoming fully human means constantly fulfilling what we are; maturity means becoming what we are not yet. It does not mean a finished state but a process of developing more and more through different periods of life.

II. Now in today's Second Reading, Paul gives us a panoramic view of Christian life:

[A]re you unaware that we who were baptized into Christ Jesus were baptized into his death? We were indeed buried with him through baptism

into death, so that, just as Christ was raised from the dead . . . we too
might live in newness of life. . . . Consequently you too must think of
yourselves as [being] dead to sin and living for God in Christ Jesus.

In this short passage and often in his other writings, when Paul
speaks of our dying with Christ, he uses the *past* tense, indicating that
this was accomplished once for all in Baptism; but when he speaks of
our Resurrection with Christ, the verbs are hypothetical and *future*
and depend on our living out that rising with Christ. For example, he
teaches not only that we Christians already possess a new life in
Christ, but we must "live in newness of life"; not only are we each a
new creature, but we must learn to put away the old pagan creature
(cf. 2 Corinthians 5:17–21); not only do we have life in Christ, but we
must continually "put on . . . Christ" (Romans 13:14); not only are
we holy, but we should finish off that holiness (1 Thessalonians 3:13);
not only are we dead with Christ, but also "living for God in Christ
Jesus" (Romans 6:11). In other words, Paul presents endless connections between the ritual of being born in Christ and the living out of
that commitment, between beginnings and development, between
being and becoming. By all these means, he urges us to deepen, to
grow, to progress to that reality, to become ever more what we are.

III. Certainly Paul did not have in mind what is described in
Seasons of a Man's Life or what modern psychologists are describing
about different periods of adult life. But as we learn more about the
regular development of human life, we can better understand what
Paul's teaching implies. For our Christian life includes our whole life;
it is identical with the one real life that we live; in includes all the
stages of human life. And so our development in Christ also develops
through a sequence of seasons or periods of life. In each of these
seasons, we try to deal with those tasks of adult life in a Christian
way. And through all these periods of human and Christian living,
our life in Christ is intended to grow, to progress, and to deepen.
In our Christian life too, we are meant to become forever more what
we are. In fact, all these Sundays after Pentecost encourage us to do
just that, by indicating how we can develop our life in Christ through
the various phases of human living.

YEAR B

Wisdom 1:13–15; 2:23–24; 2 Corinthians 8:7, 9, 13–15; Mark 5:21–43

CHRIST, SIN, AND DEATH

I. I have always been very impressed with the facade of Chicago. Over the years, I have often walked along the lakefront and been taken with the Chicago skyline and especially the downtown area. I am proud of that view; it is one of the finest facades of any city in America and I'm happy to have a framed picture of it in my room. Frequently I have gazed at that downtown skyline and realized that there are more than a million people in those buildings—working and living there. And I mused that it is so easy to be entirely taken up with this great city. Many of the people in those buildings are completely engrossed with this city and their life in it; they are preoccupied with their work; what little free time they have is distracted by the music and noise around them; and even at home they are taken up with the activities of their family or with TV It is so easy for all these people to ignore God entirely. Occasionally however, one fact of life, one human limit keeps bringing them back to God—that is death. And with thoughts of death and the questions it raises, they occasionally glimpse the emptiness of their lives. As Rollo May, the great psychologist, puts it: "The chief problem today is emptiness. [The repression of death] is what makes modern life banal, empty and vapid." That is, because so many people have discarded the old religious assurances about death and life after death, life itself becomes bleak and meaningless.

II. Today's readings deal with death, sin, and immortality. I would like to consider items without reference to Adam and Eve and try to put them together in a modern theological context. The first reading, from Wisdom, tells us:

> God formed [us] to be imperishable;
> the image of his own nature he made [us].
> But by the envy of the devil, death entered the world,
> and they who are in his possession experience it.

That is, human beings were created immortal and in God's image; we were not alienated from God either here or hereafter. Death was even then a biological fact but it was unimportant; for human beings lived in union with God in both lives. The point is simple: because we are in God's image and united to him, we are immortal. But then human beings sinned. And because sin entered the world, we became alienated from God, no longer simply in his image, no longer clearly immortal. Death then became a sign of sin, a seal of our alienation from God. That is, sin alienated us from God and destroyed God's image in us; therefore, we were no longer immortal. The biological fact of death did not change but the significance of it did; it became a sign of sin and alienation.

Then Christ came with his victory over sin and death—as intimated in today's Gospel. Because of Christ, all human beings were again essentially united with God and so immortal. Jesus our Savior restored us to communion with God and to life that cannot be destroyed even by physical death. Paul proclaims this amazing victory in Christ: "Where, O death, is your victory? / Where, O death is your sting . . . ? / Death is swallowed up in victory. . . . / [T]hrough our Lord Jesus Christ" (1 Corinthians 15:55, 54, 57).

III. It is easy to see how modern people can be totally taken up with this great city and surroundings. And if they do that, they surely want to repress death, for thoughts of death lead to God and religion—which might disrupt their life-style. Yet if they repress all this, then their life can become empty and meaningless. But we Christians can accept the whole of reality—including death and all the limits of human life. For the whole of reality includes Christ and his victory over sin and death. Because of Christ we are again in the image of God and so are immortal. We try to live according to the assurance that for us Christians, "Death is swallowed up in victory" (1 Corinthians 15:54).

Year C

1 Kings 19:16b, 19–21; Galatians 5:1, 13–18; Luke 9:51–62

Following Jesus

I. How easy it would be to preach a sermon on this Gospel in the middle ages! For those who wish to follow him, Jesus sets out his requirements: leave your home, give up your past life, cut off former relationships; that is, make a complete break with your past way of life. All of this made sense in the spirituality of the Middle Ages up to Vatican II. Because then devout Christians considered the world to be suspect, in keeping with Saint John's Epistle: "Do not love the world. . . . For all that is in the world [is] sensual lust, enticement for the eyes, and a pretentious life" [Old translation: "the lust of the flesh, the lust of the eyes, and the pride of life."] (1 John 2:15–16). So the ideal thing for a Christian, then, was to take today's Gospel teaching literally, in all its stark simplicity by fleeing the world as much as possible. The development of this theme is found in countless books of the twelfth and thirteenth centuries entitled, *De Contemptu Mundi* [On the Contempt of the World]. In such books, not only excessive love of the world, but all love of pleasure, riches, self was to be avoided. This teaching was the basis of monkish spirituality, which was the normative spirituality of the Middle Ages; it taught simply that poverty was the ideal, possessions a receding from the ideal; celibacy was the better way, marriage was an inferior compromise; obedience helped us rid ourselves of self-will and self-love, while ambition and seeking success were almost certain evils. So if married people, and laity in general, could not follow this way of the three great vows—the way of perfection—then they could only follow a watered-down version of these vows as best they could in their worldly lives. Such spirituality stressed human sinfulness and the evils of the world; it was an eschatological religion, looking toward the other world. The problem with such spirituality was that it was only possible for one percent of Christians; for everyone else, it was an impossible ideal that could only be practiced on the margin of their lives.

It was an effective way of spirituality for that one percent, but it was not very helpful for the other 99 percent of Catholics.

II. Let me try to draw a different view of the world and of Christian spirituality. For the modern Christian, after Vatican II, *the world is to be loved*; in Jesus' words, found in John's Gospel: "God so loved the world that he gave his only Son . . . not . . . to condemn the world, but that the world might be saved through him" (John 3:16–17). That is, God's purpose in the incarnation was to show his love for the world and sinful people, not to condemn it. So it is quite reasonable for a Christian to love this world. Those who have families need possessions, pleasure and worldly achievement; they cannot give up these things totally, nor does Christ ask them to do so. He wants them to enjoy them and use them for others, to meet the needs of family and neighbor—as long as they do not surrender themselves to them. Thus, the best thing for a Christian to do is to love this world; in the words of Pope Paul VI: "We will love our time, our community, our technical skills, our art, our sport, our world." What is pleasing to God then, is for us to grow and become mature human beings after the model of Jesus and to feel responsible for our world, seek to direct it, give meaning to it, work to develop it. So our family, home, job, free time, spiritual activities, sexual life, relationships to others are all essential to holiness and wholeness in Christ. Such a spirituality is *life-affirming*—accepting the reality of our lives. It stresses the need to love sinful people and form this imperfect world in the spirit of Christ. It is an *incarnational* spirituality, concerned with forming this present world. It is not a spirituality on the margin of our existence but at the *center* of our living, involving every moment of it. What Jesus wants of us in following him is the gift of our whole person, not by abandoning the world but by living our entire life in the spirit of Christ, accepting all of life just as it comes to us.

III. In today's Second Reading, Paul gives us a kind of summary of such a modern spirituality:

> [Y]ou were called to freedom, brothers [and sisters]. But do not use this freedom as an opportunity for the flesh; rather, serve one another through love. For the whole law is fulfilled in one statement, namely, "You shall love your neighbor as yourself."

Fourteenth Sunday in Ordinary Time

Year A

Zechariah 9:9–10; Romans 8:9, 11–13; Matthew 11:25–30

Religion Is Essentially an Attitude toward God

I. Religion is essentially an attitude toward God. Our personal faith consists in our attitude before God and our personal relationship to Jesus. For me, there is no better passage in all of Scripture to lead us to a fully Christian attitude than this Gospel today.

II. "Father . . . although you have hidden these things from the wise and the learned you have revealed them to the childlike." "The wise and the learned" here are those who feel comfortable with their own wisdom, satisfied with themselves and their own achievements, content with their own skill and technology. Because of their knowledge and ability, they feel adequate in life; because they limit their focus to practical questions, they can handle them quite well. They usually feel in control of life; as long as life itself does not force them to consider other human needs, deeper realities, ultimate questions, they are self-reliant and independent. Because they do not feel their ultimate inadequacy, they feel no need for God and religion. So God's ultimate wisdom is hidden from them.

The opposite attitude is that of those who feel their need and inadequacy. As children of God, they know their absolute dependence on his grace; they cannot stand on their rights before God their creator; they know they cannot control life; they see all ultimate questions answered in God alone; they know they are nothing before God, for they are saved and blessed only by the mercy of God. This is the *essential attitude* before God; it is simply standing before this truth: that he alone is God, and we are his creatures. In this profound sense, religion is only for the needy, for those who see themselves as children of God, totally dependent on his grace, his mercy, his gratuitous salvation.

III. The rest of this Gospel today is more satisfying and comforting. It is Jesus' personal invitation to relate to him, found only in Matthew's Gospel. Listen to our gentle friend, Jesus, in this passage. "Come to me, all you who labor and are burdened"; there is *no* human situation that is excluded here. Those "who labor" are all who struggle to carry their daily crosses, their many obligations without much respite. Those who "are burdened" include those with great human loss or pain or those with severe handicaps or the elderly and lonely. Jesus does not promise to take away the cross or restore what was lost, but only, "I will give you rest"; he will lead us to gentle acceptance, to personal peace together with him. "Take my yoke upon you"; this yoke is *not* some extraordinary burden added by Jesus; in general it is the same human yoke that all must carry, the same kind of trials as any human person has; it refers to just ordinary human existence, but especially the most burdensome. "[L]earn from me, for I am meek and humble of heart." Jesus here is *not* directly telling us to imitate him; rather he is assuring us of what kind of person he is. To paraphrase Jesus' words: Know that I, who love you, am gentle and kind; I am never harsh and demanding but very understanding and accepting; I am the kind, sensitive and forgiving Jesus. "[Y]ou will find rest for yourselves." The implied comparison here is to the Old Testament wisdom books. Just as the books of wisdom were a source of comfort and peace to God's people, so Jesus' wisdom school will bring refreshment and rest, not by removing the yoke, but by the assurance of his grace, comfort, and love. The physical burdens do not change, but when they are yoked to Jesus, they are bearable. In a word, Jesus wants us to know that all who search for human wisdom and comfort in human living now, can come to him, for in Jesus we find a gentle master, in him we have the entire wisdom of free, peaceful living.

IV. So our Christian faith has a wondrous attitude toward God. We are happy to stand before our God in absolute dependence on his mercy. And no matter what the burden of our life, we bring it to the gentle Jesus to be refreshed by him.

YEAR B

Ezra 2:2–5; 2 Corinthians 12:7–10; Mark 6:1–6

A PROPHET WITHOUT HONOR

I. What an amazing scene in today's Gospel! Jesus is rejected by of his own hometown, Nazareth! They heard him in the synagogue and couldn't accept him or believe him. "Who does he think he is? This is our neighbor; we know him; we are familiar with him and his family. This is too much!" They were quite familiar with Jesus, so they saw him as quite ordinary. What he claimed about himself was not possible; what he asked of them was too much. They could not see the deep-down reality of him. Familiarity was a great obstacle for them. Jesus recognized their lack of faith and could do nothing to overcome it; for they freely chose to reject him. He understood very well that "a prophet is not without honor except in his native place and among his own kin . . . ." Still Jesus was greatly disappointed by them, for they should have been the first to believe and commit their lives to his cause. Mark related this scene for a definite purpose. In the early church, many countrymen, especially Jews, rejected the apostles' message and disdained the apostles themselves. Such a rejection and lack of faith distressed Mark's contemporaries. He reminds them here that the same thing happened to Jesus himself.

II. Jesus is rejected in our time also. There are many obstacles of faith for modern men and women. For example, many Christians have a wrong *concept of God*. They see God as the great manipulator in the sky, the impersonal force they have to placate so that he can make things go well for them. They feel that if they obey God's laws, he should take care of them. And if he doesn't take care of them or sends them suffering, they give up on him and on religion in general.

Our modern theology has a profound cure for such an attitude. It tells us that we are really free—free to build the kind of world we hope for, but also free to fail and to suffer humanly. For God does not play games with our freedom and our human lives. Once God created human beings free, he could not change our freedom into a phony life, one that was entirely manipulated by him.

III. Another modern obstacle to faith is a wrong *concept of the world*. Years ago, many Catholics saw the world as evil, and they were induced into that view by the church itself. If the world was filled with sin and evil, they could only retreat from the world and live a separate, monastic, pious existence as best they could. They felt they had to choose between living in the world on the one hand or renouncing the world to follow Jesus by means of the vows of poverty, chastity and obedience. But our modern spirituality does not reject ordinary human life in the world. The basis of Catholic spirituality today is the conviction that "God so loved the world that he gave his only Son so that everyone who believes in him . . . might have eternal life" (John 3:16). That is, like God, we should love this world of ours, this world of sinful people, and try to build it into a more human, Christian world with all our living. So we accept this world as it exists and labor to make it more Christian. Such a spirituality is a much better melding of our faith and our modern world.

IV. A final obstacle of faith is our modern American way of being *too familiar with Jesus*. Many Catholics today are quick to assert their familiarity with Jesus: "Yeah, I believe in Jesus Christ." But they never understand the deep-down reality of him; they have no idea what he asks of them beyond a superficial faith. They don't hear what faith in him demands. "If anyone wishes to come after me, he must deny himself and take up his cross daily and follow me" (Luke 9:23). For here Jesus invites everyone who believes in him to offer their life for his cause, to commit their whole life to him and his way. Jesus means that he himself becomes our plan of life. He wants us to try ever more to live with his values and his model for living. He wants to be our way, our truth and our life.

V. Like the people of Nazareth in Jesus' time, we are free to choose or not to choose Jesus. But we should be clear about the choice. It is not a choice of knowing *about* Jesus and his teaching. It is a choice of knowing *Jesus* himself, making him the center of our lives, relating to him as our great friend, our constant model.

Year C

Isaiah 66:10–14c; Galatians 6:14–18; Luke 10:1–12, 17–20

Love and Ministry

I. A great movie musical of the past is "Fiddler on the Roof." At one point the leading character, Tevya, asks Golda, his wife of 25 years, "Do you love me?" And Golda responds, "For 25 years I washed your clothes, cooked for you, consoled you, bore your children. Do I love you?!" But he kept asking her again and again, "Do you love me." The affective words, "I love you," were important to him. But an effective love and shared life was proof enough for Golda. Such is human love; at times the words of affection are important; but often we have to do for the other, fulfill certain needs. I suspect Golda's form of love is more necessary for us today, especially for faith and religion. What I mean will be clearer with the help of today's Gospel.

II. In Luke's Gospel, Jesus sends out 70 disciples as his ministers. Here Luke envisions the mission to the nations of the earth—for they do not represent the twelve tribes of Israel but the "seventy" nations of the world. Luke gives no attention to the actual mission of the disciples but concentrates on the nature of their mission; that mission is simply to represent Jesus himself and to overcome the power of evil. That is, they are to announce the reign of God and to help those in need. Jesus' approach to mission here is quite instructive for us in modern America. For modern Americans are generally pragmatic, concerned with this world; they tend to judge things by their effects. Just because Americans are so pragmatic, they need Christians to be practical and real—to be witnesses to that love of God in their lives; to be ministers to one another. As one recent author put it: ". . . the Christian burden in the future will be different from that of the past: less to proclaim Jesus by word than to follow him in deed and loving service." Especially today, actions speak louder than words.

III. That leads to the one point I would like to make today: we are all ministers of Jesus, ministers to one another. To the extent that we minister to human needs of all kinds, to that extent we are ministers of Jesus. For example, the jobs we do each day minister to some human needs; not just jobs that obviously serve others—such as nurse, social worker, doctor—but all jobs minister to human needs. Even jobs like accountants, computer operators, or garbage collectors minister ultimately to people. If only we could get that sense about our work, so that it would be a positive motivating force for us. And similarly with the care we take of our family—which we can easily see as a form of love and service. Or the courtesy, kindness, friendliness, and acceptance toward others all day long are forms of ministry. Or just listening to others' troubles. Or putting up with boring, self-centered people. All of these are everyday forms of serving one another. There is no preaching involved here; there is only human, Christian response. Similarly, we occasionally minister to pain or sorrow, by visiting the sick or going to a wake or helping people in need. All of these are effective ways of caring; all are forms of Christian ministry and following Jesus. The model for such acts— whether we consciously reflect on it or not—is Jesus himself, who came "not . . . to be served but to serve" (Matthew 20:28).

IV. Admittedly, this is a view of Christian ministry that is common and ordinary. This turns the call of discipleship into simple, common activities. That's just the point; we don't have any life but an ordinary one; we don't engage in any activities but common, human ones. We are merely responding to human needs in Christian ways. And occasionally people may realize that our Christian faith and commitment is about living, not about pious practices; it involves our whole lives, not just "holy actions"; it requires effective following of Jesus by doing, not just by preaching. Jesus would say to us today: Just because you effectively try to live your Christian faith, "rejoice because your names are written in heaven."

Fifteenth Sunday in Ordinary Time

Year A

Isaiah 55:10–11; Romans 8:18–23; Matthew 13:1–23

The Word of God Bears Fruit

I. Today's Gospel is the most familiar one of the sower and the seed. We all know the general outline and meaning of the parable, for Scripture itself explains it to us. The seed is the word of God. We receive the word in faith. The seed sewn along the path represents those who hear the word but never come to believe in it; for them, the whole message of Jesus is rejected; their heart is so hard, the seed cannot even begin to take root. The seed sown among the rocks are those who believe for a short time but then give up because of trials; if God does not remove great obstacles or make things easy for them, they won't even listen to him. The seed sown among thorns are those who believe somewhat but then give up because of worldly preoccupations; the young plant of faith is choked out because the primary concern of their life is fulfilling the American dream; they have little room for God in their lives. Finally, the seed that falls on good ground are those who believe the word and live according to the word; they struggle to live their faith and grow in it all life long—with varying degrees of fruitfulness.

II. There may be one thing lacking in our understanding of this allegory, the one thing I want to emphasize today. It is the answer to the question: What is the faith that Jesus is speaking about here? In Scripture, faith is the one means of salvation; it is the only thing necessary—not the works of the law, nor even success or achievement—but only faith. What kind of faith? It is not an intellectual faith that might protest: "Sure, I believe all that stuff, Father; I've been a Catholic all my life." In fact, there is not one New Testament passage in which faith is described simply as an intellectual act. Faith in the New Testament is much more than professing the teaching of Jesus, much more than accepting Jesus' claim as Messiah and Lord, much more than submission to his commandments. Rather, faith is an act which establishes a personal union between us and Jesus; it is a surrender of self; it is a *life*, as Saint Paul puts it: "I live by faith in the Son of God who has loved me and given himself up for me" (Galatians 2:20). It is an attitude, the way we look at the world and everything in it. It is a commitment of love, as the old English word, "be-lief" implies, for "lief" means "love" and "be-lief" means complete love. It is an acceptance of Jesus with the totality of our own person. This is the sense of faith that we learn from Scripture and theology.

III. But what would Jesus tell us about this faith of ours, if he were here before us today? I imagine he might say something like this:

Nothing that you possess means more to you than this faith in me. By this faith alone you relate to me intimately, just as you do to your spouse of members of your family. This relationship to me is meant to grow and become ever more deep all your life long. Everything that happens to you in ordinary human living can be a means of bringing you closer to me in faith. I want you to bring all the joys and sorrows of your life to me; it is this very acceptance of your life, just as it comes to you, that draws us closer together. Let me assure you: no one is more gentle, understanding, patient and forgiving than I am. I ask only that you continue to try, to struggle, to pick yourself up, to come to me in all your failure and success. Then I guarantee your fruitfulness.

IV. In this spirit, listen to God's word in the First Reading today:

[J]ust as from the heavens
the rain and snow come down
And do not return there
till they have watered the earth,
making it fertile and fruitful . . . .
So shall my word be
that goes forth from my mouth;
It shall not return to me void,
but shall do my will,
achieving the end for which I sent it.

As long as we let his word take root in our life, it will bear abundant fruit.

Year B

Amos 7:12–15; Ephesians 1:3–14; Mark 6:7–13

Middle-class Christianity

I. There is a strange phenomenon in America today; it has been growing slowly for the last two decades; it is called middle-class Christianity. This is the sociological evidence. All the mainline Protestant churches are experiencing a disturbing decrease in actual membership; I believe this includes Episcopalians, Presbyterians, Lutherans, Methodist, Baptists, and others. For Catholics, though our membership continues to increase from year to year, the regular attendance at Sunday mass is at an all-time low of twenty-five percent. These statistics are rather constant throughout the entire United States.

II. Some sociologists refer to this phenomenon as a new kind of faith or religion—that of the American practical mind. That is, many modern Americans are happy to believe in a God who leaves them alone, lets them live their own life, lets them free to live without all kinds of demands and restrictions. They believe in God in his heaven but not a God who dominates human life. They have a vague appreciation of the commandments, but otherwise they believe they can handle their lives quite well without magical solutions or interventions from God. Such people tend to be moderately affluent, who can control their own lives economically. They feel generally self-reliant and self-sufficient. They work hard to maintain their lives, and as long as there is no serious disturbance in their lives, they can be rather comfortable and self-assured. With a rare gesture to God on holy days or when they experience tragedy, they can possess their own lives. As long as their family is intact, their home is not threatened and their health is secure, they can manage life without regular need for God.

III. Today's' reading from Ephesians and its context offer
a commentary on this religion of the American practical mind.
The entire reading speaks about five blessings that come to us from
God, all of them brought about by Christ. First, we have been chosen
by God from all eternity, to be holy and completely free from sin.
Second, we are God's adopted sons and daughters, meant to grow in
the likeness of his Son Jesus; such is our model for life and our high
calling. Third, we are redeemed through the blood of Jesus Christ
himself as long as we live out this way of salvation. Fourth, God has
shown us his plan for the entire history of our human race, which is to
reunite all things in Christ; there is no greater goal for the whole
human race that what we are called to in Jesus Christ. Finally, we
have heard the word of God and received his Spirit in baptism,
leading to complete redemption. The point of all this is that these are
the greatest blessings, the most amazing calling, the powerful, eternal
plan of God. Later this same epistle tells us what this plan of God
asks of us: Lay aside your former way of life . . . or you will have no
inheritance in the kingdom of God. Put on a new person created in
God's image. Follow the way of love even as Christ loved you (taken
from chapters 4 and 5). The remaining part of this epistle to the
Ephesians is filled with the goal of living after the way of Christ.
No one can read it and still believe in the superficial Christianity of the
American practical mind. I hasten to add that there is endless room
for failure and forgiveness as we try to follow Jesus. But there is only
one kind of Christian struggle: to make Christ the center of our lives,
to learn more and more how to live as Jesus lived, to live a life worthy
of this amazing love of God for us.

Year C

Deuteronomy 30:10–14; Colossians 1:15–20; Luke 10:25–37

The Good Samaritan

I. Today's Gospel is probably the most significant story told by Jesus,
the master storyteller. It is my favorite parable. Let us try to understand it in the spirit with which Jesus spoke it. The story is told in

answer to the question: "[W]ho is my neighbor?" That is, whom must I love to fulfill the second great command of God?

II. In answer, Jesus speaks of a Jew and a Samaritan. He chose this example deliberately, because there was a deep enmity between Jews and Samaritans; for Samaritans were considered half-breeds, outsiders, not God's chosen people, not to be loved. And yet the Samaritan treated this poor Jew, who had been beaten up by robbers, with great human kindness and care; he went through a lot of trouble to care for his wounds and provide for his continued recovery. His help was not merely negative, that is, by not adding to his harm; but it was active and positive, helping to right the wrong done to him. And all this in a general way was Jesus' point in telling the story: "Go and do likewise."

III. What did this story mean in Christ's own milieu? Jesus taught this revolutionary norm in a world filled with division, cruelty, and hate. To the Jew everyone not circumcised was a "gentile," an unbeliever. To the Greeks everyone not speaking Greek was a "barbarian," an illiterate. To the Romans, every non-Roman was inferior and often a slave. Our modern milieu is not entirely different. For our world is similarly tough and cruel; people of certain nationalities are often described with derogatory terms; certain races are seen as threats and treated with prejudice; injustice and hatred are often defended with a cliche or slogan. In such a world today, if Christians do not try to live these words of Jesus, then evil will continue to be met by evil, hatred met with hatred, violence will arouse violent reaction, injustice will lead to more injustice. Only if we understand this revolutionary example of Jesus, can we escape this vicious cycle; only if we refuse to surrender Jesus' criteria of conduct, can we hope to Christianize this still-cruel world.

IV. One other point in this allegory is important. Remember the two men who passed by, that is, the priest and the levite. Jesus clearly meant that they were *not* good neighbors to the man who was beaten and robbed. But they didn't do anything wrong to the man; they were not the ones who beat him, robbed him, trampled on his rights as a human being. No, they just left him alone. It was not what they did but what they failed to do that was uncharitable. That tells the lie to such claims as: "I didn't hurt my neighbor, so don't blame me"; or, "I didn't force him to live in poverty and misery, so I have no responsibility to help him out." *No*, Christian love must be a positive thing. And this means more than prayer for others. It involves kindness in speech; it involves rooting out our own prejudice; it means treating each person as a respected human being; it means trying to understand one's plight and showing some compassion. It includes helping organizations that work for human rights. It might mean working together, learning together, living together. Some of these actions involve immense, real, practical problems. I don't deny such problems or claim they don't exist. Yet, despite these real difficulties, we must try to work toward their solution. Jesus' teaching is revolutionary; as a people, we Christians have a long way to go to fulfill it. Let us begin today by accepting this counsel of Jesus, our model: "Go and do likewise."

Sixteenth Sunday in Ordinary Time

Year A

Wisdom 12:13, 16–19; Romans 8:26–27; Matthew 13:24–43

The Patience of God with Weeds and Wheat

I. The general theme of today's readings from the book of Wisdom and from Matthew's Gospel is the forbearance of God, his patience, his readiness to forgive. The reading from Wisdom expresses this theme well: "[T]hough you are master of might, you judge with clemency, / and with much lenience you govern us."

II. Let us concentrate on Matthew's Gospel. It is a good example of the different levels of meaning we find in the Gospels. There are three levels of meaning to this parable. The first level is the meaning intended by Jesus himself. Jesus, in speaking this parable, was responding to criticism from the Jewish authorities that he invited the outcasts to eat with him. He answers this criticism with this parable of the weeds and wheat. The point of his parable is that it is for God alone to make the distinction and separation between the weeds and the wheat, and he will do so only at the end, when it will be ultimately clear who are the weeds and who are the wheat. So for Jesus, the weeds and wheat refer to the outcasts and the Jewish authorities. The second level is that intended by Matthew who places this parable here in his Gospel. In this context Matthew also includes the parables of the mustard and the leaven, as we would read in the long form of the Gospel. So Matthew is trying to explain a situation in the early church, at the time of his writing this Gospel; he is concerned about the slow conversion of the Jews and the surprising conversion of the Gentiles. For Matthew, then, the weeds and the wheat refer to non-believing Israel and those who believe in Christ, especially the Gentiles. He points out that the weeds are presently indistinguishable from the wheat, but they will grow together and at the end God will separate them.

III. But the third level of meaning is of most value to us. It is the significance that the Church has generally used regarding this parable. That is, the weeds and the wheat refer to the good and the bad in the Church. We are taught that there is no need to separate the weeds from the wheat in the present life of the church, nor can we accurately distinguish the weeds from the wheat. We do know clearly right from wrong, but we cannot judge a person or his conscience. Only God can make that distinction of persons in the end. Meanwhile, we must imitate God's forbearance and patience and love—all of which are without limit for his people in this life. In other words, we must be slow to point the finger, to judge, to condemn people, even though we know that many of their actions are objectively very wrong. As the Jewish authorities in Jesus' time were often wrong in condemning the "outcasts" and the "irreligious," so also we can easily be wrong in our facile distinctions of good and bad and quick condemnation of the "bad." And today there are so many ways that we condemn others in the Church as weeds. One way we fail is by making quick *judgments* about people without understanding all the circumstances of their life. Not everyone in a second marriage, or who is homosexual, or has AIDS is in a state of grave sin; with great personal struggle, they may be in God's good grace. Only God can finally judge them. And we also fail those who are caught in habitual drug use or sexual scandals. Certainly we must condemn the grave harm they do to themselves and others. But we still must show forbearance for the individual persons and treat them with Christian decency. In general, Christ's parable of the weeds and the wheat cautions us, first, that we cannot always accurately distinguish the weeds from the wheat, and, second, that we must not separate out or destroy the weeds in the present life of the Church.

IV. In summary: thank goodness we have such a God: "[Y]ou judge with clemency, / and with much lenience you govern us." And the very next sentence in the book of Wisdom asks us to follow this example of God: "[Y]ou taught your people by [your own] deeds, / that those who are just must be kind."

Year B

Jeremiah 23:1–6; Ephesians 2:13–18; Mark 6:30–34

Christ Is Our Peace

I. In Greek mythology there is a famous story about Ariadne, the daughter of Minos, king of Crete. Ariadne was in love with Theseus, who was determined to kill the Minotaur, a death-dealing beast. In order to destroy the beast, Theseus had to pursue it into its lair along a labyrinth of underground passages from which no one had ever returned. It was impossible to find a way out of the maze of tunnels. But Ariadne found a way. She tied a spool of thread to the belt of Theseus as he entered the labyrinth. After he had found the Minotaur and slew him, he guided himself back to safety and sunlight by following that thread. Ever since, the expression "the thread of Ariadne" has been applied to any means by which one finds the way out of difficulties and confusion.

II. In today's reading from Ephesians, the word, "peace," appears four times relating to Christ; for example: "[Christ] is our peace, he who made both one and broke down the dividing wall of enmity." The author praises Jesus as the source of two kinds of peace: peace between divergent groups of people, and peace between God and us.

Consider, first, the peace between God and us: Christ reconciled us "with God, in one body, through the cross." In a similar passage, Paul assures us this peace between us and God has been accomplished once and for all: "God . . . has reconciled us to himself through Christ and given us the ministry of reconciliation, namely, God was reconciling the world to himself in Christ" (2 Corinthians 5:18–19). That is, our relation to God, destroyed by original sin and personal sin, is now restored by the redemption of Christ. Because of Jesus, the basic harmony between God and us is permanently restored. We Christians are forever "a holy nation, a people of his own" (1 Peter 2:9). "Making peace" is a synonym for reconciliation or turning hostility into friendship. Because of Jesus' work of reconciliation, we have a constant means of reconciliation, *a permanent source of peace with God.* Any time we destroy that peace by serious sin, we can easily have it restored by the inexhaustible forgiveness of Christ, our peace.

III. Second, consider the peace that Christ achieved between Jews and Gentiles:

> [Y]ou, Gentiles . . . were at that time without Christ, alienated from the community of Israel and . . . . without hope . . . . But now in Christ Jesus, you . . . have become near [to God]. For he is our peace, he who made both one and broke down the dividing wall of enmity . . . that he might create in himself one new person in place of the two, thus establishing peace (Ephesians 2:11–15).

Notice exactly the point of Scripture here. Christians who are either Jews or Gentiles still maintain their historic distinction. But now they are formed into "one new person"; that is, they form one body in Christ though distinct members of that body.

IV. Now what does this peace between Jews and Gentiles mean for us today? What Scripture says here about Jews and Gentiles forming "one new person" in the peace of Christ applies strongly to enmities among any Christian groups; it offers a solid motivation for peace among all Christian groups, whether they are different ethnic groups, or different races, or have different theological outlooks. As long as you or I claim to be Christians, there can be no groups who are foreign to us. The conviction that we all form "one new person" in Christ is our "thread of Ariadne." This might be our only way out of the labyrinth of ancient hostilities, of historic enmities, of theological quagmires.

Here is our "thread of Ariadne:" "[Jesus] is our peace, he who made both [of us] one and broke down the dividing wall of enmity, through his flesh."

Year C

Genesis 18:1–10a; Colossians 1:24–28; Luke 10:38–42

Martha and Mary

I. This short Gospel from Luke offers a lot of thoughts for serious Christians. By way of introduction, notice how women play a prominent part in Luke's Gospel. In this particular narrative, Jesus accepts the invitation to a women's home; Mary adopts the posture of a disciple before the master by sitting at Jesus' feet; Martha takes up the role of so many women in their homes—she dedicates herself to hospitality and prepares the meal.

II. Let us concentrate first on Martha. This passage in Luke follows immediately after the parable of the good Samaritan, who helped the man beaten by robbers (last Sunday's Gospel). Martha is the one here who attends to the needs of others, so we would expect Martha to be praised for her practical service to Jesus. But in fact, she is neither praised nor condemned. Rather she is challenged to consider her priorities; that is, even though loving service to others is at the heart of our Christian life, also essential is our personal love of Jesus.

One other point about Martha. She is an active person, busy with cooking and setting the table. Yet, in the midst of actively serving Jesus, she is cautioned to consider her priorities. In her agitated state, with frustration building for some time because she alone had to prepare everything, she finally confronted Jesus; her mood was very dark. But this seemingly trivial incident became a real moment of grace for her. She worked through the dark moment and made her attachment to Jesus more personal, instead of just active. And, in fact,

Martha has a feast in our liturgical year, while her sister, Mary, does not! This challenging and difficult moment may have led Martha to whole-hearted personal love for Jesus.

III. Now consider Mary, who "sat beside the Lord at his feet listening to him speak." Often in history, Mary and Martha are seen as types for the contemplative and the active life. Those concepts did not exist in Luke's time. But what did exist was Jesus' teaching about hearing the word of God and acting upon it. Twice in Luke's Gospel this example is brought up. You remember the incident:

> [Jesus'] mother and his brothers came to him but were unable to join him because of the crowd. He was told, "Your mother and your brothers are standing outside and they wish to see you." He said to them in reply, "My mother and my brothers are those who hear the word of God and act on it" (Luke 8:19–21; cf. Luke 11:27–28).

This incident is of supreme importance in the synoptic Gospels; it shows us that we can be as close and intimate with Jesus as are his mother and brothers. If we "hear the word of God" and try to live it, then we are brother or sister to Jesus, who is our most loving brother. In the synoptic Gospels, this relationship of brother or sister of Jesus is the primary and wonderful basis for our *intimacy* with Jesus! Now we see better what Jesus means in our Gospel today. Mary "sat beside the Lord at his feet listening to him speak," and that is the "one thing" that is required of any of us disciples of Jesus: besides ministering to others, we need to listen to Jesus, to "hear [his] word," and to draw close to Jesus, our brother.

IV. Most of you women here today, I dare say, are Marthas, because you are so good at caring for your family, helping others, and showing compassion. Generally speaking, you do that so much better than we men do. Jesus challenges you and all of us today to become more intimately his brother or sister as we "hear the word of God and act on it." One way we learn to do that is to come here each Sunday; here we seat ourselves "beside the Lord at his feet listening to him speak"; we hear God's word and pray to Jesus as our loving brother. This reason alone, offers us a strong motive for Sunday mass.

Seventeenth Sunday in Ordinary Time

Year A

1 Kings 3:5, 7–12; Romans 8:28–30; Matthew 13:44–52

He Sells Everything with Joy

I. Charles Colson was a very successful and important man in President Nixon's cabinet. In his words, he had "an office next to the president of the United States, a six figure income, a yacht, a limousine and a chauffeur." But he was also an unhappy man; as he put it, he had a "gnawing hollowness" deep inside him; something was missing from his life, but he didn't know what. Some time in 1973, Colson was at the home of Tom Phillips, the president of a large company. Phillips told Colson about his own life. Though he was hugely successful, he felt something was missing from his life; he was downright unhappy. Then, one night, on a business trip to New York, Phillips had a religious experience that changed him forever: "I saw what was missing [from my life; it was Jesus Christ.] I hadn't ever turned my life over to him." The more Colson listened, the more he became convinced that Phillips had put his finger on what was causing him the "gnawing hollowness" inside him. For the first time in his life he had an insight into what it was. Driving home, he suddenly pulled over to the side of the road and began to cry. In Colson's own words, "I prayed my first real prayer: 'God, I don't know how to find you, but I'm going to try! Somehow I want to give myself to you.'" He concluded by saying over and over, "Take me." That was the beginning of his religious conversion that surprised the White House and the whole country. The so-called hatchet-man of the Nixon administration had a true conversion. For several years he crisscrossed the country, explaining his own conversion to others.

II. Today's Gospel, in the short form, consists of two parables with one and the same message. The first one is about a poor farmer who finds a treasure in a field and joyfully sells everything he owns in order to buy that field. The second one is about a rich merchant who finds a very valuable pearl and sells everything he owns to possess that pearl. This double parable, then, speaks of selling everything a person owns and doing it joyfully. It suggests to us a great, boundless joy that seizes a person, overwhelms him and carries him away—so much so that everything else is of little value in comparison. The decisive element in this double parable is not what he gives up, but the great value of what he obtains. Jesus has only one point to teach us in this parable: that the Kingdom of God can be an overpowering joy, once we realize the gift that is ours. That is, the Good News of Jesus can make every other value small, every sacrifice minor, if only our commitment to Jesus is real.

III. Today we might ask ourselves: what happened to our joy in finding this treasure of Jesus? Perhaps we are just too much taken up with our selves and our troubles. I myself think that my occasional sadness comes from making too much of my self. Or perhaps we are concentrating on the rules, commandments, and responsibilities of our Catholic life and not on the loving Christ. Some of us, I believe, get disgusted with the institutional church; we have gotten the institutional church mixed up with Christ. We need to remember it is Christ himself who is the source of our joy.

On the other hand, in all honesty, many of us might admit that we never really found a treasure; we never had a faith that was more than superficial. We might try Colson's prayer: "God, I don't know how to find you, but I'm going to try." Or we might hear Jesus himself who assures us of the unconditional love of God for us, and the pearl of great price he offers us.

IV. Chesterton claimed, "The secret of a Christian is joy." The more we realize the love of God for us, the more we find the secret of peace and joy.

Year B

Kings 4:42–44; Ephesians 4:1–6; John 6:1–15

That All May Be One

I. Today's reading from the Letter to the Ephesians expresses well the real unity we have as Catholics throughout the world. What we may not realize is that it also expresses the basic unity we already share with other mainline Christian Churches. Seven unities are mentioned here; they are central to our Christian faith; they would cause no discord at an ecumenical gathering of mainline Christians. 1) There is "one body" refers to one external, visible community—the Christian Church; 2) "one Spirit"; this Holy Spirit is the single, inner source of all our spiritual life in Christ; 3) "one hope of [our] call" means that we all have this same hope of eternal life; 4) "one Lord" who is the living center of our faith, the unique Lord and Savior of all the world; 5) "one faith" summarized in our Apostles Creed; by this faith we are saved; 6) "one baptism" by which we have all been plunged into Christ and become his followers; 7) "one God and Father of all" in whom we are forever bonded as equal children of our Father.

II. In the last 30 years, there have been many high-level efforts to increase this basic unity among our mainline Christian churches. In October 1999, representatives of the Lutheran and Catholic Churches met in Augsburg, Germany. They signed a joint declaration of the doctrine of justification: "Together we confess: by grace alone in faith in Christ's saving work and not because of any merit on our part [we are justified]." This agreement means that a new day has dawned in Lutheran-Catholic relationships, because the representatives have been able to work out an agreement on the central Lutheran teaching of "justification by faith alone." Earlier in that same year, Anglican and Catholic leaders issued an agreement on authority in Christ's church. In 2000, there was a "call to common mission" agreement between Episcopalians and Lutherans, which allows both churches to share clergy and worship in some instances. Several agreements among other Christian churches have been made on important theological doctrines that hold great promise for the future of ecumenism and unity.

Also during these years after Vatican II, our Catholic Church has a renewed appreciation of Scripture as the unique norm of faith; Scripture is now clearly primary in our theology, our worship, and our Christian spirituality. There has been an explosion of understanding of Scripture for our church and for the mainline Christian churches.

III. The recent successes of the ecumenical movement should be exciting for all Christians, because such union is in keeping with the intention of Jesus himself: "I pray [Father] . . . that they may all be one . . . that the world may believe that you sent me" (John 17:20–21). That is, if Christianity is to convince the modern world of its truth, meaning, and value, then it must present real unity among its members; it cannot be disjointed and divided, but rather a coherent whole. Only then can Christianity effectively speak to our modern world and present Christ and his Church as fully adequate to the needs, the desires, the experiences, and the hopes of all people today. All of that becomes more attainable not by denying the differences that exist between churches or trying to play them down as insignificant; rather it flows from the conviction that what unites Christians is much more important than what divides us, and that we have no reason for remaining permanently separated, since God and Christ intend us all to be united in him. This hope for further unity is not chimerical or unrealistic. We may be much closer to the intention of Jesus our Savior: "That they may all be one . . . in us" (John 17:21).

YEAR C

Genesis 18:20–32; Colossians 2:12–14; Luke 11:1–13

LORD, TEACH US TO PRAY

I. Today Jesus teaches us how to pray. This may be the best passage in all of Scripture on "how to pray," especially regarding prayer of petition. Let us try to take a fresh look at the master teacher of prayer. Luke begins: "[Jesus] was praying . . . and when he had finished, one of his disciples said to him, 'Lord, teach us to pray.'" That is, the disciples are struck by Jesus' example (especially in Luke's Gospel) of his frequent need to pray.

II. It is worth noting the difference between Luke and Matthew here. In Luke's Our Father, there are only 5 petitions, not 7 as in Matthew. Scholars claim that Luke's form is probably closer to the wording of Jesus himself, for Matthew often adds phrases to Jesus' speech. One other difference: in Matthew, the Our Father is presented as simply one example of Christian prayer; in Luke the Our Father seems to be presented as a *model* prayer for Christians. For in Luke the disciples ask Jesus, "Teach us to pray," and he answers, "When you pray, say . . . ."

III. The first petition begins by addressing God as "Father." In the whole Old Testament, such an intimate form of address is never used by an *individual* in speaking to God. This familiar approach in prayer seems to be original with Jesus. Jesus' whole prayer here is simple and quite familiar, one in which Jesus encourages us to have his own personal attitude toward the Father. His first petition, "hallowed be your name," asks that God himself be vindicated in our world and proclaimed as holy. The second petition, "your kingdom come," asks that God's kingdom on earth be brought to its full realization. As spoken to the apostles, Jesus' first two petitions referred immediately to the work of Jesus and the apostles as a means of vindicating God and realizing his kingdom. In Luke's day and ours, it encourages us all to have a part in furthering God's work. The third petition, "Give us each day our daily bread," refers to material bread or food (not directly to the Eucharist); and it asks for food one day at a time. The fourth petition, "Forgive us our sins for we ourselves forgive everyone in debt to us," does not make our own forgiveness a condition for God's forgiveness; but rather impels us to realize that God's forgiveness cannot be expected if we withhold human forgiveness when we are asked. The final petition, "do not subject us to the final test," hides an Old Testament protological way of thinking; that is, in the Old Testament all things were seen as effected by God—both the good and the bad; God was seen as the cause of everything. In the New Testament, Jesus corrects this early belief and teaches that evil is not sent by God as a punishment for sin; nor does God "subject us to . . . the test" So the sense of this petition is: give us your grace that we may resist all temptation.

IV. Jesus continues his instruction on prayer by urging us to pray with great confidence that God will hear our prayer. His triple way of petition—asking, searching, knocking—encourages us to unwearying prayer. His conclusion sounds like a universal law, so that each of these three petitions always meets with a corresponding response from God. Scripture scholars agree that this *is* a universal promise for God's help as long as we ask properly. That proper attitude of prayer is variously described by them in terms such as these: if it is according to the will of God, if it furthers the kingdom of God, or if it reflects the spirit of Jesus' prayer. These conditions are all similar; they remind us that we can ask God for anything, but we should always add this bottom line to our prayer: if it be the will of God for us.

V. Jesus concludes by comparing our heavenly Father with an earthly parent. He notes that when a child asks his father for food, no human parent would deceive the child by giving him something harmful. He would never be so devious and deceitful as to give his child something that looks like food but is really poisonous or harmful. Most certainly, then, God our Father will only give good gifts to us, his children. As long as we pray in the spirit of Jesus, everything will be for our good. Jesus himself teaches us today: "When you pray, say . . . ."

Eighteenth Sunday in Ordinary Time

Year A

Isaiah 55:1–3; Romans 8:35, 37–39; Matthew 14:13–21

Who Will Separate Us from the Love of Christ?

I. Christianity is filled with signs and symbols. These signs and symbols assure us of God's salvation already accomplished in this world of ours. Throughout the year, we recall these marvelous works of God: creation, his Old Testament covenant, the incarnation of Jesus, his redemption of us from sin and death, his Resurrection and Ascension which complete his work of salvation. This faith of ours is much more than an intellectual acceptance of these signs and symbols; it is more than simply plugging into God's salvation by affirming, "Yes, I believe God did that for us in Christ." If faith is no more than an intellectual assent, then these signs and symbols are merely abstract, ethereal, removed from present human living, unreal in daily life.

II. Saint Paul's theology in the Second Reading today goes far beyond such an abstract Christian faith. For Paul, our whole life is a living out of these mysteries. So for us, Jesus is not just a Savior in history, but someone we personally accept as Savior with living faith; Jesus did not only die for our sins, but we try to die to sin in our own lives and rise with him to new life by committing our lives to him. For Paul, Jesus is the light of the world only if we accept him as our interpretation of life's meaning. He is the way to God for us only if he himself becomes our plan of living by making his attitudes and values our own. He becomes the model for all our living, if we freely choose to try to live his way.

III. Earlier in this Epistle to the Romans, Paul hints that without our personal choice and commitment to God involving all of our life, all kinds of things can cloud over God's love for us or separate us from him. Such things as a constant way of sin, or a continued ignoring God can weaken our faith. Also, a major illness or great suffering can embitter us and turn us away from him, especially if it is not seen as part of our life in Christ.

But everything changes if we maintain our real faith in God's love for us manifested in Jesus. Then, Paul assures us today, we have been freed from sin and death and from all forces imaginable that tend to drag human life down and doom us to frustration and destruction. First, he affirms that none of the dangers or troubles of human life can make us forget the love of Christ for us; we are guaranteed ultimate victory over them all. Second he insists "neither death, nor life"—no cataclysmic power, no fear of death, no human evil can overcome our hope in Christ. Third, even cosmic rulers, powerful spirits and mysterious forces—all of them are under the dominion of God. Fourth, neither the present unstable age nor any future uncertainty or apocalypse can overcome our courage and hope in Christ. Finally, "nor any other creature"—any conceivable alien being, any invisible power—can destroy or disturb the rock-solid power of God's love for us in Christ.

IV. Paul intends his assurance even for us imperfect, sinful and struggling Christians. Let him speak to you personally:

> What will separate us from the love of Christ? Will anguish, or distress, or persecution, or famine, or nakedness, or peril, or the sword . . . ? I am convinced that neither death, nor life . . . nor present things, nor future things . . . nor any other creature will be able to separate us from the love of God in Christ Jesus our Lord.

Such is already the victory of our faith and the power of God's love for us in Christ.

YEAR B

Exodus 16:2–4, 12–15; Ephesians 4:17, 20–24; John 6:24–35

JESUS, OUR HUMAN MODEL

I. In the New Testament, there are 13 epistles connected to Paul; they make up the Pauline corpus. Seven of these are recognized as authored by Paul; the other six are only probably his or merely written in the style of Paul. This Pauline corpus contains many remarks similar to the one in today's Second Reading: "[P]ut on the new self, created in God's way" (Old translation: "Put on the new man, created in God's image"). There are many references to the new life we have as Christians; we are often encouraged to walk in newness of life; 165 times he tells us we are "in Christ." Often this central idea of Paul is explained by theologians as referring to sanctifying grace as the essence of that new life in Christ. And many of us get the idea that grace is a thing, a new entity added to our human nature. Or our new life in Christ is explained by referring to the commandments and to avoiding sin. We can easily conclude that our new life only requires us to avoid sin and live according to God's law. Neither of these explanations is false, but in recent years I have found a better way of explaining our life in Christ.

II. What distinguishes us Christians from the disciples of all other religious leaders is that we follow a person, not a teaching. For us, Jesus himself is "the way . . . and the life." For us, his very person is the living embodiment of his cause, the model for our view of life and way of living. What I mean is that the person of Jesus is inseparably united with his teaching as our way of living. Yet as a human model, he does not command us, force us or demand our obedience. Rather, he draws us, calls us, encourages us to live as he lived. His influence on us is not a force of commandments or the pressure of abstract principles or ideals. Rather, Jesus' influence is the appeal of a person, the power of a lover. Only a living person—not a principle—can call, invite, challenge and summon us. Only a concrete, historical person—not an abstract ideal—can encourage us to attainable human ideals, to realistic norms and values. The human

Jesus himself is the model for our human life. His teaching, his life, his person is the way of human wholeness. Trying to live as Jesus lived is the sum of Christian holiness, the practical summary of the new person we have put on.

III. Let me suggest one way in which Jesus is a model for us and which constitutes our life in Christ as Paul describes it. Jesus is our model by exemplifying norms and values for us. Regarding material pleasures and possessions, Jesus was not an ascetic; he shared the ordinary life of men and women; he took pleasure in friends; he did not demand actual renunciation of material pleasure in order to follow him. Regarding doing the will of God, his life was characterized not by God telling him what to do nor by careful observance of minute laws. Rather he carried out God's will by living out his Father's way of love with kindness, justice, and compassion; he carried it out by accepting his human condition with the exacting requirements of love. Regarding suffering, he did not deal with it by denying it or doing away with it; he did not offer a chimerical life but only a human life, filled with the normal pains of human existence.

IV. This is what Paul means when he urges us: "[P]ut on the new self, created in God's way." He means that Jesus our model does not force us to follow him; he only calls, invites and challenges us with his loving example: "[L]ove one another as I love you" (Jo. 15, 12).

Year C

Ecclesiastes 1:2; 2:21–23; Colossians 3:1–5, 9–11; Luke 12:13–21

Vanity of Vanities

I. One Summer, years ago, I studied over in Austria. Many times during that Summer I talked to Europeans who had been to America. Among those who had visited our country, the frequent comment was, "The pace of life in America is so hectic. Americans seem to be filled with anxiety, always rushing around." And since I was then experiencing their relatively slower and calmer pace, I had to agree with them.

II. The pace of life in America *is hectic*. And we have many reasons for this hectic pace. First, our society is very *mobile*; we are always traveling from place to place; almost one-quarter of us change our place of residence each year. Our suburban living is complex— standing in lines, filling our forms, following town requirements, dealing with organizations and agencies, delivering children from place to place. Our society is *technological* and pragmatic. Life is a set of problems to be solved and worked out; we are oriented to getting things done quickly, accomplishing many chores within one day. Our society is *noisy* and distracting. We have radio or music on everywhere—at work, in the stores, even in elevators; we are sur- rounded by cell phones and ipods. Our society is *affluent*. We consider more and more possessions now as necessities; so many material things that other societies consider luxuries, for our children and us are things we must have. Finally, our society is *competitive* and demanding. If we want so many things for our homes and our fami- lies, then we have to work long hours and struggle to be more success- ful; and if we are married, then both of us must work. These are some of the things that make American life hectic. In such a milieu, it is so easy for us to be caught up with the problems, the activity, the competition, the demands of work and family; consequently, we have no time, desire or inclination to ask other questions of life. Many Americans generally avoid reflecting on the sense of it all.

III. Today's First Reading is a classic reflection on life and can be a valuable comment on modern American life. Ecclesiastes is actually a ruthless exposure of what human life is, *apart* from God. It is not a religious reflection on life at all, but a materialistic critique of life. It is not so much Good News but the bad news that has to be heard before the Good News becomes audible, before we can really be open and receptive of the Good News.

[V]anity of vanities! All things are vanity! . . . (1:2b)

For what profit comes to a man from all the toil and anxiety of heart with which he has labored under the sun? . . . even at night his mind is not at rest. This also is vanity! (2:22–23)

In the rest of this book, Ecclesiastes considers all the other human concerns: family, children, love, riches, long life, friendship, learning and achievements. And his conclusion is that all of life is ultimately futile and meaningless, if viewed in itself; it does not carry sufficient weight and meaning for the human person.

Then in the Gospel, Jesus' parable tells of the rich fool who lived his life without reference to God and was caught in the toils of futility and meaninglessness. He organized his life without reference to the transcendent, as an autonomous existence. So comes the crushing judgment of God: "You fool! This night your life will be demanded of you." "Vanity of vanities."

IV. The Second Reading ties all this together for us. The author urges us to "seek what is above"; he reminds us of the transcendent quality of living. This transcendence is not an escape from this world of ours, a copping out on our American existence. Rather, it is a living out of all this existence as also related to God. Our relation to God is not only a religious relationship to the highest, most wondrous being imaginable but is the comfortable existence of one who is loved by God unconditionally as a precious child. It is not a relationship added to our hectic life, on the margin of our existence, but a relationship that is central to our lives and involves all of this hectic life. It is meant to be the heart of this whole life, the unifying element that leads to peace and meaning and hope. "[Y]our life [even this hectic American life] is hidden with Christ in God. When Christ your life appears, then you too will appear with him in glory."

Nineteenth Sunday in Ordinary Time

Year A

2 Kings 19:9a, 11–13a; Romans 9:1–5; Matthew 14:22–33

Tell Me to Come to You

I. Dr. Thomas Holmes, several years ago, did a very significant study on change in our human lives. He studied common changes in certain people's lives, such as marriage, death of a family member, birth of a child, loss of a job, serious illness, change of home, divorce, and so on. After carefully studying change in the lives of hundreds of people, he concluded: "Any great change, even a pleasant change, produces stress in a person." And he verified that a large amount of stress within one year is very trying for the human psyche. In fact, eighty percent of those who had experienced great changes within a single year suffered pathological depression or heart attacks or serious ailments.

II. Today's Gospel is an account of a vivid and engaging event. The apostles are in a boat on the Sea of Galilee in the midst of a fierce storm. In their struggles, Jesus comes to them, walking on the water. Peter, in his enthusiasm, gets out of the boat and begins to walk toward Jesus. But then he becomes disillusioned and begins to doubt. In his fear, he reaches out to Jesus who "stretched out his hand and caught him." Matthew's intention in relating this event is to offer a paradigm of discipleship. The boat represents the Church; the storm is the persecution through which the early church was passing; the action of Jesus shows his assurance of help and the wisdom of trusting in him.

III. This passage, I believe, is one of the most helpful for us today. The storm refers to so many difficulties and changes in our lives today. Modern life in general is characterized by constant change. Some of the changes we experience are somewhat common to all lives, such as a death in the family, a serious illness, change of work, trouble with children, children leaving home as they grow up, or just the loneliness of old age. Some of the changes are exacerbated by our modern life-style, for example regarding marriage. Some psychologists today question the very possibility of long-term commitments. They report new approaches to relationships and to sexual ethics. Our society makes divorce easy, so that there are many single parent families with all the stresses that result in such situations.

Even in our church, long after Vatican II, we continue to experience many changes. We see dramatic changes in ministry with much greater lay involvement; also a serious lack of priests and sisters; numerous scandals within the Church and priesthood; continual moral problems especially in sexual ethics and genetics. These changes are so disturbing that some doubt or question their religious commitment. Some cry out, "What have they done to our church?" We seem to be rowing hard in a storm and getting nowhere. Like Peter, some of our original enthusiasm has changed to disillusion and fear.

IV. We need to realize in any storm that Jesus is there in the boat with us, to take our hand and restore our trust. However, his help is usually like God's presence in the First Reading; he is not in the violent wind, the earthquake, or the fire; rather he is in the gentle breeze, the whispering sound. His presence, his word, his grace is peaceful, calm, and constant. Whatever our situation, we can reach out and touch, we can trust in his grace and love that never fails us. We reach out and touch his hand when we realize that he never asks the destruction of the human person in any relationship. We reach out and touch, when we are determined to make the great human effort that is sometimes needed. We reach out and hold his hand when we open ourselves to our own difficult life reality. We reach out and hold his hand when we come to terms with the changes in our church. We reach out and hold his hand when we trust his love that never fails us.

V. This Gospel event can be a great source of comfort and courage for us. It does not remove all the problems and changes in our lives magically. But it can lead to a calmness and trust in the midst of great change and difficulty. It does not affect us externally and dramatically but only internally and quietly. But that is the way God's word reaches us now and his love touches us now.

Year B

2 Kings 19:4–8; Ephesians 4:30—5:2; John 6:41–51

I Am the Bread of Life

I. "I am the bread of life," asserts Jesus today. How is he the bread of life for us? He is not referring to the Eucharist here; that is the topic of the following section in John's Gospel that we will read next Sunday. Nor is he referring to physical bread—not like manna in the desert in the Old Testament.

II. The clear background for Jesus' assertion is found in the wisdom books of the Old Testament, where wisdom is said to nourish all who accept it. For example, in the Book of Proverbs, wisdom invites: "Come eat of my food, / and drink of the wine I have mixed" (Proverbs 9:5). In a similar way, Jesus asserts that he is the bread of wisdom and revelation, who nourishes all who come to him in faith. His strong claim here is that he is the bread of life, because he is the best and complete revelation of God to us; he personifies the divine revelation, and his teaching is all the wisdom and nourishment we need for eternal life. And the *way* we consume him is through *faith*. Four times in this passage, Jesus indicates that he is consumed through belief. And every time he speaks of accepting his teaching in faith, he notes the eternal quality of that faith; that is, it leads to Resurrection, life without death, "eternal life." Jesus concludes this part of his discourse with the assurance that the one who accepts him unreservedly in faith "will live forever."

III. What does all this mean practically? Some time ago our Vincent de Paul Society [a group of parishioners] was reading this Gospel at their regular meeting. I asked them how Jesus is bread for them. They answered that he is strength for them in difficult times; he is a source of courage to follow in his way; he helps them grow spiritually throughout their life; he nourishes them with what they need for daily human living. Those are incisive and real answers! Notice the words they used: "strength, growth, nourishment." That's exactly what material food does for us: it gives us strength, helps us grow, nourishes us and keeps us physically healthy. They meant that Jesus is all the spiritual food we need to be spiritually healthy.

IV. Not everyone who heard Jesus then, found in him the "bread of life." Some of his listeners said, "This saying is hard; who can accept it?" (John 6:60) "As a result of this, many [of] his disciples returned to their former way of life and no longer accompanied him" (v. 66). They could not believe in this preacher who promised them food for eternal life. In our day, many are preoccupied with all kinds of human wisdom. Never before, could they plug into most of the wisdom of the world just by going to the Internet; in this communication age, people easily have a full menu that is more than they can consume. Surrounded by all that knowledge, all that food, they feel no hunger for an entirely different kind of food—the food that promises eternal life.

Fortunately, it is not like that for us. We come here to listen to Jesus each week; we believe in him as the bread of life now and for eternity. We know that all the ultimate questions about human life are answered in Jesus our "bread of life." We know that only in Jesus can we find all the wisdom and revelation about our God and Father. We pray to him together with Peter: "Master, to whom shall we go? You have the words of eternal life" (v. 68). Lord, we believe that you alone are the complete wisdom and revelation of God; you alone are the bread of eternal life.

Year C

Wisdom 18:6–9; Hebrews 11:1–2, 8–19; Luke 12:32–48

Faith Is the Realization of What Is Hoped For

I. Langdon Gilkey, the theologian, paints this stark picture of younger Catholics today:

> In the span of [one] generation, the absolute authority of the church regarding truth, law and rules of life has suddenly vanished. Few contemporary younger Catholics recognize inwardly the authority of the *magisterium*

over their thoughts. . . . Few regard the dogmatic statements of the church's
faith as unequivocally binding on their own [faith]. . . . The sense of
historical relativity of all human statements has, for many, undermined
completely the traditional authority of the church . . . over faith and
morals alike. The supernatural authority of the church . . . has disintegrated
in the chill air of modern relativity.

That's quite a mouthful! I understand that some of the background
of this observation can be found in Vatican II. For Vatican II was
a watershed moment in the Church, a turning away from the hierarchical model of the church in which the laity were merely passively
obedient to higher authority. But sadly, one extreme reaction to
such dramatic change was the renunciation of all institutional authority as such. That leaves many Catholics today with an individualistic
faith in which everything is relativistic. Many are inclined to select
and choose what seems individually right for them.

II. Consider today's reading from Hebrews. It begins with
this classic statement about our faith: "Faith is the realization of what
is hoped for and evidence of things not seen." (The old translation is
"Faith is confident assurance concerning what we hope for and conviction about things we do not see.") That is, our faith in Christ is
marked by assurance that the goods promised by God will be fully
possessed in the future and also the conviction that the facts on
which this assurance is based are indeed facts and not an illusion, not
just relative. This is the solid ground of our faith and life in Christ,
so the foundation of our faith is absolute and rock-solid. But it would be
wrong for the teaching church to claim that *everything* in our church
is dogmatic or absolutely certain. There are many, many teachings and
practices of our faith life that are not dogmatic or absolute.

III. The rest of this reading from Hebrews today is often
referred to as "the role call of the heroes of faith." Yet strictly speaking, the Bible knows no heroes, for heroes are witnesses to their
personal achievements, whereas these great figures of salvation history,
from Abraham through the great prophets of the Hebrew Covenant,
are honored not for their heroism but precisely for their faith, for
taking God at his word and living a faith-filled existence. That is, for
all these actual historical people, faith was the dominant feature of
their life; they lived by faith and hope for the future. And that faith

and hope were only possible because they belonged to a community of faith, the people of Israel. The Letter to the Hebrews knows no great people of faith except those who belong to God's people. Hebrews would completely reject the modern American notion of individualistic or selective faith. It would reject outright the modern suggestion that faith can prosper in individuals without a supportive church; it denies that we are capable of an unmediated and direct relation to God without a church community as the visible manifestation of Christ on earth. Hebrews concludes by encouraging us all: "[S]ince we are surrounded by so great a cloud of witnesses [as these heroes] let us . . . [keep] our eyes fixed on Jesus, the leader and perfecter of faith" (Hebrews 12:1–2). We can only do that as members of God's people, the community of Christians.

Twentieth Sunday in Ordinary Time

Year A

Isaiah 56:1, 6–7; Romans 11:13–15, 29–32; Matthew 15:21–28

Christ Calls All to Salvation

I. The readings today deal with the universal call to salvation. They hint that Christ's church is catholic, that is, universal. The first reading indicates that foreigners, non-Jews may be acceptable to the Lord, as long as they are just and righteous. This reading is one of the few instances in the Old Testament of a qualified universalism. It is one of the exceptions to the general Old Testament norm that salvation is for the Jews, God's chosen people. Today's Gospel goes a little farther. Here we find the only instance in Gospels in which Jesus deals with a Canaanite woman, with that Gentile nationality. To our ears, he seems to be dealing harshly with her. Actually, their dialogue is the kind of wit that was admired in the Near East then—a game of wits that matched riddle with riddle or one wise saying with another. This Canaanite woman seems to win the debate with Jesus—that is a victory no one else achieved in the Gospel. Consequently, Jesus heals her daughter, because of her faith. This is a rare instance in the life of Jesus, for here he departs from his essential mission—to preach salvation to the jews. Then in the Second Reading, Paul goes much farther. He teaches that the Jews' rejection of Christ's teaching has led to "reconciliation of the world," that is, for Gentiles and for all people. In a word, today we hear that God's call to salvation is really universal, for all peoples.

II. We proudly call our Church and ourselves "Catholic." But we seldom reflect on the meaning of that word. We generally think of that word, "Catholic," as referring to a *geographic* universalism; that is, we think of our church as Catholic because it exists all over the world. That's correct, but it's inadequate, and in terms of Jesus' preaching and ministry, it is not even the primary sense of the word. For what Jesus preached was that the kingdom of God is for all people *qualitatively*, that is for sinners and the just, for rich and poor, for slave and free, for Scribes, Pharisees as well as non-observers of the law, for the intelligent and the ignorant, for young and old, for Jews and for Gentiles (though clearly for Gentiles only after his Resurrection). For the first time in history, a religion was started that was not just for the elite, those who were of a particular race, those who followed a rigid way of worship and righteousness, or those who opted out of ordinary life to live a monkish or separate existence. His kingdom was really for all people; it was Catholic.

III. But strangely, we individual Catholics and even our Catholic Church in general have contorted this wondrous quality of universalism. As early as the third century, Saint Cyprian gave us the slogan *Extra ecclesiam, nulla salus* (outside the church, there is no salvation). His dictum has survived to our time. It can be properly understood, but generally it is more misleading than helpful. After Vatican II, it is time for us to bluntly disavow Cyprian's maxim and affirm clearly that outside the church there is plenty of salvation. Our Catholic theology certainly emphasizes the extraordinary value of our Catholic way of salvation. With Jesus and his sacraments, we have numerous helps to salvation that non-Christians do not have. But as long as they live according to their faith in God, they can certainly be saved. God's mercy is really universal. For we will all be judged by the same norm, as we see in Christ's graphic painting of the Last Judgment (see Matthew 25:31–46)—by how we have treated our neighbor.

IV. And we contort the quality of "Catholic" in another way today. In so many ways, our Church tends to be a white church and a masculine church. Often women, Blacks, Hispanics and Orientals are seen as second-class members of this Catholic Church. We as individuals add to this confusion by narrowing our sense of who belongs, according to race, gender and moral code. When our official church does this, it is a grave scandal. When we individuals do this, we are contradicting our own assertion, "I am a Catholic and I am proud of it." For in the church of Christ all people are equal, welcome and called to salvation. This is clearly what Christ's teaching and his own life require of us. We all must learn to be *Catholic*.

Year B

Proverbs 9:1–6; Ephesians 5:15–20; John 6:51–58

Unless You Eat My Flesh, You Do Not Have Life Within

I. "[U]nless you eat the flesh of the Son of Man and drink his blood, you do not have life within you. . . . [T]he one who feeds on me will have life because of me." This is an astounding assertion of Jesus himself today. He clearly connects our life in him and the Eucharist. Let me try to explain it in simple, human terms.

II. We begin with the notion that all human friendship and love demands *presence and signs of affection*. This is most obvious in a child, who comes to his mother to be embraced, kissed, consoled, and loved by her. He constantly needs her actual presence, her personal care and her individual attention to his needs. And married partners need frequent signs of affection and actual presence. If a husband is hardly around because of his work, he puts a great strain on the marriage. If the wife is never kissed anymore, she wonders: Does he still love me? All friends need regular contact and presence. If friends no longer share any of their lives together by doing things together, they can only keep that friendship alive by writing, phoning, or e-mailing. If they do none of these things, their friendship dies or at best is dormant. This is the universal law of human friendship; all friendships demand some presence, some signs of affection.

Now our relationship to Christ is a human friendship; it too demands presence and some signs of affection. We can experience that presence and affection in many ways: private prayer, reading Scripture, sharing with other committed Christians, receiving other sacraments. But the strongest and most constant source of presence and affection for most of us is mass and communion. Most people who do not have regular contact with Jesus in mass and communion, don't have adequate external contact with him in those other ways either. And so time and distance destroy that love and friendship—as they do all human friendships. They may hang on to a minimal faith in Jesus, but they do not maintain real friendship with him. In simple, human terms then, this is what Jesus means in today's Gospel: "[U]nless you eat the flesh of the Son of Man . . . you do not have life within you." He assures us that the Eucharist is the strongest means of our constant unity and friendship with him.

III. Why is this true? How does what Jesus proclaims here happen *humanly*? First, because of the Eucharist, we have an *individual*, personal relationship with Jesus our Lord. It's not enough for us to know that Christ redeemed us all. We need a personal, visible, individual assurance of that love. And this is the genius of our sacraments; they make Jesus' redemption individual for us. The sacraments are the face of redemption turned visibly toward us. Saint Ambrose put this well 1600 years ago: "You have shown yourself to me, Christ, face to face; it is in your sacraments that I meet you." The second human explanation is that in the Eucharist Jesus *shares his life with us* as individuals. We believe that the most critical relationship we share is that he redeemed us by his suffering and dying for us. And it is particularly in mass and communion that we recall this critical part of his life: "The cup of blessing that we bless, is it not a participation in the blood of Christ? The bread that we break, is it not a participation in the body of Christ?" (1 Corinthians 10:16). Thus, the Eucharist is the constant experience of what Jesus has done to make us his friends.

IV. So when Jesus proclaims: "[U]nless you eat the flesh of the Son of Man . . . you do not have life within you," he means that the Eucharist is morally necessary for our life now and in eternity; it is the best source of our friendship with him. This is why we come here week after week to maintain our individual friendship with Jesus. "Whoever eats my flesh and drinks my blood remains in me and I in him [her]."

Year C

Jeremiah 38:4–6, 8–10; Hebrews 12:1–4; Luke 12:49–53

The Way of Faith

I. Today's readings seem low-key, unrelated and even confusing. Despite that, there is a common thread that leads to a central truth about our life of faith. The First Reading reminds us that Jeremiah's prophesying almost led to his death; that is, his proclamation of the word of God brought him rejection and suffering. The Second Reading is from Hebrews; it is really the conclusion of a long list of Old Testament heroes of our faith; it is a roll call of witnesses of the faith who endured against every temptation. All these heroes of the faith lead us to conclude that the Old Testament way of faith includes suffering as a common lot. In our reading today, we are asked to envision these heroes as a host or "cloud" of witnesses standing at the side of the racecourse, cheering us on, so that we will persevere in our race and reach the goal of our faith-life. To help us persevere, we are urged to keep our eyes fixed on Jesus, who is called the "leader" and "perfecter" of this way of faith. He is the leader or pioneer because he initiated this way of living our Christian faith—through suffering to glory. He is the perfecter because he completed the course. In Luke, today, Jesus tells us that his work and life is leading to suffering and death; he speaks of his suffering as a divine destiny. Luke makes this his central theme of redemption: God willed that Jesus should come to glory only through the cross.

II. There is one other reason for such Christian living. Hebrews mentions Jesus' own motivation: "For the sake of the joy that lay before him he endured the cross." That is, Jesus' motivation included this realization: no cross, no crown. This same motivation is found in the beatitudes he taught us: "Blessed are the poor in spirit, / for theirs is the kingdom of heaven / . . . . / Blessed are they who are persecuted . . . / for theirs is the kingdom of heaven" (Matthew 5:3 and 10). He assures us that we are all blessed who follow him in his way, because of the great reward that will be ours; that great joy which lies before us is why we are blessed.

III. Let me add one more teaching of Jesus that is found again and again in the Gospels. Jesus teaches: "[W]hoever wishes to save his life will lose it, but whoever loses his life for my sake will save it" (Luke 9:24). Scripture scholars have various ways of explaining this saying. One that I prefer is this: only those who lose their self-centered independence and selfishness can learn concern for others and gain human maturity, Christian holiness—and life everlasting. On the other hand, those who live their own, self-centered way, who depend only on their own strength and ability for everything, who have no need of God, they will lose their best self and their life in Christ.

IV. To sum up then. 1. The central mystery of Christianity is that of the redemption of Christ—through his suffering and death to resurrection and glory. 2. The constant way of all heroes of our faith shows that faith includes suffering. 3. The way of Christ is the way for us all: no cross, no crown. Our whole spirituality is Christological. "Let us . . . persevere in running the race . . . while keeping our eyes fixed on Jesus, the leader and perfecter of faith."

Twenty-first Sunday in Ordinary Time

Year A

Isaiah 22:15, 19–23; Romans 11:33–36; Matthew 16:13–20

You Are Peter, the Rock

I. This Gospel is the most vigorously discussed passage in all the Gospels and most important for the Church. We are all very familiar with this passage, and we each have our feelings about it. But we almost never hear a careful exegesis of it. Let me do that today, so that we can be confident about what exactly this passage claims and what it does not say.

II. Jesus presents a challenge for his apostles: "[W]ho do you say that I am?" Peter alone responds, "You are the Messiah, the Son of the living God." In the other Gospels, Peter answers simply, "You are the Messiah." This simpler answer is probably the exact response of Peter. That is, Peter expresses the essential faith in Jesus as the expected Messiah. The rest of this passage has Jesus' response to Peter in three parts. First, Jesus changes Simon's name to Peter. These words must come from Christ, for there is no other passage in all of Scripture that explains the change of his name. In English, the word, "Peter," loses all significance as "Rock." Jesus himself spoke Aramaic and actually called Simon "*Kephas*," which means foundation stone. It is clear that Jesus makes Peter the foundation stone upon which the church is to be built. Still, *how* he is the foundation is not entirely evident here. We assume that Peter and his faith in Jesus as the Messiah is to be the enduring principal of the group Jesus formed.

Secondly, Jesus gives Peter "the keys of the kingdom." In the first reading today—from Isaiah—Shebna is made master of the palace by receiving the keys of the royal palace:

I will . . . give over to [Shebna] your authority . . . .
I will place the key of the house of David on his shoulder;
when he opens, no one shall shut,
when he shuts no one shall open.

This First Reading is chosen today precisely to show that the confer-
ral of the keys is the symbol of office for the master of the palace,
and similarly, that Peter here is declared master of the "palace," the
Church. So Peter is not only the leader in faith as the Rock, he is also
a clear figure of authority in the church. This metaphor of the keys
is the clearest image of authority Jesus could have used. Peter's office
must be seen in terms of the Church and its mission of proclaiming
the word and baptizing, along with binding and loosing.

Finally, notice that Jesus describes the power conferred
on Peter as one of binding and loosing. This certainly indicates some
power of decision, some exercise of authority. But, since the phrase
has no background in the Bible, we cannot specify the nature and
manner of this authority. We can only add that all we know about
Peter in the rest of Scripture shows that he did have a special position
in the early church; no one else appears in an equivalent position of
leadership. However, his authority is not absolute; his decisions were
made in association with others.

III. Along with many exegetes today, I suggest that is what
this passage essentially says. That means it says a great deal more than
many Protestants are willing to admit, for it does give Peter a primary
position, authority and decision-making status. But it says a great
deal less than many Catholics would wish, for it is far from establishing an absolute monarchy of authority in the pope over all facets of
church life.

Just two further comments. First, from Chapter 20 in
Matthew's Gospel, we know that Jesus intended all authority in the
church to be not one of power and domination *but* one of service and
love in faith (Matthew 20:25–28). That norm includes the authority
of Peter and his successors. Secondly, the detailed form and structure of authority in the Church was *not* determined by Christ and, in
fact, has followed the cultural changes of history. Thus, in the Acts
of the Apostles and in the early Church, it was a loose, collegial type
of authority. In the Middle Ages, it took the form of a feudal state.

In the time of the Renaissance, it took the form of an absolute monarchy. In our lifetime, it still is very centralized. But there are signs of hope that the authority in the Church is developing some openness, collegiality, and freedom, with fewer laws. Let us pray that this trend may continue and that Peter's leadership in faith may become more effective and ever more reflective of the spirit of service and love that Jesus intended.

Year B

Joshua 24:1–2a, 15–17, 18b; Ephesians 5:21–32; John 6:60–69

You Have the Words of Eternal Life

I. According to recent surveys (throughout the 1990's), on any one Sunday in America, only twenty-five percent of Catholics actually attend church. Some of these twenty-five percent go every week, some occasionally, and some rarely. That means that the twenty-five percent does not represent the very same people each week. It probably means the thirty-five to forty percent attend mass with some kind of regularity. Other surveys indicate that sixty to seventy-five percent of Catholics disagree with some important moral teaching or doctrine.

II. *Why?* Why are such people falling away from active participation in the church? The reasons are varied, but many of them can be combined under the heading of the American practical mind. That is, more and more American Catholics seem to believe that they can have *faith without religion*. So, they believe in a God who leaves them alone, lets them live their individual lives without all kinds of institutional demands and restrictions. They believe that God is in his heaven, but has little influence on human living. Direct interventions by God are not realistic or expected. The general outline of the commandments is enough for ethical living. They reject rigid sexual morality regarding marriage or abortion. Their faith is internal, believing that simple faith, along with baptism, is sufficient for salvation. And their faith is individualistic, without the need for the Church community and common worship. They believe that a compassionate and loving God will save them because of their basic faith. So they can live their own individualistic life now and still hope to be saved.

II. How can we respond to such an attitude of the American practical mind? For me, the best reasons are found in Scripture. Actually this is my sense of how *Jesus* would respond to such an attitude. First, the Old Testament is filled with the history of a people God made his own. Without the corporate history of God's chosen people, there would have been no clear faith in God, as we see in today's First Reading. In the New Testament, the Acts of the Apostles makes clear that the way of Christ is entirely centered on the community of believers. Ever since that time, our whole tradition of faith is living in the history of our Catholic community; we are constituted by these traditions and take our identity from them as Christians.

Second, Scripture also testifies that our faith is centered on God's word and sacrament. Without word and sacrament, there is no Catholic faith. All that we believe comes from God's revealed word, found only in the living tradition of his church. The constant challenge of Jesus is to "hear the word of God and act on it" (Luke 8:21). And sacraments are essential to our following of Jesus our Lord; we Catholics are a sacramental people, more than any other believers. Scripture presents Jesus' mission statement: "[M]ake disciples of all nations, baptizing them" (Matthew 28:19), and his insistence, "[U]nless you eat [my] flesh . . . you do not have life within you" (as in last Sunday's Gospel, John 6:53). These sacramental actions make the reality of Jesus present to us as individuals. Scripture presents them as necessary for us according to the mind of Jesus, our Savior. In a word, Scripture and Jesus himself make clear that we Christians cannot have faith without religion. Only by regular contact with God's word and sacraments can we maintain our friendship with Jesus. That word of God is maintained only by a living community; those sacraments are administered only within a community of believers.

IV. In today's Gospel, "[M]any of [Jesus'] disciples who were listening said, 'This saying is hard; who can accept it?' . . . As a result of this, many [of] his disciples . . . no longer accompanied him." They found his teaching foreign to their way of thinking, quite unintelligible, even repulsive. Jesus did not try to stop them by toning down his teaching; he just let them go. Today many Americans find much in Jesus' Church that is too hard to endure: inadequate leaders, rigid authority, hide-bound morality, boring liturgies, scandals. But only with the word and sacrament of that community can they connect with Jesus and follow him, the unique Savior of the entire world. Today, let us affirm our own faith along with Peter: "Master, to whom shall we go? You have the words of eternal life."

Year C

Isaiah 66:18–21; Hebrews 12:5–7, 11–13; Luke 13:22–30

Whom the Lord Loves, He Disciplines

I. A common Catholic conviction about suffering goes something like this: Suffering is directly sent to us by God as either a form of discipline or a punishment; so we should accept suffering of all kind as the mysterious, direct will of God for us. Today's reading from Hebrews seems to express this conviction well: "[W]hom the Lord loves, he disciplines; / he scourges every son [or daughter] he acknowledges. / Endure your trials as 'discipline'; God treats you as [his children]." The trials that Hebrews refers to here are probably not physical persecution for the faith but rather the criticism, scoffing, and unbelief by their unchristian neighbors and the common difficulties of constant Christian living. But I would suggest that there is a different Catholic way of looking at suffering and God's will. We need to remember in all this, that the Church has not defined what is God's part in suffering and how his providence works.

II. Let us begin by looking at the life of Jesus and his attitude toward suffering. Throughout his life, Jesus merely accepted suffering, he did not seek it out. The sufferings he endured were a part of his human condition, a part of his commitment to serve and love others; they were not a part of his personally chosen asceticism or his personal conviction of God's direct will. Jesus was not an ascetic who sought suffering. Regarding the sufferings of others: though he did cure some, he did not take away all the sickness and troubles of life, nor did he come for that purpose. He taught that suffering is not overcome by doing away with it but by accepting it. Finally, he clearly rejected the notion that suffering is a punishment for sin. Twice in the

Gospels, he deliberately rejects the connection between suffering and God's punishment. For example, in John he affirms, "Neither he nor his parents sinned . . . that he was born blind" (John 9:3 and then 2; cf. Luke 13:2–5). In terms of God's will, I believe Jesus saw God's will not so much in *what* he did but in *how* he did it. That is, he carried out God's will by accepting his human condition with all its pains and by fulfilling the exacting requirement of love for others.

III. Our Christian attitude toward suffering follows Christ's. We carry out God's will by accepting the reality of our human condition with all the pain and suffering that is a part of our individual lives, with all the troubles, tensions and monotony that is part of modern human living. We carry out his will by accepting our individual circumstances with the attitudes, values and motives of Jesus.

Just as most of Jesus' suffering in his public life came from others, so most of our suffering comes from trying to live out his command: "[L]ove one another as I love you" (John 15:12). The sum of Christian living is to love as he loved; such a love of neighbor demands some suffering, requires a denial of self-interest, and entails a constant giving of self. For we cannot be thoughtful of others without thinking a little less about self; we cannot help anyone without some personal effort; we cannot be kind to them unless we overcome our aversions; we cannot be patient unless we control our anger; we cannot tolerate their unchristian attitudes without pain.

To my mind, this is why a saint is a saint: because he or she was cheerful when it was difficult to be cheerful, patient when it was hard to be patient, considerate when it demanded a lot, kept silent when it would be natural to complain, was helpful when it was inconvenient, kept trying rather than give up. *This* is the will of God for us: that whatever happens to us as a result of our human condition is *accepted* after the model of Jesus.

IV. You and I need to hear the word of God today: "[S]trengthen your drooping hands and your weak knees (v. 12) . . . / do not disdain the discipline of the Lord . . . / for whom the Lord loves, he disciplines" (vv. 5–6). "[Keep your] eyes fixed on Jesus, the leader and perfecter of faith" (v. 2).

Part VII

The Twenty-second through Thirty-third Sunday in Ordinary Time

Twenty-second Sunday in Ordinary Time

Year A

Jeremiah 20:7–9; Romans 12:1–2; Matthew 16:21–27

Whoever Wishes to Follow Me

I. Have you ever noticed that Jesus never says, in exact words, "imitate me"? Never once does he encourage all his followers to imitate his lifestyle. But he does invite us often to "follow me." In today's Gospel, for example, he invites all Christians: "Whoever wishes to come after me must deny himself, take up his cross, and follow me." In fact, 19 times in the Gospels we hear the invitation of Jesus, "follow me." Let us take a fresh look at these words of Jesus our Lord. What is the exact meaning of Jesus' invitation to all of us?

II. When Jesus spoke these words in his lifetime, I don't think he was referring to his own crucifixion, which was not known yet. Rather, he was probably referring to a common expression of Jewish and Greek leaders of his day. From Plato's time down to Jesus' day, "take up [your] cross, and follow me" meant "be ready to offer your life for my cause."[1] So for Jesus it meant: be willing to live or die for the cause of the kingdom of God. It meant a thorough commitment of one's whole life to the way of Jesus. By the time Matthew wrote his Gospel, his readers certainly read it with Jesus' death in mind and with their own actual persecution already a reality. But during his lifetime, Jesus was simply making it very clear for all his followers that following him involves far more than believing in him intellectually or having a lukewarm attachment to his way. Rather, Jesus meant that any Christian should be ready to live his life for Jesus and his kingdom.

---

1. Edward Schillebeeckx, God Among Us: The Gospel Proclaimed (New York: Crossroad, 1987), pp. 202–03; see footnote on p. 59.

III. Let us try to understand better this constant call of Jesus to all of us Christians. His general sense involves sharing his cause all our lives, wherever it leads us. Karl Rahner explains his call this way: "The Christian, every Christian, follows Jesus by dying with him." He calls it "dying by installments." This does not mean seeking out suffering, for throughout his life, Jesus did not seek out suffering; he merely accepted it. The sufferings he endured were a part of his human condition, not part of a personally chosen asceticism. Bearing the cross of Christ, then, means bearing our personal crosses as they come to us; it means accepting what we would like to avoid; it means steadfast loyalty to the way of Jesus in all our daily living. These are the crosses that weigh heaviest on us, and we would like to be rid of. So in simplest terms, conformity to the cross of Christ is entirely individual and unique for each one of us; it is accepting the will of God as seen in the ordinary daily life that comes to us humanly.

IV. Jesus continues in this Gospel to offer similar cautions: "[W]hoever wishes to save his life will lose it, but whoever loses his life for my sake will find it." Jesus frequently expressed such paradoxical sayings. Saint Paul adds his own metaphor: "If . . . we have died with Christ, we . . . shall also live with him" (Romans 6:8). All of these sayings are at the heart of the mystery of Christian living. They have allied meanings; they all refer to spending ourselves, to putting ourselves out, to selflessness in our service of Jesus and his cause. They are the opposite of sin, of selfishness and self-centeredness.

V. This is my understanding of Jesus' invitation, "follow me." It is addressed to *all* of us: "Whoever wishes to come after me . . . ." It does not demand a particular lifestyle; it does not require retreating from the world or a monastic existence; it does not seek an elitist way of life. It is simply a call for all of us to follow Jesus by living his way of loving others and accepting the unique human life that comes to us. This is how we "carry our cross" and offer our life for the cause of Jesus our Lord.

Year B

Deuteronomy 4:1- 2, 6–8; James 1:17–18, 21b–22, 27; Mark 7:1–8, 14–15, 21–23

The Misuse of Religion

I. In today's Gospel Jesus excoriates the Pharisees for their misuse of religion. He condemns them for their scrupulous concern with minute pious practices and external rituals, while disregarding essential commitments of faith. He quotes Isaiah: "[T]his people . . . / honors me with their lips alone, /though their hearts are far from me'" (Isaiah 29:13). He calls them "hypocrites," because they misuse religion.

II. In our day, some Christians misuse religion in a similar way—as an *escape from the world*. They escape from the harsh reality of this world and its responsibilities into a world of mysteries, candles, special prayers, and rites. They avoid the great problems and needs of the world around them by means of a pious face, religious words and a quiet retreat. For them, religion is filled with saints in another world, instead of with real people who are their neighbors in this world. Such pious activities can be helpful, but they are not the essence of our Christian religion. For our religion deals with life here and now; and that very life is something good, holy and Christian in itself. Our following of Christ deals essentially with love and deep concern for one another. Jesus' one command is, "[L]ove one another as I love you" (John 15:12).

III. There is another misuse of religion that is even more common today. Other people use religion as an *insurance policy*, as some kind of insurance for the next life. That is, they are careful to be baptized, married, and buried in the Church; they want to be "hatched, matched and dispatched" religiously. But that is about all the influence that religion has in their lives. They want to be considered Catholics, but just enough for them to cash in on their policy after death. They don't want religion to interfere too much with their business or with their freedom of choice now. They choose their own practical value system for dealing with others. They look to the prevailing attitudes of society to judge other groups and races. So for them, religion is merely their assurance that everything is going to be all right for them in the next world—while they take care of this world in their own way.

IV. Saint James, today, has a clear answer for such attitudes. His entire epistle is dominated by one concept: "[F]aith without works is dead" (2:26). He means that we must live our faith each day or it is meaningless, it is a false escape, it is an insurance policy that will never pay off. In today's reading, James tells us that our faith must be acted upon or we are fooling ourselves if we think we are real Catholics. As he puts it strongly: "Be doers of the word and not hearers only, deluding yourselves." He means that our faith must be a *life*— a life lived in an entirely Christian way; otherwise, "his religion is vain" (James 1:26b). And he concludes that religion that is pure and undefiled before God is to help those in need. James is quite demanding here, for he wants our faith to be real not phony. Let me, finally, alleviate his demand by adding a word of comfort: we Christians know that our God is endlessly tolerant and understanding about our failure to live the way of Jesus.

Year C

Sirach 3:17–18, 20, 28–29; Hebrews 12:18–19, 22–24a;
Luke 14:1, 7–14

Humility Is Realism

I. One of the most unpopular virtues in America today is humility. For Americans value highly success, achievement, scientific knowledge, social status, and technological progress. And all of these seem far removed from humility. In the face of all that, I would like to suggest one notion to you: humility equals realism. That is, humility involves measuring myself by reality; it involves relating myself realistically to God and to others.

II. First, regarding our relationship to *God*. In today's Gospel, Jesus is not just offering a bit of prudential advice, telling us how to behave at a dinner party in order to avoid embarrassment. Rather, he offers a parable about our relationship to God. That is God, in the person of Jesus as the host, is inviting us all to the Messianic feast. The only way to respond to this invitation of God is by renouncing any claim or merit of our own. The Pharisees "were choosing the places of honor at the table"; they expected the best seats because of their righteousness. Jesus' parable cautions them not to expect salvation on their own merits; they must learn that salvation only comes to them as an unmerited gift. His parable speaks to us as well; it reminds us that none of us is ultimately saved or justified because of our own righteousness or because we keep the laws of God or because of our achievements in the world—our success, our riches, our worldly accomplishments. Each and every one of us is saved *only* by the saving mercy of God. It is God's grace alone that justifies us; it is our total dependence on his mercy that gains our salvation. There is no other possible position to take before God, our creator. As Van Kaam, a modern spiritual writer, suggests: There is only one thing that God cannot stand—self-sufficiency. He means that sin does not stop God, as long as we are sorry, but self-sufficiency does block God's forgiveness and saving grace. Notice in the Gospels, that Jesus had only anger and condemnation for the Pharisees, but compassion and forgiveness for repentant sinners.

Despite all this, let me quickly add that our relation to God also inspires confidence and peace, because in his mercy, he has made us his sons and daughters in Christ, so we can approach him with great confidence and hope.

III. Also let us consider our relationship to *others*. The first reading urges us: "[C]onduct your affairs with humility / . . . / and you will find favor with God." This attitude describes a person who is not proud of his own accomplishments, who does not feel superior to others because of his social status. The wisdom of Sirach here encourages us all to be contented with our lot and not consumed with the desire for worldly success. Beyond all that, we need to learn what Jesus in scripture means by the notion of "Catholic." For Jesus himself was Catholic first and foremost in his universal acceptance of all people. That is, Jesus accepted *all people equally*; he recognized no special preference or superiority of any group; he gave no weight to individual differences based on social position or possessions. He wants us, his followers, to be Catholic in the same way. As Saint Paul expressed it, "There is neither Jew nor Greek, there is neither slave nor free person,

there is not male and female; for you are all one in Christ Jesus"
(Galatians 3:28). Jesus seems to be the *only* religious leader in history
who did not establish an elite group, separate and superior to other
groups. He knew very well that individual differences are real in our
society, yet he still insists they are not important for us Christians.
The only thing important for us is that we are all one in Christ.
That is one reason for our humility before others, for in Christ Jesus,
no one is elite and no one is superior to others. For Jesus, then,
humility is realism.

Twenty-third Sunday in Ordinary Time

Year A

Ezra 33:7–9; Romans 13:8–10; Matthew 18:15–20

Love Is the Fulfillment of the Law

I. As a young priest, my favorite comic strip was Peanuts. No adults
ever appear in the strip, but I viewed it as a comic strip for adults.
One episode made a lasting impression on me. It concerned Linus and
his big sister, Lucy Van Pelt. Linus had just told Lucy that he would
like to be a doctor when he grows up. "You, a doctor! Ha, that's a big
laugh," complains his loud-mouthed sister. "You could never be a
doctor," she continues. "You know why? Because you don't love mankind, that's why!" Then she starts to skip away from him. In the last
frame, Linus yells after her, "I do love mankind . . . ; it's people
I can't stand."

II. Paul today asserts. "[W]hatever other commandments
there may be, are summed up in this saying . . .' You shall love your
neighbor as yourself.' . . . hence, love is the fulfillment of the law."
Paul is speaking in a typically Greek fashion, trying to find a single

unifying principle behind all the commands of the law. He concludes that there is really only one commandment; it is universal and covers every situation: the commandment of love. He implies that the separate commandments of the law are no more than illustrations of what love may mean in particular situations.

But there are two points we can easily miss when we hear this teaching of Paul. First, Paul is talking about love of *neighbor*. He is not really concerned about people in general, about the remote countries of the world or about universal humanity. Rather he is speaking about our neighbor, those with whom we are personally involved, those we meet and relate to every day. Paul's teaching brings to mind Jesus' parable of the Good Samaritan; in that parable our neighbor is anyone who needs us here and now. Secondly, Paul sums it all up by urging, "You shall love your neighbor as yourself." He does not refer to some poetical or abstract norm for our love; his teaching is very concrete: "*as yourself* (emphasis added)." You and I know well what we owe ourselves; we tend quite naturally to understand ourselves, be sensitive to our feelings, care for our physical needs, protect ourselves, respect ourselves. And this is his norm for loving others: to understand them, to be sensitive to their feelings, to care for their needs, to protect and respect them. "[L]ove your neighbor as yourself" makes Christian love very clear and concrete.

III. But there is one point about Christian love that is almost never spoken about. It is this: is Christian love only *agape*, selfless love, or is it *eros*, desire and passionate love as well? The fact is, the word *eros*, or love, of desire does not appear in the entire New Testament and only appears twice in the Old Testament—where it is rejected. Most likely *eros* was never used in the New Testament because early Greek usage of this word connected it with morbid eroticism and purely instinctive sexuality. But if we simply understand *eros* as the very human love that includes desire and passion, then we can realistically find a lot of *eros* in the Bible. In fact, God in the Old Testament is a God who loves his people passionately and jealously, even as a man might love his faithless wife. And in the New Testament, God is a passionate father who wants his prodigal son back. Also, Jesus shows a constant warm friendship for children, for women and especially for the apostles, whom he so loving calls "friends." What I mean is this: neither the Old Testament nor the New Testament is interested in the distinction between a "heavenly" and an "earthly" love. Genuine human love of husband and wife, father, mother, child, friend is not opposed to love of God but is set within the context of that love.

In the past several centuries, the main emphasis in Christianity was on charity, and perhaps it made little impression on some of us, because charity seemed to have so little humanity. It seemed often dehumanized and spiritualized, with no vitality, emotion, affection, and warmth—and so was unattractive. Recently we use the word love rather than charity to indicate that our Christian love should be truly human—with depth, warmth, intimacy, tenderness, cordiality, passion, and desire.

IV. What all of this means is that we cannot say with Linus, "I love all mankind; it's people I can't stand." But we have to listen to Paul: "[L]ove your neighbor as yourself." Most of all, we try to love as Jesus loved, accepting all those near to us with a warm, practical, passionate human love.

Year B

Isaiah 35:4–7a; James 2:1–5; Mark 7:31–37

Unable to Speak and Believe

I. In the Northwoods of Wisconsin, a hunter once trapped a large eagle. He kept the eagle chained by one foot to a post in his yard. For years the eagle lived that way. No one ever noticed him make an effort to fly; he seemed content to walk around as far as the chain would let him. Eventually, the man was going to move to another town and decided to let the eagle go free. Those who watched expected the eagle to fly away as soon as it was given its freedom. But the bird continued to walk around, apparently unaware of his new freedom. After several minutes, he rustled a wing. He began to feel his freedom, and then he tried his wings. In a moment he was off—slowly at first, then steadily higher and higher, until he flew out of sight.

II. Today's Gospel is notable in some ways. It is one of the two miracle stories peculiar to Mark alone. In it Mark describes the deaf man with an unusual Greek word, *mogilalon*, meaning "with a speech

impediment" or "with difficulty of speech." This word is hardly ever
used in the New Testament; but it is the same word used in the Greek
translation of Isaiah 35, the First Reading today. Perhaps Mark
wanted to show by this healing that Jesus is the messianic healer
predicted in Isaiah. Also *where* Mark places this event in his Gospel
is notable. He uses this story to symbolize what is happening to
the disciples of Jesus at that time in his Gospel. Earlier in this same
chapter, they had been deaf to Jesus' word and unable to profess
their faith in him. In the next chapter, Peter makes his famous profession of faith in Jesus as the Messiah, and the disciples along with
Peter have their ears opened and their tongues released, so they
can profess their faith in Jesus.

III. Many Catholics found themselves in a similar situation in
the old church. That is, they felt bound and restricted by a church
that strongly emphasized rules and sometimes abused authority. They
saw the hierarchical authority making policy from above, without
consultation and little shared responsibility. But since Vatican II,
many things are starting to change. Authority in the church is beginning to evidence some openness, freedom, and democracy. Institutions
change slowly, but Jesus' spirit of service and love seems to be a little
more evident. Perhaps it is time for such people to reconsider, for now
many of the old restrictions are taken away, and there is more room
for individual freedom.

But some of us Catholics feel bound in another way. Before
the Vatican Council, our theology was so complex and tied up with
scholastic terminology that it sounded esoteric and difficult to understand. The emphasis was on intellectual assent to supernatural
mysteries. As a result, many of us had "difficulty in speech" trying to
express our faith to others and even for ourselves. Besides that, our
Christian spirituality was largely tied to the monastic ideal of retreat
from the world, and our morality seemed quite rigid and absolute.
Since Vatican II, our theology is not so complex; Scripture is not so
esoteric; morality is more understandable; spirituality is more affirming of ordinary human life. The more we learn about our faith
today, the more we get a feeling of newness, openness, and freedom.
There is a sense of our "speech impediment [being] removed." Just
as a bird is made to fly, so we are made to understand human life and
freely live the life of Christ. I hope we will continue to grow in this

feeling of freedom in the church of the twenty-first century. As our Catholic church slowly becomes more open, collaborative and free, may we all feel freer to offer our talents to build up the Body of Christ.

Year C

Wisdom 9:13–18b; Philemon 9–10, 12–17; Luke 14:25–33

The Cost of Discipleship

I. Today's Gospel is Christ's warning about the cost of discipleship. It is a very real warning, but it is frequently misunderstood. Let us try to take a fresh look at these words of Christ. First, Jesus cautions that whoever wants to be his disciple, must take up his cross and follow him without letting any family relationships or selfish concerns interfere with following him. When Jesus asks each Christian to "carry [one's] cross," he is not referring to his crucifixion. Rather he seems to refer to a common saying of the Greco-Roman world meaning to "offer one's life for a cause."[2] So Jesus' real meaning is that following him means the surrender of the whole of one's life. In a parallel passage, Luke alone adds one word to Jesus' invitation: "daily" (see: Luke 9:23, emphasis added); by that one word, he clarifies that Jesus means a constant, daily following of him. In simple terms, Jesus warns that our following of Christ should come first over any material concerns. Then Jesus offers two parables to illustrate the necessity of facing the cost. He implies: know the cost of following me; if you think it is too much, then don't be my disciple.

II. What is this cost of discipleship? What is the cross we are asked to bear? Without trying to be complete, let me make a couple points that are applicable to us modern Americans. First, taking up one's cross does *not* mean seeking suffering. Pure asceticism or inflicting pain on our selves is not necessary for following Christ. For throughout Jesus' life, he merely accepted suffering; he did not seek it out. The sufferings he endured were a part of his human condition, not a chosen form of asceticism. Following Christ, then,

---

2. Edward Schillebeeckx, *God Among Us: The Gospel Proclaimed* (New York: Crossroad, 1987), pp. 202–03; see footnote on p. 59.

means rather bearing our personal crosses as they come to us; it means enduring everyday, common troubles; it means accepting what we would rather avoid: all our daily obligations, demands, and trials. These are the personal crosses that weigh heaviest on us, and that we would like to be rid of. Simply said, this is essentially what carrying the cross of Christ means.

III. But Jesus seems to say that the cost of discipleship *adds* a cross to ordinary human existence. For his early followers this added cross was obvious. It was the cross of being divided from family and friends because they chose to follow this new way. For many, it even meant martyrdom. None of that is likely to be our situation. What is the added cost for us today? One added cost of discipleship for us modern Americans is to affirm our identity in this secularist society, not to sell out to a whole new set of values common in America today. Our society is an efficiency-oriented society, which affects us all. It has its *own set of values*: the prime virtue is ability; the supreme law is achievement; the organizational norm is profit; the goal is success; the meaning of life is improvement of material living and prosperity. Now none of these values is bad, by any means. But if they lead us to lose sight of higher Christian values and our Christian meaning of life, then we can lose our own identity, our own selves. Jesus' words do apply here: "Whoever finds his life will lose it" (Matthew 10:39). That is, if economic values are primary, if profession determines social status, if prosperity and achievement determine a person's value, then we lose our true humanity. We Christians reject the efficiency-oriented society as the highest human value, and we insist on a society centered on the meaning of the whole person, in Christ.

IV. So Christ asks a simple question of us today: "Do you really want to be my disciple; do you want to be a real Christian?" We know from the beginning that being a Christian will cost something. It clearly means accepting the daily obligations, demands, and responsibilities that come to us as our cross. It means living by Christian values that are different from the common American values. It means that we try more and more to make Jesus the center of our life. Jesus tells us that's what it means to follow him.

Twenty-fourth Sunday in Ordinary Time

Year A

Sirach 27:30—28:7; Romans 14:7–9; Matthew 18:21–35

So Will My Heavenly Father Do to You

I. All the readings today deal with forgiveness. I myself find forgiveness a very difficult Christian virtue at times. I suspect most of us do. Let us consider our Lord's teaching with an open mind.

II. Peter puts this question to Jesus: "Lord . . . how often must I forgive [someone]? As many as seven times?" The number of seven means "quite a few times"; the implication is that then the duty to forgive ceases if the offense continues. Jesus answers, "Not seven times but seventy-seven times." That is, Jesus makes the number huge, so that forgiveness should be without limit. Then Matthew inserts a parable of Jesus, which does not exactly inculcate repeated forgiveness but rather the need for us to show mercy if we expect mercy from God. The parable describes the minister of a king. The minister owed the king a huge sum of money, but when he cried for mercy, the king forgave the whole debt. Yet this same minister went out and demanded a minor payment from a servant. When the servant asked for mercy, he refused it and punished the servant severely. Jesus' conclusion to the parable is: "[I]n anger, his master handed [his minister] over to the torturers until he should pay back the whole debt. So will my heavenly Father do to you, unless each of you forgives his brother [or sister] from his heart." This parable, like every parable, has only one point to it: our forgiveness of one another is a condition of God's forgiving us. This is the same point Jesus teaches in the Our Father: Forgive us as we forgive others. In other words, Jesus urges us to imitate God's mercy to us; just as we have been forgiven by God, so we should forgive others. He also warns us against refusing to show mercy, for if we consistently fail to forgive others, then God will not offer his forgiveness in the last judgment.

III. Now what does all of this say to us humanly and practically? All of us experience minor hurts almost every day: slights, lack of consideration, acts flowing from prejudice, unkindness, and annoyance. On occasion these hurts are very deep and continuous. This is bound to happen to us, for all human beings are somewhat selfish, inconsiderate, prejudiced. So, if we do not learn readily to forgive, we will have few friends and close relationships.

But there is one point about Christian forgiveness that is seldom spoken about. Isn't there some condition for the one who offends us to receive mercy? Are we asked to forgive immediately, no matter what? Notice in this story, that both men *ask* forgiveness. And whenever Jesus speaks about God forgiving sins, he always requires sorrow for sin. God does not forgive our sins unless we show real sorrow and so ask forgiveness of God. Even in the sacrament of reconciliation, without some kind of *contrition*, there is no forgiveness from God. Surely, Jesus does not ask us weak human beings to go beyond God's forgiveness, only to follow his example. What this implies is that, according to Jesus, we are only expected to forgive whenever we are asked to forgive. The one who offended us, especially if he hurt us greatly, should show some sign of sorrow. We are not expected to do *more than God*, are we? Just as God requires contrition for his forgiveness of us, so we need some sign of sorrow from the one who offends us—even if it is indirect or implicit. But then and only then, are we urged by Jesus to forgive without fail and without limit.

IV. The genius of Jesus' way of living is to break through the vicious cycle of repaying evil with evil. What he asks us today is that whenever anyone asks us to forgive, we quickly forgive and reestablish our relationship. And Jesus asks us to do that again and again, as God does to us. This is still very difficult for us Christians at times, but it is not unreasonable. Jesus wants us to forgive others as God forgives us; he doesn't expect us to go beyond God's forgiveness; but he asks us to approach that ideal. That's hard enough for me—and for you.

YEAR B

Isaiah 50:4c–9a; James 2:14–18; Mark 8:27–35

OUR SPIRITUALITY IS CHRISTOLOGICAL

I. Our entire spirituality is Christological. Recently, I have understood this better than ever before. This one conviction can give us a simple and authentic way of Christian living. It follows Jesus' invitation in today's Gospel: "Whoever wishes to come after me must deny himself, take up his cross, and follow me." Jesus himself tells us what is the cost of being his disciple, what it means to be a Christian, how our entire life is meant to be a following of Jesus. Let us try to understand Jesus our Lord as he teaches his way of holiness.

II. The first scene in the Gospel is the familiar one of Jesus asking his disciples what people believe about him and then what the apostles believe about him. This whole scene is the center and highpoint of Mark's Gospel; it is the revelation of Mark's "messianic secret;" in it Mark tells us just what kind of messiah Jesus is. After Peter answers with inspiration, "You are the Messiah," Jesus goes on to explain that he would soon suffer, be rejected and be put to death. Peter could not accept this kind of messiah, so he took Jesus aside and "rebuked" him. Jesus responded to Peter: "Get behind me, Satan. You are thinking not as God does, but as human beings do." This is the harshest word Jesus uses in all the Gospels. Why did he use such language, especially to Peter? Because Peter could accept the idea of Jesus as the Messiah but *not* as a suffering messiah. Jesus shockingly rejects Peter's kind of messiahship, because it seemed to include a political, nationalistic character. He rejects it as a diabolical attempt to divert him from his God-given mission. He is not a divine miracleworker; he is not a political messiah; he is a Messiah who saves by his suffering, death, and Resurrection. This is Mark's "messianic secret": that Jesus our Lord is *this* kind of Messiah—the Messiah of suffering and death.

III. Then, in the second scene of the Gospel, Jesus our Lord tells us that as he redeemed us by suffering and dying, so all of us who want to be his disciples must follow him in suffering: "Whoever wishes to come after me must deny himself, take up his cross, and follow me." Jesus was referring to a traditional saying in the Greco-Roman world, that meant "to offer one's life for a cause," or in this case, "to commit one's whole life to the cause of Christ."[3] There is a powerful passage in the First Epistle of Peter that clarifies this passage for us: "Christ also suffered for you, leaving you an example that you should follow in his footsteps" (1 Peter 2:21). Notice Peter's wording is very similar to Jesus' words in our Gospel today. Peter asserts that Jesus, our suffering Messiah, is our model for suffering. In a word, our constant daily struggles and ordinary human trials, just as they come to us individually, make up our following of Christ. They are the "stuff" of our modeling our lives on Christ, our being disciples after the pattern of Jesus our Master.

IV. Mark joins these two scenes together in this Gospel and so draws a powerful parallel between Jesus as Messiah and us as his disciples. Mark first makes clear that Jesus is not a miracle-worker but a suffering Messiah, who offers his life and passion for our redemption, according to the plan of God. And this way of redemption is also the pattern of our Christian existence; this suffering Jesus is the model for Christian holiness. So our spirituality is totally Christological: Christ our Savior redeemed us by suffering for us and left us "an example that [we] should follow in his footsteps" (1 Peter 2:21).

YEAR C

Exodus 32:7–11, 13–14; 1 Timothy 1:12–17; Luke 15:1–32

GUILT AND RECONCILIATION

I. Dr. Carl Menninger observed that many Americans have a problem with guilt. In his medical, psychological experience, he found that many people cover over their guilt and refuse to admit it. They do not want to face God or themselves with such an admission. They handle guilt by suppressing it, by forcing it into the subconscious. But it

---

3. Edward Schillebeeckx, *God Among Us: The Gospel Proclaimed* (New York: Crossroad, 1987), pp. 202–03; see footnote on p. 59.

cannot stay suppressed, he says; instead it festers in the subconscious and becomes toxic.

The opposite extreme regarding guilt is to see faults and guilt everywhere. Such oppressive guilt does violence to us and stunts our psychological growth. Such people expend all their energy and nerves in avoiding offense against endless laws, rules, and imagined requirements. They demand perfection of themselves and cannot tolerate the flaws of their human condition. Anxiety hangs like a fine mist over their lives. Their capacity to enjoy life is impaired. Their guilt infects their finest human relationships and achievements.

II. A Christian sense of guilt understands that to be human is to be imperfect. We Christians have a benign view of human beings; we know that human nature is basically good but imperfect. We expect all of us to fail, to be weak at times, to be selfish, to hurt others, to sin. We are not really surprised at our faults; we can be compassionate of others' faults. And our Catholic sacraments are built on the acknowledgment of the flaws of the human condition. The genius of the sacrament of reconciliation is that it permits us to face ourselves with compassion, to acknowledge our guilt and then to be healed with God's certain forgiveness. For us Christians, there is no lingering guilt, no fear, only the comforting assurance of God's forgiveness and total healing.

III. This Gospel is from Luke. It contains three parables, two of them found only in Luke. All three make one major point: the boundless, humanly incomprehensible joy in heaven over the conversion of one sinner. The first parable of the lost sheep (which is also found in Matthew) stresses God's great concern for the individual sinner. It focuses on heaven's almost irrational joy over a converted sinner. The second parable is about a woman with ten coins. (Luke often parallels a "male" parable with a "female" parable.) Again, the effort to find what was lost is extraordinary, and the joy is exceptional. This parable underscores God's unlimited love and concern for the sinner.

But the third parable is a masterpiece about guilt and reconciliation. Concentrate, if you will, on the reception of the prodigal son by his father. The father shows his complete acceptance of his son in three ways. First, he embraces his son; he welcomes him back with open arms and a ceremonial robe. The embrace and welcoming kiss take place without any words. Second, he puts shoes on the boy's feet. The significance here is that bare feet were a sign of slavery; while the shoes are a sign that he is a free and welcome son of his father. Third, the father gives his son a ring, probably a signet ring containing the family seal. Such a ring means that the son has the power to act in the family's name. In a word, the ceremonial robe, the sandals and the signet ring all show that the son is personally restored to his place in the family by a loving father. In all three parables, nothing is sad or half-hearted; there is only joy and relief.

IV. Such is often our experience in the sacrament of reconciliation—a sense of joy and relief. This is why we Christians can admit our guilt. This is why we can face ourselves compassionately, despite our faults. For we have only to go back to our Father to be embraced and forgiven, to be welcomed with joy.

Twenty-fifth Sunday in Ordinary Time

Year A

Isaiah 55:6–9; Philippians 1:20c–24, 27a; Matthew 20:1–16a.

The Laborers in the Vineyard

I. Of all the parables of Jesus, this one probably causes the most confusion. Some of the confusion is reasonable and flows from the text itself. Let us try to recover the different levels of this parable of Jesus, and in doing so, learn how the early Church transformed many parables of Jesus addressed to the crowd or his opponents into a lesson for the apostles and disciples.

II. Begin with the original historical setting and see why *Jesus* told this parable. Concentrate on the second part of the parable, in which the laborers are indignant; they rebel and protest; they receive

the humiliating reply, "Are you envious because I am generous?"
This all refers to those who resemble the murmurers in the parable,
those who criticize the good news of God's generosity; it refers directly
to the *pharisees* who complain that Jesus is a companion of sinners, the
poor and the outcasts, those not keeping the law of God or are lazy
in carrying it out. We might imagine the complaint of the Pharisees:

> How can the master give the same pay to these lazy or unworthy people?
> How could such people be rewarded with entry into the kingdom of God?
> To let them be saved just as us Pharisees is a piece of purely arbitrary
> injustice, a capricious equality.

With this parable, Jesus tries to teach the Pharisees that
everyone who responds to the call of God—even tax-collectors and
sinners—will be given a place in the kingdom, as long as they believe
and reform their lives. God is not arbitrary or capricious; rather he is
large-hearted, compassionate, and "generous" to all—as long as they
believe and repent. Implied in all this is that Jesus too is compassionate and generous like God and should not be condemned by the
Pharisees for his openness and compassion for all.

III. But this in not Mathew's purpose in telling this parable
here; *Matthew* changes this apologetic parable into a moral parable.
He places this parable immediately after Christ's sermon about the
rich having great difficulty in entering the kingdom and the apostles'
receiving a hundredfold for giving up all to follow Jesus. Then he
relates this parable out the laborers in the vineyard. In Matthew's
scheme, then, the *disciples* are the ones who are being warned not to
presume any preference because they are called first, nor are they to
complain about the latecomers and sinners who will be received into
God's kingdom, just as they may be. Perhaps he even hints that they
should follow him out of love not for a greater reward.

IV. Our whole exegesis, here, presents this parable as a prime
example of what the Gospel writers did with many of Jesus' parables.
That is, the evangelist often took a parable addressed to the scribes,
Pharisees or the crowd, and changed the lesson of the parable to
relate to the disciples of Jesus or the readers of their Gospel. And it is
primarily the expression of the evangelist that is the inspired word of
God, so this is clearly the authentic meaning of the parable.

V. We can even go one step farther. The *Church* of the second and third centuries reapplied this same parable to their then current concerns; they related those who worked the whole day to the Jews who followed God's call from the beginning, and recognized the latecomers as the *gentiles* who answered God's call so late in the day. Though that is not the original meaning of Jesus' parable, it is a valid practical application. Similarly in our day, we might well apply this same parable to the Church's concern for the outcasts of society—for street people, for addicts, for AIDS sufferers. This too can be a valid application of Jesus' original parable about the generosity, forgiveness, and compassion of our God to all who sincerely answer his call.

In *every* understanding of this parable, the conclusion is: Our God is wondrously generous to all who repent and believe, no matter who they are!

Year B

Wisdom 2:12, 17–20; James 3:16—4:3; Mark 9:30–37

Servants, Not Ambitious People

I. Mark's Gospel has three predictions of Jesus' Passion; in each context, he follows a pattern. First, Jesus predicts his suffering and death; second, he mentions the misunderstanding of the apostles; and third, he instructs them about discipleship. Today's passage is the second passion prediction and contains these three elements. First, Jesus predicts his passion; then he notes the misunderstanding of the apostles. The apostles don't even try to understand Jesus' shocking warning about his coming suffering; instead they argue about who is the most important among them! So Jesus instructs them about priority in the kingdom; he tells them directly that importance does not consist in being first or having authority, but in being a humble servant. Then he gives a concrete example of such humble service— that of a child who has no importance or rights in their society, but still represents Jesus himself. In a word, this Gospel reminds all of us not to argue about rank or authority, not to be contentious or self-serving, but rather to be humble servants.

The reading from James today makes an allied point: Christian wisdom is peaceful, sincere and agreeable, but pride and selfish ambition lead to conflicts, disputes, and fighting.

II. Let me apply what Mark and James teach us today to the general situation in our modern Church. Many things in our two Catholic worlds are disputed, argued and almost irreconcilable. It is easy for us who care about the Church to insist on our sense of what is right for the church and to reject any other approach. It is natural to insist on our truth and not be open to or accepting of people who sincerely differ from us. In the spirit of the Word of God today, let me try to find some common ground for all of us; let me point to some things that are commonly developing and can be generally agreed upon by all sincere Catholics.

III. The first common ground in our church today is directly related to our Gospel today. It is that our Church is to be one of *service* not triumphalism. Authority in the church today is somewhat less monarchical and is beginning to listen and to share decision-making; our liturgies are less triumphal and more commonly shared, with all kinds of people in ministry; clerical and religious states in the church are no longer referred to as higher ways of life but only as a different way of living the Christian commitment.

The second agreement in the church is that *scripture* is the foundation of our faith. Our knowledge of scripture is growing dramatically in the last 50 years. All Catholic groups now appreciate its primary place in theology. And the more we know scripture, the more we know Christ.

The third agreement is an acceptance of *pluralism*, an understanding that there are numerous approaches and descriptions of theology, expressions of faith, liturgical forms and church discipline. As Karl Rahner put it: "Theological pluralism can no longer be turned back." There is more tolerance of conservative and liberal theologies, of Hispanic, African, and Oriental expressions of faith. No longer must the church in the East, West, North, and South all look just like the European church. We no longer look for a lock-step uniformity; we only require unity in Christ.

Finally there is agreement that faith is a commitment of life, not a set of intellectual truths. We have found a new focus of the Gospel; it is not about special, magical, mysterious truths, but about human life, about following Christ as the model and motive of life. It is no longer the individual approach of "me and you, God," but the communal service of our neighbor and trying to live as Jesus lived.

IV. These are the developments that are in process now in the church; they are far from complete, but they are real. They are the common ground for all of Jesus' disciples who care about building up his church. They can lead to a church of people who are not self-righteous or ambitious but only humble servants.

YEAR C

Amos 8:4–7; 1 Timothy 2:1–8; Luke 16:1–13

THE CHILDREN OF THIS AGE ARE SHREWD

I. Some years ago, I was at a testimonial dinner for a classmate of mine, Fr. Dan Mallette. Dan had spent 11 years in, perhaps, the toughest parish in Chicago. At this testimonial dinner, there was an amazing variety of people from around the city. I happened to be sitting at a large table with an African-American judge and a successful Jewish businessman. We talked constantly during the meal. At one point, the businessman made this bold assertion: "To get ahead in this world, to have any influence, money is really all that talks. Those who have money have to be very shrewd to make a lot of it, and when they do, they have real power." He concluded that, in our capitalistic society, you had to be shrewd to make money, and if you did, you had real power.

II. Today's Gospel implies a critique on such an attitude, and it is not all negative. This parable of the dishonest steward is confusing, unless we understand the common economic system of the time. Rich landowners would have stewards who managed their property. The steward's job was to make money through binding contracts for the master. It was entirely acceptable for him to charge usurious interest, up to double the original amount; and the whole amount owed would be included in one lump sum. For example, if someone owed 100 gallons of oil, because of fifty percent interest, the contract could state that he owed 150 gallons of oil. The steward possessed great liberty and full responsibility to collect what was owed; if he collected much more, it was rightfully his (something like our modern debt-collection agencies).

In this parable, however, the steward knows he is about to be dismissed; he does not engage in self-pity or indecision but decides to act shrewdly and make some provision for his own future. He cancels his own *usurious* profit and makes friends for himself with the debtors. The master is not cheated out of anything that is rightly his, and the steward shrewdly hopes that the debtors will reciprocate his largess: "[W]hen I am removed from the stewardship, they may welcome me into their homes." Jesus concludes by praising the shrewdness of the steward; he was not dishonest, only clever in his use of money. Jesus wants his followers to be just as clever in making money and in using it. In the rest of the reading today, Jesus adds three morals about using money prudently in our ordinary living, in constant subordination to God and in preparation for the end of life.

III. What do this parable and Jesus' three additional morals say to us today? Like the steward we can be bold, resolute, and shrewd in our business and at work; it is prudent to make a success of our business. Second, we need to be just in our daily work and business; this rules out graft, cutting corners, fraud, putting in an inadequate day's work. Third, we can use our limited wealth and convert it into heavenly capital by sharing it with others. Fourth, we can serve God first by not being preoccupied with luxury, material possessions and conspicuous consumption. Finally, we can make our commitment to Christian living a constant value even in our business or our daily work.

IV. In a word, in today's Gospel, Jesus is not mouthing some innocuous platitudes. He is challenging us to be shrewd in work, to be just in business, to acknowledge God first in all our living. "[S]eek first the kingdom [of God]" (Matthew 6:33).

Twenty-sixth Sunday in Ordinary Time

Year A

Ezra 18:25–28; Philippians 2:1–11; Matthew 21:28–32

Have the Same Attitude as Christ

I. "Have among yourselves the same attitude that is . . . in Christ Jesus." Surprisingly, this is the only passage in all of Paul's writings where the imitation of Christ explicitly appears. He encourages all of us Christians to have the same attitude toward others that Jesus showed when he humbled himself to become man, to serve others and finally to die on the cross. That is, as he shows throughout this reading, he wants our relationship to our fellow Christians to be marked by unity, love, humility, and consideration for others. This comes close to defining our Christian way of life: to live as Jesus lived. Paul is not concerned with intellectual faith here but with living that faith in all our relationships.

II. The Gospel is a simple parable found only in Matthew and only recently included in our cycle of Sunday readings. In this parable of the two sons, the first son agrees to the father's command but then fails to act. The other son verbally rebels against his father's request but then ultimately obeys him. There are different levels of meaning to this parable. *Christ* himself is contrasting the Jewish leaders who affirm God's way but don't do it, to sinners who reject God's law but eventually repent and obey God. *Matthew* in the context relates this parable to the Jews in general who think of themselves as God's faithful people but do not accept his new way in Christ, to the Gentiles who were unbelievers but came to accept the kingdom of God in Christ.

III. *For us* the application is similar. Many Christians are like the *first son* in today's Gospel. As a child they say, "Certainly I will go and work in your vineyard, Lord—I will live my life as a real Christian." But as an adult, they forget what it means to be a Christian. They think it means little more than a child's faith; they are quick to affirm, "I went to a Catholic school;" or, "I was an altar boy when I was a kid." Their adult lives are empty of a real sense of Christian living, and they don't even realize it. One example would be the pragmatic businessman who is totally focused on success in business. Another example is the satisfied American who does not feel any need for God in his daily life. For such people, faith is primarily intellectual. Their life is empty of any sense of Christian commitment. They are not doing their Father's will.

Other Christians today are like the *second son* in the Gospel. As a young person, they moved away from their practice of faith and for various reasons went their own way. Now as an adult with children of their own, they are inclined to reexamine their lifestyle and commitment again. They begin to realize that faith in God is essential for their own living and for raising their children. The rebellion they felt as a young person is being reconsidered in a more adult and responsible context. They see vaguely that Christian faith life is very concrete and explicit, for it is simply following the attitude and life of Jesus: "Have the same attitude that is . . . in Christ Jesus."

III. Paul reminds all of us today what is the sum of our Christian living. It is to strive for the attitude of Christ in all our relationships, particularly in terms of unity, love, humility and consideration for others. And the Gospel reminds us that no matter what we did in the past, now as adults we can strive to be like the second son and respond to God our Father: "Behold, I come to do your will, O God" (Hebrews 10:7).

Year B

Numbers 11:25–29; James 5:1–6; Mark 9:38–43, 45, 47–48

Whoever Is Not against Us Is for Us

I. Some Sundays the scripture readings have an obvious unity to them; they have a dominant theme and make one strong point.

Today's readings are not like that; they include several ideas that
are disjointed. But we can use these readings as a form of Scripture
study, which may help us understand the Sunday readings throughout
the year.

II. Start with this question: How are the readings for each
Sunday chosen? Do they all belong together and teach the same
truth? Actually, the First Reading, the one from the Old Testament,
usually belongs together with the Gospel reading. That is, it emphasizes much the same point as the Gospel, or it gives the background for the teaching of Jesus found in the Gospel. If you haven't
noticed that before, watch how the First Reading and the Gospel
fit together on the next few Sundays. On the other hand, the Second
Reading—taken from one of the epistles—is not chosen because
it belongs together with the others; in fact, it rarely matches the other
two readings. Rather, week after week, it is a *continuous* reading from
one of Paul's letters; often it will be the very next passage or the
next chapter from the previous Sunday reading.

III. Now consider today's readings. The first reading is from
the Book of Numbers. It describes God's giving the gift of prophecy
to many others who were to assist Moses. But two men were not
included in that divine action, yet they still began to prophesy.
So Joshua, Moses' aid, insisted on some institutional control and he
wanted to stop them. But Moses would not place limits on the action
of the spirit. Rather, he encouraged an attitude of tolerance.

Then consider the Gospel. It consists of several sayings of
Jesus that have no consistent theme. But the beginning of the Gospel
makes the same point as our first reading. Thus, the apostles are
disturbed because a man who was not a follower of Jesus was expelling
demons. Perhaps he was just an oriental holy man using Christ's name
as an incantation. Whatever the case, Jesus' response is filled with
tolerance and acceptance: "Do not prevent him . . . [W]hoever is not
against us is for us." So Jesus shows a great tolerance of other people
and their sincere efforts—no matter what their personal convictions.
Here we come to recognize Jesus as very humane and free of rigidity.

IV. What the church wants to teach us in these readings is
a deep-down tolerance for others, even if they do not believe what
we believe or if they are very different from us. The tolerance of Jesus
should be our norm with people of other faiths. As long as they

sincerely follow their way of belief, we can only respect their convictions. Jesus' tolerance can also be our model for treating all kinds of Christians who are different from us—by race, culture, class, or gender. We need to understand that Jesus came to form an inclusive community, a fully *catholic* or universal church. In his Church all of us are called to solidarity with one another across all barriers of race, sex, culture, and class. In Jesus' church there can be no superiority or preference, no rejection of differences, no rigidity or prejudice. Such tolerance is most evident in Jesus, but it was a major struggle for the post-apostolic church. It is still an immense challenge for us, 2000 years later. We all have some way to go, in order to imitate the spirit of tolerance of Jesus our model. "[W]hoever is not against us is for us."

Year C

Amos 6:1a, 4–7; 1 Timothy 6:11–16; Luke 16:19–31

Dives and Lazarus

I. This Gospel is quite familiar to us and we immediately grasp the central point of it, which is the complete reversal of fortune in the next world for these two people. The rich man, the man of luxury, who "dined sumptuously each day," who seems to have no concern for others, finds himself in hell; the poor man, who is helpless in his poverty and suffering but who seems to be a just man, is in heaven and actually in the highest place of honor ("the bosom of Abraham"). What a complete reversal of fortune! How wondrous is God's mercy!

II. But when we take a closer look at this parable, we find a wealth of meaning besides. The first surprise here is that Jesus is appropriating a well-known folk tale. There was a common Palestinian folk tale that concludes with the words, "He who has been good on earth, will be blessed in the kingdom of the dead, and he who has been evil on earth, will suffer in the kingdom of the dead." So Jesus is drawing on material known to his hearers, but then he adds his own twist to this folk tale. He calls the poor man, "Lazarus," which means "God helps." He doesn't name the rich man at all; we call him

Dives, which is just the Latin word for "rich man." Jesus' point seems to be that God is the God of the poorest and most destitute. But we cannot imagine he is teaching here that wealth in itself merits hell or that poverty in itself is rewarded by paradise. Never does Jesus teach this. But what he does indicate is that unconcern for others and impiety are punished by God, while piety and humility or simply faithful living is rewarded by God. Notice also, the "great chasm" that Jesus speaks of; it expresses the irrevocability of God's judgment; there is simply no recourse after death.

III. Let me change gears here and talk about one of the great figures of the twentieth century, Albert Schweitzer. As a young man, Schweitzer was already acclaimed as a philosopher, a Christian theologian, an historian, and a concert soloist. But, already at the age of 21, he had a dream, a plan of life; he promised himself that he would devote himself to art and science until he was 30 years old. On his thirtieth birthday (October 13, 1905), he sent letters to his parents and closest friends, telling them that he wanted to devote the rest of his life to working among the needy and serving the poor. By the time he was 38, he became a medical doctor, and at 43 he left for Africa and opened a hospital on the edge of the jungle in Equatorial Africa. He died there at the age of 90. In 1952, he was awarded the Nobel Peace Prize and was called "the man of the century."

What motivated this brilliant man to turn his back on worldly fame and work among the poorest in Africa? He explained that one of the great influences on him was his meditation on *today's Gospel* about the rich man and Lazarus. He seemed to realize that the sin of the rich man was simply that he never noticed Lazarus or accepted him; his sin was one of omission, that is, not doing something he should have done. He said: "It struck me as incomprehensible that I should be allowed to live such a happy life, while so many people around me were wrestling with . . . suffering."

Let me add here the words of Pope John Paul II, delivered in a homily at Yankee Stadium in New York in 1979:

> We cannot stand idly by, enjoying our own riches and freedom, if in any place the Lazarus of the twentieth century stands at our doors. The poor of the United States and of the world are your brothers and sisters in Christ. You must never be content to leave them just the crumbs of the feast.

Twenty-seventh Sunday in Ordinary Time

Year A

Isaiah 5:1–7; Philippians 4:6–9; Matthew 21:33–43

God's Vineyard

I. It's an old story but a classic. A man fell over a cliff. As he fell, he was able to grab a branch. Hanging onto the branch, he yelled out for help, "Help! Isn't there someone up there who can help me?" Then he heard a voice saying, "Here I am; I will help you." "Who is that?" he asked. "I am the Lord. I will help you. All you have to do is trust me." "I trust you; just tell me what to do." "All right . . . just let go of the branch." There was silence for a while, as he thought about it. Then he asked, "Is there anyone else up there?"

II. Today's Gospel is about God's vineyard. It is not a parable, which makes a single point. Rather, it is an allegory, in which all the elements are significant. In Matthew, here, it describes the whole of salvation history. Thus, the vineyard is Israel; the vinedressers or tenant farmers are the religious leaders of the Jews; the successive emissaries are the Old Testament prophets; the son is Jesus, the Messiah; his murder is the crucifixion. "A people that will produce its fruit" are the Gentiles, after many of the Jews reject Jesus. The rich harvest refers at least partially to the last judgment.

One point needs further explanation; the tenants say to one another, "This is the heir. . . . [L]et us kill him and acquire his inheritance." Is this a realistic plan? Well, consider that foreign land-lords owned much of Galilee. They hired out tenants to care for their vineyards. But if the owner dies intestate—without an heir—the property became ownerless and could be claimed by anyone, and the tenants could easily claim it first. So in Jesus' day, this allegory was quite realistic and readily understood by his hearers.

III. Jesus directed this allegory to the leaders of the Jews who rejected him. Because of their rejection, the kingdom would be given to the Gentiles, as the concluding verse indicates. The application to us is not so apparent, for we do not reject Jesus. Rather, our failure is similar to the man in the story who fell over the cliff and held onto the branch. We do believe and trust God, but only half-heartedly. In varying degrees, we hold onto our ways of life, our secularistic lives, our superficial Christianity. We are not willing to trust God completely or to commit ourselves to him wholeheartedly; we do not let go of the branch.

But is it realistic to let go of the branch? *No*, if we mean by that to let go of every human support, every source of security for our selves and our families. I don't believe that God expects that of us. But the answer is *Yes*, if it means that Jesus becomes our interpretation of life's meaning and our plan of life. *Yes*, if it means that we are willing to accept all that happens to us in the spirit of Jesus: "[N]ot my will but yours be done" (Luke 22:42).

IV. Jesus assures us that we are children of a loving God, that his love never fails us, that "even the hairs of [our] head have all been counted" (Luke 12:7). His love does not keep our hairs from falling out (How well I know that!). His providence does not keep suffering away from us. He only assures us that no matter what happens, his grace will enable us to accept it in the spirit of Jesus.

IV. All of this brings us to Jesus' final words in this Gospel: "The kingdom of God will be . . . given to a people that will produce its fruit." The harvest Jesus refers to is not ultimately success or achievement in this life. The only harvest Jesus wants is our very selves, putting our lives in his hands.

Year B

Genesis 2:18–24; Hebrews 2:9–11; Mark 10:2–16

Catholic Marriage and Annulment

I. My sister first married when I was a young seminarian. Her husband was in military service at the time. He was an agnostic and an alcoholic. He was given a less-than-honorable discharge from service. With his alcoholism and work record, their marriage lasted about one more year; eventually they were divorced. They had been properly married in the Catholic Church, and there was nothing I could do as a priest to set her free to marry again. For thirty years she lived a single life. Her faith was a strong support for her through all that time, but she found it very difficult not be free to marry. Only with the modern means of annnulment was there anything that could be done for her. Several years ago, she finally got an annulment from her husband on the grounds of psychic incapacity. Then I was able to marry her to a fine Catholic man. It was a great relief to her to be properly married in church.

II. Today's readings cry out for some explanation of our Catholic rules for marriage. In the Gospel, Jesus refers back to the Book of Genesis, which is our first reading today: "[T]hey are no longer two but one flesh. Therefore what God has joined together, no human being must separate. . . . Whoever divorces his wife and marries another commits adultery against her." Four times in the Gospels, Jesus states such an uncompromising norm for marriage. It's hard to believe that the gentle Jesus could give us such a demanding norm. Yet over two thousand years, the Church has not found a way around these words of Jesus. Even with our modern knowledge of Scripture, we cannot dismiss his words. So the church teaches the following norms on marriage: 1) All marriages of Christians are intended for life; 2) Catholics must be married before a priest (or deacon for a valid marriage; 3) All first marriages of non-Catholics are always presumed valid.

III. What can be done for Catholics who are now divorced or find themselves in an impossible marriage situation? Until recently, very little could be done. After decades of frustration and pain for many sincere Catholics, we have found a way of helping people in intolerable situations. One of the best means is that of annulment on the grounds of psychic incapacity. That is, just as a marriage could always be declared null because it was entered into by force or because one party was physically impotent, so also it can now be declared null because one party was psychologically incapable of a mature adult relationship. In addition, there are other more sensitive solutions for some cases. Our Church wants to alleviate, where possible, the pain connected with broken marriages.

IV. A few practical solutions. 1. Catholics who are in a first marriage but were never married in Church can easily do so in a simple, quiet ceremony, without any cost. 2. Catholics who are divorced and would like to seek an annulment should come in and talk to us about a solution; we can often find one. 3. Catholics who are away from the sacraments for a long time because of a second marriage and would like to straighten out things should come in and talk to us. Each case if different and will be seriously considered.

IV. To sum up. Jesus' teaching on marriage is meant to be an inspiring ideal for couples to live their lives with generosity and intimate love. Yet in his Church we try to make room for everyone, for Jesus is a most compassionate Lord. Recently, the church has found ways to respond to people in broken marriages in accord with the compassion of Jesus himself.

Year C

Habakkuk 1:2–3; 2:2–4; 2 Timothy 1:6–8, 13–14; Luke 17:5–10

Increase Our Faith

I. Listen to the complaint of the prophet Habakkuk today:

> How long O Lord? I cry for help
> but you do not listen! . . .
> Why do you let me see ruin;
> why must I look at misery? . . . .
> Then the Lord answered me and said,
> 'Write down the vision . . .
> [which] presses on to fulfillment, and will not disappoint . . . .
> [I]t will surely come . . . .
> [T]he just man, because of his faith, shall live.

Habakkuk cries out against very real injustices that are coming to God's people. The Babylonian invasion will be violent and devastating;

Judah and Jerusalem will be destroyed. How long will Yahweh let this violence go on and not intervene? The Lord's answer is that he *will* intervene in his own good time, but only after the suffering runs its course. God tells Habakkuk to write down the promise of deliverance and underscore his fidelity, "[I]t will surely come." God will be faithful to his word and promise. Then God's final word is both a warning and an assurance: "[T]he just man, because of his faith, shall live." Here faith means holding on in the midst of adversity; it means trusting the word of God as absolutely reliable.

II. One sentence in the Gospel is also a cry for faith: "[T]he apostles said to the Lord, 'Increase our faith.'" Here too faith includes trust in God's promises. Together with the words of Habakkuk, we are urged to have strong faith in God's promises; our faith should be real even in adversity; we should be true to our own words of faith.

III. Consider, for a moment, the importance of our own words. They are the most critical means of communicating and revealing ourselves. Our words indicate what kind of person we are. Sometimes our words are almost sacred, as indicated in the saying: "He is a man of his word." By our words we reveal our own view of life, our values, our promises, our commitments. If we do not live up to our words, then people believe us less and less. If we do not prove our words by our actions, then people realize our words are phony—as they often are for politicians running for office. If we do not honor our commitments, then we are judged irresponsible.

Words of faith are no different. We use words to express our faith; we affirm, "I am a Catholic; I believe in the truths of our faith." Such words of faith include an attitude about this world, a philosophy of life, a value system or ethic of life. If we do not live according to that value system, then we give the impression that such a value system is false. Our words of faith imply promises or vows taken at baptism; if we do not keep those vows, then we are not faithful to that extent. Finally, our words are essentially a sign of commitment to Jesus and his way of life. If we do not honor that commitment, then, to some degree, we are false to Christ.

IV. Today, I suspect, we are all willing to cry out with the apostles, "Increase our faith." Like the apostles, we are already people of faith, but like them we need to grow in that faith. So we ask Jesus to add greater depth to our words of faith, so that we can be more faithful to our words. We each want to be "a man of his word" with Christ. We know that Jesus makes endless allowances for our failures and weaknesses. But even he is helpless with those who refuse to be open to him or make a serious effort to follow him. So we ask our Lord, today, "Increase our faith"; help us to mean what we say and prove our words of faith more and more by our actions.

Twenty-eighth Sunday in Ordinary Time

Year A

Isaiah 25:6–10a; Philippians 4:12–14, 19–20; Matthew 22:1–14

Come to the Wedding

I. Today's First Reading is taken from Isaiah; it is commonly referred to as the "little apocalypse" of Isaiah; it is a very vivid and earthy presentation of the end time as a sumptuous banquet: "On this mountain the Lord of hosts / will provide . . . / A feast of rich foods and choice wines."

II. Matthew's Gospel today uses this image of a wedding banquet and expands an original parable of Jesus into an outline of the whole plan of redemption. It has been highly allegorized by adding many elements that refer to various people. Thus, the one who prepares the wedding feast is a king, God the Father; the feast is for his Son, Jesus, the Messiah; those invited first are those leaders of the Jews who persecuted the Christian apostles and messengers. Then, "the king was enraged and sent his troops, destroyed those murderers, and burned their city." This harsh and violent note refers to God's judgment on Jerusalem and its actual destruction in 70 AD; it is clearly a note added by the later church. Then the messengers are sent out into the streets to invite others, that is, the Gentiles; their invitation into the wedding hall is a reference to baptism. The king's entry into the banquet hall is the moment of final judgment. The wedding garment symbolizes the quality of an active Christian faith; only those with an active faith are properly attired to enter the kingdom of God. Thus, the entire history of redemption is depicted in this one allegory.

III. The central teaching here is the need to accept the kingdom of God and be ready for it in faith when it comes to us individually. The image of the banquet is frequent in the Old Testament, and at the Last Supper, Jesus himself made the connection between the heavenly banquet and the Eucharist: "I shall not eat it [again] until there is fulfillment in the kingdom of God" (Luke 22:16). Let us study the connection between the two banquets, the Eucharist and the heavenly banquet.

IV. As a young priest, one day I went to visit a family I had known for twenty-five years. I had gotten to know them when they were only kids and I was a seminarian running a summer program at a Chicago park. In all that time, I would visit them every year or two. This time, I saw the two eldest children along with their mother. It was a sad occasion for me. The daughter was breaking up her common-law marriage and interested in another married man. The grown children were very disrespectful to each other. The mother was confused and disgusted by all that was happening in the family. We eventually got around to talking about the Church. They admitted they had not gone to mass for years. They claimed they didn't need mass, "It's so changed," they said; "so I pray by myself; I have my faith without that. I still live as a Christian." Despite how they acted toward each other and how their lives were all messed up, they could still offer such excuses. I tried to make the point with them that no human relationship or friendship can remain strong without regular contact and expressions of friendship. The same is true for all of us. Our faith commitment to Christ can only remain a real friendship if we express it regularly and publicly. Since for most people, the only regular external expression of our friendship with Christ is the mass and Eucharist, without that, our faith tends to fade away.

V. That is the single point I wish to make today. To respond to God's invitation and to believe in his kingdom is not accomplished once and for all. Our response must be constant, external, and often renewed, or it tends to fade away. This is why we come each week to this Eucharistic banquet. This is how we strengthen our friendship with Jesus. This is the very means he gave us to maintain our active Christian faith; this is what he means, when he assures us: "Whoever eats my flesh and drinks my blood remains in me and I in him [her]" (John 6:56).

YEAR B

Wisdom 7:7–11; Hebrews 4:12–13; Mark 10:17–30

JESUS AND MATERIAL POSSESSIONS

I. Jesus never gives us a thoroughly developed theology about possessions. But this Gospel is one of the best passages for getting a sense of his attitude toward riches and possessions.

First, he tells the rich young man, "Go, sell what you have, and give to [the] poor . . . then come, follow me." This is *not* a universal statement; it is not a requirement for everyone who wants to follow Jesus. It is clear that the reality of Jesus' wandering public life was a poor life, without home or comforts; so if anyone were to travel with him, he had to share such a life, and so give up any land-holdings and possessions. That was the way Jesus and his disciples actually lived. One implied point that Jesus makes here is that beyond keeping the commandments, the way to eternal life is to follow Jesus. To follow Jesus *is* a universal way for all to enter eternal life.

Secondly, Jesus makes some observations about riches in general: "How hard it is for those who have wealth to enter the kingdom of God!" It's almost impossible if they become attached to it. This "astonished" the disciples, for in the Old Testament the possession of riches was a sign of God's favor. Now Jesus turns upside-down this popular notion; he teaches that riches is a hindrance! It is a barrier to submitting to the kingdom of God. The reasoning behind this norm of Jesus seems to be that a rich person is easily self-sufficient, independent, disinclined to submit to God's law. To say all that another way: it is so easy to be taken up with riches and possessions and feel no real need for God and his way.

Finally, Jesus assures Peter what will happen to those who do renounce all to follow Jesus: Anyone who has left family and lands for his sake, will receive a hundredfold and life everlasting (cf. vv. 29–30). Even though Peter had left only a single fishing boat, it was still a great sacrifice, since it was all he had. We need to add that it is not the very act of leaving things by itself that matters, but following Christ. Those who leave all human attachments for Christ are promised peace, courage, grace, and God's love now—and life everlasting.

II. Now let us try to summarize Jesus' whole approach to material possessions. In general, Jesus was not an ascetic; he never demanded sacrifice for the sake of sacrifice; he shared the ordinary life of men and women; he came "eating and drinking" (Matthew 11:19). His sacrifices were merely demanded by his way of living and his constant journeys to preach the word. He did not demand the renunciation of material possessions for anyone to become his disciple. But he did see that possessions could easily fill a person's heart, so that it would be difficult to submit to God's will, to be committed to Jesus' way. We cannot adequately characterize Jesus by seeing him as an ascetic religious leader, as one who separates himself from the world, as a man who requires poverty and actual rejection of all possessions. Such is not the characteristic way of Jesus; he was not that kind of religious leader. The only thing that adequately characterizes Jesus and his way is doing the will of his Father, serving the kingdom of God on earth. No external practices, no minute laws, no renunciation of possessions are absolute requirements for following him. Only doing the will of God and living after the model of Jesus himself are absolute norms for his followers.

III. This attitude toward material things is not common in affluent America today. The pursuit of possessions—often seen as necessities—is commonly the overwhelming drive of our society today. I believe riches and our consumer society are a great hindrance to following Jesus. Not only the rich, but all who are driven toward achieving or maintaining affluence, need to listen to Jesus' words today: "How hard it is for those who have wealth to enter the kingdom of God!" His caution is not absolute, but it is a strong warning for all of us.

Year C

2 Kings 5:14–17; 2 Timothy 2:8–13; Luke 17:11–19

He Was a Samaritan

I. What are the most well-known stories of Jesus? Which parables are remembered most by Christians? Which of his parables do you remember best? Let me suggest some and see if you personally agree. One would probably be the story of the good Samaritan, who found the man who had been robbed and cared for him. Another might be the prodigal son, who took his inheritance and spent it foolishly, before he came back home to his father. You might add the parable of the good shepherd, who left the 99 sheep and went looking for the one that was lost. Another might be the recently read Gospel of the Pharisee and the publican, who went to the temple to pray; or the story of Dives and Lazarus of two weeks ago. Surely there would be others, but these would probably be mentioned often. And that's surprising, for all of these parables are found uniquely in Luke's Gospel; no other Gospel has any of these stories, only Luke! Besides that, all these stories are part of the same theme of Luke; they all deal with the universality of salvation. Luke alone makes this the prime purpose of his Gospel: salvation is for all people equally. Thus, Luke more than any other evangelist taught that salvation is even for the Gentiles, especially in the story of the good Samaritan. The Jews did not like to hear that, for they were very proud of being God's chosen people. And he emphasized that salvation is for the poor and lowly in the parable of the Pharisee and the publican, and even more forcible in the story of Dives and Lazarus. This message was not welcomed by the rich and respectable. Also, Luke stressed that salvation is for the sinner and the outcast of society in the stories of the prodigal son and the good shepherd; this was not acceptable to the righteous.

II. Now take a look at today's Gospel in Luke. The most obvious lesson here is about thanksgiving. It uses the image of being cured of leprosy as a comparison for God's forgiveness of sins. The practical message for us is that's how much we should be grateful for God's forgiveness—as if we were cured of leprosy! But Luke also makes another point here, which gathers together all these themes we are talking about. Notice that only one man came back and received praise from Jesus, and "He was a Samaritan." As a Samaritan, he was a despised non-authentic Jew; as a leper, he was poor, lowly, and ugly. As a leper punished for his sins—as was supposed by Jesus' audience—he was a sinner and an outcast. The Samaritan had three strikes against him; but he is the only one praised by the Lord!

III. If this was Luke's point again and again in his entire Gospel, then this is certainly true of our Christian faith and this must be one of the marks of a true Christian. Yet here we are 200 years later, and we Christians have not been outstanding in keeping this teaching of Luke or in following this way of Jesus our Lord. For example, we are not always kind in speaking about Jews or Muslims in general. And we have a hard time accepting Mexicans and African Americans in our midst, even if they are fellow Christians. We get tired hearing about the poor and the starving in Africa and Latin America. We would rather avoid the poor, unkept, and uneducated in our society. We even condemn people with AIDS or other outcasts of our society.

IV. Let me confess that such judgments and attitudes are not totally eliminated in my own life. If we are completely honest, we might all admit that we still have some degree of prejudice and antagonism hidden deep inside us. Jesus does not demand perfection in us; but he does want us to admit his Christian ideal and continue to work on this attitude. Luke reminds us today that there is only one way of Jesus our Savior: acceptance of all, salvation equally for all people, no preference for any ethnic group, no prejudice or blanket condemnation toward any race. We need to realize that we all belong to the class of those ten who were made clean by Jesus. And we thank him for his gift of grace and salvation by trying to love him in his non-Catholics, his people of color, his poor, and his sinners. There is no other way for us if we want to be genuine Christians.

Twenty-ninth Sunday in Ordinary Time

Year A

Isaiah 45:1, 4–6; 1 Thessalonians 1:1–5b; Matthew 22:15–21

God and Caesar

I. The question of today's Gospel deals with God and Caesar or with separation of church and state. How are church and state separate? How are they related? Over the centuries, there have been numerous solutions to this question. Let us take a look at history and try to form our own solution.

II. How are church and state to be separated? The first answer is intimated by those who ask the question of Jesus in this Gospel. For some Jews, God alone was their king; they were God's chosen people; a secular Caesar could have *no real authority* over them. They simply did not accept the power and authority of Caesar; they tried to avoid payment of taxes, military service, or any allegiance to the governing power. Jesus' answer to them in the Gospel is more clever than clear; but at least he does not accept their position.

The second answer is that of the middle ages; it is one of *theocracy*. The king rules by divine right, and he is subordinate to the church. God is the supreme ruler of everything; the pope is his vicar on earth; the king must obey God and the church. In a word, church and state are united in one theocratic power.

The third solution grew very slowly from the second. In the last 200 years, it reached the opposite pole: church and state are quite *separate*; each has its own proper domain; the church rules over the sacred, the state rules the secular. This dichotomized solution has led to extreme positions lately in the United States. For example, it has led the supreme court to interpret the first amendment to the constitution so that they refuse all possible aid to non-public schools and they reject any possible prayer in public schools. It has also led politicians and many American to decide questions of war, justice, and foreign aid on a purely secular basis: what's good for the image of the U.S. or for our economy is absolutely good.

III. But there is one final solution that is becoming more obvious lately. It concentrates on the fact that *all our actions are human actions* and cannot be totally separated into sacred and secular. Everything we do, we do as Christians. Church and state are separate realms; but any human action of ours is both a secular and a Christian action. The basis for this solution is that Christian living is human living; it is not a Sunday morning activity or a vague keeping of the commandments, but a way of life that includes everything we do. And every action of a citizen involves justice, human rights, and personal responsibility. Many decisions involve complex moral issues; for example, nuclear armaments, civil rights laws, abortion laws, support or control of totalitarian regimes, humanitarian or military aid. Not every issue is a strictly moral issue, but every issue deals with human values and human needs.

Such are the four views of church and state throughout history. More than 200 years ago, in President Washington's farewell address, he asserted: "reason and experience both forbid us to expect that national morality can prevail in exclusion of religious principle." Neither George Washington in that address nor Jesus in today's Gospel had clearly in mind the union of church and state that I just suggested; but such a union is in keeping with their remarks. In a word, I maintain that for us Christians, church and state are inextricably united, because the Christian way of life includes all of our value judgments and human concerns.

Year B

Isaiah 53:10–11; Hebrews 4:14–16; Mark 10:35–45

What Is Christian Greatness?

I. In today's Gospel, Jesus describes his notion of greatness. His entire teaching is clear and forthright. Let us try to understand him with an open mind. Jesus begins by describing greatness among secular states or in the political realm: "You know that those who are recognized as rulers . . . lord it over them, and their great ones make their authority . . . felt." His language is particularly strong: lording "it over them" and making "their authority . . . felt"; he refers to great men wielding their power with authority. We can easily agree with this when we consider our modern world. Totalitarian rulers dominate and tyrannize their people fiercely. Even in democratic countries, those who have the power rule and manipulate others. In a word, among secular rulers: greatness equals power.

But there is another form of greatness that is particularly American. The most prominent form of greatness in America is measured by status and economic influence. Americans are considered great precisely by being successful, by being one of the richest people in America, by ruling over others and having all their needs fulfilled. In a word: greatness equals riches and *status*.

II. Christ's notion of greatness in this Gospel is diametrically opposed to all of this. First, he responds directly to James and John and their ambition to be first, to be powerful: "[I]t shall not be so among you." That is, though great men of the world lord it over their subjects and tyrannize them, it must not be that way with you; "Rather, whoever wishes to be great among you will be your servant." Here Jesus deliberately contrasts domination and power with service and being a servant to others. He does not rule out authority, but he does rule out domination. He knows that James and John will have some authority—in fact even given by himself—but they must use that authority to serve the rest. For them and for all who are in authority in the church, he has a profound caution. In a word, for Jesus, greatness equals *service*.

Secondly, Jesus makes a universal statement for all Christians: "[W]hoever wishes to be first among you will be the slave of all." That is, any Christian who wants to be first, must serve the needs of all. I believe Jesus' answer responds particularly to our American sense of greatness. For in America, riches and possessions equal greatness, precisely because they make us independent, able to satisfy our needs, able to have others serve our needs. Clearly, they are not looked upon as a means of serving others. So Jesus implies that riches and success are often a hindrance of greatness.

Finally, Jesus offers a *model* of greatness for all Christians: "[T]he Son of Man did not come to be served but to serve and to give his life as a ransom for many." That is, Jesus' mission as Messiah consists precisely in his serving, in his reconciling us to God by his death, in his being the suffering servant who redeems us. His greatness is that of profound service, compassion, and love. We might readily agree that what Jesus did for us deserves absolute prominence as the unique redeemer of the world. But we are slow to accept that this is also *our way* to greatness. We need to accept Jesus as our model for human greatness: greatness equals *service*.

III. Jesus' teaching about greatness becomes practical and clear when we consider people we know who followed his way of greatness. Here in our parish we have had some wonderful examples of greatness after the model of Jesus. Their greatness has nothing to do with their social position or status; it is not based on their personal success, fame, or power. No, it has everything to do with their compassion, service, and love, after the model of Jesus. They realize that such was the only kind of greatness that Jesus taught and lived. Such people inspire us all to follow the model of Jesus as our norm of greatness.

Year C

Exodus 17:8–13; 2 Timothy 3:14—4:2; Luke 18:1–8

Pray Always without Becoming Weary

I. Today's Gospel has two purposes. Saint Luke's purpose centers on the woman and emphasizes perseverance in prayer, as he indicates at the beginning: "[Jesus] told them a parable about the necessity . . . to pray always without becoming weary." Jesus' purpose centers on the judge as an image of God and emphasizes the assurance of God's help: "Will not God then secure the rights of his chosen ones, who call out to him day and night? Will he be slow to answer them?" In the context, just before our reading, Jesus is talking about the parousia, the tribulations at the end of the world. So his message, by means of this parable, is: Have no anxiety in the face of persecution and the final tribulation. You are God's elect; he will hear your cry and save you, despite persecution. These two purposes are not unrelated and both suggest to me the question: Why should we trust God in prayer? Why does perseverance in prayer make sense?

II. The first answer to this question is the one that Jesus intends here; that is, God does hear our prayer and will certainly help us, giving us the *victory in the end*; no matter what our trials, he most certainly will save us and deliver us from the trials in the end. Every time we say the "Our Father," we pray for just this final help: "[D]o not subject us to the final test, /but deliver us from the evil one" (Matthew 6:13; or, more familiarly, "Lead us not into temptation but deliver us from evil").

III. The second answer to why we should trust God and persevere in prayer faces the essential problem that so many of us have about prayers of petition. Many of us believe that trusting God in prayer means he will take care of the things we pray for, give us the things we want, make our way smooth and untroubled. I suggest that such an idea is not Christian, for Jesus himself did not come to make our world a Utopia, and God himself cannot force all people to be good to us, for then they would not be free. Earlier in Luke's Gospel, Jesus goes so far as to promise: "[A]sk and you will receive; seek and you will find; knock and the door will be opened to you" (Luke 11:9). This verse is so strong that it sounds like a universal law. Then he concludes his instruction on prayer by assuring us: "[H]ow much more will the Father in heaven give the holy Spirit to those who ask him" (11, 13)? I suggest from all this that our prayer will not keep tragedies and accidents from happening to us; nor will it make people unfailingly kind to us; nor will it make our little part of the world all sweetness and light. But prayer will always result in some help, if not specifically what we ask for, then certainly the help of the Spirit of Jesus to have *the courage we need to follow him* in whatever comes.

IV. The third answer to why we should trust God and persevere in our prayer is that *right in our prayer God helps us*. For me the primary purpose of prayer is exactly this: to understand our relationship to God, to open ourselves to his love and his way. That is, right in our prayer, he constantly helps us to be aware of our relationship to him, to accept Jesus as the meaning of our lives, to surrender ourselves to his way of life, to open our hearts to Jesus' way of compassion, forgiveness, and love, to be convinced that we are valuable to him and that he cares for us.

V. Let me conclude with some of my experience of prayer. I am convinced that I need regular contact with God to be aware of him in my life, to accept his way, to be open to his love, to be assured that he cares for me. At times in my life, when I did not pray for a while, this assurance faded a little and my relationship to God was not as strong and conscious. This is similar to how all human friendships work; without regular contact, the friendship fades away. That's why we need "to pray always without becoming weary" (Luke 18:1).

Thirtieth Sunday in Ordinary Time

Year A

Exodus 22:20–26; 1 Thessalonians 1:5c–10;
Matthew 22:34–40

Christian Life Takes This Life Seriously

I. Christianity is a religion that takes this life seriously; it insists that every person and this world of ours have great value and meaning. And the most common alternatives to real Christian living today do not take life seriously. For example, hedonism or "eat drink and be merry" does not take this world seriously; it claims that life is for satisfaction, for self-gratification. The "American Dream" does not take life seriously; it is concerned with material success, possessions, and status—all external qualities only. Spiritualistic religion does not take this life seriously; it is a fantasy approach to life that underplays the value of this world, stays aloof from it and tries to live in another world. And legalistic religion does not take this life seriously; it identifies religion with laws and religious practices that only touch a small part of our existence now. But Christianity is serious about this world and the value of our life in it; the Christian knows that the eternal meaning and value of his life is worked out only in this world; he knows that what he hopes to become is only accomplished here and now; he takes seriously both God and our human life and connects the two inseparably.

II. Consider today's Gospel. The Pharisee presents Jesus with a moral or legal problem, a typical concern for legalistic religion; that is, among the many laws, which is the greatest? Jesus' answer raises the whole issue to a different plane; it summarizes in a unique way what our entire Christian life is meant to be. This summary of the law is not altogether original with Jesus. What *is* unique and distinctive in Jesus' response is the implied radical *interconnectedness* of the two: you cannot have one without the other. For love of God is illusory, if it does not issue in love of neighbor, and universal love of our neighbor is impossible, if it does not proceed from love of God.

Let me explain what I mean. Love of God is illusory without love of neighbor. As St. Teresa of Avila explains:

> The most certain sign that we are keeping these two precepts [of love of God and neighbor] is our love of our neighbor, for whether or not we love God cannot be known, but neighborly love is unmistakable. If we fulfill this precept very perfectly, we have done everything.[4]

To say this in other words: there is only one *means* of loving God: it is by loving our neighbor; there is only one *way* to prove our love for God: it is by loving our neighbor; there is only one *medium* by which we serve God: it is by serving our neighbor.

On the other hand, love of neighbor is impossible without the love of God. For only our common bond as sons and daughters of God and our motive: "[I]f God so loved us, we also must love one another" (1 John 4:11), can overcome our separateness, our isolation, our selfishness, our unconcern. Humanism alone is not enough.

III. There is one argument against Christianity we still need to consider. Isn't it true that Christianity deals with laws and rituals and keeping the commandments and these are mostly external actions? YES, we do have to keep the commandments; as Jesus says,

---

4. Teresa of Avila, *The Interior Castle*. See: *The Complete Works of St. Teresa*, 3 vols. (London: Sheed and Ward, 1944–46), pp. 261–262.

"If you love me, you will keep my commandments" (John 14:15). But the commandments are merely the negative, external and minimal requirements; negative, because they indicate what we should avoid; external, for they are definite, expressed laws to be lived; minimal, for they only deal with essential morality. But we Christians are called to live the life of Christ not only by avoiding sin as it becomes a problem perhaps a few times a day, but also by trying to live as Jesus lived every moment of our life, wherever we are, whatever we are doing; these are the positive, internal and maximal requirements. We Christians go far beyond concern over sin, when we take as the norm of our life, ". . . love the LORD, your God, with all your heart, and with all your soul (Deuteronomy 6:5) . . . [and] love your neighbor as yourself" (Leviticus 19:18). To do that well, we must take the world and the human person very seriously.

YEAR B

Jeremiah 31:7–9; Hebrews 5:1–6; Mark 10:46–52

OUR COMPASSIONATE SAVIOR

I. Father Raymond Brown is a moderate and cautious scripture scholar. This is what he says about the humanity of Jesus: "Unless we understand that Jesus was truly human, we cannot understand the depth of God's love . . . [for] God so loved us that he subjected himself to our most agonizing infirmities." Last Sunday and today, we are reading from the Letter to the Hebrews. This letter gives us a most consoling description of Jesus, our very human and compassionate Savior.

II. It begins: "Every high priest is taken from among men . . . [and so] is able to deal patiently with the ignorant and erring, for he himself is beset by weakness." Then he insists that Jesus is such a high priest. His point is that Jesus can fully sympathize with sinners because he knew temptation as we do, he was acquainted with the trials of human nature, he experienced our fear of death. Because he too experienced suffering, weakness, human trials and fear, he can be really compassionate with our human failures and struggles. Just because he is a truly human Savior, we can be sure that his compassion for us is deep and real.

But this letter to the Hebrews emphasizes another facet of Jesus' humanity. Three times it describes Jesus as being made perfect through suffering; for example: "[I]t was fitting that [God] . . . in bringing many children to glory, should make the leader to their salvation perfect through suffering" (2:10; cf. 5:8–9 and 7:27–28). That is, through suffering, Jesus our model learned obedience, fulfilled his mission and attained the goal and perfection of his moral life.

III. This leaves us with the implied conclusion: if Jesus himself only became perfect through suffering, then we too can only become perfect or complete through the trials of our lives. But the first letter of Peter makes this conclusion explicit and powerful: "[T]o this you have been called, because Christ also suffered for you, leaving you an example that you should follow in his footsteps" (1 Peter 2:21). That means that we too are perfected by obedience as Jesus was. Jesus is our model of holiness by his suffering. Because Jesus became morally perfect through suffering, so we also become morally whole by the ordinary trials of our life.

Looking over this assembly here today, I have known some of you for 18 years. During that time, so many of you have had some major trial: a serious illness or operation, the death of a family member, becoming widowed or very elderly, heartache with your children or loss of your job. Add to that, the ordinary struggles of daily living—your daily work, family difficulties, disappointments, physical ills, loneliness, prejudice—these are all ways to imitate Jesus in his suffering. We do that especially by accepting the reality of our individual life, just as it comes to us.

IV. To sum up what the letter to the Hebrews tells us today: The compassion of Jesus our Savior is real, because he suffered just as we do. He is our model for holiness by his very suffering. We can become perfect or complete, if we "follow in his footsteps."

Year C

Sirach 35:12–14, 16–18; 2 Timothy 4:6–8, 16–18; Luke 18:9–14

The Pharisee and the Publican

I. Especially in Luke's Gospel, the parables of Jesus teach religious and moral examples for Christians of every century. Last week's parable about persistence in prayer and today's parable are both unique to Luke, and both deal with our attitude toward God in prayer. When Jesus first spoke this parable, it sounded outrageous to his listeners. For the Pharisee was a righteous man, not a sinner; he was quite moral in performing his religious duties; society judged him to be one of the "good guys." But the tax collector, by his very occupation, was a sinner, one who collaborated with the Romans in cheating his own people by extortion and graft. Society judged his as a swindler and a "bad guy."

Jesus does *not* mean that the Pharisee was wrong in his deeds of morality and piety or that the tax collector was right in being a swindler. Rather, the whole point of this daring parable deals *only* with the proper attitude in prayer, with the way to approach God in prayer. Just as last week's parable taught perseverance in prayer, this parable teaches the proper attitude for prayer.

II. The entire point of Jesus' parable here deals only with our attitude before God in prayer. The Pharisee considered himself good and righteous, because he religiously tried to keep all the Old Testament laws and traditions. So he set before God all his merits and trusted in God's help because of his own righteousness. Jesus condemned him for that, because he felt self-justified; his prayer was self-serving from beginning to end; he believed that he deserved God's grace.

The tax collector, on the other hand, knew he was a bad lot; he beat his breast and said *Kyrie Eleison*; he asked only for forgiveness; he depended only on the mercy of God. That is the attitude that wins praise from Jesus: "I tell you the [tax collector] went home justified, not the [Pharisee]."

III. What Jesus teaches so strongly here is another form of Saint Paul's fundamental teaching of justification by faith apart from the works of the law. Paul insists that none of us is justified or ultimately saved because of our righteousness or because we keep the law or because of our wisdom and achievements in the world, or because of our success and status in the world. Rather, each and every one of us is saved and blessed *only* by the saving mercy of God. It is God's grace alone that justifies us; it is our total dependence on his mercy that saves us. There is no other possible position for us to take before God. Religion is only for the poor in spirit; salvation is not our right but purely God's grace. And here in this parable, Jesus teaches this fundamental stance of Christians, not in the complicated, technical exposition of Paul, but in the concrete, pictorial language of this parable.

IV. Notice, finally, how comforting this teaching of Jesus is for us. It tells us the almost nothing stops God's grace—not sin, failure or weakness—as long as we are sorry. Rather, the only thing that God cannot tolerate is self-righteousness and self-justification. For then God would not be our God of pure mercy and free grace. So our only approach to him in prayer is as his creature, as one who is nothing before him. Of if you will, as his child who has no strict right to his saving grace but is still filled with trust in a loving Father. The source of our confidence in not our good actions but only God's mercy and love—which never fail us.

Thirty-first Sunday in Ordinary Time

Year A

Malachi 1:14b—2:2b, 8–10; 1 Thessalonians 2:7b–9, 13; Matthew 23:1–12

Only One Way to Love

I. Modern life tends to separate us from one another. Those who live in cities learn to be unconcerned about their neighbors, lest they get caught up in their problems. Those living in apartments, often don't even know the one living next door. Since the average family moves every four years, many relationships are very temporary. Our technological world tends to isolate us farther. Our social housing patterns still tend to divide us by race and economic status. Even in a suburb (or city), our complicated life-styles and time-demands incline us deliberately to seek quiet and privacy.

With such a split-up society, it seems natural to ask, "Why should I care about my neighbors? I am not really bound to them. In a few short years, they or I will be moved. Our free time is so limited, we can hardly make the effort necessary for friendship." And such negative feelings become even stronger when others do not respond well to us, when others take advantage of us, when we go through some crisis of loneliness or depression without much support from our neighbors.

II. The readings today are some help. Malachi asks, "Have we not all the one Father? / . . . / Why then do we break faith with each other, / violating the covenant of our fathers?" Here the fatherhood of God is stressed as a covenant relationship, so that when we break faith with one another, we break the covenant with our Father. In the Gospel, Jesus reminds us, "[Y]ou have but one Father in heaven . . . . The greatest among you must be your servant." That is, God alone is the great and loving Father; our greatness comes from serving his children. I am reminded here of the strange logic of Saint John: "[I]f God so loved us, we also must love one another" (1 John 4:11).

II. One poem I have liked since I was a youngster is "Abou-ben-Adam" by Leigh Hunt. The poem tells the story of a rabbi in the East who wanted to feel sure that he loved God. One night he had a dream in which an angel appeared to him holding the "Roll of Life," in which were written the names of those who loved God. The scroll was unrolled before him, and he looked at the names but could not find his own name there. He was deeply disappointed. As the angel was departing, Abou-ben-Adam looked at him sadly and said, "At least write down my name as one who loves his fellows." Next night, he dreamed again, and the angel with the scroll appeared once more. He unrolled it before the rabbi, and to his delight, Abou-ben-Adam saw that his name was at the head of the list.

III. Our Christian faith teaches us that there is only one means of loving God; it is by loving our neighbor. There is only one medium by which we can serve God; it is by serving our neighbor. There is only one way we can prove our love for God; it is by loving our neighbor. This is also what the saints teach us. Saint Teresa of Avila, the great mystic, teaches:

> The most certain sign that we are keeping these two precepts [of love of God and love of our neighbor] is our love of our neighbor. For whether or not we love God cannot be known, but neighborly love is unmistakable. If we fulfill this precept perfectly, we have done everything.[5]

And St. Catherine of Siena relates these words as the words of God to herself:

> To Me, in person, you cannot repay the love which I require of you, and I have placed you in the midst of your fellows, that you may do to them that which you cannot do to me . . . and what you do to him, I count as done to Me . . . [as Jesus] said to Paul, "Saul, Saul, why do you persecute Me?"[6]

---

5. 1. Saint Teresa of Avila, *The Interior Castle;* see: *The Complete Works of St. Teresa*, 3 vols. (London: Sheed and Ward, 1944–46), pp. 261–62.

6. 2. Saint Catherine of Sienna, *The Dialogue of St. Catherine of Sienna* (Westminster, MD: The Newman Press, 1950), pp. 155–56.

Even in our modern, disjointed life, the words of Jesus are true: "The greatest among you must be your servant."

Year B

Deuteronomy 6:2–6; Hebrews 7:23–28; Mark 12:28b–34

The Greatest Commandment

I. Our American culture is very concerned about laws and morality; the media constantly report tragedies resulting from a breakdown of law and order. Newspaper commentators remind us, especially after another senseless shooting or violent rampage, that we are easily the most violent country in the world. Politicians seeking election wax eloquent about the breakdown of family life, including unwed mothers, physical abuse and ever- increasing broken families. Our Catholic Church seems to claim that sins against the sixth commandment are the greatest source of evil; so many pronouncements deal with problems of premarital sex, abortion, obscenity, and pedophilia. Now, early in this twenty-first century, historians proclaim the twentieth century to be the worst in history in number of wars; at almost any time in your lifetime, there have been up to 40 conflicts or wars going on simultaneously in our world. It would be easy for anyone of these groups to claim this specific breakdown of law and morality is the most important concern for our society today.

II. In today's Gospel, *Jesus* is asked what aspect of law and morality does he rate as the most important: Of the 613 laws of the Old Testament—some of them dealing with murder, divorce, sex, and religious practices—what would be the number one law? Jesus' answer left no doubt. He said the greatest law is love of God and love of neighbor; he joined them together as one commandment, because they are radically interconnected. This is precisely the contribution and *originality* of Jesus' response: you cannot have one without the other. What he seems to affirm is that the love of God is illusory, if does not issue in love of neighbor, and also the universal love of our neighbor is impossible, if it does not proceed from love of God.

That is, love of God is a sham without love of neighbor. As Teresa of Avila teaches:

> The most certain sign that we are keeping these two precepts [of loving God and our neighbor] is our love of our neighbor, for whether we love God can not be known, but neighborly love is unmistakable. If we fulfill this precept very perfectly, we have done everything.[7]

On the other hand, universal love of neighbor is impossible without love of God. For only our common bond as sons and daughters of God and our motive, "[I]f God so loved us, we also must love one another" (1 John 4:11), can overcome our selfishness and our unconcern for others.

III. So Jesus requires that our faith be humanly authentic and completely real. That means that pious religiosity alone is phony; devotions and private prayers by themselves do not make us good Christians. But it also means that humanism alone or great efforts to help cure human ills are not enough; we also need faith to love God himself. Let me summarize this teaching of Jesus in one sentence: Jesus taught only one word: love, and he meant that love of neighbor and love of God make up the essence of our morality, so that we cannot be authentic Christians unless we have both.

Year C

Wisdom 11:22—12:2; 2 Thessalonians 1:11—2:2; Luke 19:1–10

You Love All Things That Are

I. The phone call came in the middle of the night. Kathy needed to talk to me, because she had attempted suicide again and wanted someone to convince her to stop the actual bleeding of her wrist and to assuage the desperate psychological hurt she felt. For two hours, I listened to her self-loathing and to the psychological abuse her friends had inflicted on her. For months before this night, she had poured out her story to me over many sessions, in person or on the

---

7. St. Teresa of Avila, *The Interior Castle*; see: *The Complete Works of St. Teresa, 3 vols.* (London: Sheed and Ward, 1944–46), pp. 261–262.

phone. She had been an adopted child; her adoptive parents felt that her real mother was a tramp, so she herself could not be any good. Her recent husband was really a bigamist and a wife abuser. Though they were separated, he still managed to disrupt her life. Her little girl was autistic and could not respond to her in any positive way. Her acquaintances were either on drugs or were all mixed-up themselves. They were often rotten to her; it seemed that every couple weeks, one of them would take advantage of her in some way. One of them had raped her recently. No wonder she had tried to commit suicide three times. She put no value on her life. She had no self-respect and received very little human love from others. Her painful tale finally wore herself down emotionally. Then I had a chance to remind her that so much of this unspeakable life was not her doing but was done *to* her. I tried to assure her of her essential goodness and value. By the end of our conversation, she was only minimally comforted. In the next three years, we talked for more than 400 hours! Slowly, she began to be convinced of her worth as a human being. After she moved away from her companions, she was slowly able to believe in herself and in God's love for her. Eventually, she married a decent man and was able to begin a new life in another state.

II. The First Reading today is a powerful argument from the book of Wisdom on the universal mercy and love of God. The sense of the entire reading is that human beings have made such an awful mess of God's creation, yet it is still his creation, it still has his spirit of life and goodness. Humanity can always count on his mercy, care and forgiveness. Here is what Wisdom tells us:

> [Y]ou love all things that are
> and loathe nothing that you have made;
> for what you hated, you would not have fashioned . . . .
> [Y]ou spare all things, because they are yours, O LORD and lover
> of souls.

The argument here is this: just as a painter or sculptor could not bear to see the product of his genius smashed to pieces, so God could not destroy what he had made.

III. And the conclusion of the Gospel makes a similar point: "The Son of Man has come to seek and to save what was lost." By eating with outcasts and sinners and by his acceptance of Zacchaeus,

Jesus leads us to conclude that it is not the observance of the Mosaic Law or perfect moral righteousness that determines our relation to God, but our attitude toward Jesus and our sincere effort to follow his way, despite our faults. To say that another way: social outcasts, unappealing people, even sinners who are repentant—all of us are valuable and loved by God because of this one quality: our attitude toward Jesus, our faith in him, our struggle to follow him. As Jesus says in John's Gospel, "[W]hoever loves me will be loved by my Father, and I will love him [her]" (John 14:21). No one can destroy that value and goodness we have as followers of Jesus and children of God. Only we ourselves can destroy it by giving up on our faith in Jesus and not trusting God's love for us.

IV. We all know from experience that human love is often fickle and unreliable. If we depend on that for our self-love, we are bound to be disappointed at times and possible devastated. We all *need* that human love and esteem from others, but it cannot be the foundation of our self-esteem. Rather, our indestructible self-esteem comes from the assurance that God always loves the children he created, especially when we have a commitment to Jesus our Savior.

Thirty-second Sunday in Ordinary Time

YEAR A

Wisdom 6:12–16; 1 Thessalonians 4:13–18; Matthew 25:1–13

WISE AND FOOLISH VIRGINS

I. Today's Gospel is based on a simple parable about ten virgins. As a parable it has only one point, which might be paraphrased: Be prepared for death, for you don't know when the end is coming. Saint Matthew however, developed this simple parable into a longer allegory, in which all the elements are symbolic and significant. Thus, the bridegroom is Jesus himself; the ten virgins are the expectant Christian community; Jesus' coming is the end of life or the end of the world; the delay of his coming is the waiting time before the end; the suddenness of his coming is the unpredictability of the end; the rejection of the foolish virgins is their rejection at the last judgment, because they are not ready. All of these allegorical details constitute Matthew's redaction criticism; that is, Matthew himself expands Jesus' parable by giving it a fresh meaning to fit the context of his Gospel. So for Matthew, the division between the wise and foolish virgins becomes the division between those in the church who respond to the teaching of Jesus and those whose failure to follow him, makes them not ready for the last judgment. To sum all this up for Matthew's time and for our time: this allegory deals with our Christian stance regarding death. It counsels us: Be always prepared; live a life of readiness, for you never know when the end is coming.

II. Such a warning of Jesus is very appropriate for modern America. As Rollo May, the popular psychologist, claims: "The chief problem today is emptiness. [The repression of death] is what makes modern life banal, empty and vapid." That is, because so many Americans have discarded the old religious assurances, life itself becomes bleak and meaningless. They run away from death, becoming lost in work, or caught up in their busy life, or take as their goal the "good life." Life for them is a cross-country race in search of a finishing line. Others side-step death by believing in the slogan, "Eat, drink and be merry, for tomorrow you die," or the more modern slogan, "If it feels good, do it." Consequently, many Americans try to avoid thoughts of death and so are not prepared for it.

III. Our Christian approach to our mortality is quite different. We face up to the reality of death throughout our lives. For us the uncertainly of death—that is might come at any minute—is the reason why we try to live all our life with meaning, purpose, and direction. For us the closeness of death makes all human life crucial, for we have only a few, uncertain years to become what we will be for all eternity. And for us, the life after death for which we hope is a dominant fact of our life; it pervades all our living now. Our amazing hope of everlasting happiness is the great proof of God's love for us. Because of that hope, all our sufferings—even the senseless and absurd ones—can have some redeeming feature. Because of that hope, all our troubles as well as our joys have a different horizon and background; we try to live our whole life against that horizon of ultimate hope. Because of that hope, nothing in life can destroy our sense of God's love for us. Matthew concludes with the oft-repeated caution of Jesus: "[S]tay awake, for you know neither the day nor the hour."

Year B

1 Kings 17:10–16; Hebrews 9:24–28; Mark 12:38–44

Politics and Religion

I. Often in November, Americans exercise their right to vote. In different years, they choose a new president, senators, and representatives, as well as state and local leaders. For several months before this election, all of these candidates express their plans for social reform, for laws that would be more just, for programs to help all classes of people. Many of these laws have moral implications; some deal with matters of justice; others try to reform social institutions, such as social security, medicare, and medical insurance. So today might be an appropriate time to consider politics and religion.

II. What kind of guidance does our faith offer us, when we consider justice issues and reform of social institutions? Let me begin by admitting that sincere Christians who want to reform social institutions are sometimes disappointed that the New Testament has nothing *directly* to say about social reform. For example, the New Testament is silent on politics and government. Scripture is unsatisfactory regarding the problems of slavery and unjust labor practices. The New Testament says very little about war and violent revolution. Scripture does not strongly defend the equal rights of women. But *indirectly* Jesus' teaching can lead to reform of social institutions. For example, if justice and peace are Christian values for all situations, then politicians and governments cannot rule outside these values. If all Christians are "one in Christ Jesus," then it is impossible for one person to own another or abuse their employees. If "there is not male and female; for you are all one in Christ Jesus" (Galatians 3:28), then there must be no subordination or inequality for women in society. In a word, the values of Jesus are values for all Christians in all situations. To the degree that we are motivated by the Spirit of Jesus, to that degree we will insist on equal rights for all and will try to cure these social ills that are so contrary to the norms of Christ.

III. Today's Gospel is a good example of Jesus' teaching about motivation and social conscience. The scribes are Jewish religious leaders who are condemned by Jesus for their pride and ostentation. Because of their unjust treatment of widows, "They will receive a very severe condemnation." In the second scene, after some wealthy people contributed large sums of money for charity, a poor widow put in about a penny. But Jesus praises her because only her gift was a real sacrifice. Jesus wants us to know that any alms is measured not by the amount but by the sacrifice involved. Notice how Jesus here emphasizes the individual and her motivation.

This same thrust is found consistently in the Gospels—the reformation of the individual, not the reform of institutions. So Jesus' reform has nothing directly to do with government laws and social order; rather it is accomplished by the free decision and motivation of the individual person. That is, Jesus—and Saint Paul too—does not set up laws to bridle cruelty and injustice, for such laws would still leave us with a cruel world. Rather, Jesus positively teaches kindness and justice, so that the people—and ultimately the institutions—might really be changed internally. He wants us not only to bridle injustice but also to change ourselves from the insides. He implies that social action by itself is not sufficient to cure our social ills. We also need compassionate, kind, and just human beings. As followers of Jesus, we are all urged to be integral, just Christians and to find our own way to work toward justice for all.

Year C

2 Maccabees 7:1–2, 9–14; 2 Thessalonians 2:16—3:5;
Luke 20:27–38

Who Is Jesus Christ?

I. The central question of our faith is this: Who is Jesus Christ? For
Christ is the distinctive feature of Christianity; he is the center of our
faith; he is the image of God for us. For us Christians, he is the model
for our living, the way of fulfilling our amazing hope. So we need to
answer the question: What kind of leader is Jesus? Throughout these
2,000 years, Christians have seen him in one role or another, and that
role determined to a large extent the form that Christianity took for
them. One reason for considering this question today is that recent
Sunday Gospels help us to answer this central question.

II. A. Most often in history, Jesus has been appealed to as the
foundation of the *establishment*. That is, he was seen as the reason for
maintaining the religious or political status quo. For example, the
Holy Roman Empire dominated the entire western world for centuries and was the sovereign church and state in one; it included the
philosophy that it ruled according to the will of God and Christ. And
the power it wielded was often one of dominance, not service. But the
historical Jesus was not concerned with the political Roman rule or
even with Jewish religious hierarchy, but only with the kingdom of
God now and at the end of history. His message was simply the
human message of justice, freedom, forgiveness and service of neighbor. In today's Gospel, Jesus rejects the theology of the Sadducees and
never does accept their general approach to aligning themselves with
the Roman authorities in order to maintain their own power as a
priestly aristocracy.

B. Secondly, Jesus has often been seen as a *social revolutionary*,
one who wanted the social order suddenly and violently overthrown.
This is how he was looked upon in his own time. The Jews expected a
messiah who would be the long-awaited one to restore their country
and freedom and to destroy the godless rule of Rome. But Jesus
constantly had to teach the apostles that he was not that kind of

messiah; three times in each synoptic Gospel, Jesus rejected this kind of messiahship; he was not a social liberator or political messiah, but a Messiah who saves by his suffering and death.

C. Thirdly, Jesus has often been presented as a *religious ascetic*, one who dissociates himself from the world, one who seeks perfection by retreating from the world. Such were the Essenes of his time; they isolated themselves from the world and sought salvation as an elite group who observed religious laws and ascetic practices. Such also were the religious zealots throughout history who taught that the only proper way to follow Jesus was by a monastic existence including severe ascetic practices, rigid rules, and retreat from the world. But Jesus did not opt out of ordinary life; he was normal in his general behavior and did not require of his followers special vows, practices, rituals or living separate from the rest of the world. Notice the recent Sunday Gospels of the lost sheep (Twenty-fourth Sunday in Ordinary Time) and the cure of the ten lepers (Twenty-eighth Sunday in Ordinary Time). They imply that his way included worldly people, sinners and outcasts.

D. Finally, Jesus is often seen as a *moralist*, as one who teaches righteousness, which consists of observance of God's laws along with pious practices, even while living in the world. Such was the way of the Pharisees, who found their righteousness in a complex casuistry of detailed good actions, ascetic practices, and pious observances; by carefully observing the written and oral laws of God, they became worthy of salvation. But Jesus condemned them severely, because they found their righteousness before God in these very legal observances, instead of entirely in the mercy of God. Recall the Gospel of the Pharisee and the publican (Thirtieth Sunday in Ordinary Time); the Pharisee was not justified because of his self-righteousness, while the publican was justified by God's mercy.

III. What we have said so far is that Jesus fits none of the ordinary categories for a religious leader—not establishment, revolution, a retreat from the world or righteousness. Rather, he is entirely unique in his way. What kind of leader was Christ; what did he stand for? His cause is simply *the will of God or the kingdom of God*: "As is written of me . . . / Behold, I come to do your will, O God" (Hebrews 10:7). Jesus taught us to commit our entire life and being to God. That does not require a retreat from the world or a narrow form of asceticism. It requires only that we do God's will by accepting the reality of our lives just as it comes to us. It means that we become whole by practicing justice, forgiveness, acceptance, and love. For us here, all of this becomes concrete in the person of Jesus himself, for he himself is our "way," the model of our living. As disciples, no matter what our circumstances of life, we follow his way by trying "to live as Jesus lived."

Thirty-third Sunday in Ordinary Time

YEAR A

Proverbs 31:10–13, 19–20, 30–31; 1 Thessalonians 5:1–6; Matthew 25:14–30

BURYING YOUR TALENT

I. Today's Gospel is the origin of the English word, "talent." In most translations, the servants are given 5, 2 or 1 talent; a talent was a large amount of money, in fact, the largest unit of currency known at the time. Each servant was given these talents "according to his ability." So the talents had a direct reference to ability; in time, talent meant ability, as it does with our English word.

II. When Jesus first told this story, the crux of the meaning was found in the third servant. That negligent servant saw valuables as best protected by burying them. Knowing that his master expected some return with interest, he decided to make no investment at all, lest he lose some of it. So his talent remained unproductive of any gain at all. For *Jesus*, the unprofitable servant represented the Jewish religious leaders who refused to accept Jesus' message and so buried their talent. That is, without faith in Jesus, all their talents were worthless and achieved nothing for God. But *Matthew* places this parable toward the end of his Gospel, just before the last judgment scene. So he intends it as a *parousia* parable, relating to the last judgment; that is, how each one used his talent would lead either to reward ("Come, share your master's joy."), or to punishment ("[T]hrow this useless servant into the darkness outside"—meaning assign him to eternal damnation.) For Matthew, then, the profitable servants stand for all those Christians who hear the teaching of Jesus, believe in him, and follow his new way of life. And the unprofitable servant refers to those Christians who do not follow the way of Jesus; they carelessly disregard the Word of God by their self-seeking and unconcern.

III. Matthew's parable has much to say to modern American Catholics. I believe it says something to the totally pragmatic businessman of today whose work takes all his time and energy so that he never questions his own values in relation to Christ's; he never seeks any other meaning to his work; he only sees its practical value, its material result. For him, Jesus is not the meaning to his life nor the goal of his human activity.

This parable is also meant for those Catholics who see their faith only in terms of occasional mass on Sunday and, when convenient, keeping the commandments. They feel no compulsion to live their faith consistently or to grow in their faith.

IV. But Jesus wants us all to give ourselves to his way with real dedication. He expects us to grow and mature in the grace of God and to use our talents for good, not just for profit. He wants us to use our gifts or nature and grace to touch the lives of others. To paraphrase the positive meaning of the parable: our talents increase in value as long as we use them with some of the values and attitudes of Christ. That is, he wants us to build on our baptismal commitment by a steady and active growth in virtue and Christian dedication. And to the degree that we use our talents in a way that is humanly and spiritually profitable, we will be more than adequately rewarded by him. This is one of the reasons we come here week after week; we come to study Jesus and model our lives on him. We all fail somewhat in this, of course; but as long as we struggle to use our talents after the model he left us, he will judge us with compassion and generosity. Even the mediocre use of talents will merit his invitation: "Well done, my good and faithful servant. . . . Come, share your master's joy."

Year B

Daniel 12:1–3; Hebrews 10:11–14, 18; Mark 13:24–32

Continuing Human Tension

I. Both the first and the third readings today are apocalyptic, taken up with the cosmic events at the end of the world. In the early Church, such passages were most relevant, for Christians really expected the end of world to come soon. However, since the second century, such readings only related directly to a remote consummation of history in the distant future; so they lost their sense of urgency. How can they be relevant for us in the twenty-first century? In general, as soon as we focus on the end of our individual life, which is certainly coming, we are immediately confronted with the essential tension of the Christian life; I mean the tension between life now for a short time and life after death for all eternity.

II. Authentic Christianity asks us to take both this world and the next very seriously and never take away that tension. However, many modern Americans take away this tension by ignoring all thought of eternity. They have no sense of urgency about the next life; they are not moved by the shortness of life now. They may follow Christ in a minimal way, but they want to make sure they get all they can out of life now. Their motto seems to be: "Let us eat and drink, / for tomorrow we die" (1 Corinthians 15:32).

Some old church Christians often offended at the other extreme; they overemphasized life after death. They tried to live only for eternity and lost a healthy concern for this life now. Their motto might be, "Don't be concerned about material possession or even about trying to improve social conditions here; just set your heart on spiritual things and on your hope of eternal life."

Authentic Christianity insists on the essential connection between life now and life after death. The connection is this: just because we believe in eternal life, our life now is more critical and filled with meaning. For all our daily work is an effort to make the quality of life on this earth more human and more Christian. Also, all our efforts for material progress and psychological understanding are attempts to help people be more free and capable of becoming whole as human beings. And on the personal level, how we live now, what we become here and now, is the measure of our merit before God; however much we learn to "put on the Lord Jesus Christ" (Romans 13:14); that will determine our capacity to love God for all eternity. What we become here, will determine what we will be for all eternity. As the First Reading today suggests: "[E]veryone who is found written in the book" by their life here, will come to everlasting life.

III. This First Reading from Daniel ends by referring to "those who lead the many to justice." This hints at the second tension between this life and the next: a continuing tension between self-centeredness and concern for others. The American Dream, in its extreme form, is only concerned with self—with possessions, status, success and ambition. Authentic Christianity begins with love of self: "You shall love your neighbor as yourself" (Galatians 5:14). But then it draws us to be deeply concerned about others, because they are of great value personally, and because they are Christ to us. So we have to balance our concern for others with our personal problems; we have to make choices between spending time on altruistic causes and making time for our family. As long as we are Christians, we live with that tension between care of self and of others.

IV. In the context of today's Gospel, Jesus remarks: "[T]hose times will have tribulation such as has not been since the beginning of God's creation . . . nor ever will be" (Mark 13:19). He clearly warns about the trials that are sure to happen, about cataclysmic events, about distressing failures and defeats. Even his Church can suffer grave setbacks and failures. Yet none of those events can supersede the victory of our God. No devastating surprises, no human evils in our world or in our church can prevail over the ultimate victory sealed for us in Christ. So we Christians can live with all these tensions, because we know that our hope will conquer all in Christ Jesus our Lord.

Year C

Malachi 3:19–20a; 2 Thesslonians 3:7–12; Luke 21:5–19

Apocalypse and Us

I. Apocalypses follow a regular pattern in Scripture. First, the apocalyptist recounts some historical events up to the time of his writing; secondly, he indicates future events rather vaguely; finally, he really takes flight by foretelling the cosmic events of the end: resurrection, judgment, and the consummation of this world. Both the first and the third readings today deal with this final stage of apocalypse, the judgment and the consummation of the world. In very picturesque language, we hear only that this world as we know it will come to an end, and there will be a universal judgment, including reward and punishment. In the next few weeks, we will have additional apocalyptic readings. The problem we always face with apocalyptic readings is this: How do we make them relevant to our contemporary Christian life? In the early Church, such passages were most relevant, for they were understood in the sense of literal, imminent expectation; that is: The end of the world is really coming soon; be ready for it. Paul's Letters to the Thessalonians, the earliest New Testament writings, are filled with such imminent expectation. But since the second century, the Church has mainly understood this material as a prediction of a remote consummation of history. Accordingly, apocalyptic merely became the last chapter of our dogmatic system, lacking existential relevance for the present life of the church. Isn't there some other way of treating such apocalyptic so that it has more relevance to our present Christian life? I think there is. Let me offer two ways for your consideration.

II. The last part of the Gospel today refers to troubles at the end time: earthquake, famine, persecution, and trials. Then it concludes, "By your perseverance you will secure your lives." That is, God's saving purpose will certainly be achieved, despite all these trials, if we only endure in faith. Now we see troubles of our time and they are not minor. Thus, we see major problems with the *Catholic Church*: divisions between the old church and the new church, widespread uncertainty of exactly where we are going, grave inequality of women in the Church, a distressing lack of vocations, and even scandals. Also, Christianity seems to be moving backwards in terms of what percentage of the world is Christian; it seems the population of the world is becoming less Christian. What apocalyptic offers us is the certainty of Jesus' promise that out of all these troubles too, there will come vindication and the final achievement of God's saving purpose. These troubles in our church are real and deep, but they are much less than the final ones and they *will not* destroy God's saving purpose in our world.

III. The second way of making such apocalyptic relevant to our life today deals with the general problem of evil in *our world*. We wonder where our God is, when the evil in the world doesn't seem to lessen and, in some ways, seems to get worse. Thus, wars and the threat of wars seem to increase; terrorist groups become more active and destructive; the number of starving people throughout the world seems to grow, so that some predict it may be catastrophic; there is no equality among the races; the rich continue to get richer and the poor poorer, even in our country; so often the unscrupulous seem to get ahead and the good suffer. And in our personal lives, things do not get better for us when we try to follow God's laws. Now what does apocalyptic and our Christian faith offer in the face of so much evil? In my sense of Christian theology, there is nothing in our Christian faith that promises justice *now*. Our faith does not ensure punishment or reward *here*. Nothing in our Christian faith assures us that God shall work his will on the world and make it *conform* to his will. In a word, this is simply not the time of reward or the place of justice. But *there is* a time for reward and a place of justice; there *will* be vindication; our hope in God *is* secure and certain.

IV. Let me conclude this way. We Christians must continue to work for peace, justice, and love; and with confidence in God's help, we have some hope of attaining these in some notable way in this life. But the great promise of God is for the next life; the vindication and reward are only certain then; our hope in only *absolute* in the risen Christ.

Part VIII

Solemn Feasts

Our Lord Jesus Christ the King

Year A

Ezra 34:11–12, 15–17; 1 Corinthians 15:20–26, 28;
Matthew 25:31–46

Christ the King and His Disciples

I. This Gospel is the famous scene of the last judgment. It is one of the most picturesque passages in all of Scripture. It paints a colorful, surrealistic picture of Christ, the King, who will finally judge all nations. In this very colorful image, Jesus assures us that there will be an accounting for each of us, and a time for making things right. Our own life experience teaches us that there is no justice for people in this world. Time after time, we see the poor and the innocent suffer and the unscrupulous get ahead. Tragedies, accidents, natural disasters affect us all. Every time we watch the news on TV, we increase our conviction that there is no justice in our life here. What Jesus makes certain here is that there is a place for justice, there is a time to set things right—by a just and merciful God. Notice the critical factor in Jesus' description. How are we judged? By our actions, by the kind of person we were in our deeds; by how we lived our Christian life. The emphasis here is stark and simple: we are judged by our good deeds or our lack of them. Certainly faith in God is presupposed; but our actions are critical.

II. The shocking point of Jesus' description is that what we do to others, Jesus our King considers as done to himself. The sheep didn't know they were helping Jesus; they did not even think about him in their good deeds. Yet Jesus considers all those good deeds as done to himself: "[W]hatever you did for one of these least brothers [or sisters] of mine, you did for me." Even more surprising, the goats are accused of harming Jesus, because of what they did to the least of his disciples. They protest, "Lord, when did we see you hungry or thirsty . . . or ill or in prison, and not minister to your needs?" How can they be condemned for doing harm to Jesus himself, when they never encountered him at all?

This very issue is the primary and directly intended point of this whole passage. Jesus bases his assertion here on a traditional Jewish principle: the *shaliach* principle. *Shaliach* is the Hebrew word for "agent." According to this principle, a person's accredited agent was equivalent to himself. That is, the acceptance or rejection of an accredited agent involves the acceptance or rejection of the sender. In the Old Testament, this principle was used regarding Moses, Elijah, Elisha, and Ezekial. Because they were God's prophets or agents, they acted in the person of God, and if anyone accepted God's agent, he accepted God; it anyone rejected what God taught through his prophet, he rejected God himself.

Jesus refers to this same principle at least two other times in the Gospels. In Mark, he asserts, "Anyone who gives you a cup of water to drink because you belong to Christ . . . will surely not lose his reward" (Mark 9:41). And again in Matthew: "[W]hoever receives one child . . . in my name receives me" (Matthew 18:5).

Now here in this colorful description of the last judgment, Jesus proclaims that whatever is done to any of his disciples is done to him. The sheep didn't know that they were helping Jesus; they freely admit that they did not even think about Jesus in their acts of kindness. Still, Jesus insists, what was done to them, was done to him. Jesus so identifies with his followers that what is done to them is done to him. It doesn't matter whether his followers are good or bad, saints or sinners, respected or despised, he so identifies with the least of them, that anything done to them is done to himself. And the goats are even more shocked. How can they be judged as having harmed Jesus when they never recognized him in others? They certainly didn't mean to harm Jesus himself. Yet his answer is just as strong: "[W]hat you did not do for one of these least ones, you did not do for me."

III. Christ our King makes it very clear: whatever we do to other Christians in terms of accepting them, respecting them or caring for them, we are actually doing to Jesus himself. We don't have to realize we are doing it to Jesus; most of the time we never imagine such an identification with him; but it's enough that he identifies with each of us. In a word, for us Christians, everything has a relationship to Christ our King. On that judgment day, there will be a time for justice, there will be a place for setting all things right. Then there will be a wondrous reward for our life and love, because all we did for others was done to Jesus himself.

Year B

Daniel 7:13–14; Revelation 1:5–8; John 18:33b–37

What Kind of King Is Christ?

I. It is beyond doubt that Jesus was crucified on the charge of being a messianic pretender. So many things about Jesus' trial and condemnation are uncertain or disputed. But this one point is clear: both the Jewish and the Roman authorities condemned him as messiah and king. The word, "king" was merely the Roman equivalent of "messiah." And the title on the cross: "King of the Jews," was a realistic charge, not a smart invention of Pilate. Now today's Gospel focuses on the notions of messiah and king. Let us see how this passage in John offers Christ's own interpretation of what kingship means for him.

II. Christ's view of his kingship is not *political*. In Jesus' first response, he refuses to affirm kingship on Pilate's terms. This means Jesus is not a political king. And I suggest that Jesus did not intend to do any of the things that kings or government properly do for us. What are the functions of political leaders and governments? Governments protect us against wars and foreign enemies; they protect against crime and physical harm; they protect against natural disasters such as floods or drought. And governments promote the commonweal by strengthening the economy, providing food and fostering jobs; they promote medical aid and health care. Now when Jesus implies he is not that kind of king, that means none of these functions are direct effects of his kingship.

III. Secondly, Christ's view of his kingship is that it is not *of this world*. His second response is simply, "My kingdom does not belong to this world." This suggests that Jesus is not a builder of Utopia, not one to change this world into a perfect human society. He does not offer any certainty that this world will be peaceful, kind, and loving. What would a Utopia look like? It would do away with all suffering and illness; it would stamp out injustice and dishonesty; it would cure all poverty and starvation; it would rid the world of prejudice and enmity; it would require all people to be caring and loving. Now when Jesus denies that he is a king of this world, I believe he means that none of these conditions is a direct function of his kingship. So we should not look for him to be such a king.

IV. But Jesus finally affirms that he is a king in one sense—in terms of *witness to the truth*. In his third response to Pilate, he asserts, "[F]or this I came into the world, to testify to the truth." That is, Jesus redefines his messiahship and kingship to mean that he is a bearer of divine revelation, a witness to the truth. And truth here means the reality of God as seen through Jesus' revelatory and redemptive action. This description of his work is constant in John's Gospel. That is, though John does portray Jesus as redeemer by his suffering and death, much more often he portrays him as the Messiah who teaches the total truth about God and human life, or simply as the Word of God. What John means by this is that Jesus came to give us all we need to know, in order to become whole human beings in the midst of the struggles and trials of human living. What do we need to know to become whole as human beings? First, we need to know that this world and our life is from a loving Father; consequently, our world is a benign world not an evil one. Accordingly, Jesus taught that the creator is our loving Father. Secondly, we need to know what God is really like; we need a tangible, understandable revelation of God. And Jesus himself IS that revelation and that clear image of God. Also we need to know what we can become—that we can become whole through the reality of our human existence; that we can learn to be selfless, kind, accepting, just and understanding. He offers us a human model, "I am the way" (John 14:6). Also we need a motive that is strong enough to love all our neighbors; that motive also centers on him: "[L]ove one another as I love you" (John 15:12). Then we need a hope that is certain and satisfying—a destiny that is worthy of human life, that is to be worked out now and will continue after death. Finally we need constant encouragement to build a world that is ever more just, peaceful and loving; "[T]ake courage," he tells us, "I have conquered the world" (John 16:33).

V. So when Jesus redefines his kingship and messiahship, he asserts: "For this I was born . . . to testify to the truth." He means that this is the direct function of his kingship. And I believe that this is all we really need to have fullness of life now, even in our very defective world. "I came so that they may have life and have it more abundantly" (John 10:10).

Year C

2 Samuel 5:1–3; Colossians 1:12–20; Luke 23:35–43

Our Human King and Kingdom

I. Christ our King was a very human king. One anonymous writer describes him this way:

> He was born in an obscure village, the child of a peasant woman. He grew up in another obscure village. He worked in a carpenter shop until he was thirty, and then he was an itinerant preacher. He never wrote a book. He never held an office. He never owned a home. He never had a family. He never went to college. He never traveled 200 miles from the place where he was born. He never did one of the things that accompany greatness. While he was still a young man, the tide of popular opinion turned against him. His friends ran away. One of them denied him. He was turned over to his enemies. He went through the mockery of a trial. He was nailed to a cross between two thieves. His executioners gambled for the only piece of property he had on earth, while he was dying, and that was his coat. When he was dead, he was taken down and laid in a borrowed grave.

II. See how *human* he was! He was poor, obscure, and unimportant politically, even scandalous and repulsive in dying. How hard it was for some people to see him as Son of God. As Paul points out, "Christ crucified [is] a stumbling block to Jews and foolishness to Gentiles" (1 Corinthians 1:23). Also in our day, for all non-Christians and even for some marginal Christians, such a human king cannot be divine. But for us, this human Christ is also *divine*. As the Letter to the Colossians describes him today, "He is the image of the invisible God, / the firstborn of all creation. / For in him were created all things

in heaven and on earth. . . . / He is before all things." For us Jesus
is the revelation of God and the Word of God. For us he is the
center of human history, the redeemer of the world, our only Savior.
For our human life now, he is the model for our living, the meaning
and value of life, the goal and end of our existence.

III. Christ's kingdom on earth is a very *human kingdom*.
His Christian Church, which is a prominent form of that kingdom,
is a very human church. It is made up of millions of poor, obscure,
uneducated, unimportant people. Worse than that, it is made up
of scandalous, sinful, even repulsive people. For example, some church
leaders abuse their authority and make it a means of autocratic rule
instead of effective service. Others in the church take rigid moral
positions and condemn others self-righteously. Others are proud of
their racial standing and quite prejudiced. Others are often selfish,
mean, offensive, petty, thoughtless, unkind. To many people, this
human element in the church of Christ is a "stumbling block." They
protest that they cannot belong to such a faulty, sinful, proud, legalistic church of Christ. But for us, this Christian Church, so very human
and faulty, is also *divine*. It is the Body of Christ on earth; its soul
is the Spirit of God. It teaches the message of Jesus which can only
perdure in a community of faith. It is the means of our relating to
Jesus, which we cannot do alone. It is the source of grace and salvation
according to the intention of Jesus. It is our spiritual home, in which
all the ultimate questions about human life are adequately answered
for all ages. It is the supporting group that moves us to a love of God
and our neighbor, after the model of Jesus. It is the enduring source of
hope in Jesus, who conquered the world and rose from the dead.

IV. Christ our King is very human but he is also divine.
And we love him more for being entirely one of us as well as divine.
The Christian Church—which is a notable form of his kingdom on
earth—is very human and faulty but also divine. And we love this
pilgrim people of God made up of people like us who feebly struggle
to follow Christ our King.

Immaculate Conception of the Blessed Virgin Mary

Years A, B, and C

Genesis 3:9–15, 20; Ephesians 1:3–6, 11–12; Luke 1:26–38

Mary Immaculate

I. This feast of the Immaculate Conception is the most confused feast of the year. The secular media always get it wrong; they think it means Jesus was conceived without a human father. Let me simply explain the meaning of this feast and what it implies for us. The Immaculate Conception refers to Mary's own conception in the womb of her mother. It affirms that Mary was filled with sanctifying grace from the first moment of her conception, because of the foreseen merits of Jesus our savior. In any theology, old or new, that's what this feast affirms: that Mary was a child of grace from the first moment of her conception in her mother's womb; she was conceived immaculate, free of all sin. That's the essential theology of this feast.

II. But this feast also says something about original sin and Mary. And here I think the new theology is more helpful than the old. In the old theology, we learned that Mary was conceived without original sin, meaning that she was without the guilt and stain of the first parents, Adam and Eve. She was preserved from this sin because she was to be the Mother of Jesus.

In the new theology, original sin is simply our common, sinful human condition; it is the imperfection of our common nature; it is the fight within us between flesh and spirit; it is the inclination to put ourselves first and to be inhuman to others. This Mary was without, in the sense that she so accepted the will of God and loved others, that she was like Jesus, "the man for others." She overcame this sinful, human condition, this original sin.

III. Saint Paul recognized this struggle within us, this sinful, human condition with surprising honesty: "I do not do what I want, but I do what I hate" (Romans 7:15). We all have this primary, human defect of selfishness, which is the source of all sin; it leads us to harm others, to use them, to sin. Paul also knew that this universal inclination to selfishness could be partly overcome by the grace of God and the model of Jesus our Savior. As today's second reading teaches: "[God] chose us in [Christ] . . . to be holy and without blemish before him." It does not say we *actually are* holy and blameless, but only that the moral qualities of holiness and purity are expected of God's chosen ones. The emphasis here is on the *agency* of Christ; it is by reason of Jesus that we are made children of God and can aspire to holiness; it is his grace that makes it possible for us to gradually overcome our selfishness, insensitivity and sinfulness.

IV. This leads us to what this feast implies for us, especially in the new theology. First, this feast leads us to *praise* Mary. We praise her not only because she was the Mother of God, but also because she is our model for living our faith. For she accepted the will of God so well in her life that she lived the Christ life as well as any human being could. Her whole life was sinless; today's Gospel hints at this sinlessness: "Hail, favored one! The Lord is with you." Throughout her life Mary accepted life just as it came to her, with all its confusion, uncertainty and suffering. And so she became—as the poet expressed it—"our tainted nature's solitary boast."

But in this theology we can do more than admire Mary, the Immaculate Conception. We can also try to *imitate* Mary. We can find in her life a way of life for us; we can learn to live the Christ life more faithfully. For us too, doing God's will means accepting the reality of our individual existence just as it comes to us, in the Spirit of Christ. God's will is not so much *what* happens to us but rather *accepting* what happens to us in the spirit of Christ.

V. On this feast of the Immaculate Conception, we affirm that Mary was conceived in grace from the first moment of her existence. And we also recall that she lived her entire life according to the will of God, after the model of Christ. We admire her in this. But we also try to imitate her—for this is simply what it means to be a Christian. Imitation is the sincerest form of flattery—and of praise.

Assumption of the Blessed Virgin Mary

YEARS A, B, AND C

Revelation 11:19a; 12:1–6a, 10ab; 1 Corinthians 15:20–27; Luke 1:39–56

MARY'S MAGNIFICAT

Many years ago, there was an interesting TV program with Leonard Bernstein, the great conductor. He was giving his musical interpretation of the "Magnificat" by Beethoven. He claimed the leitmotif of the Magnificat was the constant interplay of pride and humility; the pride was in God's accomplishing so much in Mary; the humility was in her insignificance. I dare not quarrel with Bernstein's musical interpretation of this masterpiece, but as a theologian I must insist that Mary's Magnificat contains not one expression of pride; every word of praise and glory is directed to God. Though she mentions the goodness of God in her regard and is aware that "from now on will all ages call me blessed"; yet she never attributes this goodness to herself or seeks any praise for herself. She is not afraid to admit the great good that God has done in her, because she realized so well that all the good in her is in her not of her.

II. This Magnificat is wonderfully instructive for us. It teaches us the essential religious attitude toward God. The very heart of Christianity consists of our attitude before God and our personal relationship to Christ. Consider, by contrast, the attitude of those without religion; those who feel they can live very well without God. To some degree, such people feel comfortable with their own wisdom, satisfied with themselves and their own achievements, content with their skill and personal resources. They are almost exclusively concerned with the practical questions that they can usually handle well. As long as life does not force there to consider other human needs, deeper realities or ultimate questions, they feel self-reliant and independent. Since they do not feel their human need and inadequacy, they feel no need for God and religion. They are infected with what Victor Frankl calls "the principal malady of [modern life]: an existential vacuum."

III. Contrast this attitude with that of Mary: "[God] has looked upon his handmaid's lowliness / . . . / The Mighty One has done great things for me, / and holy is his name." She affirms here that only God could do all these things, and the reason why he did them is simply because he is good. She affirms that all grace is from God—both ordinary and extraordinary, and she does not strictly deserve, merit or produce any grace on her own. This is the number one lesson of the spiritual life: that we are God's children in total dependence on the free grace of God. This is our essential attitude before God; it is simply standing before the truth: that he alone is God and we are his creatures. We cannot stand on our rights before God; we know that we are saved and blessed with any grace at all, only by the mercy of God. We understand the precise meaning of the first beatitude in Matthew's Gospel: "Blessed are the poor in spirit" (5:3), for in Matthew, it has nothing to do with money or possessions and everything to do with our sense of complete *dependence on God* for all good and all grace. In this profound sense, religion is only for the needy, for those who are totally dependent on God for all grace. All of us humans are needy; those who recognize their need are religious people or good Christians.

IV. Our Christian religion has a wondrous attitude toward God; we are happy to stand before God in complete dependence on him. Mary's attitude in the *Magnificat* is a powerful model for us; she teaches us the essential thing that God asks of us, which is simply to affirm whole-heartedly that he is God and we are his creatures. "[M]y spirit rejoices in God my Savior."

All Saints

Years A, B, and C

Revelation 7:2–4, 9–14; 1 John 3:1–3; Matthew 5:1–12a

The Beatitudes of Matthew

I. The beatitudes are filled with mystery and idealism. They are addressed to "the disciples" who have personally chosen to follow Jesus and so also to us. Together, they make up the spiritual charter of Christ's kingdom, a program of life that is in fact modeled by the life of Jesus himself. This feast of All Saints is a good day to study them, for they contain the heart of Christian holiness for us.

II. In Latin, each beatitude begins with the word *beati*, which means blessed or happy or, more accurately, fortunate. There are always two parts to a beatitude, indicating: *If* you do this, *then* that will follow. The first part of each beatitude: "[Fortunate are those] who are poor, who mourn, who hunger and thirst, who are persecuted," is *absurd* for those without faith. On the natural level such assertions are preposterous and contradictory. And even for us Christians, they only begin to make sense with the second part: "They will be comforted; they will inherit the land; they will be satisfied; they will be called children of God; they will see God." All of these conclusions are only variations on the promise of Jesus in the first and last beatitudes: "Theirs is the kingdom of heaven." That is, Jesus relates all these beatitudes to the next life and the reward that God offers to those who follow Jesus and his way. That is why they are *beati*.

III. Jesus' logic, expressed in these beatitudes, is not easily grasped. We can try to understand Jesus' logic with the help of Scripture and by reflecting on the actual lives of the saints whom we honor today. Begin with Paul in his letter to the Romans: "I consider that the sufferings of this present time are as nothing compared with the glory to be revealed for us" (Romans 8:18). That is, we Christians live our entire life against the horizon of hope; for us, everything has an added value because of what it will mean for us for all eternity. And when we encounter suffering in our life and accept it willingly, we are fulfilling the will of God in a notable way, perhaps even a heroic way. Such actions are especially rewarded by God, for they are our way of living out the following of Jesus in difficult circumstances.

The Letter to the Hebrews describes Jesus' own motivation: "Son though he was, he learned obedience from what he suffered; and . . . was made perfect" (Hebrews 5:8). That is, by the obedience learned through suffering, Jesus was brought to the full perfection of his humanity; or: Jesus followed the way of human suffering in order to be the first to achieve perfection by means of a human life. We are to follow this same way of human purification and spiritual maturity.

Finally, the Letter to the Hebrews teaches that Jesus himself followed the motivation of the beatitudes: "For the sake of the joy that lay before him he endured the cross" (Hebrews 12:2). Jesus' motivation here models for us the last of Matthew's beatitudes: "Blessed are they who are persecuted . . . /for theirs is the kingdom of heaven."

IV. This is the wisdom of the beatitudes and the way of the saints. For each of the saints, this following in the footsteps of Jesus meant practicing some of these beatitudes. They did not deliberately plan to practice this or that beatitude; they found their sanctity in accepting the reality of their individual lives just as it came to them. The same is true for us. We can only try to do whatever we are - given to do, in the Jesus way. What makes this entire effort "blessed" is this hope of eternal life; what makes us "happy" is that we are following the example of Jesus; what makes us "fortunate" is that our human perfection is won only in this way of Jesus.

Years A, B, and C (Alternate Homily)

Revelation 7:2–4, 9–14; 1 John 3:1–3; Matthew 5:1–12a

Plain Talk about Sanctity

I. So much has been written about the saints which makes them seem to be plaster-cast saints, saints without humanity. So much has been preached about sanctity that seems to demand extraordinary lives—lives removed from our world or from our experience. For once today, let me use plain talk about sanctity.

II. You probably have very grave doubts about the possibility of sanctity for people like you and me. You might protest that we are people who live without great success, recognition or acclaim. We are people who do common, ordinary things, monotonous and routine things, without any splendor or great achievement. Mother Teresa of India has a great answer for people like us. One day she was asked about being discouraged in her work with the desperately poor and the dying. Such work was so obviously dreary and repulsive; it was filled with only failure and death. A reporter asked her, "How can you continue doing such unsatisfying and miserable work? You must get very discouraged living without any measurable success." Mother Teresa answered, "God has not called me to be successful; he only called me to be faithful." She meant that success or public acclaim is not the hallmark of a Christian saint, fidelity is—constant fidelity to the will of God as it comes to us naturally in our daily lives. We might add that holiness does not require great achievement, public notice, popularity, charm or status. It only requires that we "hear the word of God and act on it"(Luke 8:21); that one quality alone makes us sisters , and brothers of Jesus.

III. There is another problem with the possibility of sanctity for us. It comes from the way sanctity has been described for the last 1000 years in our Catholic Church. Ever since religious or monastic life developed in our Church, especially since the twelfth century, "the way of perfection" included the three vows of poverty, chastity, and obedience. If lay people could not keep these three vows, this way of perfection, they could only imitate the vows in some watered-down way in their secular lives. But that seemed to leave them far from sanctity. Only recently are we getting over this singular approach to perfection and affirming a way of spirituality that is quite proper to our lives in the world. After a thousand years, modern spirituality is finally positive and affirming of such a life.

IV. Let me describe this new spirituality that grew out of Vatican Council II. To keep it uncomplicated, let us concentrate on just two elements. First, consider that our lives consist of constant relationships to people. All day long we have contacts with people on various levels: incidental contact, business relationships, regular acquaintance, real friends, and family. We are never without people. We Christians are told by Jesus himself that all of these people are related to him: "[W]hatever you did for one of these least . . . you did for me" (Matthew 25:40). We need to grow in our understanding that what we do to them, we do to Jesus himself. Jesus even adds that it doesn't matter that we generally don't think about this relationship to him; as long as we serve others with the habitual sense that they are members of Jesus, he sees it as done to himself.

Secondly, we can have a different view of our daily work, whatever it might be: homemaker, social worker, factory worker, businessman, or whatever. We need to realize that all our daily work is not just something to "offer up," as we thought previously. Rather, the *work itself* is valuable, because all of it is some kind of *service* to God's people. Whatever our job, it offers some service to others even if it is far removed from the actual people helped by it. We need to grow in this awareness of serving Christ by our work.

V. All that we've said here about our modern spirituality is summed up in one sentence in the Letter to the Colossians: "[W]hatever you do, in word or in deed, do everything in the name of the Lord Jesus" (Colossians 3:17). That includes the people we meet and the work we do each day.

Acknowledgments

Grateful acknowledgment is made to the following publishers and authors for permission to reprint sections from copyrighted material:

All scripture texts are taken from the *New American Bible* with revised New Testament and Psalms, Donald Senior, general ed. Copyright © 1991,1986, 1970 by the Confraternity of Christian Doctrine, Inc., Washington, D.C. No portion of the *New American Bible* may be reprinted without permission in writing from the copyholder.

America Press, for *The Documents of Vatican II,* edited by Walter Abbott, SJ. Copyright © 1966 BY America Press, New York, NY.

Chappell Music Ltd., for "If I Ruled the World" from *Pickwick,* words by Leslie Bricusse, music by Cyril Ornadel. Copyright © 1963 by Chappell Music Ltd. Copyright renewed; international copyright secured; all rights reserved.

Doubleday Publishing Co., publishers of *The Anchor Bible,* for *The Gospel According to John, XXIII–XXI (vol. 29A)* by Raymond Brown. Copyright © 1970 by Doubleday Publishing Co., New York, NY.

Doubleday Publishing Co., for *Jesus of Nazareth* by Pope Benedict XVI. Copyright © 2007 by Doubleday Publishing Co.

E. P. Dutton, publishers of *Passages* by Gail Sheehy. Copyright © 1974, 1976 by Gail Sheehy.

ICS Publications (Institute of Carmelite Studies), for *The Collected Works of John of the Cross,* translated by Kieran Kavanaugh and Otilio Rodriguez, OCD. Copyright © 1991 by Washington Province of Discalced Carmelites ICS Publications, Washington, D.C.

Sheed and Ward (an imprint of Rowman and Littlefield Publishers, Inc.) for *The Interior Castle,* by St. Teresa of Avila, translated by E. A. Peers. Copyright © by Sheed and Ward, Chicago, IL

Scriptural Index

NOTE: This index includes only those passages used as a basis for a homily.